North Carolinians *in the Era of the*
Civil War & Reconstruction

North Carolinians

in the Era of the

Civil War

and

Reconstruction

Edited by

PAUL D. ESCOTT

The University of

North Carolina Press

Chapel Hill

Laura F. Edwards's essay in this book is a revised
version of Laura F. Edwards, "Status without Rights:
African Americans and the Tangled History of Law and
Governance in the Nineteenth-Century U.S. South,"
American Historical Review 112, no. 2 (April 2007):
365-93; reprinted with permission.

The paper in this book meets the guidelines for
permanence and durability of the Committee on
Production Guidelines for Book Longevity of the
Council on Library Resources.

The University of North Carolina Press has been a
member of the Green Press Initiative since 2003.

Library of Congress Cataloging-in-Publication Data
North Carolinians in the era of the Civil War and
Reconstruction / edited by Paul D. Escott.
p. cm.
Includes bibliographical references and index.
ISBN 978-0-8078-3222-6 (cloth : alk. paper)
ISBN 978-0-8078-5901-8 (pbk. : alk. paper)
1. North Carolina—History—Civil War, 1861-1865.
2. North Carolina—Politics and government—1861-
1865. 3. North Carolina—History—1865- 4. North
Carolina—Politics and government—1865-1950.
5. Reconstruction (U.S. history, 1865-1877)—
North Carolina. 6. African Americans—North
Carolina—Social conditions—19th century. 7. African
Americans—Segregation—North Carolina—History—
19th century. 8. Women—North Carolina—Social
conditions—19th century. 9. North Carolina—
Biography. I. Escott, Paul D., 1947-
E524.N67 2008
973.7'456—dc22   2008005592

cloth   12 11 10 09 08   5 4 3 2 1
paper   12 11 10 09 08   5 4 3 2 1

Contents

North Carolinians *in the Era of the* Civil War *&* Reconstruction

Introduction

The era of the Civil War and Reconstruction was a crucial period in U.S. history and in the history of North Carolina. More was at stake than the fate of the Union and the future of slavery, vitally important though these questions were. The fundamental character of southern society—its dominant values as well as its race relations, class relations, and gender relations—also was in flux as impersonal forces and human efforts created enormous pressures for change. In North Carolina, people at all levels of society reacted swiftly to events. Some seized their opportunity to promote long-desired alterations in the social structure, while others fought back, working to block or negate change. These struggles ultimately shaped the state's politics and its social landscape for decades to come.

Throughout the South, both the war and Reconstruction shook the foundations of the social structure. War's privations and disruptions brought conflicts to the surface, challenging conventions and empowering groups that had been without influence, and from the start Reconstruction was a battleground over the future of social relations. To the extent that fundamental change became a reality, that fact in turn stimulated efforts at profound resistance. Thus, it is no mystery why this period remains a crucial and fascinating one for historical investigation. The era attracts many of the best minds in the profession and constantly inspires innovative, original scholarship.

In studies of the Civil War and Reconstruction, North Carolina attracts more than its share of attention and is the focus of a great deal of exciting new scholarship. One reason for this phenomenon is the fact that events in the Tar Heel State revealed with special clarity the basic conflicts that dominated both eras. Whether the topic is emancipation and race relations; class conflict or white solidarity; the status, rights, and roles of women; or the struggles in society to mold an ideological consensus, North Carolina's history throws a revealing light on vital social processes. The struggles over change were especially visible, and often very bitter, in the Tar Heel State.

During the Civil War, North Carolina became an unexpectedly important source of strength for the new southern nation, supplying one-sixth of the Confederacy's soldiers and nearly one-fourth of all its conscripts. Forty thousand soldiers from North Carolina died, fully a third of all those from the state who served in the army. Although Federal forces captured Roanoke Island and nearby coastal regions, most of the state remained under southern control and thus furnished to the Confederacy an uninterrupted stream of tax revenues, food from the tax-in-kind, and impressed commodities of all sorts.

But along with these enormous contributions of men and matériel came strong protests from the state—against conscription, impressments, suspension of the writ of habeas corpus, and other policies—as well as large-scale desertion of troops and internal class divisions on the home front. Thus, North Carolinians did much to sustain the Confederacy, but at the same time they exhibited a great deal of disaffection. Slaves in the eastern part of the state ran away to gain their freedom, while some white Tar Heels aided the Union, tried to find neutral ground, or joined a rising chorus of complaints from the war-weary. Despite the state's immense contributions to the southern war effort, by 1864 many observers questioned whether there was enough loyalty in North Carolina to hold it within the Confederacy until the end of the conflict.

The key issues of Reconstruction also developed and played out in a dramatic way in the Tar Heel State. During Reconstruction, established leaders resisted congressional Reconstruction, while newly enfranchised African Americans joined with a substantial number of white citizens, particularly in the piedmont, to form a strong Republican Party. But despite the biracial cooperation within the state's Republican Party—or because of it—North Carolina became the site of a large amount of Ku Klux Klan terrorism and violence. North Carolina's women sought new influence, some acting within a patriarchal context while others struggled to expand the boundaries of gender roles. Sharp differences of class interest contended with pressures for white racial solidarity. The nature of social relations would affect not just Reconstruction but the New South, in which North Carolina would soon become both a leader of industry and a center of the farmers' Populist revolt.

These dramatic and important events are a magnet for historical talent, attracting ambitious scholars who want to test their understanding of key issues and build new theories on the data of North Carolina's past. Award-winning scholars and talented newcomers are focusing on North Carolina in order to understand the Confederacy's life and death, the realities of emancipation, the struggles for and against a more democratic, liberated society during Reconstruction, and the agonized birth of the New South. What were the sources of change, and who were its agents? Who orchestrated resistance to change, and what were their weapons? This volume brings together some of the most valuable new scholarship on a vitally important period and an unusually revealing state. Nine new and original essays shed light on emancipation, loyalty and conflict among white Confederates, challenges to racial and sexual mores, the uses of racism by key politicians, the sources of change in women's social position, and the contest to develop a historical consciousness and social ideology that would shape the future. They also remind us that the world of these North Carolinians, in contrast to our own, was intensely local. Many Tar Heel citizens were protective of their homes and their state, and they viewed regional or national issues through a North Carolina lens that gave a distinctive character to their perspective on southern culture.

The volume is arranged chronologically and begins with David Brown's reinterpretation of loyalty and disaffection in the North Carolina piedmont. It has long been known that several piedmont counties produced disproportionate numbers of deserters and resisters to Confederate authority, but Brown seeks a new understanding of this phenomenon by focusing on the social reality and political outlook of the region's small farmers. Arguing that existing interpretations have become too polarized between notions of deep class conflict on the one hand and unfaltering loyalty on the other, Brown explores the local and family-based outlook of piedmont whites. He argues that ambivalent or ambiguous attitudes emerged naturally from the context of their lives and that the factor that most shaped their actions was "the overriding significance of the family." Brown provides a new understanding of these Confederates who took an ambivalent position toward the war and their government, and he reminds us that they should not be written out of the era's history, for a large number of people occupied that middle ground.

Barton A. Myers's essay focuses on a remarkable wartime event: the Federal raid by black North Carolina troops into their home counties in northeast North Carolina. This region of the state, like the central piedmont, was characterized by divided loyalties among the white population and a flagging commitment to the Confederacy. Residents of the northeast counties found themselves caught between two armies and suffering severely from both. The raid by General Edward A. Wild's brigade of liberated slaves struck at the foundations of the old order and heralded a new reality while it flouted long-established racial and sexual assumptions. The reactions of local whites were telling. When these Tar Heels sought to negotiate a truce for their counties between Union and Confederate authorities, they revealed much about the nature of southern Unionism and Confederate loyalty. "Community safety and stability" became their goal, much as localism had predominated in the piedmont. These events also showed how quickly a limited counter-guerrilla operation could evolve toward unrestrained violence.

Judkin Browning's essay on the quest for freedom by black people in occupied Carteret and Craven counties deepens our understanding of the meaning of emancipation. It details the strategies and goals pursued by black Tar Heels who were experiencing freedom for the first time and trying to build a foundation for future independence while they maneuvered among two groups of whites—the native residents and the occupying northerners. As freedmen worked to construct a new and more favorable social order, both groups of whites reacted out of their racial worldviews. The initiatives of African Americans led to considerable success. But the responses of Confederates and their conquerors ultimately had more influence on the racial and social landscape of the future.

What the changes brought by emancipation could mean to white southerners becomes the focus of Chandra Manning's innovative research on the 1864 gubernatorial election in North Carolina. Amid a discouraged and war-weary populace, Zebulon Vance sought reelection against William Holden, editor, vocal critic of Confederate policies, and instigator of scores of peace meetings that had expressed the desperate unhappiness of the home-front voters. Analyzing this election more fully and convincingly than anyone has done before, Manning focuses on race as the key factor in Vance's victory. Her analysis underlines the importance of racism and racial fears among the white population as the slave South stood on the brink of change.

The next three essays make important contributions to our understanding of gender roles, gender issues in politics, and women's history. By focusing on Cornelia Phillips Spencer and her history of *The Last Ninety Days of the War in North Carolina*, John C. Inscoe demonstrates how someone who undoubtedly saw herself as a patriotic Confederate lady could expand the accepted roles for women while simultaneously defending the male political elite, its lost cause, and the honor of her state. Spencer pioneered in a kind of public advocacy that would become identified with subsequent generations of privileged white women. But she also helped prominent males shape the ideology of the defeated South and the image of North Carolina's elite.

Laura F. Edwards breaks new and fundamental ground in her analysis of the roots of female assertion during Reconstruction. She finds an ironic connection between the traditional past and a changing future. Although civil war, destruction, and defeat had certainly brought change, Edwards argues persuasively that women's efforts to raise their status in the postwar world proceeded, in vitally important ways, from certain characteristics of the regressive social system and legal culture that had previously bound them. Her essay looks anew at the way society and the legal system of pre-war North Carolina had defined family and the boundary between private and public matters. Focusing particularly on the concept of the "peace" of the community, Edwards offers a convincing new interpretation of a dynamic that encouraged women to use the courts and thus led to change.

Taking another approach to changes in gender relations, Karin Zipf dissects and analyzes the unexpected amount of attention—and action—that the North Carolina Constitutional Convention of 1868 devoted to issues of marriage and divorce. Zipf finds evidence that women were taking new initiatives and that delegates to the convention reacted with a surprising degree of support. Their decisions largely rejected the state's existing statutory principles and case precedents on divorce and suggested changing social attitudes. Here, too, race emerges as an important social variable, for it was black delegates who took the lead in supporting improvements to the legal status and rights of women.

Paul Yandle's essay locates the roots of the New South's segregationist ideology in the racial politics of the 1870s, which were exacerbated by Congress's passage of a national civil rights bill. In North Carolina, this bill forced Republicans to search for a formula by which they could defend the essential rights of black voters without being crushed by racist white reactions. Through careful analysis of rhetoric, he connects the politics of the 1870s with the formulations of segregation that became codified in Booker T. Washington's address at the Atlanta Exposition in 1895. By analyzing the voting of legislators, he also lays bare the tensions within the Republican Party between officeholders of different races and regions and explains the dilemmas facing black Republicans.

The importance and political uses of race also figure prominently in Steven E. Nash's perceptive analysis of the tributes to Zeb Vance upon his death in 1894 and in the years following. Tar Heel Democrats had relied on Vance's record during the key election of 1876, reinterpreting it for their political benefit. After his death, they again seized upon his memory and his long career as an entertaining politician to create a symbol that could help their party weather the storms of the 1890s. History is written, at least initially, by and for the victors, and North Carolina Democrats used commemorations of Zeb Vance to reconstruct the historical memory of their state and the Civil War in ways that supported Democratic hegemony. By emphasizing Vance's labors for the common white man and his defense of local interests against Confederate demands, the Democrats burnished their party's image and appealed for white unity at a critical time when that solidarity was crumbling. While honoring a deceased leader, Democrats fashioned popular conceptions of history designed to buttress a repressive racial and class hierarchy.

Events in North Carolina during the era of the Civil War and Reconstruction had a powerful impact on the future of the state. They also illustrated the effect of forces at work throughout the South. The rights of black people, the roles of women, the influence of gender, and the nature of the class system were all in flux and moving toward definition through the political system. The racial norms that would replace the world of slavery were in formation. Historians face a large challenge in understanding the dynamics of this crucial period, both for North Carolina and for the South. These new essays, through their original research and perceptive interpretations, significantly advance that important agenda.

DAVID BROWN

North Carolinian Ambivalence

Rethinking Loyalty and Disaffection
in the Civil War Piedmont

The issue of southern loyalty (or loyalties) during the American Civil War has been a perennial staple for nineteenth-century historians since Robert E. Lee's surrender at Appomattox. But in the past decade, it has evoked particular interest and controversy. The extent to which southerners rallied to the Confederate cause and sustained their commitment to the war—especially southerners who did not own slaves—has been the focus of considerable debate and much excellent work. Even so, there are few signs of general agreement: scholars remain bitterly divided on the question of southern lower-class loyalty during the war. On one side, historians like Paul D. Escott, Wayne K. Durrill, and most recently David Williams argue that class divisions seriously undermined the Confederate cause. On the other, Gary W. Gallagher, William Blair, and Brian Steel Wills argue for the strength of Confederate unity and the particular resilience of the plain folk. In their view, war weariness should not be mistaken for a lack, or even a loss, of will. Commitment to the Confederate nation was enduring, they suggest, despite the immense sacrifices demanded by a war wreaking terrible devastation in both emotional and material terms in many parts of the South.[1]

This robust historiographical debate, linking home front to the battlefield, has been invigorated by reference to an increasingly sophisticated literature devoted to the study of nationalism. Stimulated by a lively debate among historians of early modern and modern Europe about the origins and consequences of national identity and civic affiliation, Civil War scholars have probed the strength and vitality of southern nationalism. Did the political hierarchy in Richmond convince southerners that the Confederacy was a nation with core beliefs and a distinctive identity? Was this enough to sustain morale and maintain the war effort until the South was eventually overwhelmed by superior northern forces?[2]

This essay considers these issues within the confines of a single location:

the North Carolina piedmont. It seeks a middle ground between the two competing historiographical positions that, in broad terms, emphasize the significance of a debilitating class antagonism on the one hand and on the other stress the unfaltering loyalty of lower-class whites (or, at least, that disaffection and internal conflict, which most historians would agree increased after 1863, was a result of the strains of war and did not necessarily indicate diminishing support for the Confederacy). This historiographical impasse has become too polarized and is in danger of distorting and oversimplifying a complex situation. It is a false dichotomy to posit class antagonism or strains of war as rival explanations of increasing internal problems, much less as an explanation for Confederate defeat: both were important and each tended to reinforce the other. To be sure, there were many North Carolinians in the piedmont committed to the Confederacy, and they remained so for the duration of the war. Equally, many others stuck with the Union in large part because they were not enthusiastic about a war that they regarded as engineered by slaveholders defending an institution peripheral to the piedmont's economy.

Other North Carolinians in the piedmont, however, just like countless others across the South, did not neatly fit into either one of these positions. Wartime situations can elicit an extraordinary level of sacrifice and unshakeable commitment, but for every southerner who was staunchly Unionist or Confederate, there were others, perhaps a majority, whose loyalty fluctuated, who equivocated, and who did what was best for themselves and for their families. This group is difficult to discern and even more difficult to quantify—historical evidence is heavily slanted toward bold statements of support for the "cause," however that is defined—and has tended to be overlooked in the current historiographical debate. Southerners taking what might be called an ambivalent position might be elusive, but they should not be written out of the Civil War story.[3]

A more nuanced approach must also take greater consideration of prewar conditions than is often the case. The impression can sometimes be given that political loyalties and prevailing attitudes were formed only after the attack on Fort Sumter in April 1861. This essay pays particular attention to the continuities and discontinuities of class relations in the late antebellum period and the wartime responses of civilians on the home front. While not denying the importance of forging an overarching sense of Confederate identity, moreover, the essay argues that the recent focus on nationalism tends to obscure what is really significant to understanding the actions of North Carolinians in the piedmont during the war: local conditions and, above all, the overriding significance of the family. Ideological attachments to the Confederacy, or to the Union, were significant in broadly generating loyalty and sustaining a sense of purpose. In the end, however, familial ties, community bonds, and the ways in which the war played out at the local level were more important factors influencing the responses and actions of yeomen families trying their best to cope with the unprecedented burdens placed on them between 1861 and 1865.

The Peculiar Nature of
the Antebellum Piedmont

The North Carolina piedmont occupies a distinctive place within the Old North State. As historical geographer D. W. Meinig succinctly put it, the settlement of North Carolina's interior was made "by peoples whose origins, social character, economic interests, and political concerns differed sharply from those of the older coastal societies." Caught between the eastern plantation economy and the more isolated mountainous west, the region was in the midst of a transformation from a self-sufficient farming economy to a more commercial, market-focused orientation by the mid-nineteenth century, stimulated to a great extent by the building of the North Carolina Railroad. Turpentine and gold mining were also valuable businesses in the piedmont, and there were a number of textile factories.[4]

Even so, the majority of whites were small farmers cultivating a variety of crops. Slavery did not underpin the piedmont economy, as it did in many other parts of the South. There were exceptions to this rule, and cotton and tobacco were grown in the 1850s. However, piedmont slavery was heavily concentrated in counties on the northern and southern extremes: tobacco on the Virginia border and cotton on the South Carolina border. It was on the edges of the piedmont, then, that slavery was most entrenched. Slaves were present in the counties of the central piedmont, but they were proportionally not more than one-third of the total population and in many counties considerably less than a third. In 1860, just 15–20 percent of whites in the central piedmont owned slaves. Even allowing for those not owning slaves but who were involved with slavery (overseers, for example), it is fair to say that for about three-quarters of the central piedmont's white residents, slavery was not central to their immediate economic concerns.[5]

The *mentalité* of the piedmont is more difficult to characterize than its economy. There is no question that the central piedmont counties remained especially receptive to antislavery ideas long after the southern wing of the movement had supposedly withered in the proslavery onslaught after the Virginia emancipation debates of 1832. This partly reflected a distinctive, if not peculiar, religious composition (by comparison with other parts of the South) that included Quakers, Moravians, Lutherans, Dunkers, and other sects. The American Missionary Society openly preached an abolitionist message in the piedmont during the 1850s, focusing on the central counties, which some have called the Quaker Belt. The piedmont also exhibited an intellectual strain of antislavery thought exemplified by the abolitionist proponents Hinton Rowan Helper and Benjamin S. Hedrick. Helper was born close to Mocksville, in what became Davie County in 1836, while Hedrick hailed from Salisbury in Rowan County. Both regarded slavery as an impediment to economic diversification and future progress.

To what extent others shared this view is impossible to gauge with any precision. In 1860, Hedrick estimated that between five hundred and a thousand men in Guilford County had read Helper's antislavery tract *The Impending Crisis of the South*, suggesting that yeomen in the piedmont were at least willing to contemplate slavery's utility and, perhaps, its future. Jesse Wheeler, a friend of Helper's and Hedrick's from Greensboro who covertly distributed *The Impending Crisis*, wrote that the book was "eagerly sought after by many men" but, in response to the optimism of his friends that a more hard-line stance against slavery might be developing in the piedmont, sounded a note of caution. Wheeler declined to become involved with a Republican Party initiative because he believed there was "not the least idea that they can carry this state."[6]

Wheeler's caution is important. Slavery was so central to southern life, so ingrained in the texture of daily routine, that while substantial numbers of whites in the piedmont were not directly connected to the institution, they nonetheless mostly accepted its presence without thinking. Abolitionists were overwhelmingly the exception. There is reason to speculate, however, that the status quo was in flux by the late 1850s and that the economic position of the lower classes gradually became worse in the decade before the Civil War.

Landless poor whites, mainly tenant farmers and laborers, made up between 30 and 40 percent of all free white households in the central piedmont in 1860. Their chances of accumulating sufficient money to buy or rent land diminished in the 1850s, as the presence of slaves both lessened the need for, and drove down the price of, casual wage labor. While the proportion of slaves in the central piedmont was low compared with elsewhere in North Carolina and across the South as a whole, the unsuitability of cotton and tobacco ensured that slave owners, lacking a staple plantation crop, put their bondspeople to a variety of diverse tasks and hired many out. Casual work, routinely required by the agricultural economy (during harvesting in particular) and in building the railroad, was one way that poor whites might eventually accumulate enough savings to become upwardly mobile. Other potential avenues of employment, such as working in the mining or turpentine industries, were also subject to competition from slave labor. As railroads made the piedmont more accessible to distant markets, moreover, the shift to widespread commercial farming raised the average purchase price of land. Historian Charles C. Bolton concludes that there was a permanent and growing class of landless whites in the central piedmont whose only option was migration, and many left in the decade before the Civil War.[7]

The position of yeomen farmers who owned their own land was much better than that of poor whites. Rising land prices increased the value of their property, and the railroad made it easier to sell surplus products on wider markets. Despite the prospect of increased affluence, however, slavery remained an institution of little utility to farmers whose main cash crops were wheat and corn—the soil and environment of the central piedmont simply did not encourage plantation agriculture. Moreover, the prospects of yeoman sons and daughters looking to establish their own households in the local area were uncertain at best and were seemingly diminishing as the cost of buying land, which was in short supply anyway, went up. Without land or suitable opportunities of alternative employment, yeomen as much as poor whites had to consider leaving the place of their birth. Martin Crawford's study of Ashe County (in the mountains) argues that "for all households land ownership remained the guiding star of domestic ambition, for only then could social dependency be avoided." This was equally true of the piedmont, where the short supply of good farming land was a serious problem.[8]

Thus, while only a committed few demonstrated overt dissent, declining economic opportunity as well as slavery's limited significance and uncertain future in the central piedmont economy arguably sustained a feeling of ambivalence toward slavery. Like other parts of the Upper South, slavery was not economically vital and was naturally withering in many respects. Ira Berlin has emphasized the crucial distinction between a "slave society," in which the present and future depended on slave labor, and a "society with slaves," in which the enslaved were present but were of peripheral and, in the case of the mid-nineteenth-century Upper South in particular, declining importance. William W. Freehling develops this interpretation more fully for large sections of the Border South by the late antebellum period, using the apt term "semi-slavery" to characterize the trajectory of economic development. Quite simply, the northern extremes of the

South were becoming more like the Middle Atlantic states and less like the plantation societies of the Lower South. The central North Carolina piedmont most closely resembled these Border South regions on the eve of the American Civil War.[9]

Perceptions of economic well-being were critical to individual responses to the onset of war, but there was also an important political edge to piedmont society that was equally significant. Throughout the antebellum period, the region battled with the planter elite of North Carolina's eastern counties who controlled state government on issues of political representation, taxation, and internal communication, seeking to counter the privileges that slaveholders enjoyed within the state's governmental system. In contrast to other southern states (with the exception of South Carolina and Virginia), North Carolina resisted making democratic changes to its political system, retaining property qualifications for voting and for officeholding. For example, approximately half the white male population was barred from voting in state senate elections until the abolition of the fifty-acre rule in 1857.[10] The dispute over an ad valorem tax had been a cause of antagonism, since the revised constitution of 1835 not only failed to tax slaves according to their value but also exempted slaves younger than twelve and older than fifty from taxation altogether. What Paul D. Escott and Jeffrey J. Crow term an "intensifying series of class conflicts" during the 1850s placed the divergent interests of the non-slaveholding majority and the planter minority in unusually sharp relief. To an extent, the second party system contained overt sectional and class conflict within North Carolina, as the Whigs and the Democrats maintained coalitions of different interests, including slaveholders and non-slaveholders, from different sections of the state, albeit with much difficulty at times. Undeniably, though, planters wielded disproportionate power within North Carolina.[11]

Planter control came to the fore during the secession crisis. The majority of North Carolinians were against immediate secession, and a substantial number were unconditional Unionists reluctant to leave the Union even if negotiations to resolve the sectional dispute failed in the spring of 1861. Things came to a head in February 1861 over the question of whether to hold a secession convention. "More than any previous election since the formation of the second party system," argues Robin E. Baker, "the secession delegate election served to polarize the North Carolina electorate along class lines." Slaveholders overwhelmingly voted for secession delegates and non-slaveholders for Unionist (even those previously supporting

John C. Breckinridge in the 1860 election). Results in the central piedmont left no room for ambiguity. Approximately 19,000 votes were cast against holding a convention, while only 3,000 were in favor. By a margin of six to one, the central piedmont voted against immediate secession. By contrast, the slaveholding counties on the edges of the piedmont unanimously voted in favor of the convention, overwhelmingly so in some cases: Anson (520–460); Caswell (692–137); Granville (1,056–743); Mecklenburg (1,448–252); Richmond (383–251); and Warren (774–33).[12]

As the first shots were fired at Fort Sumter on April 12, 1861, the commitment of those in the central piedmont to a war protecting slavery was uncertain to say the least. Unlike their peers in the Deep South, who overwhelmingly saw their economic success resting on the promise of slave ownership, yeomen in the piedmont had little reason to consider slavery central to their future prospects. Moreover, the piedmont as a whole had spent many years battling with the eastern planter establishment on a variety of issues. These were serious impediments to Carolinian unity, especially in galvanizing support for a war that few in the piedmont regarded as anything else but a war to defend slavery. Even though there were concerns over the intentions of Abraham Lincoln and the Republicans, secession was regarded as a drastic step, and for many a step too far. The Union was too cherished an institution to break apart.

Taking Sides, 1861–1862

Jonathan Worth, senator from Randolph County, was the piedmont's, if not the state's, leading Unionist. He staunchly opposed secession in a series of speeches in 1860–61. He also believed that the majority of his constituents—yeomen from the piedmont—shared his view. As long as Lincoln made plain that he would "respect property and discountenance rebellion or insurrection among our servile population," then "many of our people will not willingly take arms," Worth wrote. Worth's optimism was dashed, however, in wake of Lincoln's request for volunteers to suppress what he called a rebellion after the attack on Fort Sumter, and Worth was forced to acquiesce to the wishes of the eastern planters. After that, a wave of secessionist fervor swept over the Upper South. It had always been likely that any coercive measure to prevent southern states from leaving would be decisively rejected by Upper South states, but few could have predicted how strong the reaction would be. Unionists were dismayed and could not prevent a popular surge toward the Confederacy. Worth's fellow piedmont Unionist, John Gilmer from Guilford County, believed that after Lincoln's call, he "could do nothing more with the people. My voice was hushed."[13]

It was within this emotionally charged atmosphere that North Carolinians were asked to vote again in May 1861, this time for delegates to the secession convention. Most Union sympathizers were resigned to defeat, although as late as May 6, Jesse Wheeler maintained that "the people of Guilford, Randolph and other adjoining counties are unshaken in their devotion to the Stars and Stripes."[14] However, there was no real campaigning in this election, as the result was perceived to be inevitable; the intimidation of Unionists was also reported, ensuring that potentially important figures like Worth and Gilmer remained silent or else risked jeopardizing their position. Voter turnout was very low, indicating a lack of enthusiasm for an election in which the outcome was already widely anticipated, but, even then, some Unionist delegates were elected from the central piedmont (unfortunately, a full record of the results was not preserved). Unionist representatives who attended the convention in Raleigh on May 20 had little influence, however, as a secession ordinance was ratified unanimously at the convention. Unionists tried to delay the inevitable by suggesting that a second proposal, the adoption of the Confederate constitution, be put to the people for ratification, but that proposal was defeated, and the convention voted to accept the Confederate constitution.

North Carolina thus seceded from the Union by a decision that had not been democratically endorsed, although one that undoubtedly reflected the popular mood of the moment. In the short run, this was of little consequence in the heady excitement of the summer of 1861 as North Carolinians rushed to join up, anxious for the chance to "whip the Yankees." Everyone anticipated that the war would be extremely short, and soldiers on both sides worried that they might miss out. In the long run, however, as it became clear that the war was not going to be over in six months, the failure to democratically endorse secession would not be forgotten by many Tar Heels, especially those in the piedmont.

Approximately ten thousand volunteers had gathered in Raleigh before the secession convention, heeding Governor John W. Ellis's call in late April for a militia force to be ready to meet the Federals. It is impossible to know precisely how many of them were from the piedmont, but without doubt a sizable number were. Whether these men could have been any more enthusiastic about the war than Presbyterian minister James Sinclair is unlikely. Sinclair wrote to the governor from Robeson County, on the southeastern edge of the piedmont, unequivocally supporting secession.

"Halting between two opinions at the present day is both criminal & cowardly," he suggested, and "he who is not today with the South is against it." Sinclair offered "services, my life[,] my all, to be placed on the altar of my adopted country. In making this offer I ask for nothing but an opportunity, even in the humblest capacity, to vindicate the honour, the integrity and sovereignty of N. Carolina." He did not for a moment question the governor's power. "There is a peculiar propensity in ministers of the gospel, I think, at this time in giving up to the will of the Executive. Ritual principles of morality and religion underlie the questions at issue in the present struggle. . . . I have therefore no sympathy with the super-hyper sanctity which snivels and fawns over bloodshed and strife *when great principles are at stake*." Such sentiment was perhaps to be expected from a Presbyterian minister. By the late antebellum period, the Presbyterians were known as the denomination of the planters (an exclusivity emphasized by the fact that just 7 percent of southern churchgoers were Presbyterian).[15]

Other early recruits were perhaps not so emphatic in their conviction but nonetheless displayed similar commitment. Devotion to the state's cause, a desire to meet the "threat" posed by the Republicans, and a manly calling to duty were important motivating factors. Private James William Gibson, from Iredell County, told his parents that "it may be a long time before we get back to the old north state we will go back a free people when we do. We come here to be free or die if old Abe Lincoln sits his foot in our soil we will have to fight or die." Edmund Shoe, from Cabarrus County, told his gloomy sweetheart that "I have to be here now to fight for our homes and firesides[,] for freedoms[,] cause we must fight." Similarly, William Clement of Davie County comforted his beloved by telling her that it was his duty to join the cavalry: "You said that if I were to feel as much sorrow about leaving as you did, I could not go. Mattie, do not think I do not sorrow at the thought of parting with you, for I assure you I feel it more than any can imagine. But a sense of duty drives me on. I believe that we will not come out conquerors unless we turn out and meet the invaders man to man." A sense of obligation was paramount for Clement, as it was in many other similar letters written by volunteers. Staying at home was not an option for him, because if "the worst was to happen, I would never feel right afterwards, but if I go and do my duty, I will feel that the blame does not rest upon me if we are defeated."[16]

It is equally clear, however, that for every forthright declaration of loyalty from a piedmont volunteer, there were many others who chose to ignore the call. Charles C. Bolton calculates that fewer than 20 percent of eligible men in the central piedmont actually volunteered for service in

1861.[17] Less than one in five is an undeniably low figure, especially in comparison with other Confederate states where recruitment rates were much higher. Explaining with any precision why this was the case is exceedingly difficult. Uncovering and characterizing the complex personal, emotional, economic, political, and familial factors involved in each individual case is hard enough, let alone making sweeping judgments for the whole of the central piedmont. Nonetheless, two important observations stand out in considering who volunteered in the first year of the war.

First, poor whites in the piedmont probably came forward more readily than yeomen, or at least more readily than yeomen with family commitments, although the evidence is far from conclusive. Poor whites did not have an economic stake in society that needed tending and protecting as yeomen did. A wage of eleven dollars a month was attractive to them. B. M. Edney of Henderson, a mountain county bordering the western edge of the piedmont, was commander of a Confederate camp. He requested a bounty for his recruits, or "*destitute* soldiers," as he put it, because "they are poor many of them and . . . greatly in need of that money I have promised them." Some petty criminals, overwhelmingly from the lower rungs of society, were simply coerced into the army in lieu of other punishment.[18]

Second, yeomen were reluctant to volunteer because they regarded their primary duty to be protection of the family. Decisions taken by yeomen in the piedmont were heavily determined by the needs and circumstances of their families. The vast majority of yeomen were tied to the farm: they had far more responsibilities than poor whites and risked their coming harvest if leaving. It was not only economic interest that influenced their decision, however. The uncertainty of the war, especially the unpredictable response of the enslaved, heightened the emotional attachment between men and women and emphasized the patriarchal responsibility of men to take care of their dependents. Not all yeomen, of course, were married or even property owners—as mentioned earlier, a growing number were looking to establish their own households, having come of age. In the cases of the three volunteers mentioned above, for example, Gibson was a widower, Shoe was unmarried, and Clement a law student, which undoubtedly made their choice easier. Moreover, some yeomen were fortunate enough to have friends or extended family too young or too old to join and were in a position to leave the farm in the hands of others if they wished. They might also be part of families large enough to cope with the absence of some members. Others perhaps wanted to join but were compelled not to do so because of their circumstances.[19]

Undeniably, though, the overwhelming majority in the piedmont stayed at home. This surely cannot be explained by circumstance alone and indicates that large numbers of yeomen and poor whites were not prepared to support the Confederate cause or held sufficient reservations not to volunteer. Unionism was undoubtedly a major factor in the North Carolina piedmont. Throughout the central piedmont in the aftermath of secession, there were signs of discontent over joining the Confederacy. Many were not persuaded by secessionist arguments, essentially remaining committed to the Union, and were anxious, if not angry, at the news coming from Raleigh. Although it had long been thought that the mountain region of North Carolina was more staunchly loyal to the United States, recent scholarship suggests that Unionism was actually much stronger in the piedmont.[20]

Thus, while incidents of Unionist outrage can be identified across the state in the wake of secession, they emerged with most vehemence and with more sustained force within the piedmont, especially within the central counties. Surprisingly, in terms of the conventional story of the early months of the war, but unsurprisingly, given the piedmont's economic circumstances and political experience, it was not just non-slaveholders who remained steadfastly Unionist but also some slaveholders as well. In April 1861, Colonel Caleb Bohanan, slaveholder from Yadkin County, informed his local militia "that no man ought to support" the Confederacy. He hoped that volunteers would indeed heed Lincoln's call, because "every secessionist ought to be hung." That feeling was enduring and continued to be openly expressed in places. On the occasion of an election for constable in Alamance County in 1862, for example, "one of the candidates announced himself as still devoted to the union and his supporters voted for him with ballots having on them the Eagle, as emblematic of their attachment to the Union." Unionist sentiment was sustained in no small part by the undemocratic way in which the state joined the Confederacy. As one claimant from Rowan County stated to the Southern Claims Commission after the war: "My feelings and language was for the Union all the time. The secession ordinance was not submitted to the people. I did not go with the state after it was declared out of the union by the rebels." Some of these piedmont Unionists were among the minimum number of five thousand North Carolinians who fought in the Federal army.[21]

It was a group in Davidson County, a few miles from High Point, who illustrated the extremes of piedmont Unionism. In July 1861, James H. Moore informed Governor Henry T. Clark that there was "a combination of persons opposed to the Southern Confederacy and who openly advocate the Union and express sentiments favorable to the policy of the old government and in favor of the coercion policy of Lincoln." He estimated about 150 in total, "some of whom are men of considerable property (not slave owners)" who had forged links with other Unionists within the piedmont. Moore's estimate of numbers is conservative; other accounts suggest up to around 500 men were involved. What is not in question is the devotion of these men to the Union. "They have been in the habit of mustering under the old U.S. flag, and have expressed determination to do it two days ago at their militia drill, but was prevented by the rain. We sent men from this place to their muster ground to take note of the proceedings and they report that the officers of the company openly declared they would muster under the U.S. flag and would kill any man or set of men that should attempt to prevent it." This group was a persistent thorn in the side of the Confederate authorities. More than likely, these men were founding members of the Heroes of America, an organization actively opposing the Confederacy and seeking to aid the Union effort throughout the war. They forged links with similarly minded groups within the piedmont and across and even beyond the state as pockets of Union supporters organized themselves for mutual protection and armed resistance.[22]

How should the dichotomy between willing volunteers and died-in-the-wool Unionists in the piedmont be interpreted? In the absence of precise figures, historians are forced to rely on vague terms such as "many" or "most," which is at the root of the historiographical disagreement over lower-class loyalty: both sides can marshal substantial evidence supporting their position, and each lacks a reliable method of quantification. In the case of the piedmont, the statistic of one in five volunteers could be taken as evidence that four-fifths of men were hostile to the Confederacy. Without much evidence to go on, this figure certainly should not be ignored. James M. McPherson contends that those entering service after the passage of conscription laws in April 1862 were much less patriotic than genuine volunteers; in effect, they were ambivalent about participating in the war. McPherson calculates that 57 percent of yeomen volunteers in the Confederate army in 1861–62 expressed "patriotic convictions" compared to just 14 percent of conscripted men after 1862.[23] But, then, the elusive nature of individual motivation makes it dubious at best to think that those men remained at home solely because they were anti-Confederate—there were surely many factors at work in their decision. It is probably safer to assume that about a fifth of eligible males in the piedmont were unhesitatingly committed to the Confederacy at the outset of the war. If historians want to cite examples of willing commitment, they will find many letters that provide this. Equally, if they want to find evidence of uncertainty and out-right hostility and noncompliance, that exists in abundance as well.

To escape this dichotomy, a different approach might consider enthusiastic volunteers and defiant Unionists as *both* constituting "extreme" positions rather than being typical or representative. Most men and women in the piedmont stood somewhere between the two. Focusing on the gushing letters of new recruits or the dramatic actions of armed resisters ignores the outlook of the majority, who cannot comfortably be placed in either camp. If we look very carefully, we can discern the existence of an ambivalent majority.

Take the earlier example of Mattie Martin, the tearful sweetheart of William Gibson, who joined the cavalry. She did not have a strong ideological connection to the Confederacy or to the Union but was very concerned about the life of one particular man caught up in the war. More tellingly, James H. Moore's description of the Davidson Unionists provides an indirect comment on the position of the majority. "In almost any other community," he wrote, "no difficulty would exist in arresting the parties and bringing them to trial, but it is a fact that a great number of citizens outside of those who are connected with this affair, and who profess to be southern in feeling, assume a neutral position, and would refuse to lend assistance to suppress the disaffection."[24] It is these "neutrals" who are generally overlooked in the historiographical debate over Confederate loyalty. Rather than being absolutely for or against the Confederacy, positions on which the terms of the current historiographical debate are predicated, a more sophisticated understanding of loyalty and dissent should recognize the wide spectrum of opinion that was ambivalent, ambiguous, and subject to rapid and frequent change. If we accept that many families in the piedmont were not decisively committed either way — and that they swayed between the twin poles of Unionism and the Confederacy — it provides a somewhat different perspective in considering the allegiances of lower-class whites during the war.

Conscription and the Inner Civil War in the Piedmont, 1862-1863

The story of the piedmont's inner civil war is not one that is very widely known among Civil War scholars, although it is well known to historians of North Carolina. This is surprising, given that events taking place between 1861 and 1865 have been outlined in detail by William T. Auman in several articles and an excellent Ph.D. dissertation, foundational work to which all interpretations of the piedmont in the Civil War are indebted.[25] It is probably because the region (and indeed the state as a whole) cannot easily be placed within the terms of the dominant paradigm of Confederate loyalty or class dissent that it has been largely overlooked. North Carolina provided more Confederate troops than any other state except Virginia, and these men died in greater numbers than the soldiers of any other Confederate state. At the same time, North Carolina also had the highest number of deserters: approximately one-quarter of the total in the Confederacy as a whole. On the one hand, the Old North State was heavily committed to the cause; on the other, that commitment was exceedingly fragile, making sweeping interpretations of loyalty or disaffection highly problematic.[26]

While Jefferson Davis attempted to marshal southern forces against the North, and North Carolina governors Henry Clark and Zebulon Vance coordinated both the defense of the state and its contribution to the Confederate war effort, a series of skirmishes took place within the piedmont between 1861 and 1865. The region was generally spared the large-scale battles that caused havoc elsewhere, but a different kind of confrontation took place. County authorities, militia officers, and the Home Guard had to deal with anti-Confederate forces of many different kinds, engaged in hostile activity ranging from withholding supplies and hiding out in the woods to more serious armed resistance. Matters became so dire that regular troops were sent into the region on several occasions in an increasingly desperate attempt to quell trouble and establish order.

For those in the piedmont who had not volunteered for service or joined rebel Unionist organizations, this was a cause of uncertainty, if not anxiety. In these circumstances, it was daily, local concerns that were uppermost. Protection of home and property was paramount in the minds of ambivalent yeomen. All southerners were called on to contribute not only manpower but supplies as well, demands that became increasingly onerous. But anti-Confederates also posed a threat, as they foraged for supplies and did not hesitate to take food and clothing when necessary. J. H. Foust complained of a "a band of desperate men" located "on the river of lower Randolph county" who, as soon as the volunteers had left for service, intended "to rob our people of property [and] commit outrages of a gross character on our defenceless citizens." In Franklinville, also in Randolph County, J. P. Aldridge reported that a Home Guard had been formed not only "for the defence and protection of the Southern Confederate states" but "also to protect the homes, lives and prosperity of this county for we have abolitionist and Lincoln among us who defy the home guards to molest them.

They say they have as many armed men as we can raise." Their efforts were hampered by confusion over the legal status of the anti-Confederates and the legality of pursuing their apprehension. Aldridge complained to Governor Ellis that "we have no power to molest them[;] if we do we lay our selves liable to the punishment of the laws. So now we want some powers to clean out all such fiends as them." Local authorities tried to deal with this problem and establish order but met with limited success.[27]

The passage of the conscription act in April 1862 marked a key moment in the history of the inner civil war. Ambivalent North Carolinians were now placed in an extremely difficult position. Hitherto, they had been able to get on with their lives as best they could and ignore the war if they preferred, but with the passage of this and later conscription laws, which allowed for the drafting of men aged between eighteen and thirty-five (later raised to forty-five and then fifty), that was no longer a safe option. Margaret M. Storey points out how all southern Unionists faced a dilemma at this point: they either revealed their true colors and risked arrest and punishment if refusing to be drafted or had to swallow their principles and serve in the Confederate cause if called.[28]

Not only Unionists faced this dilemma. Depending on age, the ambivalent came under intense pressure to take sides, or at least had to work much harder to avoid escalating their participation. "There has been a strong feeling against the conscript law among the uninformed part of the citizens here, ever since its passage," reported R. F. Armfield of Yadkin County. "Many of that class swore they would dye at home before they would be forced off and when the time came for them to go, perhaps nearly one hundred in this county took to the woods, lying out day and night to avoid arrest, and although the militia officers have exerted themselves with great zeal yet these skulkers have always had many more active friends than they had and could always get timely information of every movement to arrest them and so avoid it." The support of family was critical to those individuals who did not want to join the armed gangs. Outliers would hide in the woods and return home when they could, often under cover of darkness, for food and shelter. Armfield ruefully observed how this hampered the Confederate cause and in so doing confirmed the crucial role of intermediaries helping the fugitives: "The section of the county in which they lurk is so disloyal . . . and the people so readily conceal the murderers & convey intelligence to them, that it will be exceedingly difficult to find them, even if they do not draw together a larger force than they have yet had." In Iredell County, it was reported that "four or five hundred armed men" intended "to resist the guard by bushwhacking."[29]

John A. Craven's letter of October 1862 similarly suggested that many men in Randolph County were avoiding the draft. He requested that Vance "have arrested at once all deserters & conscripts who are at home." Craven described how the arrest of a skulker brought an immediate response from his companions, who burnt down the barn of the militia officer involved. It was clear that a large proportion of draftees were not prepared to accept their orders: of 500 conscripts in his local area, Craven estimated that just 150 had gone into service. Some had gone to work in the salt mines, but the "great bulk of all these are *Abolitionists* and *Lincolnites*, a population that is entirely unsafe amongst us," he suggested. They were responsible for all kinds of trouble and threatened the safety of every loyal person in the county.[30]

Whether Craven's description was entirely apt is debatable. Some men probably joined the Union bushwhackers, who caused such mayhem, for reasons of antipathy toward the Confederacy but also because they believed it was the best way to avoid conscription. For others, however, Unionism and abolitionism had little to do with their decision: they simply wanted to stay out of active service. It is impossible to calculate the numbers of men who hid in the woods or to generalize about their motivation. A common phrase used by witnesses in the Southern Claims Commission reports indicates that many men did not make an active or dramatic protest against the war: "I don't know that he ever contributed anything to aid the Union army or cause. I don't know that he ever contributed anything to aid the rebellion in anyway." Much depended on circumstances in specific neighborhoods. Anti-Confederates in Rowan County were afraid to make their feelings known "for fear of being imprisoned" in the prison camp located in Salisbury. Even where local feeling for the Union was strong, support was constricted at certain times, such as when the draft was called. "There were a good many union people in the neighbourhood," a witness from Guilford County stated, "but they were afraid to speak their sentiment openly, being fearful that they would be taken up." The personality of the individual was also crucial. Did they have the resolve to openly defy local officials? John Cole of Orange County was described as a "reserved man" who "was intimidated to some degree" although in favor of the Union. This evidence suggests that more men chose to hide from the draft than join organizations like the Heroes of America in the piedmont, thereby maintaining an ambivalent position as best they could.[31]

Historians tend to view all outliers, and those who aided them, as disloyal, for obvious reasons—they ultimately worked against the Confederate cause. Such a view is understandable, but whether the men involved regarded their actions in precisely this way is open to question. Once conscription was introduced, fugitives avoided the militia and draft officers as best they could. Some did not have the resolve to avoid being pressed into service; Hamilton W. Rice testified that he "was a Confederate soldier for three years but was opposed to the war all the time." It was a common complaint that men taking positions exempt from the draft, such as in the salt mines or in the Home Guard, did so to avoid fighting. Should they be considered loyal to the Confederate cause? Others no doubt decided to join armed Union gangs as the best means of avoiding being called up, but this could have been a decision based on personal preservation and immediate need more than it was a reflection of core political beliefs. Yet more men in the piedmont simply did not want to commit themselves at all.[32]

The majority of piedmont claimants to the Southern Claims Commission professed broad sympathy with the Union but were not prepared to escalate that affiliation by doing anything more than hiding out or providing food and shelter to deserters if not called up for service, choosing to see out the war as best they could. Draft dodgers in the piedmont justified and rationalized their decisions in many different ways; it is possible that some may even have been more broadly sympathetic to the Confederate than the Union cause. It was not loyalty to either side that was really important, though. The bottom line was that they were not prepared to risk their lives or leave their families behind. Outliers usually tried to remain as close to home as possible. It is no coincidence that this allowed them to continue to work on the farm at times when the militia and Home Guard were not present. Rebecca Norman of Yadkin County stated that her husband refused to be drafted and hid from the militia, but in "early 1863 he came home and worked a while in the farm."[33]

Family, Loyalty, and Increasing Ambivalence, 1863–1865

Neighbor confronted neighbor in an ugly and divisive atmosphere that threatened to split communities apart in the piedmont. It was very difficult for the ambivalent to avoid taking sides in this situation, especially if they were on the receiving end of rough treatment. Jason S. Dunn provided a frightening description of the activity of a Unionist band led by William Owens in "sections of our old N. state where Crooks[,] McBride[,] and Daniel Worth's field of operations have been" (Davidson, Guilford, Randolph, Montgomery, and Moore counties). Encouraged by "the Quaker influence[,] they have strengthened and grown," stealing guns, food, and horses, burning barns, and threatening further retribution. Dunn had been forced out of bed in the middle of the night by this gang. When he refused to hand over his gun, pistols were raised against his wife and daughter; "if I behaved myself," he said, they promised "to restore me to the Bosom of Abe. Lincoln . . . but if they herd from me anymore they would send me to the Devil where secession came from and my age only saved my life." All were afraid to report the names of these men for fear of retribution. "Things have grown so alarming and I dare not leave home as well as many others for our familys would be without what little protection we might afford[.] [T]he wretched and deplorable condition of Treason[,] Rebellion[,] Robery[,] and incendaryism with plundering and ravaging the country all around going on here is incredible."[34] Dunn was almost certainly perceived to be a Confederate sympathizer, because attacks such as this were not usually carried out on households with Unionist inclinations. Even so, it must have been difficult to distinguish friend from foe as violence, intimidation, and lawlessness became pervasive in the piedmont.

Such circumstances might have furthered support for the Confederacy as the best hope of restoring law and order, but the militia and Home Guard could cause as much trouble as renegade Unionists. The inner war was vicious in the piedmont—those aiding the outliers risked torture, imprisonment, and even death—particularly when regular soldiers, who had little hesitation in using coercive measures to obtain information, were sent in.[35] Aggression on both sides most likely encouraged the uncommitted to continue to try to ride out the war as best they could without taking sides. Confederate hopes of generating support for the cause among ambivalent yeomen were also hampered by the ways in which preexisting rivalries shaped the dynamics of politics at the local level during the war. Joshua Bonner was accused of harboring a deserter but claimed that it was the false accusation of ex-Democrats in his home town of Salem who were abusing their authority. Bonner asserted that they not only picked on their former Whig rivals but used their position to stay out of active service while forcing others to serve. How many other local officials abused their power in this way is uncertain, but the complaint that those hunting deserters were conveniently avoiding the draft themselves was regularly made.[36]

There is no question that the authorities seeking to enforce Confederate control received diminishing degrees of assistance in the central piedmont. In August 1863, J. H. Foust distinguished three different reactions among his fellow citizens, characterizing the position of ambivalent yeomen rather well. First, "the most dangerous sympathise with them [anti-Confederates] & will & do indirectly aid them." Second, some "fear to do any thing for fear of destruction both of life & property & if forced out will effect nothing." Finally, "the third class would aid in arresting them but are too weak to hope for success." Foust concluded that the Home Guard was not capable of arresting deserters and that their attempts only served to "increase the destruction of private property," unless they worked in conjunction with regular troops.[37] If the complaints of militia officers and Confederate authorities are anything to go by, more and more in the piedmont refused to help in arresting deserters and outliers. By 1864, Governor Vance was informed that not only were sections of Wilkes County (on the western edge of the piedmont) "disloyal" but that the local Home Guard and militia were "encouraging desertion and have gone under with the disloyal sentiment with at least one half of the people of the county. I am convinced that a good many magistrates have [also] succumbed."[38] The failure to establish order in piedmont counties did nothing to endear the Confederacy to ordinary whites who were uncertain that secession was a wise move in the first place.

Underlying the negative responses of yeomen and poor whites were family considerations. B. H. Kearns of Randolph County wrote to Vance inquiring if men aged between thirty-five and forty would be drafted soon as he, and many of his neighbors, wanted to know if it was worth planting a corn crop. He had been conscripted but not called up yet. "We know not what to do. Conscription is held over us. It is a folly to sow a crop and then be called away from it having no one to complete." Moreover, those who might be enlisted wanted to make "some arrangements for the protection of our families during our absence." Hugh M. May from Anson County wrote to Vance, "with reluctance," asking for exemption from further service after completing a twelve-month term. "I have got my mother and family under my charge and my sister and four little children whose father and husband volunteered for the War and died in the service and then my own wife and two little children all who look to me for support and last year I lost my crop by being in the service and I beg of you not for my sake but for the sake of those under my charge to give me a discharge until next fall if you have the power to do so for unless I stay at home they are bound to suffer." Both of these men were willing to continue with the war but were personally conflicted because of family responsibilities. Those displaying less conviction were surely more ready to place family above loyalty to the Confederacy.[39]

As the war progressed and the hardships got worse, it does indeed seem that family duty increasingly overrode other concerns. As Bill Cecil-Fronsman observes, the governors' papers are "replete with pleas to release sons or husbands whose labors were desperately needed for family support." Eliza A. Thomas described this as "the cries of the poor." She was one of countless others with children to feed who begged Governor Vance to return her husband from the front. The family "has a small crop in the field probably enough to support [the] family if it could be taken care of but the prospect is for it to remain there" because there was no one to harvest it. "If the country has come to the [point] that such a man cannot be spared to his family I suppose we must take what follows." Men and women in the piedmont became progressively more forthright in their discontent with the Confederacy's demands. It is too simplistic, though, to say that they withdrew their support because of war weariness or that they never had much support to give in the first place due to their class status. Both assumptions are partially correct. The debilitating effects of the war asked too much of yeomen families, and the consequent discontent inflamed preexisting social, political, and economic tensions. The exigencies of war, then, exacerbated class tensions in a region where the fault lines ran deep.[40]

It was increasingly common for yeomen to use the rhetoric of class in expressing their frustration. However, growing class-consciousness, if that is the best way to characterize this phenomenon, did not necessarily encourage allegiance to the Union or necessitate abandoning the Confederate cause. A much-cited letter, written by a disgruntled private from Fayetteville, illustrates the way in which war weariness and class tensions combined but is perhaps most revealing by the way in which it shows that family was the major concern. "Now Govr. do tell me how we poor soldiers who are fighting for the 'rich mans negro' can support our families at $11 per month? How can the poor live? I dread to see the summer as I am fearful there will be much suffering and probably many deaths from starvation. They are suffering now." This soldier predicted "a revolution unless something is done as the majority of our soldiers are poor men with families who say they are tired of the rich mans war & poor mans fight. They wish to get to their families & fully believe some settlement could be made were it not that our authorities have made up their minds to prosecute the war regardless of all suffering." The decisive factor, however, was not class or disaffection but the adverse manner in which his family was affected. "There is great dissatisfaction in the army and as a mans first duty is to provide for his own household the soldiers wont be imposed upon much longer." It was family considerations that would guide his future conduct. "If a single man is killed no one suffers but if a married man or man of family is killed many may be made to suffer."[41]

An anonymous letter was just as blunt: "The time has come that we the common people has to hav bread or blood & we are bound both men & women to have it or die in the attempt. Some of us have bin travling for the last month with the money in our pockets to buy corn & tryed men That had a plenty & has bin unable to buy a bushel holding on for a better price[.] [W]e are willing to give & obligate two dollars a bushel but no more for the idea is that the slave oner has the plantations & the hands to rais the bred stuffs & the common people is drove off in the ware to fight for the big mans negro." If prices could not be regulated, the consequences were dire. "Them that has worked hard & was in living circumstances with perhaps a good little homestead & other thing convenient for there well being will be credited until the debt will about take there land & every thing they hav & then they will stop all & if not they will hav to rent there lands of them lords[.] [S]ir we hoos sons brothers & husbands is now fighting for the big mans negros are determined to hav bread out of there barns & that at a price that we can pay or we will slaughter as we go if this is the way we common people is to be treated in the confederacy." Despite the biting class hostility displayed in this letter, its writer was prepared to see the war continue as long as prices could be regulated, for it was "not our desire to organise and commence operations." The author was ready for North Carolina to consider leaving the Confederacy—"let us try to manage & defend our own state"—but was seemingly prepared to remain within it, if grain could be sold at acceptable prices. Indeed, the priority was not really staying in or out of the Confederacy but protecting the family homestead. The greatest fear revealed in this letter was of debt and the calamitous prospect of losing the farm. It also reflected the frustrations women felt in being left to carry out the daily burden of running the household and tending crops in the absence of large numbers of men. Drew Gilpin Faust famously drew on evidence like this to argue that it was because of the alienation of elite women that the Confederacy lost the war. Undoubtedly, the hardships that women faced did not help the Confederate cause, but this particular letter was not a decisive rejection of the Confederacy, much less a move toward the Union, but was a passionate defense of home and hearth.[42]

The famous actions of a group of women in the piedmont in March 1863 during the so-called bread riots tell a similar story. The *Carolina Watchman* (Salisbury) reported that approximately "50 soldiers' wives, followed by a numerous train of curious female observers," attacked "several of our businessmen . . . whom they regarded as speculators in the necessaries of life" to "demand an abatement in prices." They threatened to take what they wanted unless storekeepers complied with their wishes. One man initially refused to sell flour at what the women considered a fair price, and they "went to work with hatchets on the store room door" until he changed his mind. These women were not outliers or criminals; indeed, they did not consider themselves to be doing any wrong. "They unhesitatingly declared their purpose and gave specific arguments to justify their acts," as Escott observes. Most likely, they did not even need to justify actions that put food in the mouths of their children. The *Carolina Watchman* sympathized with, rather than condemned, the women; "there are many families in this town and vicinity who have not tasted meat for weeks, and some times, months together." Similar demonstrations took place in the central piedmont, in High Point and in Yadkin County. Without further evidence, we cannot be sure that these women had decisively turned against the cause that their husbands fought for, but we can state with certainty that they acted to protect their families.[43]

Rather than making a decisive stand against the Confederacy, many men and women in the piedmont did what was best for their families and homes, and in the latter stages of the war, almost certainly a majority took this position. The threats (and in the case of bread rioters, actions) of the countless numbers who complained to the governor were primarily motivated by family considerations, although they are often interpreted as being political acts. To what extent they were politically motivated cannot be ascertained without further evidence. It is impossible to tell with precision exactly how many supported the Confederacy, how many supported the Union, and how many stood somewhere in between, much less quantify changing opinions and fluctuating allegiances. However, we can be fairly certain that the need to protect and to provide for their families, in the most arduous of circumstances, became the most important concern for piedmont yeomen and poor whites by 1864 and 1865; it had been that way for many of them from the beginning.

Conclusion: The Piedmont in Wider Perspective

Understanding why piedmont non-slaveholders were so reluctant to become involved in the war when compared with their peers across the South has to begin by stressing local circumstances. It is not only slavery's peripheral economic importance in the central counties but a political and cultural environment in which slavery and planters were not central to piedmont society. Planters, and their desire to protect slavery, were the driving force behind secession and defeating the North at all costs. As Victoria E. Bynum argues, large slaveholders in the piedmont "did not fit the general stereotype of the southern planter," as they were less wealthy and influential and more economically diversified than their counterparts elsewhere.[44] They were mostly located in the northern and southern extremes, where plantation agriculture existed. It is unsurprising, then, that piedmont yeomen, especially those in the central counties, did not unthinkingly follow the planters' lead, either within the state or within the South, and that the Confederacy attracted varying levels of support.

The power of the eastern planter establishment and the undemocratic nature of secession also did little to endear the Confederacy to ordinary whites in the piedmont (and to some slaveholders as well). Randolph County postmaster Emsley Beckerdite posed a difficult question to newspaper editor Marmaduke Robins in January 1865: "Was ours a republican government? You answer in the affirmative. Then I ask again if the people, the bone and sinew of this once great country[,] were ever legitimately consulted upon the question of cession. You would not like to risk your well earned title to intelligence by answering affirmatively." A minority in the piedmont felt so strongly about the undemocratic nature of North Carolina's exit from the Union that it underpinned their efforts to violently resist Confederate authority. Approximately one in five did not hesitate to volunteer, for a variety of reasons—not least the feeling that it was their duty to do so. It is not these southerners who have been the focus of this essay but the ambivalent who preferred not to take sides and avoided active participation as best they could. By 1863, there were more and more in this position. Beckerdite revealed that "I have not known a man in the last two years who would not willingly have given all he had and would have pledged all that his friends had to keep out of the army. . . . I tell you plainly that the people of the Confederate states would welcome with ovations any power upon earth that was able to deliver them from Conscription[,] impressments[,] taxation[,] and the other ills imposed upon them by those who have deceived them." The demands of the war, and local circumstances within the piedmont, worked in tandem in pushing the ambivalent to take a more critical view of the Confederacy.[45]

In this light, the debate over the success, or otherwise, of Jefferson Davis, Robert E. Lee, and other southern politicians and generals in crafting a southern identity and stimulating a nationalist fervor seems somewhat peripheral. To be sure, wider issues of Confederate leadership should not be written out of the story. Piedmont residents followed the course of the war closely. Had Davis's welfare measures been successful, substantial discontent might have been avoided. The effects of the conscription laws were immense. On balance, though, the rhythm of daily life was influenced more by family concerns and local events, not by what was happening in Richmond or on the battlefields.

This should come as no surprise when considering the nature of yeomen society before the war began. Scholars as diverse in their interpretation of yeomen life and culture as Stephanie McCurry, Lacy K. Ford, and Steven Hahn agree on the centrality of the household and the significance of family and community. The present historiographical debate over lower-class loyalty during the war tends to lose sight of this, shifting the focus from family and local community to the wider and more abstract notions of Confederate identity and allegiance. Whether this change in orientation provides a deeper understanding of the home front experience in the piedmont is debatable. Several decades ago, Orville Vernon Burton argued that residents of Edgefield, South Carolina, "interpreted the meaning of the conflict and reacted to its demands from the perspective of their own families, relatives, friends, and the local community." This was overwhelmingly the case for yeomen and poor whites in the piedmont as well, many of whom did not feel particularly strongly about either side in the war but looked to their own family concerns first and foremost. It is not class, disloyalty, or disaffection that best characterizes their position, but ambivalence.[46]

It is difficult to draw too many broad conclusions from the example of the piedmont during the Civil War because local circumstances were critical, although there were surely many other ambivalent southerners. It can be speculated, however, that had the region felt the presence of the Federal army and its destructive power, this might have stiffened the resolve of the ambivalent and bred hatred of the invaders, as in Virginia, for example. "The more I see the Yankees," wrote a resident of occupied southeastern Virginia in 1862, "the worse I *hate* them." The inner civil war did not serve this purpose, however. It encouraged families to take a middle line and avoid committing to either side. Fighting rarely had a direct impact on the piedmont, and this helped to maintain a strong sense of localism rather than identification with the Confederate nation.[47]

At the same time, there was undoubtedly a stronger underlying ambivalence toward slavery and toward the Confederacy in the piedmont than there was in most other parts of the South. Unionism was particularly strong. Few historians of North Carolina would dispute Cecil-Fronsman's contention that there was a "growing sense of class consciousness" among non-slaveholders between 1861 and 1865.[48] Even so, this development manifested itself in many different ways, and recognition of common interests as yeomen or poor whites in a slaveholder's war did not always conflict with support for the Confederacy. The piedmont contributed men and materials, even when the demands placed on the region became virtually intolerable. Some yeomen chose to support the Confederate cause to the end, despite the hardships and the food shortages. We need to move beyond the either/or mode of thinking that categorizes southerners only as loyal or disloyal during the war and rediscover the large number who occupied the middle ground.

Notes

I gratefully acknowledge the support of an Archie K. Davis Fellowship from the North Caroliniana Society that allowed me to carry out research for this essay.

1. Key works emphasizing class and a lack of will include Richard E. Beringer, Herman Hattaway, Archer Jones, and William N. Still Jr., *Why the South Lost the Civil War* (Athens: University of Georgia Press, 1986); Wayne K. Durrill, *War of Another Kind: A Southern Community in the Great Rebellion* (New York: Oxford University Press, 1990); Paul D. Escott, *After Secession: Jefferson Davis and the Failure of Confederate Nationalism* (Baton Rouge: Louisiana State University Press, 1978); David Williams, *Rich Man's War: Class, Caste, and Confederate Defeat in the Lower Chattahoochee Valley* (Athens: University of Georgia Press, 1998); and David Williams, Teresa Crisp Williams, and David Carlson, *Plain Folk in a Rich Man's War: Class and Dissent in Confederate Georgia* (Gainesville: University Press of Florida, 2002). The opposite view is given in Gary W. Gallagher, *The Confederate War* (Cambridge, Mass.: Harvard University Press, 1997); William Blair, *Virginia's Private War: Feeding Body and Soul in the Confederacy, 1861–1865* (New York: Oxford University Press, 1998); and Brian Steel Wills, *The War Hits Home: The Civil War in Southeastern Virginia* (Charlottesville: University Press of Virginia, 2001). See also William W. Freehling, *The South vs. the South: How Anti-Confederate Southerners Shaped the Course of the Civil War* (New York: Oxford University Press, 2001), which makes an astute analysis while leaning toward the class interpretation.

2. The most recent book on southern nationalism is Anne Sarah Rubin, *A Shattered Nation: The Rise and Fall of the Confederacy, 1861–1868* (Chapel Hill: University of North Carolina Press, 2005). Many of the essays in Lesley C. Gordon and John C. Inscoe, eds., *Inside the Confederate Nation: Essays in Honor of Emory M. Thomas* (Baton Rouge: Louisiana State University Press, 2005), discuss the themes of nationalism and allegiance; see, in particular, Brian Steel Wills, "Shades of Nation: Confederate Loyalties in Southeastern Virginia," 59–77.

3. In *Southern Outcast: Hinton Rowan Helper and the Impending Crisis of the South* (Baton Rouge: Louisiana State University Press, 2006), I argue that yeomen

and poor whites in the piedmont were ambivalent in their view of slavery. This argument is extended to the Civil War years in this essay. Victoria E. Bynum also makes use of this term but in different contexts. She argues that "the ambivalence of the state's citizens and political leaders toward disunion—manifested by North Carolina's late entry into the Confederacy—has long been recognized by historians" and that "southern women had expressed an ambivalence about the war from its inception." Bynum, *Unruly Women: The Politics of Social and Sexual Control in the Old South* (Chapel Hill: University of North Carolina Press, 1992), 130, 133.

4. D. W. Meinig, *The Shaping of America: A Geographical Perspective on 500 Years of History. Volume One: Atlantic America, 1492–1800* (New Haven: Yale University Press, 1986), 292–93; Paul D. Escott, "Yeoman Independence and the Market: Social Status and Economic Development in Antebellum North Carolina," *North Carolina Historical Review* 66 (July 1989): 275–300; Allen Tullos, *Habits of Industry: White Culture and the Transformation of the Carolina Piedmont* (Chapel Hill: University of North Carolina Press, 1989), 77–82; Bess Beatty, *Alamance: The Holt Family and Industrialization in a North Carolina County, 1837–1900* (Baton Rouge: Louisiana State University Press, 1999), 15–29, 53–71.

5. Rosser Howard Taylor, *Slaveholding in North Carolina: An Economic View* (Chapel Hill: University of North Carolina Press, 1926), 35–36, 48–49; Charles C. Bolton, *Poor Whites of the Antebellum South: Tenants and Laborers in Central North Carolina and Northeast Mississippi* (Durham: Duke University Press, 1994), 11–12, 20. Counties in the central piedmont include Alamance, Chatham, Davidson, Davie, Forsyth, Guilford, Iredell, Montgomery, Moore, Orange, Randolph, Rowan, Stanly, and Yadkin. Caswell, Granville, and Warren counties to the north predominantly grew tobacco, while Anson, Mecklenburg, and Richmond counties to the south grew cotton. The figure of 15–20 percent owning slaves in the central piedmont contrasts with the norm of 25 percent across the South as a whole in 1860; in the Lower South, more than a third of whites owned slaves. Peter Kolchin estimates that perhaps as many as 50 percent of all white southerners actually held "an economic stake in slavery" through family ties or connections to the plantation economy, even if they did not own slaves. Since North Carolina lacked a fully fledged plantation economy, this applied to few yeomen and even fewer poor whites in the central piedmont. Kolchin, *American Slavery, 1619–1877* (New York: Hill and Wang, 1993), 181.

6. Benjamin Sherwood Hedrick to John A. Gilmer, January 19, [1860], Benjamin Sherwood Hedrick Papers, Southern Historical Collection, University of North Carolina at Chapel Hill (hereafter SHC); Jesse Wheeler to Hinton Rowan Helper, September 10, 1859, William Henry Anthon Collection, New York Public Library.

7. Bolton, *Poor Whites*, 12–41.

8. Martin Crawford, *Ashe County's Civil War: Community and Society in the Appalachian South* (Charlottesville: University Press of Virginia, 2001), 3. For an extended discussion of these issues, see Brown, *Southern Outcast*, 80–87, 118–23.

9. Ira Berlin, *Generations of Captivity: A History of African-American Slaves* (Cambridge, Mass.: Harvard University Press, 2003), 209–30; William W. Freehling, *The Road to Disunion: Volume Two, Secessionists Triumphant 1854–1861* (New York: Oxford University Press, 2007), 14 and passim.

10. Ralph A. Wooster, *Politicians, Planters, and Plain Folk: Courthouse and State-house in the Upper South, 1850–1860* (Knoxville: University of Tennessee Press, 1975), 40; Fletcher M. Green, *Constitutional Development in the South Atlantic States, 1776–1860: A Study in the Evolution of Democracy* (Chapel Hill: University of North Carolina Press, 1930), 232–33; Thomas E. Jeffrey, "Beyond 'Free Suffrage': North Carolina Politics and the Convention Movement of the 1850s," *North Carolina Historical Review* 62 (October 1985): 387–419, and " 'Free Suffrage' Revisited: Party Politics and Constitutional Reform in Antebellum North Carolina," *North Carolina Historical Review* 59 (January 1982): 24–48.

11. Paul D. Escott and Jeffrey J. Crow, "The Social Order and Violent Disorder: An Analysis of North Carolina in the Revolution and the Civil War," *Journal of Southern History* 52 (August 1986): 379; Donald C. Butts, "The 'Irrepressible Conflict': Slave Taxation and North Carolina's Gubernatorial Election of 1860," *North Carolina Historical Review* 58 (January 1981): 44–66, and "A Challenge to Planter Rule: The Controversy over the Ad Valorem Taxation of Slaves in North Carolina 1858–1862" (Ph.D. diss., Duke University, 1978).

12. Robin E. Baker, "Class Conflict and Political Upheaval: The Transformation of North Carolina Politics during the Civil War," *North Carolina Historical Review* 69 (April 1992): 159; Bolton, *Poor Whites*, 143; R. W. D. Connor, ed., *A Manual of North Carolina* (Raleigh: E. M. Uzzell and Company, 1913), 1013–15.

13. Jonathan Worth to Dr. C. W. Woolen, May 17, 1861, in *The Correspondence of Jonathan Worth*, ed. J. G. de Roulhac Hamilton (Raleigh: Edwards and Broughton Printing Company, 1909), 1:147–48; John Gilmer, cited in Bolton, *Poor Whites*, 144–45. Marc W. Kruman, *Parties and Politics in North Carolina, 1836–1865* (Baton Rouge: Louisiana State University Press, 1983), 213–21, provides a lucid analysis of the abrupt switch of support within North Carolina in April 1861.

14. Jesse Wheeler to Benjamin Sherwood Hedrick, May 6, 1861, Benjamin Sherwood Hedrick Papers, Duke University.

15. James Sinclair to John W. Ellis, May 4, 1861, Governor's Papers, box 151, North Carolina Division of Archives and History (hereafter GP and box number); Bruce Collins, *White Society in the Antebellum South* (London: Longman, 1985), 154; T. Watson Street, *The Story of Southern Presbyterians* (Richmond: John Knox Press, 1960), 52. Approximately one-half of Southern Presbyterian families owned slaves, estimates Andrew E. Murray, *The Presbyterians and the Negro—A History* (Philadelphia: Presbyterian Historical Society, 1966), 65.

16. Private James William Gibson to parents, August 11, 1861, in *The Civil War in North Carolina: Soldiers' and Civilians' Letters and Diaries, 1861–1865*, ed. Christopher M. Watford, vol. 1, *The Piedmont* (Jefferson, N.C.: McFarland, 2003), 19; Edmund Shoe to Esther Barrier, October 23, 1861, in ibid., 24; William Clement to Mattie Martin, October 25, 1861, in ibid., 26.

17. Bolton, *Poor Whites*, 157.

18. B. M. Edney to John W. Ellis, July 11, 1861, GP 152. Bolton, *Poor Whites*, 158, notes the cases of two poor whites coerced into service. See also the letter of a poor white, charged with murder in Goldsboro, asking for a pardon in order that he might join the militia in South Carolina. He apologized for his actions and hoped that he

would "have the chance of killing one yankey if you pleas before I dy" months before the war had actually begun. William Sauls to John W. Ellis, December 12, 1860, GP 149.

19. Without a detailed socioeconomic breakdown of initial volunteers from the piedmont, their status is open to conjecture. A study of the First North Carolina Regiment, composed of men from the eastern counties, suggests that it was yeomen who volunteered more readily than poor whites: Alan Craig Downs, "Enlistment into Confederate Military Service: The First Regiment North Carolina State Troops as a Test Case" (M.A. thesis, University of North Carolina, Chapel Hill, 1982). Based on this, Bolton speculates that poor whites were less likely than yeomen to volunteer, but he also presents many compelling reasons why poor whites were more likely to come forward in the central piedmont, outlined in the previous paragraph of this chapter, which seem more convincing. Bolton, *Poor Whites*, 157–58. There is limited archival evidence on this question, but it suggests that it was those without a household to support and maintain who chose to join the Confederate army. Martin Crawford's analysis of Ashe County volunteers concurs that family responsibilities were significant, as more single men volunteered than married men. Crawford speculates that volunteering "provided an opportune escape route for young men who had failed to establish themselves economically," although he also notes "that Confederate recruits derived from progressively poorer families as the war continued into and beyond its second year." Crawford, *Ashe County's Civil War*, 90–91. It is worth remembering that the dividing line between poor white and yeoman is anything but clearly defined and that the key point is how few men came forward in the piedmont in comparison to elsewhere.

20. John C. Inscoe and Gordon B. McKinney, *The Heart of Confederate Appalachia: Western North Carolina in the Civil War* (Chapel Hill: University of North Carolina Press, 2000), 84; Kruman, *Parties and Politics*, 211–12.

21. H. C. Wilson to Governor Ellis, April 22, 1861, in Noble J. Tolbert, *Papers of John Willis Ellis* (Raleigh: State Department of Archives and History, 1964), 2:662–63; William K. Ruffin to Thomas Ruffin, February 14, 1862, in *The Papers of Thomas Ruffin*, ed. J. G. de Roulhac Hamilton, 4 vols. (Raleigh: Edwards and Broughton Printing Company, 1918–20), 3:215–16; Claim 2114, John Julian, Rowan County, March 19, 1876, Settled Case Files for Claims Approved by the Southern Claims Commission, 1871–80, Record Group 217, National Archives, Washington D.C. (hereafter SCC; for more scholarship about this institution, see note 31 below). Richard Nelson Current, *Lincoln's Loyalists: Union Soldiers from the Confederacy* (Boston: Northeastern University Press, 1992), 216–17, speculates that 5,000 was the minimum number of North Carolinian Federal soldiers but that the total was probably much higher, especially because many were counted as recruits from Tennessee.

22. James H. Moore to Henry T. Clark, July 18, 1861, GP 152; William T. Auman and David D. Scarboro, "The Heroes of America in Civil War North Carolina," *North Carolina Historical Review* 58 (October 1981): 327–63.

23. James M. McPherson, *For Cause and Comrades: Why Men Fought in the Civil War* (New York: Oxford University Press, 1997), 102.

24. James H. Moore to Henry T. Clark, July 18, 1861, GP 152.

25. William T. Auman, "Neighbor against Neighbor: The Inner Civil War in the Central Counties of Confederate North Carolina" (Ph.D. diss., University of North Carolina, Chapel Hill, 1988). See also Auman, "Neighbor against Neighbor: The Inner Civil War in the Randolph County Area of Confederate North Carolina," *North Carolina Historical Review* 61 (January 1984): 59-92.

26. Hugh T. Lefler, *History of North Carolina* (New York: Lewis Historical Publishing Company, 1956), 2:494; Ella Lonn, *Desertion during the Civil War* (New York: Century Company, 1928), 231.

27. J. H. Foust to John W. Ellis, June 10, 1861, GP 151; J. P. Aldridge to John W. Ellis, June 22, 1861, GP 151.

28. Margaret M. Storey, *Loyalty and Loss: Alabama's Unionists in the Civil War and Reconstruction* (Baton Rouge: Louisiana State University Press, 2004), 57, 66.

29. R. F. Armfield to Zebulon Vance, February 19, 1863, GP 162; J. C. McRae to Silas Alexander Sharp, September 17, 1863, John McKee Sharp Papers, SHC.

30. John A. Craven to Henry T. Clark, October 21, 1862, GP 160. It should also be noted that after joining the Confederate army, large numbers of men in the piedmont chose to desert. Auman, "Neighbor against Neighbor," 69 (*NCHR*), estimates that just less than a quarter of men from Randolph County deserted.

31. Claim 8797, Joseph Ivery, Orange County, March 27, 1875; Claim 743, Michael Shuding, Rowan County, March 29, 1877 (a similar view is given in Claim 3483, John Carson); Claim 3044, Jeruia A. and Julia D. McGrady, Guilford County, December 1878; Claim 12789, John Cole, Orange County, March 14, 1872, all SCC. Frank W. Klingberg has written the basic study of the Southern Claims Commission; see *The Southern Claims Commission* (Berkeley: University of California Press, 1955). Michael K. Honey, "The War within the Confederacy: White Unionists of North Carolina," *Prologue* 18 (Summer 1986): 75-93, remains the fullest study of the cases made by North Carolinians to the Southern Claims Commission during Reconstruction seeking recompense for property and materials taken by Federal soldiers during the war.

32. Claim 10730, James M. Lindsey, Davidson County (testimony of Hamilton W. Rice), SCC.

33. Claim 3508, Rebecca Norman, Yadkin County, March 19, 1875, SCC.

34. Jason S. Dunn to E. J. Hale and sons, January 8, 1863, GP 161.

35. See, for example, Mary Browne to Vance, September 15, 1864, GP 180, for an account of how women, children, and old men were spared no mercy by militia officers in Davidson County. She hoped Vance would do all that he could "to protect the civil laws and writs of our country." The relations of suspected rebel leaders were especially vulnerable; William Owens's wife was strung up by her thumbs. Bynum, *Unruly Women*, 143-44.

36. Joshua Bonner to Henry T. Clark, January 16, 1862, GP 157.

37. J. H. Foust to Vance, August 29, 1863, GP 168.

38. S. A. Sharpe to Vance, September 5, 14, 1864, GP 179.

39. B. H. Kearns to Vance, February 26, 1863, GP 162; Hugh M. May to Zebulon Vance, January 5, 1863, GP 161.

40. Bill Cecil-Fronsman, *Common Whites: Class and Culture in Antebellum North*

Carolina (Lexington: University Press of Kentucky, 1992), 212; Eliza A. Thomas to Vance, October 25, 1864, GP 181.

41. O. Goddin (Fifty-first North Carolina Regiment) to Vance, February 27, 1863, GP 162. This letter has been reprinted in W. Buck Yearns and John G. Barrett, eds., *North Carolina Civil War Documentary* (Chapel Hill: University of North Carolina Press, 1980), 97–99, but it has not been transcribed entirely accurately or fully. The last quotation cited here is from Goddin's postscript to this letter that is not reprinted in Yearns and Barrett.

42. Anonymous to Vance, February 17, 1863, GP 162. This letter may or may not have been written by a female, and it is possible it even had multiple authors (it is signed "Regulators"). The content is most reflective of a female voice, however. The letter also originated from Bladen County, just outside the southeastern corner of the piedmont. It nonetheless aptly captures the concerns of yeoman families from the piedmont and, indeed, across the state, whose worst fear was losing their home and farm. Drew Gilpin Faust, "Altars of Sacrifice: Confederate Women and the Narratives of War," *Journal of American History* 76 (March 1992): 1228.

43. *Carolina Watchman* (Salisbury), March 23, 1863; Paul D. Escott, *Many Excellent People: Power and Privilege in North Carolina, 1850–1900* (Chapel Hill: University of North Carolina Press, 1985), 65–66.

44. Bynum, *Unruly Women*, 20.

45. Emsley Beckerdite to Marmaduke Robins, January 21, 1865, cited in Escott, *Many Excellent People*, 82.

46. Orville Vernon Burton, *In My Father's House Are Many Mansions: Family and Community in Edgefield, South Carolina* (Chapel Hill: University of North Carolina Press, 1985), 225–26; Steven Hahn, *The Roots of Southern Populism: Yeoman Farmers and the Transformation of the Georgia Upcountry, 1850–1880* (New York: Oxford University Press, 1983); Lacy K. Ford, *The Origins of Southern Radicalism: The South Carolina Upcountry 1800–1860* (New York: Oxford University Press, 1988); Stephanie McCurry, *Masters of Small Worlds: Yeoman Households, Gender Relations, and the Political Culture of the Antebellum South Carolina Low Country* (New York: Oxford University Press, 1995).

47. Mattie Prentiss, June 1862, cited in Wills, "Shades of Nation," 65. Echoing the conclusions of William Blair in *Virginia's Private War*, Wills argues that "as Union actions became increasingly heavy handed, the reactions they provoked often reinforced a sense of Confederate nationalism among the civilians they encountered." Ibid, 66. The opposite view, however, is given in a study of Alabama: Malcolm C. McMillan, *The Disintegration of a Confederate State: Three Governors and Alabama's Wartime Home Front, 1861–1865* (Macon: Mercer University Press, 1986).

48. Cecil-Fronsman, *Common Whites*, 209.

A More Rigorous Style of Warfare

Wild's Raid, Guerrilla Violence, and Negotiated Neutrality in Northeastern North Carolina

During the final days of December 1863, Union brigadier general and Massachusetts abolitionist Edward Augustus Wild was a thoroughly frustrated man. By his own admission, Wild had undergone a major change in recent weeks. When he sat down on December 28 to pen the official account of his recent operation into Pasquotank, Camden, and Currituck counties, part of the Albemarle region in rural northeastern North Carolina, he tried desperately to explain (in eighteen handwritten pages and three appendices) his aggravation with waging counterguerrilla war on the southern home front.[1] Wild had just led the first major Civil War operation in the eastern theater using a full brigade of African American troops in a counter-guerrilla effort against companies of Confederate irregulars, and by the general's account, his men had done their duty well.[2]

Wild described to Major General Benjamin Butler, his superior at Norfolk, Virginia, how he and his soldiers had conscientiously followed the broad directives they received before the expedition: protect the loyal Union population along the coast of North Carolina, free the remaining slaves held in the northeastern counties, and destroy the menacing guerrilla force operating there.[3] But Wild had "found ordinary [military] measures to little avail" in his three-week expedition. As his black soldiers entered Pasquotank at the beginning of the raid, his brigade had at first adopted a strategy of "judiciously discriminating in favor of the worst rebels." Proceeding cautiously, Wild's troops impressed crops and livestock and punished only the disloyal, burning three buildings that were homes for two guerrillas and the barn of a Confederate supporter.[4] General Wild even drew up a list of fifty-three Unionists in Pasquotank with their addresses. After the raid, he suggested to his commander that these Unionists of Pasquotank be protected.

But when Wild left Pasquotank and entered Camden and Currituck, where guerrilla resistance stiffened, he "adopted a more rigorous style of warfare." After this point, his command demonstrated less and less restraint in dealing with the civilian population and moved toward a strategy of punishing the entire civilian community through increased property destruction and burning relatively large numbers of private residences for a rural area. Although his men never completely abandoned restraint toward civilians, they did adopt a scorched-earth policy that seemed to ignore the loyalty of the homeowner. In a desperate attempt to eradicate local support for the Confederate irregulars, Wild's troops burned over a dozen houses, including every home in the four-square-mile area around Indiantown in Currituck County.[5] In fact, the only military directive that Wild did not reevaluate over the course of his three-week expedition was Butler's instruction to enforce the Emancipation Proclamation. This order Wild carried out regardless of loyalty.

The historiography of the Civil War does not easily accommodate the rapid change in military policy toward southern civilians that is described in General Wild's report. Historians who have focused on Union military policy in the occupied South have tended to develop broad national narratives for how and when military policy evolved gradually toward a harsher strategy, leaving out the many local contexts where policy moved at an uneven rate.[6] While much important work has created general periodizations for when Union military policy shifted from a conciliatory "rosewater" stance to a harder strategy of increased violence and economic pressure against all civilians regardless of loyalty, it is important to ask how Union officers' policies evolved in specific southern communities.[7] Wild's raid in northeastern North Carolina illustrates how rapidly the transition to harsher warfare against the civilian population could occur in the context of a guerrilla war, and it highlights the impact of guerrilla tactics and punitive countermeasures on the local population. The evolution of military policy from discriminating on the basis of loyalty to employing harsh measures of widespread economic destruction and confiscation could occur over only a few days' time in the mind of an independently operating commander. In short, what Wild struggled to explain to General Butler was his own frustrating transition from a strategy of protecting Unionists and rooting out Confederate guerrillas to a less discriminating, more aggressive, and far more destructive policy aimed at crushing the guerrilla resistance in North Carolina's Albemarle region. Harsh as Wild's measures were, they moved local residents to seek a negotiated neutrality that brought some benefits to them and to the Union cause.

For Civil War scholars studying occupation, Wild's brief incursion into the northeastern region of North Carolina demonstrates the difficulties of waging a limited war against resisters on the Confederate home front. In Wild's response to the irregular problem, one can see initial attempts to limit violence in dealing with guerrilla forces and efforts to retain Unionists' loyalty in a politically divided community. But, one can also see how easy it was for a commander in a difficult position to become less restrained in his treatment of innocent civilians while fighting an irregular war. Wild's personal experience in northeastern North Carolina shows that Union military policy was not always created in Washington, D.C., or even at the headquarters of the army theater commander in the field. Policy could be created by any local commander operating independent of the larger field armies, and his policy did not have to conform to the dominant doctrine of the Federal government. Wild's raid into North Carolina reminds us that the recalcitrant problem of guerrilla activity in no-man's-land communities, like Pasquotank, Camden, and Currituck counties, was a key element that pushed Union commanders in many localities across the South toward the harder tactics that became dominant by 1864.

In the aftermath of the raid, the efforts by Pasquotank's Unionists, Confederates, and disillusioned citizens to negotiate a neutral position between the North Carolina government in Raleigh and General Butler's headquarters in Norfolk also illustrate how a community divided in its loyalties but deeply frustrated by guerrilla war could cooperate when threatened with complete social and racial disorder. When Pasquotank citizens came together and responded to Wild's raid at a town meeting held in late December 1863, Unionist and Confederate citizens sought to shore up their social order. By asking Governor Zebulon Vance to remove Confederate guerrillas and at the same time requesting that General Butler cease further Union raids into the community, both Confederate and Unionist residents of northeastern North Carolina briefly made community safety and stability more important than personal loyalty to either cause.

The geography of these counties differed from that of other parts of North Carolina. Camden, Currituck, and Pasquotank were at the far northeastern corner of the state and along with Perquimans, Chowan, and Gates counties made up a remote region cut off from the rest of North Carolina by the Chowan River to their west, the Albemarle Sound to the south, and the Great Dismal Swamp and Virginia state line to the north. All of these counties included swampy terrain. Local citizens of the three county seats—Elizabeth City in Pasquotank, South Mills in Camden, and Currituck Court-House in Currituck—turned this geography to their economic benefit during the antebellum years by developing a vibrant timber and turpentine trade with bustling Norfolk via the Dismal Swamp Canal.[8]

The economy of these farming and trading communities depended on the labor of a large black population. In 1860, Pasquotank County's population included the second largest free black population in the state of North Carolina. Of 4,500 black residents, 1,507 were free and 2,983 enslaved. Free blacks did much of the work in the tedious turpentine and shingle industry of the Dismal Swamp. The black population lived alongside 4,450 whites in the county, mostly small farmers and mariners. Camden and Currituck counties both had much smaller but not insignificant free black populations, 274 and 125 respectively. Like Pasquotank County, Camden and Currituck both had large slave populations relative to the size of their white communities. By 1860, Camden slaveholders held 2,127 blacks in bondage, in a county with only 2,942 white residents. Similarly, Currituck slaves numbered 2,523, while the white population was a little larger with 4,669 residents. The slaves primarily worked as agricultural laborers on corn and wheat plantations or as hired labor to smaller farmers.[9]

The origins of Edward Augustus Wild were very different. This unorthodox Union general was born in Brookline, Massachusetts, in 1825 of sturdy abolitionist stock. Wild spent his formative years being educated first at Harvard and then as a physician at Jefferson Medical College in Philadelphia. The future Union commander left for study and adventure in Europe in 1848 and again in 1855. While on his second trip abroad, he served as both surgeon and soldier of fortune in the armies of the Turkish sultan during the Crimean War. When he returned to the United States after his travels, Wild joined a militia unit in Brookline. When the Civil War came, Wild left his successful practice as a physician to become one of Massachusetts's first volunteer officers.[10]

Wild's early Civil War service was distinguished but harrowing; he nearly lost his life on two different battlefields, one in Virginia, the other in Maryland. After a bullet crippled his right hand during the battle of Fair Oaks in June 1862, Wild went home to convalesce. He returned to the army quickly, only to suffer the loss of his left arm at the battle of South Mountain in September 1862. Nevertheless, Wild's zealous belief in the abolition of slavery kept him committed to the cause of preserving the United States government and eager to return to the war as soon as his body mended. Wild worked his way through the ranks quickly, serving first as a captain in the First Massachusetts Infantry and later, in August 1862, as the colonel of his own regiment, the Thirty-fifth Massachusetts.

Following his wounding at South Mountain, Wild was promoted to brigadier general in April 1863. Shortly after this promotion, Wild's dedication to abolitionism led him to recruit one of the first all–African American combat units, partially from North Carolina's freed slave population. This green unit, with a freshly minted brigadier general as its leader, would be referred to in official correspondence as "Wild's African Brigade."[11] By late 1863, Wild's distinguished combat record and his racial beliefs won him a spot serving under Union major general Benjamin Butler, who was then in command of the Norfolk garrison.

In December 1863, the passionate General Wild led his 1,800-man force of black soldiers, recruited from towns in North Carolina, Ohio, and Massachusetts, in an expedition to the coast of the Old North State. Some of Wild's black soldiers had even been slaves in northeastern Carolina counties but had made their way to the Union lines at Norfolk, Portsmouth, Roanoke Island, Plymouth, or New Bern, where they were recruited into combat regiments.[12] Even with the loss of these early runaways, the northeastern region of North Carolina was still populated with a large number of slaves who could easily be liberated if a Union commander were inclined to press the issue.[13] Such an operation might deny Confederate forces needed supplies from this wealthy agricultural district. Furthermore, once emancipated by their brethren in arms, the remaining male slaves might join the ranks of Wild's new command.

Another reason that Wild and Butler focused on northeastern North Carolina was the growing Confederate guerrilla resistance in the counties along the northern side of the Albemarle Sound. These irregulars were daily harassing the minority Unionist community of northeastern Carolina, especially those Unionists residing in Elizabeth City, Pasquotank's county seat and the commercial center of the Albemarle region. Wild's command hoped to stop the guerrillas and blockade-running while confiscating the surplus crops and livestock of Confederate citizens, which might otherwise fall into the hands of Confederate commissary officers. With these objectives in mind, Wild secretly prepared in the late days of November 1863 to dash into the hostile "no man's land" (communities nominally in Confederate territory but in reality under neither government's control) of Pasquotank, Camden, and Currituck counties.[14]

The communities Wild entered were teetering on the brink of social chaos in late 1863. Since the fall of Elizabeth City in February 1862 to Union gunboats, Pasquotank, Camden, and Currituck counties had been racked by a brutal guerrilla war; public executions and murder had dominated the daily lives of the politically divided communities. Beginning in the late spring of 1862, Confederate soldiers paroled after early war battles formed bands of irregulars to fend off Union naval and army incursions along the coast. Periodically throughout 1862 and 1863, Union soldiers briefly occupied Elizabeth City and attempted to recruit local Unionists into the ranks of the Federal army. By the summer of 1863, Union troops became more focused on ridding the area of the menacing guerrillas who were hindering Federal recruitment efforts. During the summer and fall of that year, several small counter-guerrilla operations meant to suppress local irregulars resulted in less than a dozen secessionists killed or captured.[15]

Wild's forces would attempt to succeed where other counter-guerrilla raids had failed. When Wild started his troops from their bases in Virginia on December 5, they marched in two separate columns. The first, which he led himself, left from Norfolk and included the Fifth U.S. Colored Troops, one hundred men from the First North Carolina Colored Volunteers, and the Fifty-fifth Massachusetts.[16] The other column left from Portsmouth, Virginia, and consisted of the First U.S. Colored Troops and the Second North Carolina Colored Volunteers.[17] During the early days of December 1863, Wild and his "sable braves" meandered their way south, past the canals and through the forests of southern Virginia, across the state line, and into the heart of northeastern North Carolina.[18] As they entered the Albemarle region, the black soldiers skirted swamps on narrow footpaths and sauntered confidently by large plantations. A *New York Times* correspondent known only as "Tewksbury" attached himself to Wild's command and described his journey into this difficult country. "The [region's] inhabitants being almost exclusively 'secesh,' the colored boys were allowed to forage at will along the road," the reporter wrote.[19] General Wild also commented that during the early days of the raid, "we were . . . obliged to live on the country for a few days; which we did judiciously discriminating in favor of the worst rebels."[20]

Wild and his soldiers congregated at South Mills in Camden County just north of Pasquotank on December 7. While at South Mills, Wild was reinforced by two companies of cavalry and a section of artillery from Norfolk. Of this group, both the Fifth and Eleventh Pennsylvania Cavalry companies had previously operated as a reconnaissance force in the northeastern region during the fall of 1863. At South Mills, Wild's men busied themselves with rebuilding a bridge across the Pasquotank River that had been destroyed earlier in the war. To do so, Wild ordered the home of a local captain of the Confederate guerrillas torn down and used as wood for the bridge.[21] Wild likely selected this home with the help of the Pennsylvania troops who had been operating in the region for several months. This was the first recorded destruction of a building during Wild's expedition, but it would not be the last. Wild then crossed the river and started southward toward Elizabeth City.

When the African Brigade arrived at Elizabeth City on December 10, General Wild established a headquarters at the home of a local Unionist, Dr. William G. Pool, a relative of John Pool, a Pasquotank native and the Opposition/Whig Party candidate for governor in North Carolina in 1860.[22] While the former Whig John Pool had fled to the interior of nearby Bertie County, some of his relatives stayed in Elizabeth City for the duration of the war. "Three years ago it was a busy and beautiful little city, noted for the number of its stores and manufactories, the extent and variety of its trade, for its enterprise and the rapid increase of its population," wrote Tewksbury. But, he continued, "now most of the dwellings were deserted; the stores all closed; the streets overgrown with grass, its elegant edifices reduced to heaps of ruins by vandal Georgian troops [who had occupied the town during 1862]; the doors of the bank standing wide open, and a sepulchral silence brooded over the place."[23]

Wild decided to determine the loyalty of the local citizens once he set up headquarters in Elizabeth City. The general had already heard about the minority Unionist population, and with the help of the prominent Unionist Dr. Pool and almost certainly his black soldiers from Pasquotank, he identified virtually every assertive Unionist who remained in the county. This list totaled fifty-three, nearly every one a head of household.[24] "After careful inquiry," Wild later recorded, "I have been able to make out a list of genuine Union citizens of Elizabeth City and vicinity." He continued by describing the loyalty of the entire region: "We found the majority of people along our track to be reasonably neutral; that is to say, although sympathizing with the South, they were tired of the war, or weary of their own distresses and privations; harassed by the frequent alternation of masters, being plundered by both sides; or despondent of the ultimate success of the South; or convinced of the doom of slavery; or aware of the mischief arising from the presence of guerrillas in their midst." With true New England skepticism, Wild further qualified his assessment of local loyalty: "or if really neutral, or sympathizing with the North, they were usually (and reasonably) afraid to speak their minds, on account of Guerrillas etc." As he soon learned, however, when the property of disloyal men was threatened, men who claimed neutrality or Confederate sympathies would rapidly shift their public political statements to support the Union.[25]

At Elizabeth City, General Wild also began carrying out his principal order to free local bondsmen. "Slaves belonging to isolated plantations were constantly coming to headquarters and asking the General to protect them in the removal of their families," Tewksbury recorded.[26] He described one incident in which a member of Wild's brigade, likely on Roanoke Island, asked the general for permission to retrieve his son who was enslaved at the farm of his own former master. In response to the black soldier's request, Wild sent him on that mission with a contingent of guards to ensure their protection. In the end, the man rescued his son from bondage.[27]

As Wild and his soldiers set about the business of removing slaves from all of the local plantations and offering them safe passage to the Union freedmen's colony at Roanoke Island, they encountered resistance from irregulars in the vicinity.[28] Since some of Wild's men had at one point been Pasquotank residents, there was an added dimension to Wild's upending of the racial order. Not only was he putting black men over white by giving black men the power to confiscate white men's property and fight them on the battlefield, but he was also placing former slaves or black employees in a position of power vis-à-vis their former owners or employers. This point clearly disturbed the local guerrilla companies and must have been on their minds as they planned operations against Wild's troops.

During one of Wild's first encounters with the local irregulars, Captain John T. Elliott's Pasquotank guerrillas captured Private Samuel Jordan of the Fifth U.S. Colored Troops. Fearing that Jordan would not be treated as a legitimate prisoner of war but as a rebellious slave, Wild used an unusual, if not unprecedented, method to ensure his protection.[29] He took two hostages, Elizabeth Weeks and Phoebe Munden, the wives of local irregulars then serving in Elliott's band. Wild also captured twenty male citizens; most were later released after a hearing on their status, but eight men were charged with "various offenses."[30]

The day after Jordan's capture, Wild sent out a party to Hertford, the seat of neighboring Perquimans County, to break up the training camp of Colonel James W. Hinton, the officer appointed by Governor Vance to organize the northeastern Carolina guerrillas into a conventional infantry regiment. The expedition succeeded in destroying two guerrilla camps in lower Pasquotank County, but when the Union soldiers arrived at the banks of the Perquimans River, they found the bridges across the waterway destroyed and the channel unfordable. They returned to Elizabeth City never having reached Perquimans County and having captured only one suspected guerrilla, a farmer named Daniel Bright.[31]

Meanwhile, the guerrillas east and west of the Pasquotank River watched, scouted, and waited for evening to fall. "The Guerrillas pestered us," General Wild later noted in his report. "They crept upon our pickets at night, waylaid our expeditions, and our Cavalry scouts, firing upon us whenever they could." Even though the Confederate guerrillas were deeply annoyed, they were not afraid of Wild's troops. No doubt, the seizure of two local women and twenty men and the destruction of Confederate property sent fear through the hearts of peaceable Confederates in the county, and the fact that all this was carried out by African American soldiers was impossible for either local Unionists or Confederates to ignore.[32]

Confederate officers in the region, however, looked on with great frustration as Wild and his black troops accosted Pasquotank's residents. During mid-December, two Confederate colonels, who were both perplexed by Wild's activities and afraid of the consequences to both men and supplies from the region, sent off a flurry of correspondence to their regional commander, Major General George E. Pickett. Pickett, who had lost his position in Robert E. Lee's Army of Northern Virginia following the debacle at Gettysburg, now commanded the southern forces in all of eastern North Carolina.[33] On December 14, 1863, worried about his inability to hold Wild and the African Brigade at bay, Colonel Hinton wrote to Pickett that "my little force—about 500 strong—are doing all they can to hold them in check, but cannot operate successfully against so large a force." Pleading with Pickett, Hinton asked, "Can you not, general, send a brigade to the relief of that community?" Fearing serious repercussions, Hinton warned that "if they are not Speedily dislodged, the Confederacy need not expect to get any more provisions from that section of country, but if they are driven off, the quantity of pork and bacon that will come to the Confederacy from the east side of the Chowan [River] will be truly incredible."[34]

The next day, another dire message came from the Confederate forces near Pasquotank. Colonel Joel R. Griffin of the Sixty-second Georgia Cavalry/Partisan Rangers, who operated independent of Hinton in southern Virginia and northeastern Carolina, also sent Pickett an urgent message. "Enemy, 1,500 strong, negroes and whites," Griffin wrote frantically. The black soldiers are "committing all kinds of excesses; insulting our ladies in the most tantalizing manner."[35]

In light of these warnings, Pickett grew deeply concerned about the further loss of resources from his theater and the continued embarrassment to his own reputation. He fired off a letter to the Confederate War Department suggesting that "we could send a cavalry expedition of our own down in such neighborhoods to collect and bring in the negroes . . . as every day loses so much valuable property to the Confederacy."[36] Aggravated with the inability of his own forces to respond efficiently and effectively,

Pickett charged that "Butler's plan, evidently, is to let loose his swarm of blacks upon our ladies and defenceless families, plunder and devastate the country." He then openly threatened retaliatory execution: "Against such a warfare there is but one resource—to hang at once every one captured belonging to the expedition, and afterward any one caught who belongs to Butler's department."[37] Writing the same day to his troops stationed in the Albemarle, Pickett reinforced his earlier statement with an unequivocal order: "Any one caught in the act (negroes or white men) of burning houses or maltreating women, must be hung on the spot, by my order."[38]

Pickett was not the only commander growing frustrated with the military situation along the Albemarle. Wild was irritated with the incessant guerrilla attacks on his troops, and on December 17, he sent a dispatch to the guerrilla captain Elliott, who operated out of the Pasquotank swamps. In the letter, Wild threatened that he held "in custody Mrs. Munden and Mrs. Weeks as hostages for the colored soldier taken by you. As he is treated so shall they be, even to hanging."[39]

Later that day, Wild busied himself with the proceedings "of a drumhead court-martial." At this hearing, he reviewed the status of the roughly twenty prisoners seized during his excursions to local farms and plantations. Most of these individuals Wild probably detained for aiding and abetting the guerrillas in the county. But, he believed that one of those captured, farmer Daniel Bright, was in fact a deserter from the Sixtysecond Georgia Cavalry/Partisan Rangers, who returned to his home to join the Pasquotank guerrillas. Wild accused Bright of engaging in pillage and other illegal activity. During the "court-martial," General Wild acted as both judge and jury. Little else is known about the proceedings except that he based his decisions largely on whether the accused could prove legal status as a conventional Confederate soldier, which could be done by producing paperwork that stated that he was given a legal furlough from the Confederate army. At the proceedings, Phoebe Munden and Elizabeth Weeks were ordered detained and eight men were sent to jail in Norfolk, the latter most likely soldiers at home who had been granted official leave from their units.[40] The rest of the twenty prisoners were released without punishment and without any further discussion of their status. Perhaps they were suspected of supporting the guerrillas, and after arraignment, Wild decided that they were not worth incarcerating.

Apparently, Daniel Bright could not produce proof of his own legitimacy as a soldier. Bright, unlike the other men, was charged with robbery and desertion from the Confederate unit to which he allegedly belonged. Wild's men captured Bright in lower Pasquotank when they were on an expedition to Hertford. More than likely, Wild's soldiers seized Bright as a suspect when they were searching for the perpetrators who had destroyed the bridge over the Perquimans River. For General Wild, Bright's inability to prove his status as a legitimate combatant led Wild to pass a sentence of execution and condemn Bright to hang. Following the court-martial, Wild began the withdrawal of his troops from Elizabeth City, which they had occupied for seven days.

"About noon" on the following day, December 18, Wild stopped on his march north from Elizabeth City and executed Bright, leaving his body to hang in the small hamlet of Hinton's Crossroads (also known as Hintonsville on contemporary maps of the county) on the edge of the Dismal Swamp.[41] His choice of where to execute Bright is telling. Wild exhibited the body at a crossroads close to the swamps of northern Pasquotank County, where many of the irregulars lived. It was also directly across the road from the dwellings of people who may have been supporting the swamp denizen irregulars. Wild obviously wanted to send a clear message to the guerrillas and the local community of Unionists and Confederates. Attached to Bright's body was a statement indicating he had been condemned for his guerrilla activities. Bright's body became a declaration about who wielded power over the community.

Wild's use of African Americans to guard the captured white wives of the guerrillas, who looked on helplessly as Bright swung in the wind, also sent a strong racial message to the few people living near Hinton's Crossroads. Those individuals who lived at the small hamlet bordering the swamp must have carried news of the hostages and the hanging to Elizabeth City, only a few miles down the road. In addition, the presence of the newspaper correspondent Tewksbury at the execution ensured that the sensational events of Wild's raid would reach regional and national newspapers within days. By January 1864, from Milledgeville, Georgia, and Charleston, South Carolina, to the Shenandoah Valley of Virginia, southern newspaper readers learned of the hostage-taking and hanging of the guerrilla Daniel Bright.[42]

Upon quitting Elizabeth City, Wild had divided his men to strike at a broader area. One of these groups went by water to Powell's Point in lower Currituck County. The other columns moved north to Hinton's Crossroads. After Bright's hanging, Wild marched his portion of the force into northern Camden and Currituck counties. Of Camden, Tewksbury thought "at first, the country was poor, and the houses were mean," but by afternoon, he noted "spacious corn-fields on every side." Finally, the black troops came upon an area of wealth and splendor. "In no portion of the South had I seen more magnificent plantations," he wrote of lower Camden.[43] A local Confederate irregular later reported that Wild burned "six or seven houses in Camden County."[44]

As the general left Pasquotank for Camden and Currituck counties, he began to slide toward a harder strategy. Between December 18 and December 24, Wild's method of "judiciously discriminating" among all civilians gave way to more callous tactics toward the guerrillas and their supporters, especially as he entered the area around Indiantown in Currituck County. Guided by a captured muster roll that his men had discovered at a guerrilla camp, Wild put roughly a dozen homes to the torch in Camden and Currituck.[45] Wild was still relying on a list of secessionist guerrillas to punish, did not systematically target civilians with violence, and clearly never adopted a policy of methodically killing citizens, but he stopped caring about discerning the loyalty of the civilians he targeted with nonhuman property confiscation and home destruction. During the second phase of the raid, Wild confiscated both Unionists' and Confederates' property. In the few days surrounding Daniel Bright's execution, one can see Wild's mindset shifting from a careful and discriminating policy in Pasquotank to a harsher and more indiscriminate strategy during the final days of the incursion.

As the African Brigade marched toward Indiantown in Currituck County on the afternoon of December 18, the troops were ambushed by three different companies of guerrillas. The following day, Wild retaliated with fire. He burned every suspected guerrilla home within a four-mile radius of Indiantown. He also detained Major D. Gregory, a man in his seventies, who was suspected of aiding the irregular forces. Wild's troops had seized Gregory as insurance, since a second black soldier of the African Brigade had been captured.[46] Wild had taken the elderly Gregory as a hostage because the man's name appeared on the muster roll of "N.C. Defenders" that his men had seized at one of the guerrilla swamp hideouts. Wild also determined that Gregory's farm was a major supplier of corn for Captain Willis Sanderlin's guerrillas. Ultimately, he released Gregory, but the old man died, probably of a stroke, not long after the traumatic experience.[47]

Wild found neighboring Camden and Currituck counties, like Pasquotank, full of hostile irregular forces living in the deepest parts of the local swamps. He also discovered that destroying the guerrilla menace could be time-consuming and difficult due to these environmental conditions. "Finding ordinary measures of little avail" in his hunt for swamp denizen irregulars, a frustrated Wild "adopted a more rigorous style of warfare, burned their houses and barns, ate up their live stock, and took hostages from their families. This course we followed throughout the trip [through Camden and Currituck]. . . . [W]e learned that [the guerrilla companies] grew disgusted with such unexpected treatment." Although he and his men clearly had changed their methods between the first phase of the expedition in Pasquotank and that later phase in Camden and Currituck, Wild did not see his own escalation in property destruction and confiscation clearly until he sat down after the raid to reflect on the matter.[48]

Wild explained that during one of the forays against irregulars, he "drove them a long chase into their swamp, and after much trouble, struck their trail . . . a succession of single felled trunks leading in to their citadel. We filed in singly, burned their camp." Following another encounter in Camden and Currituck, he wrote that "after burning the neighboring houses and giving them another chase, we . . . sent out Col. Draper with 170 to attack Captain Grandy's [guerrilla] Camp, situated like the others in the center of the swamp . . . accessible only Single file over a pathway of felled trunks, from a third to a half mile long." After destroying this irregular fortress, Wild then sent his subordinate Colonel Alonzo Draper to Knott's Island, where more slaves were in bondage and where another band of irregulars was reportedly operating. During Draper's brief independent excursion, he took another woman hostage—Nancy White, the daughter of a lieutenant in Captain Coffey's company of Confederate irregulars.[49] With three local women now in custody, Wild and his men were violating traditional gender norms, and this raised the stakes in his effort to root out irregular forces in the region.

Wild's shift in policy toward northeastern Carolinians is demonstrated by several incidents involving Unionists and neutral citizens in Camden and Currituck. One incident documented by a correspondent for the *New York Daily News* concerned a Unionist from Camden County whose property was confiscated by Wild and his troops. The reporter wrote:

Many of these people [from the northeastern region] to my knowledge, were loyal, and had been so for months. . . . They had certificates of protection from the former commandants at this post, and no man questioned their good faith. When [General Wild] took the property of Mr. Morrisetts [*sic*], of Camden County, North Carolina, [Wm. J. Morrisett] interposed his certificate of loyalty; Gen. Wild paused for a moment, took the property, however, promising to return it when he reached Norfolk. The old man followed him to this city, and again pressed to his attention this promise and the shield of a Government manifesto, but in vain. [General Wild] flatly told [Wm. J. Morrisett that] this property belonged to his negroes, and his [Unionist] loyalty did not protect him. I saw the tear gush from the old man's eye as he turned away, muttering in the anguish of his broken heart, "I am a ruined man; my children are beggars."[50]

Another Unionist, John Bottoms of Camden County, described how Wild's men came to his house and camped in his yard. While at the house, Wild's men seized "one Horse, 10 hogs, 1 sow, 5000 lbs. of fodder, and 40 barrels of corn." Likewise, Unionist R. R. Guirkin of South Mills in Camden County also had a large amount of property taken by Wild's troops, including "8 barrels of corn, 8 head of cattle, 1800 pounds of fodder, 18 head of hogs, 2 horses."[51]

Some northeastern Carolinians were clearly disillusioned with the war and desired to drop out of the conflict entirely. Yet, they were not spared the hardship of Wild's expedition. Edmond Simmons in Currituck County, who Unionist Thomas G. Munden called "a quiet citizen, who remained at home and attended to his own business and did not meddle with public affairs," had fed both Union troops and Confederate guerrillas when they came to his property, but only because "[h]e was forced to do this." Citizens who claimed neutrality made Wild's job even more difficult, and when his troops visited Simmons's property during the second phase of the raid, they seized "two horses, one yoke of oxen, two carts, fifteen barrels of corn, fifteen bushels of peas, four thousand juniper rails for fire wood, twenty-five hogs, fence rails worth one hundred dollars."[52]

These incidents show that Wild became less concerned with discerning loyalty during the second phase of the raid. But perhaps even more striking evidence is the absence of a compiled list of Unionists from Camden or Currituck like the one Wild made for Pasquotank County.[53]

Even though Wild moved away from political loyalty as a criterion for confiscation of goods during the latter part of the raid, the expedition was not an early example of what one historian has called "localized total war."[54] The line between combatant and noncombatant never completely broke down, even during the period when he adopted a harsher scorched-earth policy. Though he changed his mind about how to deal with the guerrilla threat after the execution of Daniel Bright, Wild never targeted the civilian population at any point during the raid with systematic extermination or forced depopulation. Clearly, during his second phase, Wild made a distinction between a harsher and more thorough policy of destruction/confiscation not based on loyalty and the outright annihilation of the entire civilian population in the region.[55]

On December 22, Wild again attempted to communicate with the guerrillas in the region. He sent a letter to guerrilla captain Willis Sanderlin threatening retaliation for the capture of a second black soldier from his command. According to Confederate accounts, the black soldier for whom Gregory had been taken hostage later escaped; Samuel Jordan, the first black soldier captured by the guerrillas, remained in their custody.[56] Edward Wild and his men had now been away from their base in Virginia for more than two weeks. On December 23 and 24, his men exhausted and foot-sore, Wild turned his troops back toward Virginia, laden with confiscated goods and trailed by a large assembly of blacks, a group whose number probably included both former slaves and free blacks from all three of the counties Wild visited.

Soon thereafter, Wild summarized his raid's accomplishments: "We sent by water 9 loads [of former slaves] to Roanoke Island, and two to Norfolk, besides 4 long trains overland. The exact numbers it was impossible to count, as they were constantly coming and going." Nevertheless, Wild estimated "2500 Negroes released and migrated." "But few recruits were gained," Wild complained, "as the ablebodied negroes have had ample opportunities to escape heretofore, or have been run over into Dixie." Despite this assessment of recruitment, he estimated that between seventy and one hundred African American soldiers were enrolled from Pasquotank and the surrounding area.

Wild was equally proud of his counter-guerrilla operations: "We burned 4 Guerrilla camps, took over 50 guns, 1 drum together with equipment, ammunition etc, burned over a dozen households, two distilleries etc, took a number of prisoners." Neither did he shy away from discussing his use of hostage-taking to coerce and deal with the guerrillas in his report. Wild and his troops took "four hostages for our men taken prisoner, 3 women and one old man, hanged one Guerrilla, captured 4 boats engaged in contraband trade, took many horses." He finished his official account by thoroughly endorsing the performance of his black troops. "The men marched wonderfully—never grumbled, were watchful on picket, and always ready for a fight. They are most reliable soldiers."[57]

Wild astutely discerned the nature of the guerrilla forces he faced and attempted to gauge his response to them accordingly. His brief description of the resistance provides interesting background on the composition and operations of Confederate irregular forces in North Carolina. Wild asserted in his official report to General Benjamin Butler:

> The organization of the guerrillas is loose and improper, and ought not to be recognized. Governor Vance gave commissions to the officers to raise their companies, ostensibly for State defense. They are entitled "North Carolina Defenders." Each captain is his own mustering officer; musters men into the service of North Carolina, and the men are paid, or expect pay, from the State only. Governor Vance supplied them with excellent arms (new Enfields) and ammunition. There appears to be some person acting as commissary near each company, to keep a small stock of provisions in camp: but the bands do not scruple to live on the inhabitants, individually and collectively. The captain is allowed to en-camp where he pleases, and to operate when and where he sees fit, his proceedings being as independent, arbitrary, and irresponsible as those of any chief of bandits. The men have never been obliged to report to anybody except the captain. . . . They are virtually bandits, armed and hired by Governor Vance. They have not defended and cannot defend their State, nor any portion of it. They can only harass us by stealing, murdering, and burning; by stopping negroes from reaching us, and by driving them over the lines, and harass their own State by plundering, terrifying, and even murdering Union citizens. There are jealous dis-affections among them—not only between the individuals of a company, but between one company and another—amounting to rancor. There are more than enough for one regiment of infantry between Hertford and the Atlantic. . . . Of late, attempts have been made to bring them together into a regiment. They are called the Sixty-sixth [eventually mustered into service as the Sixty-eighth] North Carolina State Troops, and the different companies are lettered. Hinton to be colonel.[58]

The guerrillas General Wild faced in northeastern North Carolina were mostly young and poor. Out of the ninety-one men who served in Elliott's company during the war, forty-one could be identified in the 1860 census. The average age of a man in Elliott's Pasquotank band was twenty-five. Of those forty-one, eleven were under the age of seventeen in 1860, the youngest being twelve years old. Those who were old enough to have an occupation in 1860 were almost all small farmers who owned no slaves. The average total property ownership of these men was less than $1,000 ($433 real and $535 personal, respectively). Of the forty-one men, twenty-eight owned less than $100 dollars in personal property, and twenty-nine owned less than $100 in real property. Moreover, only five of Elliott's men owned any slaves, and the total number of slaves owned by these five guerrillas amounted to only seventeen.[59]

For Wild and his command, violence became the most effective educational tool for a community filled with guerrillas. But violence was not the only form of power Wild wielded over these North Carolina communities. Racial and mild sexual displays of power also became ways of communicating to both the Confederate, Unionist, and guerrilla members of the population about appropriate conduct. Wild's message to the guerrillas was clear: he wanted the irregulars to abandon their activities or join the regular Confederate army. In fact, during the raid, Wild had even sent a message to Captain Elliott unequivocally stating his feelings. "Guerrillas are to be treated as pirates," Wild wrote, and "you will never have rest until you renounce your present course or join the regular Confederate Army."[60] Clearly, what Wild disdained even more than Elliott's Confederate loyalty was the irregular nature of his unit.

To the local community, Wild's message was less explicit. Blacks saw his raid as an opportunity for freedom, and by the end of it, more than 2,500 free and enslaved blacks were ushered north to Virginia under the guard of black soldiers.[61] The situation for white residents was complex, but fear was a common reaction. By capturing and guarding white women with black soldiers, Wild used race as a weapon that enraged Confederate guerrillas and unnerved local Confederate citizens. According to Tewksbury, they were "completely panic-stricken. Scores of families fled into the swamps on [Wild's] approach. Never was a region thrown into such commotion by a raid before." The Yankee journalist also believed that "an army of fifty thousand blacks could march from one end of rebeldom to the other . . . the terror they would inspire making them invincible."[62]

"General Wild . . . understands the guerrilla pathology," believed Tewksbury, "and can give prescription that will cure every time."[63] The *New York Times* reporter was clearly convinced of the racial power at play in northeastern Carolina, and he explicitly described the military prowess of black soldiers in this southern guerrilla war. "This raid possesses historical importance," he commented. "It is the first of any magnitude undertaken by negro troops . . . and by it the question of their efficiency in any branch of the service has been practically set at rest." Furthermore, Tewksbury was "confident" that black soldiers "will prove far better guerrilla-hunters than the whites." He even defiantly charged that "when the rebellion shall have subsided into partisan warfare, so far from lasting for ever, as Jeff Davis threatens, our colored troops will take care that its end is soon reached."

He concluded: "It is an instructive turn of the tables that the men who have been accustomed to hunt runaway slaves hiding in the swamps of the South, should now hiding there themselves, be hunted by them."[64] This final comment, published in the most widely read northern newspaper, focused on psychologically shaming white southerners for both guerrilla violence and their racial beliefs.

Local white Unionists faced a different problem from that confronting Confederates. When Wild discussed the situation of the Unionist minority in the region, he was empathetic. Some of these men "have hired their slaves on share of profits, a few even . . . pay them money. [Unionists] have, of course, been cautious and silent; but they have been persecuted more or less," the general thought. Moreover, "I would respectfully suggest that such men deserve some extra discrimination in their favor, in the way of protection, &c."[65]

An angry member of Pasquotank's Unionist minority, perhaps Dr. William G. Pool, suggested that Wild should issue a public message concerning the problem of guerrilla war.[66] This proposed declaration highlights two factors Wild perceived as being most important to both Unionists and Confederates in the northeastern counties: peace and property. According to Wild, the proposed proclamation was "written by a professional gentleman of excellent judgment, discretion, and experience, residing at Elizabeth [City]. He, with all the rest, supposed that we were intending to occupy the city permanently, and he urged me to issue a proclamation and follow it up by action." Wild included a copy of this letter in his official report to Major General Butler: "A TIMELY WARNING. General Butler intends to exterminate all guerrillas east of Chowan River, and will use any and all means to do so. If it cannot be done otherwise, property of all sorts will be destroyed, and the country entirely laid waste. If citizens wish to prevent such universal destruction of their property, they must aid our authorities in ridding this country of these land pirates. It now rests with them to save themselves and property, or not. We have force now here sufficient to accomplish our purpose, and we shall immediately enter upon the work. Now is the time for the people to come forward."[67]

Wild's empathy for Pasquotank Unionists like Pool caused Wild to suggest a more proactive Union military strategy in this part of North Carolina. He urged the extension of the Union lines around the northeastern region, noting that "the Pasquotank [River] is a natural barrier, being wide and deep." And, if the river were controlled by Union forces, "the advantages of such communication would be very great. It would go farther towards reclaiming the inhabitants of that region than any other measure."

Wild believed that "the only drawback or danger arising from the Guerrillas, I could rectify in two weeks of stern warfare. The included territory comprises exceedingly productive tracts which would be brought to bear next season, if the inhabitants could be assured against other alternation of masters and have confidence on protection." He asserted that in this sector of the state, "the rebels have been and still are drawing vast supplies for their Army and for their great works."[68]

Wild saw his failure to destroy the entire guerrilla population in Pasquotank and contiguous counties as the consequence of applying violence too sparingly. In his official report, he came to the conclusion that many other Union commanders were also coming to during this period: that only "stern warfare" toward irregulars coupled with support for local Unionists had a chance at solving the problem of guerrilla violence.[69]

In the aftermath of Wild's raid, the whites in Pasquotank, Unionist and Confederate alike, were at an impasse. For nearly two years, since the fall of Elizabeth City, neither the southern government in Raleigh nor the northern authorities assigned to command in the region had been successful in protecting their county from the other side. At times, both governments seemed indifferent toward the plight of this remote but prosperous agricultural sector of the state. Only one factor had remained constant in the community: a contest for power over who would dominate the politically divided population.

Prominent Confederates in Pasquotank feared further reprisal by Union troops. Their local guerrillas, who reigned supreme at night on the roads outside of Elizabeth City, had already proven unable to protect them. First, white Union officers had arrived in small numbers for recruiting, then armed black soldiers had drilled in the streets of Elizabeth City, and finally General Wild had seized their slave property. For local slaveholders, their economic system lay in shambles. With the antebellum racial, social, and economic order shattered, Confederates were ready to be rid of the Union raiders for good. Some were committed enough to preserving peace and property that they were for a brief period willing to work with Unionist community members in order to recover social stability.

General Wild's fifty-three "truly loyal" Union men from Pasquotank faced a different kind of problem once Wild and his black troops left the region. Wild had not spared their slave property, but he had shielded them from the violence of his troops and confiscation of their other possessions. The loss of slaves hurt them economically, but at least their homes and farms had been protected. When Wild left the county, they continued to fear the guerrillas. The Unionists in Pasquotank wanted to get Confederate or Union authorities to control the irregulars in order to prevent future incursions from either side that might disrupt their local economy. Since the irregulars were community members who knew the Unionists and where they lived, the shifting tides of power on the coast of the Albemarle left the Unionist population most vulnerable.

However General Wild's raid affected individuals within white society, Unionists and Confederates faced the same quandary at the end of 1863: how to stop the violence perpetuated by both sides upon their community. Having endured regular power reversals on the exposed North Carolina coast since the fall of the county seat in February 1862, many leading white citizens, regardless of political allegiance, were tired of war. The peaceful majority of this divided community was ready to see their local war end.

On December 19, one day after Daniel Bright's execution, Unionists, Confederates, and "neutral" citizens met at Elizabeth City to discuss their recourse. At the meeting, the citizens adopted a resolution, which asked the Confederate government to remove the guerrillas, condemned blockade-running, and requested that both Union and Confederate militaries "let alone" the war-torn county. Local men were appointed in each district to secure the signatures of all white men over eighteen years old. In a remarkable condemnation of the local guerrilla war, the petitions attempting to negotiate neutrality were ultimately signed by 523 citizens, all of the remaining white male residents of Pasquotank. The 1860 census returns and other local sources were used by the residents to verify the names. The signatories included prominent Confederates, Unionists, and citizens claiming neutrality. The citizens at the meeting then formed a committee to visit with Governor Vance in Raleigh and a committee to meet with General Butler in Norfolk.[70] The counties of Camden, Currituck, Perquimans, and even Chowan also held meetings where "similar" resolutions were adopted, and although little extant material from their meetings has survived, it is likely that these communities also sought protection from both the Union and Confederate armies.[71]

The Pasquotank committee sent to Butler included Unionists George D. Pool (brother of William G. Pool), George W. Brooks, and John J. Grandy. All three of these men were on Wild's list of Unionists. The committee sent to Governor Vance included Confederates Richard B. Creecy, William H. Clark, and James Shannonhouse, none of whom were on Wild's list. Governor Vance met the resolutions with skepticism, but since he still struggled to retain adequate manpower to defend the coast, he clearly did not want to lose control over the manpower that was available in the region. In the end, Vance followed the same policy he had held for nearly a year: try to enforce conscription by bringing the guerrillas under tighter control and ultimately effect their transfer into a regular Confederate unit. General Butler greeted the committee from Pasquotank with enthusiasm and guaranteed that if guerrilla violence and blockade-running ceased, he would send no more raids into the northeastern region.[72]

Butler also used this opportunity to defend Wild's military strategy and the conduct of his soldiers while in the Albemarle. "I think we are much indebted to General Wild and his negro troops for what they have done," asserted Butler in a letter to Secretary of War Edwin M. Stanton, "and it is but fair to record that while some complaints are made of the action, authorized by Gen'l. Wild against the inhabitants and their property . . . the negro soldiers made no unauthorized interference with property or persons, but conducted themselves with propriety." Yet, even Butler had some criticism of the operation. Referring to the confiscations and violence of the final phase of the raid, Butler commented that Wild operated "with great thoroughness, but perhaps with too much stringency."[73]

On January 13, 1864, the Pasquotank guerrillas executed Private Samuel Jordan, the first black soldier captured during Wild's expedition.[74] Although this angered Butler and doubtless enraged Wild, no further escalation of violence resulted from Jordan's death. Despite Butler's defense of Wild's methods and his use of force, he diffused the heightened tensions over the raid by rescinding Wild's hostage execution order and by eventually returning the local citizens seized during the raid to their homes.[75]

Ultimately, the community effort to negotiate a middle ground between the Union and Confederate forces was only partially successful. Most of the guerrilla bands in the northeastern counties were finally organized in late January 1864 into the Sixty-eighth North Carolina State Troops and by the early spring had left for operations west of the Chowan River. Ironically, these same men were sent to round up deserters in western Carolina in July 1864. Nevertheless, a few guerrilla units did remain in the northeastern counties under the command of Captains Hughes, Ethridge, and Coffey. These companies unfortunately left no other records about their activities, and they never mustered into the regular Confederate service. Union and Confederate cavalry continued to visit the northeastern region of North Carolina in 1864 to stop blockade-running or to impress supplies.[76]

In February 1864, Confederate general Matt Ransom came to Pasquotank and hauled away hundreds of pounds of supplies. Six regiments of North Carolina infantry (including the Sixty-eighth) supported by cavalry and artillery visited the county from their bases west of the Chowan River. The raid lasted seventeen days, and although few extant sources discuss the outcome of this Confederate expedition, it clearly reinforced a feeling of instability among community members.[77] Union troops also returned to Pasquotank hunting guerrillas and blockade-runners in late July 1864. Union troops also impressed supplies, finding the community war-weary. Although partially successful for local residents who desired to see the guerrillas removed, the overall plan to negotiate a peaceful middle ground failed to prevent further incursions.[78]

If General Wild's raid demonstrated how quickly Union military policy toward southern civilians of both Unionist and Confederate loyalty could evolve, the efforts of those civilians to negotiate their own neutrality in the aftermath of the raid demonstrated the lengths to which politically divided North Carolinians were willing to go in order to secure social stability and freedom from attack. In the end, Wild's raid and the response of residents in northeastern North Carolina illustrate the resiliency and ingenuity of southern communities trying to survive the internal menace of guerrilla war and the external threat of military raids.

Notes

I would like to thank John C. Inscoe, James C. Cobb, Noel G. Harrison, Paul D. Escott, and two anonymous readers from the University of North Carolina Press for providing excellent critiques of early drafts of this article.

1. Edward Augustus Wild Report, December 28, 1863 (hereafter cited as Wild Report), Edward Augustus Wild Papers, Southern Historical Collection, Wilson Library, University of North Carolina at Chapel Hill (hereafter cited as Wild Papers, SHC). Robert R. Mackey in *The UnCivil War: Irregular Warfare in the Upper South, 1861–1865* (Norman: University of Oklahoma Press, 2004), 3–23, makes a distinction between "counter-guerrilla warfare" or passive measures (like blockhouses and heavy-picketing) and "anti-guerrilla warfare" or active measures (like search and destroy missions). In Pasquotank, the Union army units often used both methods simultaneously. The term counter-guerrilla warfare is therefore used here to encompass both. In his perceptive study, Mackey outlines three forms of irregular warfare in the Upper South. According to the author, Arkansas exemplified military theorist Karl von Clausewitz's "people's war" (of self-constituted bands resisting the regular forces of the enemy); Virginia represented Napoleonic military thinker Antoine Henri de Jomini's legitimate "partisan war" (of elite cavalry units, in this case Partisan Ranger units, sanctioned for the expressed purpose of employing irregular warfare behind enemy lines); and the war waged by General John Hunt Morgan in Kentucky and Tennessee demonstrated the "raiding warfare" of regular cavalry. In northeastern North Carolina, a combination of the first two forms existed; self-constituted bands of Confederate guerrillas tried to join a state partisan ranger unit that subsequently

never mustered into service. As a result, these men end up serving under virtually no direction until most of the Confederate companies were in 1864 brought under state control as an infantry regiment. I emphasize the hybrid nature of this situation because it is important to point out the role that Confederate military policy (and specifically the 1862 Partisan Ranger Act that fostered the idea of state-level North Carolina Partisan Rangers) played in sparking interest in irregular warfare among its own civilian population.

2. General Butler was one of the first to endorse the performance of Wild's troops. Benjamin Butler Report, December 31, 1863, in U.S. War Department, *The War of the Rebellion: A Compilation of the Official Records of the Union and Confederate Armies*, 128 vols. (Washington, D.C.: Government Printing Office, 1880–1901), ser. 1, vol. 29, pt. 2, 596–97 (hereafter cited as *Official Records*). General Butler received members of the community afterward who attested to the black soldiers' discretion. Another positive endorsement of the black troops is found in the report by "Tewksbury," *New York Times*, January 9, 1864 (hereafter cited as "Tewksbury," *New York Times*). "A Wild General" in the Democratic organ the *New York World* is a disparaging account of the raid, but most northern accounts were supportive of the expedition and its objectives. Nonetheless, southern papers were highly critical in the months after Wild's expedition.

3. Benjamin Butler to Edward M. Stanton, December 31, 1863, *Official Records*, ser. 1, vol. 29, pt. 2, 596.

4. W. N. H. Smith Report, February 10–17, 1864, *Official Records*, ser. 2, vol. 6, 1127–30. These homes were that of suspected guerrilla Daniel Bright and guerrilla commissary William T. White. The barn was the property of Ed Jennings, a likely guerrilla sympathizer. W. J. Munden, an irregular and the husband of hostage Phoebe Munden, reported these homes destroyed in his official deposition to the Confederate committee investigating the Wild raid. The fact that Munden singled out Jennings's barn suggests that this barn may have been a place where local irregulars resupplied.

5. Wild Report; Tewksbury, *New York Times*.

6. Historians who have looked at Union military policy toward southern civilians on a large scale have tended toward broader national interpretations as opposed to local analysis. These scholars include Stephen V. Ash (*When the Yankees Came: Conflict and Chaos in the Occupied South, 1861–1865* [Chapel Hill: University of North Carolina Press, 1995]), who argues that the war policy of the North turns to a harsher warfare by late 1862, and Charles Royster (*The Destructive War: William Tecumseh Sherman, Stonewall Jackson and the Americans* [New York: A. A. Knopf, 1991]), who believes the war is essentially destructive from the commencement of hostilities. Mark Grimsley in *The Hard Hand of War: Union Military Policy toward Southern Civilians, 1861–1865* (Cambridge: Cambridge University Press, 1995), 3–6, 118–19, outlines three periods of Union military policy: a conciliatory phase, a pragmatic period, and a hard war phase. Although Grimsley's work allows for a period of pragmatism or judicious discernment (treatment on the basis of loyalty), he does not leave room for localized evolution in policy and does not seem to allow for rapid changes in policy over the

course of one operation. Grimsley argues that Lincoln's Emancipation Proclamation destroyed the policy of conciliation toward southern civilians in existence before July 1862. But, he argues that the Proclamation itself did not inaugurate hard war since it was not forced upon southerners at the point of the bayonet in the eastern theater until early 1864. Grimsley believes the Proclamation alone without enforcement did little to harm the southern economy and therefore did not inaugurate hard war. When I attempted initially to apply Grimsley's terminology to Wild's raid, I discovered that as a counter-guerrilla raid it would fall into Grimsley's "pragmatic" phase, but as a raid aimed at ending slavery (i.e., economic warfare aimed at the entire population of the region), it would also fall into the category of "hard war." Over the course of his three-week December 1863 raid, General Wild enforced the Emancipation Proclamation, but in respect to other types of property, he evolved from practical discernment (confiscation and destruction based on loyalty) to a harsher confiscation policy not based on loyalty. Clearly, applying just one term (e.g., "hard war" or "pragmatism") to an operation will not work in every case. Since these terms do not effectively describe Wild's three-week operation given the specific definitions Grimsley employs, I avoid using his terminology in favor of Wild's own descriptive terminology. It is clear, however, that by the end of the operation, Wild had reached the point Grimsley defines as "hard war," and the account of this raid modifies his timeline for the beginning of that policy by roughly one month. For another view of Wild's raid with respect to Union military policy, see Brian Steel Wills, *The War Hits Home: The Civil War in Southeastern Virginia* (Charlottesville: University Press of Virginia, 2001), 203. Wills employed Grimsley's "hard war" concept to describe Wild's incursion, arguing that the entire operation from beginning to end represented this policy.

7. For scholars who have focused on changes of policy toward civilians at the local level, see Kenneth W. Noe, "Exterminating Savages: The Union Army and Mountain Guerrillas in Southern West Virginia, 1861–1862," in *The Civil War in Appalachia*, ed. Kenneth W. Noe and Shannon H. Wilson (Knoxville: University of Tennessee Press, 1997); Noel G. Harrison, "Atop an Anvil: The Civilians' War in Fairfax and Alexandria Counties, April 1861–April 1862," *Virginia Magazine of History and Biography* 106 (1998): 133–64; and Everard H. Smith, "Chambersburg: Anatomy of a Confederate Reprisal," *American Historical Review* 96 (1991): 432–55. Noe asserts that the war in West Virginia makes a full transition to what he calls "localized total war." Harrison's analysis that the Union military adopted a harder style of waging war in northern Virginia in 1861 is convincing. Smith looks at Confederate military policy toward Union civilians during John McCausland's Chambersburg, Pennsylvania, raid. He asserts that the raid represented total war because of the large number of homes destroyed. In general, all of the scholars who have focused on transitions in policy at the local level have described changes over months, usually with the changes of officers in a region (e.g., Noe compares McClellan's conciliation to Fremont's notion of a war of "annihilation"). None of these historians has focused his attention on one officer undergoing such a rapid change from discernment to a harsh policy over the course of one operation as General Wild did in the Albemarle. Furthermore, none has studied areas where black soldiers were used against guerrillas to see the new policy dynamics it produced in a politically divided southern community.

8. For demographic data, see Secretary of the Interior, *Population of the United States in 1860; Compiled from the Original Returns of the Eighth Census* (Washington: Government Printing Office, 1864), 348–63.

9. On the free blacks working in the Great Dismal Swamp region, see John Hope Franklin, *The Free Negro in North Carolina, 1790–1860* (Chapel Hill: University of North Carolina Press, 1995), 74–75, 132–35; for an examination of the prewar economy and society of the greater Dismal Swamp region, see Jack Temple Kirby, *Poquosin: A Study of Rural Landscape and Society* (Chapel Hill: University of North Carolina Press, 1995); another community study of the Civil War in the greater Albemarle region is Wayne K. Durrill, *War of Another Kind: A Southern Community in the Great Rebellion* (New York: Oxford University Press, 1990), on Washington County.

10. For biographical background on Edward Wild, see Bradford Kingman, *Memoir of Gen. Edward Augustus Wild* (Boston: privately printed, 1895); Edward A. Longacre, "Brave Radical Wild: The Contentious Career of Brigadier General Edward A. Wild," *Civil War Times Illustrated* 19, no. 3 (1980): 8–19; and Frances Harding Casstevens, *Edward A. Wild and the African Brigade in the Civil War* (Jeffersonville, N.C.: McFarland, 2003), 1–35. Wild's raid is briefly discussed in John G. Barrett, *The Civil War in North Carolina* (Chapel Hill: University of North Carolina Press, 1963), 177–81; and Noah Andre Trudeau, *Like Men of War: Black Troops in the Civil War, 1862–1865* (New York: Little, Brown, 1998), 112–18. A recent local history that explores the events of Wild's raid is J. V. Witt, *Wild in North Carolina: General E. A. Wild's December 1863 Raid into Camden, Pasquotank and Currituck Counties* (Belvidere, N.C.: Family Research Society of Northeastern North Carolina, 1993).

11. Richard Reid, "Raising the African Brigade: Early Black Recruitment in Civil War North Carolina," *North Carolina Historical Review* 70 (1993): 266–301.

12. Patricia C. Click, *Time Full of Trial: The Roanoke Island Freedmen's Colony, 1862–1867* (Chapel Hill: University of North Carolina Press, 2001), 45–46. General Wild recruited the first company of colored volunteers from Roanoke Island in mid-June 1863. For a discussion of the return of these black soldiers to Pasquotank and other coastal counties after the war, see Richard Reid, "USCT Veterans in Post–Civil War North Carolina," in *Black Soldiers in Blue: African American Troops in the Civil War Era*, ed. John David Smith (Chapel Hill: University of North Carolina Press, 2002), 391–421.

13. Wild Report. General Wild estimated that he freed roughly 2,500 black people during his raid, meaning that a large number of blacks remained in the county as of December 1863.

14. Ash, *When the Yankees Came*, 99–105. Pasquotank and the contiguous counties of northeastern Carolina fall into this broad regional grouping by having a Unionist minority and Confederate majority population but with neither government nor military able to maintain permanent control.

15. Report of Col. Benjamin F. Onderdonk, August 20, 1863, *Official Records*, ser. 1, vol. 29, pt. 1, 70–72; Report of W. Dewees Roberts, August 6 and 8, 1863, *Official Records*, ser. 1, vol. 29, pt. 1, 30–31; Report of William L. Kent, October 17, 1863, *Official Records*, ser. 1, vol. 29, pt. 1, 478–80.

16. For more on the formation and history of these black units, see Regimental De-

scriptive Books, Thirty-fifth, Thirty-sixth, and Thirty-seventh United States Colored Troops, Records of the Adjutant General's Office, Record Group 94, National Archives, Washington, D.C. The First and Second North Carolina Colored Volunteers became the Thirty-fifth and Thirty-sixth United States Colored Troops in 1864. Unit histories include Jonathan William Horstman, *The African American's Civil War: A History of the First North Carolina Colored Volunteers* (M.A. thesis, Western North Carolina University, 1994); and Versalle Freddrick Washington, *Eagles on Their Buttons: Fifth Regiment of Infantry, United States Colored Troops in the American Civil War* (Ph.D. diss., Ohio State University, 1995). Also, see Reid, "USCT Veterans in Post–Civil War North Carolina," 391–421; James Kenneth Bryant II, "'A Model Black Regiment': The Thirty-sixth Colored Infantry in the Civil War" (M.A. thesis, University of Vermont, 1996); and Shana Renee Hutchins, "'Just Learning to Be Men': A History of the Thirty-fifth United States Colored Troops, 1863–1866" (M.A. thesis, North Carolina State University, 1999).

17. Wild Report.

18. Tewksbury, *New York Times.*

19. Ibid.

20. Wild Report.

21. Ibid.

22. For obituaries of members of the Pool family in Pasquotank, see John Pool Scrapbook, Southern Historical Collection, Wilson Library, University of North Carolina at Chapel Hill. John Pool's loyalty throughout the war appears to be that of a pragmatic cooperationist. Throughout the war, most of Pool's relatives in Pasquotank remained staunch Unionists. But in 1862, Pool wrote letters that can easily be judged as loyal to North Carolina or as a cooperationist with the Confederacy. Nevertheless, his chief concerns were local matters at the county level, principally improving the plight of those poorer residents who suffered from the flight of planters to the upcountry. Above all, Pool seemed committed to preserving local stability, including the system of slavery. By 1864, however, he became a principal backer of the peace candidate for governor, William Holden. Pool reentered the North Carolina legislature as a highly vocal peace advocate in 1864. After the war, he became a Republican and was elected to the U.S. Senate. Unfortunately, there are few extant papers remaining from Pool's wartime political career that can shed light on his somewhat ambiguous loyalty. For a letter of Pool's that can be taken as cooperationist, see John Pool to Zebulon B. Vance, September 18, 1862, *Official Records*, ser. 1, vol. 18, 745–48. The editors of the Zebulon Vance papers describe Pool as a "wartime Unionist." See Joe A. Mobley, ed., *The Papers of Zebulon Baird Vance*, vol. 2 (Raleigh: Division of Archives and History, North Carolina Department of Cultural Resources, 1995), 88. But, for a nuanced assessment of Pool's loyalty, see Allen W. Trelease, "Pool, John," *American National Biography Online*, February 2000 <http://www.anb.org/articles/04/04-00800.html> (June 9, 2004).

23. Tewksbury, *New York Times.*

24. Wild Report. Also, see author's database on Pasquotank Unionists developed from the 1860 census. This database will appear in the author's forthcoming book,

Executing Daniel Bright: Military Incursion, Racial Conflict, and Guerrilla Violence in a Coastal Carolina Community during the Civil War (Baton Rouge: Louisiana State University Press, forthcoming), and is presently available upon request.

25. Wild Report.

26. Tewksbury, *New York Times*.

27. Ibid.

28. For an excellent analysis of the Roanoke Island freedmen's colony and General Wild's involvement in it, see Click, *Time Full of Trial*, 48–49, 218–23. The appendices of this work refer to some freedmen who were from Elizabeth City and moved to the island during the period before Wild's northeastern Carolina raid. Wild recruited some of his black soldiers among these Elizabeth City free blacks who had fled to Roanoke Island. The presence of these free blacks in his force likely made Wild's task of determining loyalty easier during the December expedition.

29. For an explanation of the May 1863 Confederate congressional policy on black soldiers and their white officers, see Dudley Taylor Cornish, *The Sable Arm: Black Troops in the Union Army, 1861–1865* (Lawrence: University of Kansas Press, 1956), 161–62; for examples of other hostage takings as response to guerrilla activity, see Ash, *When the Yankees Came*, 66.

30. Wild Report. The women were taken on December 12 and 13, 1864, respectively; Tewksbury, *New York Times*.

31. Wild Report.

32. Ibid.

33. For an excellent analysis of General Pickett's racial beliefs, see Lesley J. Gordon, *General George E. Pickett in Life and Legend* (Chapel Hill: University of North Carolina Press, 1995), 126–27.

34. James W. Hinton Report, December 14, 1863, *Official Records*, ser. 1, vol. 29, pt. 2, 877.

35. Joel R. Griffin to George E. Pickett, December 15, 1863, *Official Records*, ser. 1, vol. 29, pt. 2, 872–73. The Sixty-second Georgia Cavalry was also known as the Second Georgia Partisan Rangers and consisted of ten companies in 1863. Three of those companies were from North Carolina and seven from Georgia. In December 1863, it had 408 effectives. Throughout 1863, this unit was assigned to the Department of North Carolina commanded by General George Pickett. Normally Partisan Ranger units did not operate outside the region from which they were recruited, but the Sixty-second Georgia spent much of its career beyond the Georgia boundaries. Since three companies of this unit were recruited later in North Carolina, it is probable that the unit left Georgia for northeastern Carolina on a recruitment expedition. For more on the Sixty-second Georgia, see Joseph H. Crute Jr., *Units of the Confederate States Army*, 2nd ed. (Gaithersburg, Md.: Olde Soldier Books, 1987), 115–16; and Stewart Sifakis, *Compendium of the Confederate Armies: South Carolina and Georgia* (New York: Facts on File, 1995), 151, 164–65.

36. George E. Pickett to Samuel Cooper, December 15, 1863, *Official Records*, ser. 1, vol. 29, pt. 2, 873. Pickett's comment about the continued presence of African Americans contradicts the October 1863 correspondence of James W. Hinton,

who had claimed that the Confederates of this region had already lost most of their slaves.

37. George Pickett to Samuel Cooper, December 15, 1863, *Official Records*, ser. 1, vol. 29, pt. 2, 873. For a study of another hanging General Pickett ordered at Kinston, North Carolina, in February 1864, see the essay by Lesley J. Gordon in Daniel E. Sutherland, ed., *Guerrillas, Unionists and Violence on the Confederate Home Front* (Fayetteville: University of Arkansas Press, 1999), 45–58.

38. George Pickett to Joel R. Griffin, December 15, 1863, *Official Records*, ser. 1, vol. 29, pt. 2, 872–73. Also, see Gordon, *General George E. Pickett in Life and Legend*, 126–27. It is not clear exactly how messages were communicated to the guerrillas; however, local citizens were the likely surrogates for General Wild. General Pickett probably used the Sixty-second Georgia Cavalry or other Confederate couriers as his go-between with the guerrillas. Clearly, some of the guerrillas acted as subsistence and commissary officers for their units, and there was probably someone in the company designated to act as a company courier. Simply posting a message on a tree or on an executed body (as Wild did with Daniel Bright and the guerrillas did with Samuel Jordan) was another gruesome but effective form of communication.

39. Edward A. Wild to John T. Elliott, December 17, 1863, Wild Papers, SHC.

40. According to Tewksbury, General Wild sent eight men to Norfolk as prisoners. Wild stated later that he "took a number of prisoners, including six Confederate soldiers, provided with furloughs, some with a printed clause stipulating that they should provide themselves with horses before returning." These six were apparently among the eight sent to Norfolk.

41. Confederate accounts refer to the site of Daniel Bright's execution as Hinton's Crossroads; see *Charleston Mercury*, January 5 and 20, 1864. Contemporary maps and the Tewksbury account refer to the site as Hintonsville. Tewksbury describes this place as having "a church and a single dwelling-house" (*New York Times*).

42. For Confederate accounts of the Wild raid, see *Republican Vindicator* (Staunton, Va.), January 29, 1864; *Southern Recorder* (Milledgeville, Ga.), January 19, 1864; and *Charleston Mercury*, January 5 and 20, 1864.

43. Tewksbury, *New York Times*.

44. W. N. H. Smith Report, February 10–17, 1864, *Official Records*, ser. 2, vol. 6, pt. 1, 1127–30.

45. Tewksbury, *New York Times*.

46. Ibid.

47. Captured Muster Rolls of "N.C. Defenders" and December 28, 1863, Report, Edward Augustus Wild Papers, SHC. Also, see Tewksbury, *New York Times*. Tewksbury asserts that Gregory was taken at his own home for supporting guerrillas. Major D. Gregory was his proper name; the "Major" was not a military rank. His name is found on the captured list of "N.C. Defenders."

48. Wild Report. For evidence that Unionists were not targeted for food and livestock confiscation during the Pasquotank phase of the raid, see the Records for Allowed Claims, Southern Claims Commission Case Files for Pasquotank County, N.C., National Archives, College Park, Md. Despite the large number of allowed claims

made by Unionists from Pasquotank County after the war, only one of these claims issued from the period of Wild's raid. This claim was made by a man named Phillip C. Fletcher. Fletcher, who was only fifteen in 1863, kept his horse at his grandfather's home in Camden County. During the December 1863 expedition, Wild and his men seized this horse at his grandfather's property. His grandfather's name was Major D. Gregory. Although the government awarded him money for his horse, it is unlikely that even this claim was valid, given his grandfather's wartime sympathies with the guerrillas. Phillip C. Fletcher (no. 21,340), Southern Claims Commission Case Files, 1877–83, Records of the Government Accounting Office, Records of the Third Auditor's Office, Record Group 217, National Archives, College Park, Md. (hereafter cited as Southern Claims). Also, see Benjamin Butler Report, *Official Records*, ser. 1, vol. 29, pt. 2, 596–97. General Butler received members of the community afterward who attested to the black soldiers' discretion.

49. Wild Report. Nancy White, like Phoebe Munden and Elizabeth Weeks, would be detained and taken to Norfolk. White was released in mid-January 1864, but Munden and Weeks were still being held in late January while Butler reviewed the situation and negotiated with the Confederate government. See Benjamin F. Butler to W. J. Munden and Pender Weeks, January 26, 1864, *Official Records*, ser. 2, vol. 6, pt. 1, 877.

50. *Charleston Mercury*, January 22, 1864, reprinted this story from a *New York Daily News* article posted at Norfolk on December 28, 1863. Also, see William J. Morrisett (no. 31,049), Southern Claims. Morrisett's claim garnered $1,918, a sizable sum for the commission to approve.

51. John Bottoms (no. 9,680), Southern Claims Disallowed. This claim was disallowed because Bottoms was forced into the Confederate militia for one month during the early period of the war. Nevertheless, short Confederate service under duress was relatively common among Unionists in the northeastern region; R. R. Guirkin (no. 19,919), Southern Claims Disallowed.

52. Edmond Simmons (no. 13,240 and 21,723), Southern Claims Disallowed. Simmons's claim was ultimately denied because his wife stated "they were opposed to the war at first, but after it began their sympathies were with their own people and they went with the state, but never did anything actively for the Confederacy."

53. Jesse Forbes Pugh, *Three Hundred Years along the Pasquotank: A Biographical History of Camden County* (Durham, N.C.: Seeman Printery, 1957), 160–66. Pugh documents at least forty-four Unionist families in Camden County during the war. Although a similar list is not extant for Currituck County, we do have the allowed claims list of Unionists from the Southern Claims Commission. Currituck had thirty-seven claims by Unionists approved after the war.

54. Noe, "Exterminating Savages," 106.

55. On the question of whether the war ever became total, my views in this essay closely parallel the thinking of Mark Neely, "Was the Civil War a Total War?" *Civil War History* 37 (1991): 5–28. Neely's article asserts that the idea of total war is both a twentieth-century construct and phenomenon. Wars must include systematic and/or indiscriminate killing of enemy civilians in order to truly embody total war; the line

between combatant and noncombatant must completely disappear. Wild's raid in its final stage was an example of harsher policy toward Confederate civilians but not total war.

56. Deposition of William J. Munden, February 10, 1864, *Official Records*, ser. 2, vol. 6, pt. 1, 1129–30.

57. Wild Report.

58. Ibid.

59. Weymouth T. Jordan Jr., ed., *North Carolina Troops, 1861–1865: A Roster*, vol. 15, *Infantry*, 528–29. John Elliott's group mustered as Co. E, Sixty-sixth North Carolina Partisan Rangers in April 1863, but like the other companies of this unit, it was never formally accepted as part of a regiment into the Confederate or North Carolina state service. It did not officially enter North Carolina service as part of a regular regiment until the Sixty-eighth North Carolina State Troops was accepted in January 1864. For economic data, see U.S. Bureau of the Census, *Population Schedule of the Eighth Census of the United States*, 1860, Pasquotank and Perquimans County, N.C.; U.S. Bureau of the Census, *Slave Schedule of the Eighth Census of the United States*, 1860, Pasquotank and Perquimans County, N.C., National Archives publication, Microfilm No. 653, Roll No. 925.

60. Benjamin Butler to Henry Halleck, January 17, 1864, *Official Records*, ser. 2, vol. 6, 847. See "Sub-inclosure" from General Wild to Captain Elliott dated December 17, 1863.

61. Wild Report.

62. Tewksbury, *New York Times*.

63. Ibid.

64. Ibid. Daniel Bright had served in a prewar slave patrol in Pasquotank County. See Slave Patrols, Pasquotank County, Records of Slaves and Free Persons of Color, 1815–61, North Carolina Department of Archives and History, Raleigh, N.C.

65. Wild Report.

66. Enclosures A, B, and C, Wild Report.

67. Wild Report.

68. Ibid.

69. General Orders No. 100, April 24, 1863, *Official Records*, ser. 3, vol. 3, pt. 1, 157.

70. Benjamin Butler Report, December 31, 1863, *Official Records*, ser. 1, vol. 29, pt. 2, 596–97. A list of the signatories can be found in Witt, *Wild in North Carolina*, 83–93. For a different type of reaction by Unionists and Confederate civilians living in occupied Carteret and Craven counties also on the eastern North Carolina coast, see Judkin Browning, "Removing the Mask of Nationality: Unionism, Racism, and Federal Military Occupation in North Carolina, 1862–1865," *Journal of Southern History* 71, no. 3 (2005): 589–620. Browning has found a different dynamic at work in occupied New Bern and Beaufort, where the Union troops garrisoned the town, whereas the no-man's-land experience of Pasquotank brought an effort to negotiate a middle ground between the two opposing governments. Browning demonstrates that anger over the Emancipation Proclamation and power abuses caused Unionists and

Confederates in the Carteret region to turn on the Union army and become "confirmed Confederates."

71. Benjamin Butler Report, December 31, 1863, *Official Records*, ser. 1, vol. 29, pt. 2, 596–97. Only one other detailed record from another county's meeting in the northeastern region has been preserved. It is a questionnaire from the Chowan County meeting where the community inquired about whether the oath of allegiance would be applied to them and if trade with Norfolk would continue. Citizens of Chowan County to Benjamin F. Butler, February 10, 1864, *Official Records*, ser. 1, vol. 33, 548–49; a copy of this questionnaire can also be found in Richard Dillard, *The Civil War in Chowan County, North Carolina* (Tyner, N.C.: Library Club of Chowan High School: 1916).

72. Benjamin Butler Report, December 31, 1863, *Official Records*, ser. 1, vol. 29, pt. 2, 596–97. Citizens' committees from Camden and Currituck also visited with General Butler, but unfortunately no record of their meetings has been preserved. On Governor Vance's reaction, see *Elizabeth City Economist*, August 31, 1900; Jordan, *North Carolina Troops, 1861-1865: A Roster*, vol. 15, *Infantry*, 509; and John Pool to David Barnes, March 28, 1863, in *Papers of Zebulon Baird Vance*, ed. Mobley, 2:101–2.

73. Benjamin Butler to Edward M. Stanton, December 31, 1863, *Official Records*, ser. 1, vol. 29, pt. 2, 596.

74. James Forbes et al. to General George W. Getty (Enclosure A), January 13, 1864, *Official Records*, ser 2, vol. 6, 846.

75. It is not clear from the extant records exactly what date Phoebe Munden and Elizabeth Weeks were released. Munden and Weeks were probably released sometime shortly after their husbands received a letter from Benjamin Butler seeking a trade of the husbands for their wives as prisoners. Since there is no further record of Phoebe Munden and Elizabeth Weeks after February 1864, it is likely they were released sometime during that month. The other hostage, Nancy White, was released on January 14, 1864. See Edward A. Wild Report, January 10, 1864, Wild Papers, SHC; and Benjamin Butler to Lt. W. J. Munden and Pvt. Pender Weeks, January 26, 1864, *Official Records*, ser. 2, vol. 6, 877–78; and Casstevens, *Edward A. Wild and the African Brigade*, 139–41.

76. Jordan, *North Carolina Troops, 1861-1865: A Roster*, vol. 15, *Infantry*, 517; Laurence Simmons Baker to James W. Hinton, July 21, 1864, Edward Clements Yellowley Papers, Southern Historical Collection, Wilson Library, University of North Carolina at Chapel Hill; Wild Report. The first names of Captains Hughes, Ethridge, and Coffey cannot be positively identified.

77. George E. Pickett to James Seddon, January 12, 1864, *Official Records*, ser. 1, vol. 33, 1083. Also, see Jordan, *North Carolina Troops, 1861-1865*, 15:517.

78. I. Vodges Report, August 4, 1864, *Official Records*, ser. 1, vol. 40, pt. 1, 820–21.

Visions of Freedom and Civilization Opening before Them

African Americans Search for Autonomy during Military Occupation in North Carolina

Wednesday, January 14, 1863, found Beaufort, North Carolina, still drying from a recent tempest and getting colder by the hour. The weather had not been the only turbulent event that week. Captain William B. Fowle Jr., Beaufort's provost marshal, sat down that morning to write a letter to his superior officer relating an event that had occurred just a few days earlier when an African American woman had encountered two prominent Unionists, Joel Henry Davis and Henry Rieger. Fowle wrote: "Mr. Davis and Mr. Rieger together tied the woman to a tree her arms over her head and then whipped her severely, the flesh on her arms where the ropes went was badly lacerated and her arms covered with blood when I saw her — She was only released upon the peremptory order of a private of the Ninth New Jersey, who says the treatment was very cruel — Her crime was that she demanded her daughter whom Mr. Davis retained in slavery; she is a smart intelligent woman and quite able to support herself and children."[1]

This story illustrates one of the ways in which African Americans asserted their independence — and the violent reactions such assertions could cause — in the wake of the Emancipation Proclamation in occupied Carteret and Craven counties. Many slaves felt emboldened by the Proclamation as a direct acknowledgment of their right to freedom and, as a consequence, their right to assert themselves. Perhaps it was under the influence of such feelings that on a brisk, early January 1863 day, this African American woman sought out Davis, a man she knew well, to insist that her daughter be released from servitude, provoking the incident that Fowle described.

The woman's ability to "support herself" and her assertion of her independence probably rankled the former slaveholder Davis as much as any Federal policy did. In southern society, whites believed a black person's proper role was as a dependent. Independence and autonomy granted blacks a new psychological footing, and if allowed to go unchecked, such black assertions could lead to a genuine belief in social equality. The woman's demand challenged Davis's traditional social authority. For financial reasons, Davis had embraced Union occupation, but he would not tolerate black expectations to equal rights. Davis's violent attack was his own personal, physical attempt to stem the tide of racial equality that the Federal government seemed to be ushering into the region. His action served a dual symbolic and political purpose. By physically scarring her body, Davis sent a visual warning to other blacks not to challenge their former masters. To fellow whites whose allegiance may be suspect, Davis's message revealed that though he had accepted Union occupation, he would not accept racial equality. To be a Unionist did not mean one forsook white superiority.[2]

Many scholars have written on those tensions inherent in the creation of a new order that began when Union soldiers arrived in southern communities. However, most scholarly works have been concerned with how Union agents proscribed black freedom and autonomy, or as Stephen V. Ash concluded, how "the Union army decreed an end to black bondage but staked out certain limits to black liberty." Even Willie Lee Rose, in *Rehearsal for Reconstruction*, the first major exploration of a black community during wartime occupation, focused much more on the role played by antislavery men and women—particularly the idealistic abolitionists of "Gideon's Band" and the often unscrupulous Union army officers—than on the slaves who gained their freedom in the region. Though scholars make the perfunctory assertions that blacks forced the administration's hand in terms of liberalizing its policy, they generally focus on the role whites played in the black emancipation experience.[3]

This essay offers a different perspective, focusing not on Union authorities but on blacks as savvy pragmatists who utilized the Union army and agents of northern benevolent societies to attain the four pillars of their empowerment: escape, employment, enlistment, and education. While whites certainly figure prominently in this story—as they were integrally involved with the black experience and much evidence of black actions come from white sources—blacks are the leading actors in this drama. Freedpeople were remarkably successful at achieving their empowerment goals during wartime occupation and hoped that that success would lead to greater opportunities for independence and autonomy once the war ended. In this, of course, they were frustrated. Once the war ended, the Federal government withdrew its wartime level of support, reneged on promises, and allowed former Confederates to regain control of their abandoned lands. Yet, this should not diminish the story of the black struggle for autonomy under Union occupation. Blacks gained much success in those years of the war when they were able to assert their independence, confident in the support of the Federal government.[4]

The Carteret-Craven county region offers a unique lens through which to examine these black efforts at independence and autonomy. The port cities of Beaufort and especially New Bern served as Union military bases and destinations for thousands of escaped slaves. In addition, unlike the situation that Rose explored in South Carolina's Sea Islands, many local whites remained in the Carteret-Craven region after Union forces occupied it. Therefore, freedom-seeking slaves had to interact with local whites as well as with Union soldiers and benevolent society members. Blacks encountered much hostility from southern and northern whites in the region but continued to utilize the Union agents and Federal policies to maximum advantage. An examination of this region not only allows for greater understanding of the black search for autonomy in North Carolina but also fills an important void left by Ash in his otherwise excellent exploration of military occupation in the South—it allows the reader to see how African Americans reacted "when the Yankees came."[5]

The Yankees came to this coastal North Carolina region on March 13, 1862, when a large expeditionary force under the command of General Ambrose E. Burnside landed south of New Bern. After a brief battle, Burnside's force captured New Bern on March 14 and Beaufort on March 25, beginning an occupation that would last the rest of the war. Hoping to escape war's uncertainty and take advantage of new economic opportunities while simultaneously maintaining the social status quo, many local whites forsook the Confederacy and pledged their allegiance to the Union—some more equivocally than others. But the most unequivocal demonstration of loyalty came from African Americans who flocked to the region to take advantage of the opportunities presented by wartime occupation. While local whites, even Unionists like Davis, were simply trying to preserve the antebellum status quo, the war had taken a radical turn; the Emancipation Proclamation was the culmination of white fears. Repudiating their slave heritage, African Americans sought personal autonomy—control over their own bodies, minds, and material conditions—and asserted their independence, especially among their former masters.[6]

Embittered local whites placed all the blame for such radical black actions on the Union soldiers and Federal government. Local slaveholders declared, like most southern planters, that their slaves were content within the confines of the peculiar institution and did not desire independence.

James Rumley, a secessionist diarist who remained in Beaufort during occupation, was convinced that slaves "would have but little of this feeling if let alone." Rumley conveniently ignored reality, however. For as he and other slave owners knew well, African Americans had been trying to ameliorate their hardships and establish some sort of self-control over their lives for decades before the Union soldiers arrived. Individually and collectively, slaves in eastern North Carolina sought to maximize their autonomy in a variety of ways—at home and at work, inside as well as outside the accepted parameters of slavery.[7]

Within the home, the dogged attachment to family, despite repeated threats to its existence, revealed the powerful desire slaves had for maintaining some degree of control over their lives. In addition to maintaining a domestic family life, slaves sought to carve out a cultural space for themselves that was not dominated by working in the fields. They clandestinely nourished social ties within the black community, often traveling away from their home grounds at night while keeping a vigilant eye out for the slave patrols. Slaves also engaged in an active, often illicit "internal economy"—trading or bartering goods with each other and with lower-class whites. Blacks did more than just exchange items of economic value with these whites; they often worked, drank, and slept with them as well. William Henry Singleton, a Craven County slave, explained that local masters feared that poor whites "might teach us to read or might give us some information about what the North was trying to do." Poor whites also would occasionally aid escaping slaves, if the whites could derive personal benefit from it. When William Kinnegay ran away from his master in 1857, he concealed himself in the swamps south of New Bern and killed and dressed hogs for nearby whites in exchange for survival supplies.[8]

Escape from the confining nature of slavery represented the most direct way of asserting one's independence. Antebellum North Carolina newspapers are filled with thousands of advertisements for runaway slaves, especially in the coastal region, where access to waterborne travel allowed abundant opportunities for escape to the North. Yet, a surprising number of slaves did not seek to abandon their home region. In the Carteret and Craven county region, kinship proved to be the tie that bound many runaway slaves to the area. Advertisements often repeated variations on the same theme, such as one Craven County master's notice for his slave who he believed was probably bound for New Bern, "at which place I think it most likely he will harbour, as the most of his family connections are there." Some runaway slaves told of remaining near family for many years. "Nights I came back to my mother's house and to the cellar and very early in the morning before the sun was up I would go to the woods and watch the men go to their work," William Henry Singleton wrote. "I would stay in the woods all day and then come back at night." Similarly, Harriet Jacobs, a slave from coastal Chowan County, escaped from slavery only to hide for seven long years in the attic of the house of her free black grandmother before finally deciding to flee north. These slaves chose to escape slavery but could not completely discard all the positive relationships at home. What was the value of freedom if one had to abandon family, community, and all the social networks one had established?[9]

Though running away might be the ultimate method of asserting one's autonomy, many other slaves sought to ameliorate their lives within the institution of slavery through acceptable practices, most often in the employment of a trade. The ability to "hire out" imbued skilled slaves with a greater sense of autonomy and independence than field hands, for they could control their time, occupation, and often their income as well as utilize their earnings to improve their family's standard of living through the purchase of goods. In Beaufort, John Pender and Henry Mathewson, slaves of the prosperous merchant and Confederate captain Josiah Pender, were carpenters who maintained a limited degree of independence through the practice of their trade. Pender remembered that his master "allowed us to make our own contracts and buy such tools as we needed." Pender achieved such a level of autonomy that he even purchased land from his master, which he used to establish his family's homestead during and after slavery.[10]

Many slave boatmen shared Pender's sense of independence. As David Cecelski has argued, few occupations allowed slaves more freedom than those that required work on the water, for "the nature of their labors meant they could not be supervised closely, if at all, for days or even weeks." They not only had a larger degree of personal freedom than most slaves but also disseminated antislavery talk among the local slaves. Boatmen traveled widely and traded information with enslaved and free blacks from all over the Atlantic region. Though not all slaves had opportunities to meet people outside their own geographic region, few were ignorant of the wider world around them.[11]

While many slaves sought to carve out cultural space within the confines of slavery, through escape or employment, nearly all slaves viewed education as one crucial determinant of their personal autonomy. As historian Janet Duitsman Cornelius has affirmed, "For enslaved African Americans, literacy was more than a path to individual freedom—it was a communal act, a political demonstration of resistance to oppression and of self-determination for the black community." Whites, of course, feared the implications of education for slaves. North Carolina slave testimony recorded during the Works Progress Administration interviews of the 1930s reveals the taboo whites placed on black education. "You better not be found trying to learn to read," recalled Hannah Crasson. "Our marster was harder down on that than anything else." Patsy Michner confirmed, "You better not be caught with no paper in your hand; if you was, you got the cowhide."[12]

Supporting testimony also comes from more contemporary informants than octogenarian freedpeople trying to remember their childhood. Horace James, a Union chaplain, heard slaves decry their masters' restrictions: "If any of them saw us with a spelling-book trying to learn to read, they would take it away from us and punish us." Even a hint of a slave seeking some reading knowledge would bring instant retribution from concerned masters. Autobiographer Singleton recounted how his master "whipped me very severely" just for opening a book. Nonetheless, many slaves still sought education because of its empowering virtues. As one clandestinely educated slave noted, "I felt at night, as I went to my rest, that I was really beginning to be a *man*, preparing myself for a condition in life better and higher and happier than could belong to the ignorant *slave*."[13]

Many slaves sought, primarily through surreptitious means, to acquire some degree of education. These efforts were surprisingly successful. Historians have suggested that between 5 and 10 percent of southern slaves had at least some rudimentary degree of literacy by 1860. Union soldiers confirmed these suspicions in the New Bern–Beaufort region. Henry A. Clapp, a Massachusetts soldier who would be part of the occupying force in New Bern in 1863, wrote: "I should say that about one in fifteen of the men, women, and children could read. We find that many learned or began to learn before they were freed by our army—taking their instruction mostly 'on the sly' and indeed in the face of considerable danger." Whether "on the sly" or through acceptable methods, North Carolina slaves, including those in the coastal region, sought autonomy and self-control over their own lives as much as possible throughout slavery. When Union soldiers began arriving in the spring of 1862, African Americans in the region recognized that they had been presented a golden opportunity to throw off the chains of slavery and embrace the independence they had long desired.[14]

When Union soldiers landed south of New Bern on March 13, 1862, they immediately encountered welcoming slaves, most of whom, as one officer remarked, were "laughing and so glad to see us." One Union soldier noted that as they marched from the boats, "a few Negroes with the liveliest joy depicted on their countenances greeted our approach." Some were more serious, recognizing the consequences of the soldiers' arrival. One slave woman, "her eyes shining like black diamonds," encouraged the Federal soldiers to defeat the Rebels, defiantly commanding, "you Bomb 'un out." A Union officer summed up the emotions in the county when he wrote, "The slaves alone seemed rejoiced at our coming, and looked upon our victorious banners as signs of their approaching millennium." Upon the approach of the Union army, many masters had fled and left their slaves. These slaves felt immediate relief from the institution of slavery and thanked the Federal forces for their release. As one slave told a Union soldier three weeks after the battle of New Bern, "it seemed like Christmas to him," for "it was the most rest that he had seen in all his life."[15]

After taking control of something as intangible as their own personal liberty, slaves turned their attention to taking more tangible items that had been so long denied them—such as their masters' property. In New Bern, General Burnside informed Secretary of War Edwin M. Stanton that "nine tenths of the depredations on the 14th, after the enemy and citizens had fled from the town, were committed by the Negroes, before our troops entered the city." The efficiency of looting by local blacks impressed Union soldiers, who displayed remarkable skill themselves in plundering. A Massachusetts soldier noted, "The Negroes take the advantage [and] became Masters of their Masters['] Houses and things and went in for spoils and things had to fly."[16]

In Beaufort, while Federal officers commandeered the comfortable home of the temporarily absent merchant Edmund H. Norcom, angry local resident James Rumley noted, "The kitchen and backyard [had] become a perfect den of thieving runaway Negroes" who "had free access to every part of the building." Some blacks took practical items from the houses of Norcom and Benjamin Leecraft, the absent commander of a Beaufort artillery company, such as food, beds, furniture, and "even the dresses of Mr. Leecraft's deceased wife and child." Other liberties were more symbolic than practical. A Massachusetts soldier reported that in New Bern, blacks "stole everything they could get hold of—some of the colored ladies now wear some very fine silk dresses—and seem to feel above the rest of man or woman kind." In Beaufort, Rumley raged, "a big buck Negro was lately seen seated in the parlor, thumming on Mrs. Norcom's piano." Perhaps more galling to Rumley's sensibilities as a patriarch and protector of the purity of white women was his comment that "even her bridal dress has been worn by negroes!" This last garb held particular symbolic importance to the plundering bondspeople. Slaves had been denied any legal right of marriage, and though they took spouses, they had no protection against separation or white male sexual exploitation. Donning the silk dresses of city elites and the wedding dress of the wife of a wealthy slave owner was more than just an appreciation of quality tailoring; it was a bold public gesture of defiance and revenge.[17]

Escape

The arrival of Union forces offered more than just prospects for plunder; it afforded slaves opportunities to attain the four pillars of their empowerment. The first and foundational pillar was escape, without which none of the others could follow. Numerous slaves in the countryside fled their masters and sought their freedom under the protection of the Union army. Union soldiers documented the flood of black refugees. Burnside's personal secretary, Daniel Read Larned, wrote, "Stealing in from every direction by land & sea—in squads from 6 to 30 each—they come and dump themselves by the side of the fence and 'wait orders from Mr. Burnside.'" A Massachusetts soldier rejoiced in their escape, declaring: "Thank God for the evidence that we here see that the day of their oppression is passed." Another soldier noted the risks that slaves took. "They are continually coming in," he wrote, "in squads of from one to a dozen threading their way through the swamps at night, avoiding pickets, they at last reach our lines." Sutton Davis, a black fisherman, led the slaves on Davis Island in Pamlico Sound to freedom in New Bern. He found a small boat and rowed it to the fishing village of Smyrna, from which they escaped to New Bern on foot.[18]

Slaves also testified to their immense desire for freedom. George W. Harris, a Jones County slave, recalled that his master had concealed George and his fellow slaves in the woods, "mindin' hosses an' takin' care o' things he had hid there." George, his father, and several other slaves decided to leave together in a gang and "ran away to New Bern," about twenty-file miles away. Mary Barbour and her family came from much farther away. They originally fled from near Raleigh to Union lines in Chowan County. While there, Barbour recalled, "De Yankees tells pappy ter head fer New Bern an'd dat he will be took keer of dar, so ter New Bern we goes."[19]

The irresistible impulse for freedom compelled many slaves to perform amazing feats to rescue friends and family members. The boldness of a slave who had just escaped to New Bern in April 1862 astounded R. R. Clarke, a Massachusetts soldier. The slave "had just heard that his wife was about 7 miles above our pickets and that [the rebels] were going to carry her off upcountry," Clarke wrote. "He wanted to go & get her—of course we gave consent & I have no doubt but that he will evade their pickets and get her within 48 hours." Testifying before the American Freedmen's Inquiry Commission at Fort Monroe, Virginia, on May 9, 1863, a Union provost was asked, "In your opinion, is there any communication between the refugees and the black men still in slavery?" He answered, "Yes Sir, we have men here who have gone back 200 miles." Slaves had discussed freedom for so long that they could not pass up the opportunity to seek it out. Alex Huggins, a slave who escaped to New Bern, remembered what prompted him to run away from his family at age twelve. "Twan'nt anythin' wrong about home that made me run away," he recalled. "I'd heard so much talk 'bout freedom I reckon. I jus' wanted to try it, an' I thought I had to get away from home to have it."[20]

Thousands of slaves likewise "wanted to try it" and flocked to Beaufort and New Bern to "have it." Beaufort, whose total white and black antebellum population numbered about 1,600 (including 600 blacks), became home to nearly 2,500 blacks by January 1864 and over 3,200 by 1865, while New Bern housed over 8,500 freedpeople in January 1864 and nearly 11,000 a year later (compared to about 3,000 blacks in 1860). Slaves readily migrated to coastal cities like Beaufort and New Bern, due to their proficient knowledge of the water routes of escape that many runaways had used in antebellum times. The escaping slaves, if they remembered the antislavery talk they had heard during the antebellum years from black sailors, may have even expected to receive favorable treatment from Union soldiers, especially those from Massachusetts.[21]

Slaves discovered that they had useful allies in these Bay State soldiers, who would often directly intervene to ensure a slave's successful escape. When slaves came into Union lines as contrabands, North Carolina's military governor Edward Stanly—appointed by President Lincoln and charged with enforcing antebellum North Carolina laws—deemed them fugitive slaves and subject to be returned to their owners. In the first test of Stanly's authority, a local farmer named Nicholas Bray visited Stanly's headquarters in New Bern in May 1862 and claimed that a northern soldier had taken his female slave against her will. After Bray took the oath of allegiance, Stanly granted him permission to retrieve his slave, which he did. Northern soldiers reacted angrily. A Union soldier readily acknowledged, "A party of our men had made [the Brays] a visit . . . held a pistol at the head of Bray and his wife—put the girl into a carriage and left—One of his houses was burned down and the fence of his own [set] on fire." Daniel Larned corroborated the story and offered advice to the distraught

Mrs. Bray: "We have promised [to] place a guard at her house, but advised her to let her slave remain where she is. I think they will soon find out that the best way is to let their slaves be where they are." Powerless to command the army, Stanly also advised the Brays to give up their quest. Stanly's impotence in the matter only emboldened soldiers further. One stated, "So this kidnapping game has been played out in a brief and summary manner—It will soon be attempted again—the feeling is deep and bitter among the soldiers and many of the officers." To native whites, such actions by northern soldiers, though contrary to formal Federal policy at that time, only portended much more ominous initiatives regarding African Americans.[22]

Indeed, Lincoln's Emancipation Proclamation reaffirmed white fears, particularly because North Carolina was not exempted from the Proclamation, unlike most other areas under Union occupation. However, by the time the Proclamation took effect on January 1, 1863, there was little uproar about it in the occupied regions of North Carolina, primarily because Union soldiers had granted slaves de facto freedom ever since they first arrived. Though they bitterly opposed it, white citizens were highly cognizant that the Proclamation would grant de jure freedom to their slaves in the New Year.[23]

African Americans were also aware of the Proclamation's meaning. One Union soldier in New Bern commented, "Although they could neither read nor write," slaves "were quite well informed upon the President's proclamation, at least the portion relating to their own immediate change of condition, viz. freedom." Another soldier concurred: "The Negroes are on the whole so far as I have seen more intelligent and clear headed than I fancied and are considerably interested in the President's proclamation, which many of them understand very well." The Proclamation had a powerful and lasting effect in African Americans' collective memory. After the war, when agents for the Southern Claims Commission asked former slave Caesar Manson of Beaufort when he became free, he answered forthrightly: "At the time of President Lincoln's proclamation went into effect." A Union soldier detected the black affection for Lincoln and declared, "Still coming generations that come up will call him blessed." Some former slaves also utilized their newfound freedom to rectify previous wrongs. William Derby, a soldier in the Twenty-fifth Massachusetts Regiment, recounted the story of James Whitby, a slave who had married Emeline thirty years earlier and had watched eight of their fifteen children sold away. In 1863, James and Emeline asked the regiment's chaplain to remarry them, making the act legal in the eyes of God *and* the law. Derby recalled James explaining, "We's want dis ting right dis time, for shu!" A new day had dawned for slaves, and their hopefulness and joy at future prospects became infectious. One northern missionary noted that blacks beheld "visions of freedom and civilization opening before them," which, he admitted, "inspired my heart with unwonted enthusiasm."[24]

Often blacks' desires to assert their independence led to confrontations with local whites over the nature of what it meant to be free and to occupy a place in this new civilization. Many confrontations were rather benign, as slaves exercised their newfound power. James Rumley complained when "negroes looked on with indifference" as "delicate women and aged men" had to perform "drudgeries, to which they have never been accustomed." Understandably, ex-slaves felt little pity when their former masters were compelled to perform daily menial tasks for survival. Slaves also engaged in verbal rows with whites. One New Bern resident complained, "It is nothing unusual for the Negroes to curse their masters & mistresses in passing along the streets. They are allowed to do so [by the Yankees]." Another white lady angrily vowed, "If any of her slaves were impudent again she 'would knock them flat.'"[25]

Throughout the time of occupation, however, some black assertions of independence led to more malevolent confrontations, as whites used violence to intimidate blacks into submission. A military court found that civilian Edward Hughes "did commit an assault with intent to kill" upon a black woman in New Bern "by shooting at her twice with a pistol, both shots taking effect upon her person." Union soldiers noted that Rebel pickets would shoot at blacks whenever they had an opportunity. In March 1865, a freed slave was "accosted by a man with a double-barreled gun, who after asking him some questions, deliberately killed him." In 1864, several blacks who tried to cultivate land outside of Union lines were captured or killed by Rebels.[26]

The most illustrative example of violent confrontation in the wake of emancipation was the story that opened this chapter, when Joel Henry Davis tied up and mercilessly beat a former slave for demanding that he release her daughter from bondage. Though he was a respected Unionist, Davis was aggrieved about the uncompensated loss of his slaves, but being a practical merchant, he recognized the benefits that accompanied allegiance to the Union forces. However, as Margaret M. Storey commented regarding Alabama Unionists, "although loyalty to the Union represented a rejection of the Confederate state, it did not necessarily represent a rejection of southern culture or values." Even though he may have saluted the Stars and Stripes, Davis did not welcome some of the government's more radical war aims, embodied in the woman's demand for her daughter. Davis had come to terms with Union occupation, but he would not allow a social leveling between blacks and whites. Davis lashed out against the woman to demonstrate that as a white man, he still enjoyed certain powers over blacks. His reaction exemplifies Ash's assertion: "To whites throughout the occupied South . . . the more violence they were able to inflict on blacks, the more thorough was their racial mastery." Indeed, violence was native whites' response to their disenchantment with a Federal policy that prevented the maintenance of the antebellum social status quo.[27]

Unlike local whites, who simply wanted to return to life in the Union as it had been prior to the war, some Federal officials desired a much greater change. Foremost among them was Horace James, chaplain of the Twenty-fifth Massachusetts Regiment who later became Superintendent for Negro Affairs for the Department of North Carolina. James asserted, "It is not enough to bring back this country to its position just before the breaking out of the rebellion. The 'Union as it was' is not what I want to see restored. Let us rather have it purified and perfected, coming out holier and freer from this dreadful ordeal, sanctified by the baptism of blood." Another soldier agreed: "The more we learn of the despicable social condition of the South, the stronger appears the need of the purification which, in the Providence of God, comes of the fire and the sword."[28]

Employment

Despite white protests, blacks hastened Union efforts at "purification" of the southern social system. In addition to escaping from their masters, they sought employment, especially such that would give them the chance for land ownership—a foundational piece of autonomy. Many tried to set up their own farms. The desire to be independent and autonomous drove some African Americans to risky lengths. Horace James declared that, with no land available on which to settle freedpeople, "some of the more fearless among them did indeed venture to hire tracts of land a little out of the towns, or on the 'debatable territory' along the railroad and the Neuse, and attempt the culture of cotton or corn, or the making of turpentine." James admitted that those who desperately sought such independence took their chances with Confederate raiders or secessionist sympathizers and often forfeited their freedom or their lives. Though some tried to maintain their independence from all whites, many others took advantage of the Union army's demand for labor.[29]

Escaped slaves began working for the Union army from the moment it first arrived. In April 1862, just a month after the capture of New Bern, one Union soldier noted that over seven hundred able-bodied black men had arrived in town looking for work. "They all find employment," he wrote. "Some work on the fortifications, some unloading ships—more are really needed to perform the labor to be done here." The government employed many freedmen in the quartermaster department as teamsters and manual laborers. Some blacks served more specialized roles. Willis M. Lewis, a free black in New Bern, served at different times as a guide and scout for Federal troops as well as a nurse at regimental hospitals. Jacob Grimes, an escaped slave, came to New Bern and "was employed by the U.S. government as a detective," presumably to monitor illicit trading or treasonous actions against the government. Union soldiers also hired black men as servants. One soldier noted that even the youngest refugees knew the value of money: "The black boys want to hire out as servants, and at such low rates that many of the men in the ranks have one to run errands, draw water, wash their tin dishes."[30]

While men worked for the army as manual laborers or servants, black women utilized their domestic skills to earn income. They provided meals, mended uniforms, and washed clothes for the Union soldiers. Others baked goods and sold them in the army camps for quite a profit. Soldiers commented on the freedpeople's good business sense. One soldier wrote, "Some are very intelligent and charge reasonable prices for things while the whites ask four times what they are worth." Another commented, "The Negro women are round every day selling gingerbread cakes pies and other things and it is remarkable how they know all about money and are so ignorant in every respect." Some women established legendary reputations as cooks. One soldier wrote a friend of how he and some friends had gone down to dinner at "Jane's" place, where they enjoyed a savory meal of pork steak, fried liver, baked sweet potatoes, hoecake, and coffee. "She was cook for one of the first families," he wrote, and "now drives quite a business on her own account." Unable to make any money as a slave, Jane parlayed her skills into a lucrative business after she gained her freedom.[31]

Slave craftsmen also took maximum advantage of their skills. Coopers, wheelwrights, and carpenters worked for the Union army. In 1865, James wrote, slaves "have come in, and among them many mechanics and skilled laborers, so that New Berne has now a good supply of tradesmen, in nearly all the different branches essential to social prosperity." Former slaves Eliza Garner and John Pender were carpenters who worked for the Union army "putting up buildings for the troops and . . . repairing navy vessels." Slave mariners converted their skills into service for the Union authorities. Caesar Manson worked as a boatman carrying the U.S. mail, while others shuttled goods and passengers between Fort Macon, Beaufort, and Morehead City. James noted the preponderance of black watermen in the region, musing, "The Negro is here an aquatic animal, and takes to the water almost as readily as the sea fowl that abound in this vicinity." He continued, "Not less than one hundred men are constantly employed in boating, this business being wholly in the hands of the Negroes . . . [a]nd a remunerative calling it proves to be, indeed." In fact, some amassed enough wealth to purchase their own boats. One slave who lived in Beaufort saved up his earnings and purchased his own boat in 1863 "for the convenience of visiting his wife," who lived on Bogue Island across the harbor.[32]

In addition to providing valuable services to the Union personnel and securing their own financial freedom, employment allowed the building of a robust free black community. One of the strongest centers of social engagement was the local barbershop. In Beaufort, David Parker, a literate freedman, opened a barbershop that served as a nexus of freedmen's activity. "Many times in my shop we talked about the war," Parker recalled. "Sometimes I received papers and could read them and tell them colored people what battles had been fought and who were victorious and all about the reports of the battles and the movements of troops. My shop was sort of general headquarters for the colored people to come to for news." Not only was it an important social center, but it also exemplified one of the most lucrative types of employment. When Horace James listed the highest grossing occupations among freedmen in 1864, barbers were near the top of the list, earning an average annual income of $675 (compared to an enlisted man, who would earn $13 a month, for a yearly income of $156).[33]

James further observed that many of the freedmen, not just barbers, were prospering under occupation. "Some of these people are becoming rich; all are doing well for themselves, even in these times," he wrote. Grocers ($678), carpenters ($510), blacksmiths ($468), coopers ($418), masons ($402), and turpentine farmers ($446) all made handsome average incomes. Some individual freedmen, primarily those engaging in the turpentine business, earned more than $3,000 in one year, while over a dozen from assorted other occupations grossed more than $1,000 in 1864. James was greatly impressed by the freedmen's innate business acumen: "They evince a capacity for business, and exhibit a degree of thrift and shrewdness, which are ample security for their future progress, if they are allowed an equal chance with their fellow-men."[34]

Enlistment

Many black men felt that enlisting in the United States armed forces allowed them the greatest opportunity for "an equal chance" to demonstrate their manhood. Some local freedmen served as sailors and seamen on military and commercial Union vessels, while others enlisted into colored infantry regiments. Few things upset local whites more. "A recruiting office has been opened today by the Yankees for negro volunteers on Front Street," the fiery Rumley wrote from Beaufort on June 1, 1863, "where the black traitors are gathering in considerable numbers." In spite of white outrage, African Americans desired to demonstrate their equality as men. Rumley recounted the speech of an African American orator who invoked the themes represented in enlistment and independence, arguing that "their race would have not only their personal freedom, but political equality, and if this should be refused them at the ballot box they would have it at the cartridge box!"[35]

African American enlistment practices became politicized to represent both manhood and the privileges that rightfully accompanied freedom. Teachers from the American Missionary Association recognized the importance of enlistment to African American psychology: "The action of the government in incorporating the colored people into the army creates a new era in their history; it recognizes their manhood, gives them a status in the nation, and is open acknowledgment of their value to the country in the time of its peril." Historian Jim Cullen has persuasively argued that enlistment in Union regiments greatly enhanced black men's fundamental self-perceptions: "As the *material* conditions of their lives changed—as they joined the armed forces, were freed from slavery, or both—so too did their ideological conceptions of themselves as men."[36]

The desire to prove their manhood prompted numerous blacks to enlist. Many had been waiting for the opportunity from the moment Union troops arrived. William Henry Singleton, a Craven County slave, claimed that over one hundred black refugees had been drilling on their own as early as the spring of 1862, anticipating the time when the Lincoln administration would allow African Americans to enlist in the army. In January 1863, one Massachusetts soldier wrote, "I think there could be here in Newbern one thousand who formally were slaves, but who are now free, enlisted in the Union army, who would fight like Tigers to defend their rights as they now enjoy them." Indeed, when the Federal government finally authorized the enlistment of black soldiers in the region a month later, volunteers flocked to the enlistment office, but only after some negotiation with Union authorities for certain rights.[37]

Massachusetts soldier Edward W. Kinsley related an encounter he had with New Bern's black leader Abraham Galloway in early 1863, regarding demands for black enlistments. Kinsley claimed that Galloway had persuaded the blacks not to enlist right away, "so great was his influence among the colored people that all matters of importance concerning them were left to his decision." Kinsley probably exaggerated Galloway's power in making all decisions, but his statement does reveal that blacks had bonded together to negotiate suitable terms with Union authorities before they enlisted in the army. When Kinsley agreed to meet with Galloway to discuss enlistment demands, he was blindfolded and carried to a secret attic room, where his blindfold was removed, revealing him to be surrounded by many blacks, while "right in front of him stood Abraham Galloway and another huge negro, both armed with revolvers." In this savvy display of intimidating negotiating tactics, Galloway was able to extract the concessions that freedpeople demanded from the Federal government. They demanded not only that North Carolina blacks should be paid the same as black soldiers in Massachusetts (where the Fifty-fourth Massachusetts Regiment had just been formed) but also that "their families should be provided for; their children should be taught to read; and if they should be taken prisoners, the government should see to it that they were treated as prisoners of war." Kinsley pledged that the government would meet all these demands and, as result, reported, "The next day the word went forth, and the blacks came to the recruiting station by hundreds and a brigade was soon formed." Even allowing for some exaggeration for the timetable, the spirit of enlistment did become quite vigorous among the black community in early 1863.[38]

In the first muster in February 1863, a Union officer reported that 413 had already answered the roll. In April 1863, a Union soldier noted, "They are enlisting Negroes here at a grate [sic] rate[.] [T]wo hundred nearly enlisted in about two days." On May 24, 1863, a Union officer reported that over 400 had enlisted that week alone. The pride and satisfaction that black men enjoyed from enlisting became apparent to outside observers. One Union soldier who had feared that freedmen could not "be converted into serviceable recruits" was amazed to see their transformation upon donning the Union bluecoats. "The National uniform was as a magic robe to them and they straightened up and stood erect in it, at once men and soldiers," he remarked. "The touch of the rifle as their hands clasped it seemed to fill their veins with electric life." Indeed, the act of enlisting served as a major source of empowerment for black men throughout the region, and the prospect of martially participating in winning their own independence prompted thousands to enlist before the war ended. Though accurate numbers of black enlistments from Carteret and Craven counties are difficult to ascertain exactly, over 5,000 blacks joined the Union army from North Carolina, almost all of them from the occupied region of the state. The majority of the black men who joined in New Bern were formed into three U.S. Colored Troops regiments that became known as the African Brigade.[39]

U.S. treasury agent John Hedrick suggested in December 1863 from Beaufort that not all of these enlistments were voluntary. He wrote that General John G. Foster "has . . . ordered all able bodied negro men between the ages of 18 & 45 to be mustered into the U.S. Services, and forbids the employment of such negroes on public works." Accordingly, Hedrick claimed that the order "created quite a stir among the darkies," since, he asserted, "[t]here are very few of them that really wish to fight." However, there is little corroborating evidence from this region to suggest that blacks were coerced into military service, which occurred frequently in other occupied areas, especially in South Carolina's Sea Islands. Hedrick's letters have numerous derogatory references to blacks and especially black soldiers. This one negative letter contrasts with much evidence, from black and white sources, that confirms a strong black zeal to enlist in the Union army. Some were undoubtedly compelled into service, but the vast majority appear to have volunteered willingly.[40]

Black enlistment efforts met resistance, as freed slaves encountered hostility from locals as well as Union soldiers. Many white soldiers, even liberal antislavery ones, maintained decidedly racist views after their arrival. On one oppressively hot July afternoon in 1862, Captain William Augustus Walker of the Twenty-seventh Massachusetts Infantry, an avowed abolitionist, sat inside a house and witnessed a "great buck nigger, very black and very fragrant," fanning the flies away from a lieutenant as he wrote. Though he agreed that "the flies are really tormenting and the heat is intolerable," he averred, "I had rather endure both, than to have one of those confounded dirty niggers anywhere within twenty feet of me." He declared, "As a class they are lazy, filthy, ragged, dishonest and confounded stupid." Burnside's aide Daniel Larned shared the captain's sentiment, remarking, "They are the laziest, and the most degraded set of beings I ever saw."[41]

White soldiers particularly resented black enlistments. One described black soldiers as "regular Congoes with noses as broad as plantains and lips like raw beefsteaks." A female observer noticed that this anger seemed to be hierarchical: "As a rule it seems to grow stronger as you descend in rank, the privates having more feeling than the officers"—though not always. Over dinner one day in 1863, Commodore H. K. Davenport, commander of the Union gunboats, asked a fellow officer, "What should you do, sir, if you were to meet a Nigger Colonel, Should you salute him?" "Certainly, I should," replied the officer, adding that rank outweighed skin color. "The commodore looked at him with horror and getting up from his chair gesticulated violently exclaiming in his indignation, 'My blood boils at the thought.'"[42]

Union soldiers eventually adapted to the presence of black soldiers and accepted them as, if nothing else, a means to help end the war. When the Fifty-fifth Massachusetts (Colored) Regiment arrived in July 1863, a Union surgeon declared, "We were very glad to see them, even if they are black, for our garrison has been quite small." He concluded, "I do not object to black soldiers, but rather, think they should do some of the fighting." A naval officer was impressed with the black troops he watched drill in June 1863: "There is a firmness & determination in their looks & in the way in which they handle a musket that I like." The officer admitted his misconception of black soldiers: "I never have believed that a common plantation negro could be brought to face a white man. I supposed that everything in the shape of spirit & self-respect had been crushed out of them generations back, but am glad to find myself mistaken."[43]

Education

Whether asserting their manhood as soldiers or simply trying to advance their material conditions within Union lines, African Americans demonstrated their fervent desire to assert their independence and improve their lives. They derived support from northern teachers who tirelessly sought not only to be "intelligent friends and counselors, to guard them against the insults, impositions, immoralities and various abuses of those who hate them," but also to educate their charges. The inability to read or write represented a tangible symbol of slavery. Therefore former slaves, whether refugees or enlisted men, embraced the educational opportunities offered by Union soldiers and members of freedmen's aid societies in the region. Indeed, one American Missionary Association teacher in New Bern wrote in September 1863 that, for local blacks, learning to read "seems to be the height of their ambition."[44]

Of course, Union attempts to educate blacks angered local whites and created conflict between Union officers and military governor Edward Stanly. In April 1862, Vincent Colyer, recently appointed Superintendent of the Poor, set up a day school for whites and two evening schools for blacks in New Bern. The black school was always "full to overflowing" with more than eight hundred students who were "joyful and bright as any young learners." It progressed well for nearly six weeks, as Colyer enlisted several Union soldiers to act as teachers. "It is a glorious work," wrote Charles M. Duren, a Massachusetts officer. "How sad that so many are growing up entirely ignorant," he wrote, "and now how joyful that a brighter day is dawning upon this down trodden race." However, when Governor Stanly arrived on May 26, 1862, he did not share Duren's joy and ordered Colyer to close the school on the grounds that teaching blacks to read was against North Carolina law. Colyer closed the school and went to Washington to protest. President Lincoln assured Colyer that Stanly had no power to close the school and furthermore that "he had given Gov. Stanly no such instructions as would justify him in these acts." Colyer returned, and freedmen schools opened again over Stanly's protest.[45]

Individual officers, soldiers, and benevolent society teachers operated makeshift schools wherever there was room. Teachers held class in churches, army barracks, barns, abandoned plantation buildings, basements, and deserted jails, and one officer taught his pupils "in the rear of the Quartermaster's office." One teacher commented, "We teach in a barn fitted up with seats for nearly four hundred persons," which during winter months "is heated by only one Sibley stove, and having no sash in the windows." Students still attended despite the fact that it was so cold that the teacher "taught every day so far in a hood, blanket shawl, and thick gloves." Instructors also improvised teaching supplies. One soldier related, "As primers were not at hand, an olive green window shutter served for a blackboard, the instruction being mainly oral." Teachers utilized Bibles as standard texts. Yet, Union agents were improving the situation as quickly as possible, constructing new schools and recruiting supplies and teachers from northern benevolent societies. By the end of March 1864, New Bern boasted eleven freedmen schools while Beaufort had three, and nine more existed in other occupied parts of North Carolina. July 1864 found three thousand black students enrolled in classes in the region.[46]

Determined freedpeople used every spare minute to study. A soldier in the Twenty-third Massachusetts wrote, "Grown men, employed in 'dug outs' to catch and raft logs, brought, on their way to the saw mill . . . [their] spelling book[s] which was speedily whipped out and zealously studied at every break, however short, in their onerous task." An officer's wife, visiting her husband at New Bern in February 1863, wrote to a friend, "I have frequently seen in the street the Negro teamster[s], poring over their primers and spelling books, while waiting for something or other." One missionary noted, "After a hard day's work, they return to their homes, take their frugal meal, change their dress when they can make a change—come to the school & devote an hour and a half to earnest study." Some adults sought individual arrangements for education, bartering practical goods for instruction. One Union soldier recounted, "Aunty Southwhite gave me a quilt tonight on condition that 'I learn her how to read.'" Freedpeople also used their hard-earned money to provide opportunities for their further enhancement. When Reverend G. N. Green arrived in Beaufort in October 1863 to set up a school, he collected $84.88 from freedpeople to defray operating expenses. The Pine Grove settlement, one of several just outside of town, raised $95, and the citizens told Green that they would raise "another hundred if necessary in order to educate their children."[47]

African American students and their white teachers persevered in spite of hostile conditions. Weather difficulties and the exigencies of wartime often halted classes. In the summer of 1864, a yellow fever epidemic hit New Bern and Beaufort, killing hundreds of blacks and whites and forcing many to flee or quarantine themselves in the city. In addition, local whites tried to terrorize northern teachers and black students to prevent them from attending schools. In 1864, three white men torched one of the freedpeople's schoolhouses and threatened the female teacher with violence unless she promised to "never again teach the niggers to read." For whites, this instruction held dangerous implications, as the northern teachers taught ideas that transcended spiritual lessons and charitable efforts to teach the "three R's."[48]

At the same time, however, northern missionaries' ideas about what was best for the blacks often conflicted with what the freedpeople believed. As Jacqueline Jones comments, the "relationship between New England freedmen's aid societies and the 'objects' of their benevolence was often fraught with tension," as frequently "the aid came with strings attached." During their experience, former slaves found that many missionaries rarely viewed them as equals. For instance, many northerners dismissed freedpeople's emotional religious tradition as "ludicrous and saddening" and full of "strange, wild ideas." Missionaries sought to educate them in order to reform their moral character, which many considered degraded or dissolute, and to try to give them some sense of social responsibility and stability in the tumultuous times. In other words, they hoped to remake them in an idealized northern middle-class Christian image, ignoring the freedpeople's own cultural mores. As Ronald E. Butchart notes, "Acceptance into white society was predicated on changing blacks, making them as much like whites as possible."[49]

African Americans, on the other hand, were quite practical, accepting a certain amount of northern proselytizing while utilizing the benevolent society members to garner the material possessions as well as the intellectual ones they needed to achieve autonomy. One northern missionary, who had hoped to convert ignorant former slaves, learned that "greater good might be done by holding a pair of shoes, or a new frock in one hand, and the Bible in the other." She noted, "It is wonderful how much more influence you can have over those who do not believe, by doing something for their souls and bodies at the same time." The young woman did not understand that this was most likely part of the freedpeople's plan. Few rejected the idea of a Christian afterlife, in which the ills of this world would be replaced by the glories of the next. However, many recognized the value of playing to northern stereotypes of their ignorance in order to help address their insufficient material possessions. Teachers slowly began to realize how they were being used. One wrote in December 1863, "Yesterday a woman came asking for a flannel for her sick babe. She seemed honest, but there is so much wrongdoing that I am compelled to ascertain always." However, freedpeople gained a certain degree of hope from their interactions with northern missionaries. Though missionaries believed they were teaching moral and social values, they served as an example of how Reconstruction might offer positive opportunities for freedmen.[50]

Missionaries not only redeemed freedpeople's spiritual souls but also heightened their awareness of their political bodies and of the rights inherent in being a free person, offering visions of a promising future in which African Americans could control their own destinies without being beholden to whites. A black soldier's comment to an American Missionary Association teacher reveals that African Americans heartily imbibed from this hopeful fount. "Do you know how responsible your situation is?" he asked. "We listen to every word that you utter to us, so that nothing that you utter is lost to any of us. If we do just as you instruct us to do, and we lose our souls, whose fault will it be?" Though this soldier perhaps did fear he would be denied entry into heaven, his quote serves as an effective metaphor for those who did not dread their eternal damnation as much as a potential worldly one. If freed people diligently followed the advice of their northern deliverers and the promised land of respect, economic independence, and personal autonomy did not emerge, their betrayal would be devastating.[51]

Ultimately, such betrayals would begin as soon as the war ended. During wartime, freedpeople had to negotiate with their white counterparts in the hostile world of occupation. After military hostilities had ended, freedpeople faced an equally difficult road, especially as native whites began returning to the area. Freedpeople encountered particular hardship in acquiring land, the foundational requirement for the autonomy and economic independence they desired. During the war, they had been able to cultivate, often very profitably, the land abandoned by secessionist owners. However, when the war ended, Federal policy was to return the land to the previous owners. "I wish the giving back of houses and property by the Department commander could be stopped," wrote Horace James in July 1865. "I am quite in the dark about our prospects" regarding land, responded Colonel Eli Whittlesey, North Carolina's Freedmen's Bureau Commissioner, to James's repeated inquiries. "The President's pardon may at any time take them out of our control," Whittlesey admitted. "I would not encourage men to build on land which they are not sure of their holding."[52]

Indeed, President Andrew Johnson's pardon for former Confederates severely limited the opportunities for freedpeople's autonomy in the region. Colonel Whittlesey protested to the bureau's national director, Oliver O. Howard, that returning the lands to their former owners, after the freedmen had improved the quality and value of the lands during the war, was ridiculous and unjust. "In the towns and immediate vicinity such property has increased in value fourfold," Whittlesey argued, "and we are to pay [the Rebels] for the privilege of making them rich." When the local whites reclaimed their land, they threatened economic retaliation against the freedmen. A Freedmen's Bureau agent predicted, "Much suffering might be anticipated among freedmen about Christmas, as planters are showing an intention not to employ freedmen or aid them in obtaining support." Another agent in coastal North Carolina warned what would happen when the Freedmen's Bureau left the region: "It is to be feared, however, that after the withdrawal of this Bureau, the violent hatred of the old Rebel Slave holders will result in injuries & insults to the poor Freedmen, & excite them to retaliation & revenge."[53]

In the face of native white hostility, African Americans tried to negotiate better deals for themselves. In late July 1865, several freedmen from coastal Hyde County met with Horace James and requested that a former Hyde

County sheriff be named their agent. James wrote that they "petitioned for the appointment of Mr. Hilliard Gibbs as their protector and magistrate as it were, stating that they had confidence in him, and believed that he would promote their interests, and do them justice." James admired their assertiveness and recommended Gibbs as a bureau agent, admitting that Gibbs was "a strong, two-fisted fellow." James hoped that such an action would foster the appointment of other native white civil agents for the bureau to help staff the hopelessly undermanned agency. His hopes were dashed in the experiment of Mr. Gibbs. Six weeks after recommending him for an appointment, James admitted that he was "surprised and chagrined" by Gibbs's behavior. "He is unpopular in Hyde Co. . . . [H]e drinks hard, and is little respected," James desponded. However, he did not give up all hope of civil agents. James considered civil appointments of the utmost importance, asserting, "If the blacks are ever treated justly it must be by and through the southern people themselves."[54]

Of course, by 1877, unconcerned about whether blacks would be treated justly or not, the northern people and the Federal government abandoned African Americans throughout the South to southerners, and disfranchisement, lynching, segregation, and Jim Crow followed. Freedpeople had strived during the war to achieve the tools necessary for autonomy and independence. After the war, they needed the support of the Federal government to solidify the gains they had made. But northerners left only civilian teachers as a token reminder of their presence. As Butchart astutely asserts, "The Afro-Americans were on the threshold of freedom. They needed land, protection, and a stake in society. They needed and demanded meaningful power. They were given instead a school." This was small consolation. Butchart declares, "The gift was vastly inadequate to the needs of men and women set free in a vengeful, vindictive society."[55] Black efforts at political and economic empowerment simply increased white hostility, and blacks found little support from local Unionists, who generally disapproved of black suffrage and preferred that blacks work as wage laborers instead of independent proprietors. Whites often proscribed black employment and limited black efforts at autonomy.[56]

The failure of blacks to gain the independence and autonomy they so desired left a lingering feeling of bitterness. One former North Carolina slave, Thomas Hall, expressed this bitterness in an interview with a Works Progress Administration worker in 1937. "Lincoln got the praise for freeing us, but did he do it? He give us freedom without giving us any chance to live to ourselves, and we still had to depend on the Southern white man for work, food, and clothing, and he held us, through our necessity and want, in a state of servitude but little better than slavery," Hall declared. "Lincoln done but little for the Negro race, and from a living standpoint, nothing. White folks are not going to do nothing for Negroes except keep them down." Hall concluded with the dismal declaration that many resentful blacks undoubtedly shared: "I don't want you to write my story, because the white folks have been and are now and always will be against the Negro."[57]

Hall, who was born around 1856, was probably too young to remember that there was a brief period of time when blacks enjoyed success and whites were not able to "keep them down." These were the years of Union wartime occupation, when African Americans actively took control of their own lives, successfully attaining the pillars of empowerment—escape, employment, enlistment, and education. Such efforts had given them a sense of hope; indeed, "visions of freedom and civilization" did appear to be "opening before them." Blacks would have to use the memory of these visions as support for the future, as they would have to discover new forms of empowerment to maintain control of their own lives as much as possible in the face of white hostility and Federal neglect in the postwar period.

Notes

1. William B. Fowle Jr. to Major Southard Hoffman, January 14, 1863, box 2, part 1, Letters Received, Department of North Carolina, Records of United States Army Continental Commands, Record Group 393, National Archives, Washington, D.C. (hereafter cited as RG 393). Weather conditions reported in John A. Hedrick to Benjamin S. Hedrick, January 11, 16, 1863, in Judkin Browning and Michael Thomas Smith, eds., *Letters from a North Carolina Unionist: John A. Hedrick to Benjamin S. Hedrick, 1862–1865* (Raleigh: Division of Archives and History, Department of Cultural Resources, 2001), 80–83. Joel Henry Davis and Henry Rieger were prosperous merchants in Beaufort. North Carolina, vol. 5, p. 175, 176-L, R. G. Dun & Co. Collection, Baker Library, Harvard Business School, Harvard University, Cambridge, Mass.

2. Manuscript Census Returns, Eighth Census of the United States, 1860, Carteret County, North Carolina, Population and Slave Schedule. For more on the use of the violent physical demonstrations against the body to send political messages, see Franny Nudelman, *John Brown's Body: Slavery, Violence, and the Culture of War* (Chapel Hill: University of North Carolina Press, 2004); and Sarah E. Chinn, "Theorizing the Body as Evidence," in Chinn, *Technology and the Logic of American Racism: A Cultural History of the Body as Evidence* (London: Continuum, 2000), 1–23.

3. Stephen V. Ash, *When the Yankees Came: Conflict and Chaos in the Occupied South, 1861–1865* (Chapel Hill: University of North Carolina Press, 1995), 153; Willie Lee Rose, *Rehearsal for Reconstruction: The Port Royal Experiment* (1964; Athens:

University of Georgia Press, 1999). For works that deal with aspects of occupation, see also Stephen V. Ash, *Middle Tennessee Society Transformed, 1860-1870: War and Peace in the Upper South* (Baton Rouge: Louisiana State University Press, 1988); Louis S. Gerteis, *From Contraband to Freedman: Federal Policy toward Southern Blacks, 1861-1865* (Westport, Conn.: Greenwood, 1973); Mark Grimsley, *The Hard Hand of War: Union Military Policy toward Southern Civilians, 1861-1865* (Cambridge: Cambridge University Press, 1995); Michael Fellman, *Citizen Sherman: A Life of William Tecumseh Sherman* (New York: Random House, 1995), esp. 136-70; Wayne K. Durrill, *War of Another Kind: A Southern Community in the Great Rebellion* (New York: Oxford University Press, 1990); Peter Maslowski, *Treason Must Be Made Odious: Military Occupation and Wartime Reconstruction in Nashville, Tennessee* (Millwood, N.Y.: KTO Press, 1978); and Daniel E. Sutherland, *Seasons of War: The Ordeal of a Confederate Community, 1861-1865* (New York: Free Press, 1995). For works that grant blacks more agency in their emancipation experience, see Ira Berlin, *Slaves No More: Three Essays on Emancipation and the Civil War* (Cambridge: Cambridge University Press, 1992); and Vincent Harding, *There Is a River: The Black Struggle for Freedom in America* (New York: Harcourt Brace Jovanovich, 1981).

4. Though much has been written about each of these themes, scholars tend to focus on them in isolation rather than as an integral whole. For slave escapes, see Loren Schweninger and John Hope Franklin, *Runaway Slaves: Rebels on the Plantation* (New York: Oxford University Press, 1999). For black employment, see Gerteis, *From Contraband to Freedman*; and Julia Saville, *The Work of Reconstruction: From Slave to Wage Laborer in South Carolina, 1860-1870* (Cambridge: Cambridge University Press, 1996). Much scholarly literature deals with black enlistment and efforts at education. For black enlistment, see Ira Berlin et al., eds., *Freedom: A Documentary History of Emancipation, 1861-1867*, series 2, *The Black Military Experience* (New York: Cambridge University Press, 1982); Dudley T. Cornish, *The Sable Arm: Negro Troops in the Union Army, 1861-1865* (New York: W. W. Norton, 1956); Joseph T. Glatthaar, *Forged in Battle: The Civil War Alliance of Black Soldiers and White Officers* (New York: Macmillan, 1990); John David Smith, ed., *Black Soldiers in Blue: African American Troops in the Civil War Era* (Chapel Hill: University of North Carolina Press, 2002); and Keith P. Wilson, *Campfires of Freedom: The Camp Life of Black Soldiers during the Civil War* (Kent, Ohio: Kent State University Press, 2002). For black education, see Ronald E. Butchart, *Northern Schools, Southern Blacks, and Reconstruction: Freedmen's Education, 1862-1875* (Westport, Conn.: Greenwood, 1980); Jacqueline Jones, *Soldiers of Light and Love: Northern Teachers and Georgia Blacks, 1865-1873* (Athens: University of Georgia Press, 1980); and Patricia C. Click, *Time Full of Trial: The Roanoke Island Freedmen's Colony, 1862-1867* (Chapel Hill: University of North Carolina Press, 2001).

5. Though Ash briefly discusses slave reactions in several places as a secondary issue, the chapter that analyzes the black experience most thoroughly is more concerned with white reaction to black assertions and is appropriately subtitled "The Struggle against Black Freedom." See Ash, *When the Yankees Came*, chap. 5.

6. For a further exploration of white reactions to military occupation in this region, see Judkin Browning, "Removing the Mask of Nationality: Unionism, Racism, and

Federal Military Occupation in North Carolina, 1862–1865," *Journal of Southern History* 71, no. 3 (2005): 589–620.

7. Entry dated March 25, 1863, James Rumley Diary, Levi Woodbury Pigott Collection, North Carolina State Archives, North Carolina Office of Archives and History, Raleigh (hereafter cited as NCSA). Though slaves developed their own methods of dealing with harsh economic and political subordination, they were unable to operate completely free from white control. Southern slaves, in contrast to bondsmen in other slave societies (notably the West Indies), lived in constant contact with their white masters. In fact, in Carteret and Craven counties, the vast majority of slaves lived in households containing five or fewer slaves. They could not simply establish a new life apart from whites. Manuscript Census Returns, Eighth Census of the United States, 1860, Carteret and Craven Counties, North Carolina, Slave Schedules. For more on the development and strength of slave communities, see John W. Blassingame, *The Slave Community: Plantation Life in the Antebellum South*, rev. ed. (New York: Oxford University Press, 1979); George P. Rawick, *From Sundown to Sunup: The Making of the Black Community* (Westport, Conn.: Greenwood, 1972); Paul D. Escott, *Slavery Remembered: A Record of Twentieth-Century Slave Narratives* (Chapel Hill: University of North Carolina Press, 1979); and Charles W. Joyner, *Down by the Riverside: A South Carolina Slave Community* (Urbana: University of Illinois Press, 1984). For more on black and white interaction, see Eugene D. Genovese, *Roll, Jordan, Roll: The World the Slaves Made* (New York: Pantheon Books, 1972). For a good synthesis of scholarly works on slavery, see Peter Kolchin, *American Slavery: 1619–1877*, rev. ed. (New York: Hill and Wang, 2003).

8. William Henry Singleton, *Recollections of My Slavery Days*, ed. Katherine Mellen Charron and David S. Cecelski (Raleigh: North Carolina Department of Cultural Resources, Division of Archives and History, 1999); David S. Cecelski, *The Waterman's Song: Slavery and Freedom in Maritime North Carolina* (Chapel Hill: University of North Carolina Press, 2001), 131. For works on the slave family, see Herbert G. Gutman, *The Black Family in Slavery and Freedom, 1750–1925* (New York: Pantheon Books, 1976); and Brenda E. Stevenson, *Life in Black and White: Family and Community in the Slave South* (New York: Oxford University Press, 1996). For more works on the slaves' internal economy, see Timothy James Lockley, *Lines in the Sand: Race and Class in Lowcountry Georgia, 1750–1860* (Athens: University of Georgia Press, 2001); Philip D. Morgan, *Slave Counterpoint: Black Culture in the Eighteenth-Century Chesapeake and Lowcountry* (Chapel Hill: University of North Carolina, 1998); Robert Olwell, *Masters, Slaves, and Subjects: The Culture of Power in South Carolina, 1740–1790* (Ithaca: Cornell University Press, 1998); and Dylan C. Penningroth, *The Claims of Kinfolk: African American Property and Community in the Nineteenth-Century South* (Chapel Hill: University of North Carolina Press, 2003).

9. *Carolina Federal Republican*, August 24, 1816, in Freddie L. Parker, ed., *Stealing a Little Freedom: Advertisements for Slave Runaways in North Carolina, 1791–1840* (New York: Garland, 1994), 525; Singleton, *Recollections*, 39; Linda Brent [Harriet Jacobs], *Incidents in the Life of a Slave Girl: An Authentic Historical Narrative Describing the Horrors of Slavery as Experienced by Black Women* (San Diego:

Harcourt Brace, 1973), 117–60. As Loren Schweninger and John Hope Franklin have noted, "The most common form of absconding was not actually running away at all, but what might be termed 'truancy,' 'absenteeism,' and in some cases, 'lying out.'" Slaves would disappear from anywhere for a few hours to a few days to avoid work, visit family, or, in some cases, try to gain concessions from their owners. Schweninger and Franklin, *Runaway Slaves*, 98–109 (quotation on 98). For published examples of slave advertisements in the Carteret and Craven county region, see Parker, *Stealing a Little Freedom*.

10. Testimony of claimant John Pender, Claim 1667, Carteret County, North Carolina, Records of the Southern Claims Commission, 1871–1880, Disallowed Claims, Records of the U.S. House of Representatives, Record Group 233, National Archives, Washington, D.C. (hereafter cited as RG 233) (quotation). The presence of hired slaves was especially prevalent in New Bern, which as early as 1794 was exempted from a state law that prohibited masters from allowing their slaves to "hire out." Singleton, *Recollections*, 5–6. For another work that examines slaves' making money and claiming some control over their lives, see Charles B. Dew, *Bond of Iron: Master and Slave at Buffalo Forge* (New York: W. W. Norton, 1994).

11. Cecelski, *Waterman's Song*, xvi.

12. Janet Duitsman Cornelius, *"When I Can Read My Title Clear": Literacy, Slavery and Religion in the Antebellum South* (Columbia: University of South Carolina Press, 1991), 3; Belinda Hurmence, ed., *My Folks Don't Want Me to Talk about Slavery: Twenty-one Oral Histories of Former North Carolina Slaves* (Winston-Salem, N.C.: Blair, 1984), 18, 77.

13. Horace James to "My Dear Friends," May 25, 1863, Horace James Correspondence, American Antiquarian Society, Worcester, Mass. (hereafter cited as AAS); Singleton, *Recollections*, 41; *The Experience of Reverend Thomas H. Jones*, in William L. Andrews, general editor, *North Carolina Slave Narratives: The Lives of Moses Roper, Lunsford Lane, Moses Grandy & Thomas H. Jones*, ed. David A. Davis, Tampathia Evans, Ian Frederick Finseth, and Andrea N. Williams (Chapel Hill: University of North Carolina Press, 2003), 220–21.

14. Henry A. Clapp to "Mother," March 14, 1863, in John R. Barden, ed., *Letters to the Home Circle: The North Carolina Service of Pvt. Henry A. Clapp, Company F, Forty-fourth Massachusetts Volunteer Militia, 1862–1863* (Raleigh: Division of Archives and History, North Carolina Department of Cultural Resources, 1998), 150. W. E. B. Du Bois suggested that about 5 percent of slaves learned to read, while Genovese believes it may be even higher. See Genovese, *Roll, Jordan, Roll*, 563.

15. Daniel Read Larned to "Sister," March 18, 1862, box 1, Daniel Read Larned Papers, Manuscript Division, Library of Congress, Washington, D.C. (hereafter cited as LOC); entry for March 13, 1862, Henry White Diary, AAS; Col. Heckman to Governor Olden, March 15, 1862, in J. Madison Drake, *The History of the Ninth New Jersey Veteran Vols., A Record of Its Service from Sept. 13th, 1861, to July 12th, 1865* (Elizabeth, N.J.: Journal Printing House, 1889), 65–66; "Extracts from Letters," April 9, 1862, William L. Norton Papers, Connecticut Historical Society, Hartford.

16. Ambrose Burnside to Edwin Stanton, March 21, 1862, vol. 9, Union Battle Reports, ser. 729, War Records Office, RG 94, quoted in Ira Berlin et al., eds., *Freedom:*

A *Documentary History of Emancipation*, series 1, *The Destruction of Slavery* (New York: Cambridge University Press, 1985), 80–81; James Drennan to Wife, March 15, 1862, James M. Drennan Papers, Worcester Historical Museum, Worcester, Mass.

17. Entry dated June 7, 1862, Rumley Diary, NCSA; I. N. Roberts to Ebenezer Hunt, May 24, 1862, Ebenezer Hunt Papers, Massachusetts Historical Society, Boston, Mass. (hereinafter cited as MHS).

18. Daniel Read Larned to Henry Howe, March 28, 1862, box 1, Larned Papers, LOC; James Edward Glazier to "Dear Parents," March 19, 1862, James Edward Glazier Papers, Henry E. Huntington Library, San Marino, Calif.; R. R. Clarke to Dr. J. G. Metcalf, April 26, 1862, box 3, folder 5, Civil War Collection, AAS; Cecelski, *Waterman's Song*, 205 (Sutton Davis story).

19. George P. Rawick, *The American Slave: A Composite Autobiography; Volume 14, North Carolina Narratives, Part I* (Westport, Conn.: Greenwood Publishing Company, 1977), 373, 81.

20. R. R. Clarke to Dr. J. G. Metcalf, April 26, 1862, box 3, folder 5, Civil War Collection, AAS; Testimony of Captain C. B. Wilder, May 9, 1863, in Berlin et al., *Destruction of Slavery*, 89; Rawick, *North Carolina Narratives*, 14:450–52.

21. U.S. Census, 1860, Carteret and Craven Counties, North Carolina, Population and Slave Schedules (1860 population figures); Horace James, *Annual Report of the Superintendent of Negro Affairs in North Carolina, 1864. With an Appendix containing the History and Management of Freedmen in this Department up to June 1st 1865* (Boston: W. F. Brown, 1865), 3, 6 (1864 and 1865 black population figures); Cecelski, *Waterman's Song*, xvi, 141–51.

22. Edward Stanly to Edwin Stanton, June 12, 1862, in U.S. War Department, *The War of the Rebellion: A Compilation of the Official Records of the Union and Confederate Armies*, 128 vols. (Washington, D.C.: Government Printing Office, 1880–1901), ser. 1, vol. 9, 400–401; R. R. Clarke to Dr. J. G. Metcalf, June 5, 1862, box 3, folder 5, Civil War Collection, AAS; Daniel Read Larned to Mrs. Ambrose E. Burnside, May 28, 1862, box 1, Larned Papers, LOC. For more on the Bray affair, see Norman D. Brown, *Edward Stanly: Whiggery's Tarheel "Conqueror"* (University: University of Alabama Press, 1974), 208–14.

23. Though the Emancipation Proclamation exempted several occupied sections of the Confederacy from its power (notably parts of Virginia and Louisiana and the entire state of Tennessee), North Carolina in its entirety came under the power of the Proclamation. See "Emancipation Proclamation" in Michael P. Johnson, ed., *Abraham Lincoln, Slavery, and the Civil War: Selected Writings and Speeches* (Boston: Bedford, St. Martin's Press, 2001), 218–19. Occupied North Carolina was not exempted from the Proclamation most likely because, to quote Stephen Ash, the residents there had not "taken steps toward reconstruction sufficient to redeem them in the president's eyes." Ash, *When the Yankees Came*, 151.

24. George H. Weston to "Dear Sir," February 15, 1863, New Bern Occupation Papers, Southern Historical Collection, Wilson Library, University of North Carolina at Chapel Hill (hereafter cited as SHC); Oliver W. Peabody to Mary Peabody, November 20, 1862, Oliver W. Peabody Papers, MHS; Testimony of claimant Caesar Man-

son, Claim 1666, Carteret County, RG 233; Entry dated January 11, 1863, Journal of Benjamin H. Day, Civil War Collection, Beverly Historical Society and Museum, Beverly, Mass.; W. P. Derby, *Bearing arms in the Twenty-seventh Massachusetts regiment of volunteer infantry during the Civil War, 1861–1865* (Boston: Wright and Potter Printing Co., 1883), 216; Letter from H. S. Beals, August 18, 1863, *American Missionary* 7 (October 1863): 231.

25. Entry dated January 1, 1863, Rumley Diary, NCSA; Ash, *When the Yankees Came*, 162; Daniel Read Larned to Henry Howe, March 20, 1862, box 1, Larned Papers, LOC.

26. General Order No. 25, April 8, 1862, Entry 3239, vol. 33, pt. 1, General Records, Correspondence, General and Special Orders, Departments of North Carolina and Virginia, 1861–1865, RG 393; Entry for August 2, 1862, J. M. Drennan Diary, J. M. Drennan Papers, SHC; Frederick Osborne to "Mother," May 30, 1862, in Frank B. Marcotte, ed., *Private Osborne, Massachusetts 23rd Volunteers: Burnside Expedition, Roanoke Island, Second Front Against Richmond* (Jefferson, N.C.: McFarland, 1999), 77; Entry dated March 20, 1865, Edmund J. Cleveland Diary, SHC; James, *Annual Report of the Superintendent of Negro Affairs*, 4.

27. Margaret M. Storey, "Civil War Unionists and the Political Culture of Loyalty in Alabama," *Journal of Southern History* 69 (February 2003): 75; Ash, *When the Yankees Came*, 169.

28. Horace James to "My dear friends," June 21, 1862, James Correspondence, AAS; Corporal [Zenas T. Haines], *Letters from the Forty-fourth Regiment . . .* (Boston, 1863), 90, as quoted in Ash, *When the Yankees Came*, 171–72. For more on the role of benevolent societies, see Butchart, *Northern Schools, Southern Blacks, and Reconstruction*; and Joe M. Richardson, *Christian Reconstruction: The American Missionary Association and Southern Blacks, 1861–1890* (Athens: University of Georgia Press, 1986). For an examination of the role missionaries played among North Carolina freedmen, see Click, *Time Full of Trial*.

29. James, *Annual Report of the Superintendent of Negro Affairs*, 4.

30. R. R. Clarke to Dr. J. G. Metcalf, April 26, 1862, box 3, folder 5, Civil War Collection, AAS; Testimony of claimant Willis M. Lewis, Claim 11730, Craven County, North Carolina, Settled Case Files for Claims Approved by the Southern Claims Commission, 1871–80, Records of the Accounting Officers of the Department of the Treasury, Record Group 217, National Archives II, College Park, Md. (hereafter cited as RG 217); Deposition of Jacob Grimes, in *Gabriel Hardison v. United States* (case file no. 8070), Records of the United States Court of Claims, Record Group 123, National Archives, Washington, D.C.; John M. Spear, "Army life in the twenty-fourth regiment, Massachusetts volunteer infantry, Dec. 1861 to Dec. 1864, 1892" (typescript), 61, MHS.

31. Edward Bartlett to Martha, November 1, 1862, Edward J. Bartlett Papers, MHS; Entry dated December 1, 1862, Journal of Benjamin H. Day; Horatio Newhall to George, November 17, 1862, Horatio Newhall Papers, Civil War Miscellaneous Collection, United States Army Military History Institute, Carlisle, Pa.

32. James, *Annual Report of the Superintendent of Negro Affairs*, 10, 19; Testi-

mony of Eliza Garner, Claim 1667 (John Pender and Henry Mathewson), RG 233; Testimony of claimant Caesar Manson, Claim 1666, RG 233; Testimony of claimant Andrew Ward, Claim 11566, RG 217.

33. Testimony of David Parker, Claim 1666 (Caesar Manson), RG 233; James, *Annual Report of the Superintendent of Negro Affairs*, 12. For more on freedmen camps and community outside New Bern, see Joe A. Mobley, *James City: A Black Community in North Carolina, 1863–1900* (Raleigh: North Carolina Department of Cultural Resources, Division of Archives and History, 1981).

34. When James called on freedmen in New Bern who worked independently— outside of the government—to report their income for 1864, he found 305 men and women, reporting a total gross income of $150,562, an average of nearly $500 a person. James, *Annual Report of the Superintendent of Negro Affairs*, 11–12.

35. Entry dated June 1, 1863, and January 1, 1864, Rumley Diary, NCSA.

36. "Notes from North Carolina," *American Missionary* 7 (March 1863): 58; Jim Cullen, "'I's a Man Now': Gender and African American Men," in *Divided Houses: Gender and the Civil War*, ed. Catherine Clinton and Nina Silber (New York: Oxford University Press, 1992), 77.

37. Singleton, *Recollections*, 188; William Augustus Willoughby to wife, January 22, 1863, William Augustus Willoughby Papers (typescript), AAS.

38. Albert W. Mann, *History of the Forty-fifth Regiment, Massachusetts Volunteer Militia* (Boston: W. Spooner, 1908), 301–2 (quotations); Cecelski, *Waterman's Song*, 181.

39. James Owens to Gen. [Henry] Wessells, February 20, 1863, box 2, part 1, Letters Received, Department of North Carolina, RG 393 (February muster); Jeremiah Stetson to "Dear ones at home," April 21, 1863, Jeremiah Stetson Papers, SHC; Spear, "Army life in the twenty-fourth regiment," 156, MHS; Mann, *History of the Forty-fifth Regiment*, 324; Michael K. Honey, "The War within the Confederacy: White Unionists of North Carolina," *Prologue* 18 (Summer 1986): 65–66; Cecelski, *Waterman's Song*, 181. See also Richard M. Reid, "Raising the African Brigade: Early Black Recruitment in Civil War North Carolina," *North Carolina Historical Review* 70 (July 1993): 266–301.

40. John A. Hedrick to Benjamin S. Hedrick, December 13, 1863, in Browning and Smith, *Letters from a North Carolina Unionist*, 172. For a depiction of coercion of blacks into military service in the Sea Islands, see Rose, *Rehearsal for Reconstruction*, 265–70. In July 1862, the Second Confiscation Act and the Militia Act gave President Lincoln the right to recruit black soldiers. Lincoln endorsed arming black troops in the Emancipation Proclamation. In February 1863, the Federal government began recruiting black troops. On May 22, 1863, the War Department created the Bureau of Colored Troops to oversee and regulate black enlistment. See Wilson, *Campfires of Freedom*, 1–2; Gregory J. W. Urwin, "United States Colored Troops," in *Encyclopedia of the American Civil War: A Political, Social, and Military History*, ed. David S. Heidler and Jeanne T. Heidler (Santa Barbara, Calif.: ABC-CLIO Press, 2000), 4:2002–3.

41. William Augustus Walker to "Sister," July 11, 14, 1862, in Nina Silber and Mary Beth Sievers, eds., *Yankee Correspondence: Civil War Letters between New*

England Soldiers and the Home Front (Charlottesville: University of Virginia Press, 1996), 61–62; Daniel Read Larned to Mrs. Ambrose E. Burnside, March 23, 1862, both in box 1, Larned Papers, LOC. For an examination of the cultural baggage that New England soldiers brought to war regarding race, see David A. Cecere, "Carrying the Home Front to War: Soldiers, Race, and New England Culture during the Civil War," in *Union Soldiers and the Northern Home Front: Wartime Experiences and Postwar Adjustments*, ed. Paul A. Cimbala and Randall M. Miller (New York: Fordham University Press, 2002), 293–323.

42. George A. Jewett to "Deck," July 18, 1863, George O. Jewett Collection, LOC; Mary Peabody to [unknown], March 1, 1863, Peabody Papers, MHS.

43. Spear, "Army life in the twenty-fourth regiment," 173, MHS; William F. Keeler to Anna Keeler, June 30, 1863, as quoted in James M. McPherson, *For Cause and Comrades: Why Men Fought in the Civil War* (New York: Oxford University Press, 1997), 127.

44. "Appeal for the Freedmen," *American Missionary* 7 (January 1863): 13; Susan A. Hosmer to "Honored Father," September 11, 1863, Document 99713, Roll 150, American Missionary Association Manuscripts, Amistad Research Center, Tulane University, New Orleans, La., on microfilm at the University of Georgia Library (hereafter cited as AMA). See also Maxine D. Jones, "'A Glorious Work': The American Missionary Association and Black North Carolinians, 1863–1880" (Ph.D. diss., Florida State University, 1982), 35–38. For more on the education of black soldiers during the war, see Ira Berlin et al., *Black Military Experience*, 611–32; and John W. Blassingame, "The Union Army as a School for Negroes," *Journal of Negro Education* 34 (Spring 1965): 152–59.

45. Special Order No. 65, March 30, 1862, part 1, General Records, Correspondence, General and Special Orders, Department of North Carolina, Departments of North Carolina and Virginia, 1861–1865, RG 393; Charles M. Duren to "Mother and father," May 2, 1862, Charles M. Duren Papers, Special Collections and Archives, Robert W. Woodruff Library, Emory University, Atlanta, Ga.; M. Jones, "'A Glorious Work,'" 29–30; Horace James to "My dear friends," June 21, 1862, James Correspondence, AAS.

46. M. Jones, "'A Glorious Work,'" 45–51; Herbert E. Valentine, *Story of Co. F, 23d Massachusetts Volunteers in the War for the Union, 1861–1865* (Boston: W. B. Clarke and Co., 1896), 65; Miss Emily Gill to the American Missionary Association, January 11, 1864, document 99734, roll 150, AMA; Sing-Nan Fen, "Notes on the Education of Negroes in North Carolina during the Civil War," *Journal of Negro Education* 36 (Winter 1967): 25.

47. James Emmerton, *A Record of the Twenty-third Regiment Massachusetts Volunteer Infantry in the War of the Rebellion, 1861–1865* (Boston: William Ware, 1886), 97; Mary Peabody to Livy, February 23, 1863, Peabody Papers, MHS; William Briggs quoted in M. Jones, "'A Glorious Work,'" 41–42; Entry for November 16, 1864, Cleveland Diary, SHC; Letter from Rev. G. N. Green, October 23, 1863, *American Missionary* 7 (December 1863): 280.

48. M. Jones, "'A Glorious Work,'" 48–51; Thomas J. Farnham and Francis P. King, "'The March of the Destroyer': The New Bern Yellow Fever Epidemic of

1864," *North Carolina Historical Review* 73 (October 1996): 435–83; Fen, "Notes on the Education of Negroes," 26n11.

49. J. Jones, *Soldiers of Light and Love*, 4; Charles Eustis Hubbard, *The Campaign of the Forty-fifth regiment, Massachusetts Volunteer Militia: "The cadet regiment"* (Boston: J. S. Adams, 1882), 82; Letter of H. S. Beals, August 1863, *American Missionary* 7 (Oct. 1863): 230; Butchart, *Northern Schools, Southern Blacks, and Reconstruction*, 23.

50. Letter from Miss Burnap, January 18, 1864, *American Missionary* 8 (March 1864): 65; Letter from Miss E. James, [December 1863], *American Missionary* 8 (February 1864): 39.

51. Letter from Chaplain Talbot, *American Missionary* 9(January 1865): 6.

52. Horace James to Eli Whittlesey, July 20, 1865, Letters Received, roll 8, Eli Whittlesey to Horace James, October 2, 1865, Letters Sent, roll 1, Records of the Assistant Commissioner for the State of North Carolina, Bureau of Refugees, Freedmen, and Abandoned Lands, 1865–70, Record Group 105, National Archives, Washington, D.C. (microfilm, M843) (hereafter cited as RG 105).

53. Eli Whittlesey to Oliver O. Howard, October 4, 1865, Letters Sent, roll 1; Fred H. Beecher to Horace James, September 13, 1865, Letters Sent, roll 1; William Doherty, "Semi-monthly Report of Outrages by Whites Against Blacks in the State of North Carolina, Elizabeth City, August 15, 1868," Reports of Outrages and Arrests, roll 33, all in RG 105.

54. Horace James to Eli Whittlesey, July 31, 1865, Horace James to Fred H. Beecher, September 18, 1865, James to Beecher, September 20, 1865, Letters Received, roll 8, RG 105.

55. Butchart, *Northern Schools, Southern Blacks, and Reconstruction*, 9.

56. The best comprehensive work on Reconstruction and its failures remains Eric Foner, *Reconstruction: America's Unfinished Revolution* (New York: Harper and Row, 1988). For a work that conveys how whites used racial violence to accomplish their conservative political ends during Reconstruction, see George Rable, *But There Was No Peace: The Role of Violence in the Politics of Reconstruction* (Athens: University of Georgia Press, 1984). For works that discuss how sectional reconciliation and postwar politics shifted the focus away from African American civil rights, see Heather Cox Richardson, *The Death of Reconstruction: Race, Labor, and Politics in the Post-Civil War North, 1865–1901* (Cambridge, Mass.: Harvard University Press, 2001); David W. Blight, *Race and Reunion: The Civil War in American Memory* (Cambridge, Mass.: Belknap Press of Harvard University Press, 2001); and Nina Silber, *The Romance of Reunion: Northerners and the South, 1865–1900* (Chapel Hill: University of North Carolina Press, 1993).

57. Hurmence, *My Folks Don't Want Me to Talk about Slavery*, 52–53, 54.

The Order of Nature Would Be Reversed

Soldiers, Slavery, and the North Carolina Gubernatorial Election of 1864

In 1864, North Carolina governor Zebulon Baird Vance faced more than the usual number of challenges. The Civil War engulfed his nation; weather, labor shortages, and the presence of armies played havoc with harvests; and food and supply shortfalls afflicted his people. On top of it all, a peace movement swept his state, and the gubernatorial election loomed. Contesting Vance for the governor's office was William Woods Holden, editor of a Raleigh newspaper called the *Weekly Standard* and organizer of the peace movement, who proposed stopping the war by negotiation. For a time, Holden seemed so sure to win that Vance made halfhearted plans to return to the army following his probable defeat.[1] Among North Carolina soldiers, the popularity of Holden's peace stance led Private George Williams to predict Holden would sweep his regiment "by a large majority."[2] Yet once the results were tallied, Vance won easily with 80 percent of the total vote, including a stunning 87.9 percent of the soldier vote.[3] The timing of the election in the summer of 1864 helped, but Vance's dramatic come-from-behind victory resulted in larger measure from a campaign speech first delivered by the governor on February 22, 1864, subsequently disseminated by newspaper distribution and by Vance's frequent repeat performances, and from the battle of Plymouth fought in April 1864. North Carolina soldiers' reactions to the speech and the battle reveal the importance of racial fear in managing Confederate patriotism's inherent tensions and in keeping enlisted North Carolinians committed to the war effort in 1864.

Soldiers' late burst of enthusiasm for Vance gets at a central tension between individual interests and national needs that rested right at the heart of Confederate patriotism.[4] Though the tension was often related to class division, it proved even more fundamental than class resentment because it was located within the very makeup of Confederate patriotism.[5] The

Confederacy earned early support among the ordinary white southern men who constituted most of its army by convincing them that an independent Confederacy would promote the interests, aspirations, and well-being of white individuals and families better than the Union would.[6] One main way in which it would do so was by preventing the abolition of slavery, an institution that even non-slaveholders throughout the Confederacy repeatedly insisted was vital to their liberty (by which they chiefly meant the unobstructed pursuit of material prosperity), crucial to the moral superiority of the South, central to the honor and equality of themselves and their children, necessary for the safety of their families, and integral to their ability to control and protect white women, an indispensable component of their identities as white men that would otherwise be under constant assault from black men if slavery disappeared.[7] The emphasis on the direct connection between Confederate independence and the prosperity, well-being, and identity of white men and their loved ones proved very effective at first, but it led to problems when the demands of the Confederacy conflicted with the needs and interests of white men and their families. In 1864, Governor Vance confronted precisely that conflict; it would shape his campaign and influence soldiers' reactions to both candidates in the race for the governor's office.

Historians have generally explained Vance's remarkable comeback either by minimizing Holden's initial support among soldiers or by attributing the lopsided vote tallies to coercion, and there is some justification for both interpretations. Even at the height of Holden's popularity, North Carolina lieutenant Macon Bonner vowed that he would "walk many a 'weary mile' to see [Holden's] body hanging food for birds of prey."[8] On the other hand, officers did sometimes prevent North Carolina troops from casting Holden ballots, either with threats or by tearing up Holden votes before they could be counted. Holden complained that fully two-thirds of soldiers in the field had their right to vote as they wished suppressed, and others without an obvious stake in the election's outcome verified incidents of coercion, if not at the rate that Holden claimed.[9] Union general Winfield Hancock even noted that two North Carolina men deserted to his lines "because they were not allowed to vote yesterday."[10] Yet reports from soldiers in the field indicate that while fraud and intimidation happened, they were not universal. Private Henry Patrick concluded "from *personal observation*" of the voting in his own company that "there never was a fairer election held that I ever witnessed." Most men simply chose Vance of their own free will.[11] Accounts like Private Patrick's suggest that longtime Vance advocates and frustrated would-be Holden voters notwithstanding, many North Carolina soldiers supported Holden, the peace candidate, for governor, then changed their minds and voluntarily voted for Vance. The shift in their views needs explaining.

The challenge is how to get at soldiers' views, especially in a war fought by citizen-soldiers who disagreed with each other regularly, making it fairly easy to find at least one soldier who said almost anything. Soldiers' own words provide the best glimpse into what they thought about the election and the war, and those words can be found in personal letter and diary collections, in newspapers, and in the Zebulon Baird Vance Papers, since many soldiers wrote to the governor. Written sources obviously privilege literate soldiers, but in the Confederate army, where 80 percent of soldiers could read and write, most men were literate, and those who were not often persuaded friends and messmates to write for them. While different men often expressed different, and sometimes opposing, views, and while exceptions to almost everything existed, dominant patterns plainly emerged in what soldiers said about the 1864 election. In addition, some regiments saved their tallies of votes cast, and those totals buttress the patterns present in the written sources.

As the war's fury enveloped the South, it exposed the tensions between the needs of families and the needs of the Confederacy that rested at the heart of Confederate patriotism. The sheer length of the conflict kept men away from the homes and communities that relied on their labor and in that way endangered rather than furthered white families' best interests. Many white southerners responded to such conflicts with resentment that did not negate their commitment to the Confederacy but did strain their willingness to continue making the sacrifices Confederate independence would require. Women of Rutherfordton, North Carolina, for example, sent an angry petition to Governor Vance in 1863 informing him that because the local tanner was in the army, "half the ladys in Rutherford county hast to stay at home from church for the want of a pear off shoes," and they were not willing to put up with the situation any longer. The women still wanted the Confederacy to win the war, but they also wanted the tanner to be relieved from the duty of fighting for it so that he could come home and make shoes for them.[12]

The army's need for manpower led the Confederate government to act in ways that violated or at least minimized individual liberty and also exposed class friction among southern whites. A conscription bill passed on April 16, 1862, drafted white able-bodied men between the ages of eighteen and thirty-five and involuntarily extended the enlistments of soldiers already in service. Later adjustments exempted one white man for twenty or more slaves for the purpose of maintaining race control at home.[13] Non-slaveholders by and large acknowledged the need to uphold race control, but they often resented the wealthy men who could stay at home, protecting and providing for their families, while men who did not own slaves were denied that same privilege. A non-slaveholder from Green County agreed that a white man should stay behind to control the local "negros," who would otherwise be "left hear to plunder an steel . . . an destroye our famely," but he saw no reason why the white man assigned to the job could not be a poor man with a family to support rather than a rich man with slaves to do his work for him while he fought in the army to protect slavery.[14]

As the Confederate government took additional steps to meet the unforgiving demands of war, it intruded into people's daily lives far more than the Union government ever had, a development that further aggravated stresses in Confederate patriotism. Tax-in-kind, which obligated families to tithe a portion of each year's crop to the government, and impressment, which allowed Confederate army officers to commandeer civilians' crops in return for virtually worthless IOUs, directly interfered with the material well-being of North Carolina families. Private James Zimmerman bitterly resented government authorities like "the tax collector and the produce gathere[r]s [who] are pushing for the little mights of garden and trash patches . . . that the poor women have labored hard and made." He advised his wife to resist Confederate authorities by saying "you thought your husband was fighting for our rights and you had a notion that you had a right to what little you had luck to make."[15] Meanwhile, despite the obvious growth in power that the Richmond government claimed for itself, President Jefferson Davis's administration seemed to neglect North Carolina when it declined to commit troops or resources to resisting the Union occupation of parts of the state's coastal plain in 1862. The Confederate government had presented itself as protector of white southerners' best interests; by ignoring or impinging on those interests, it drew its own legitimacy into question and contradicted one of its reasons for existence.

Such conflicts did not immediately turn North Carolina soldiers into Union men, but they did impair the unity and effectiveness of the army. Private John Lee soured on the Confederacy because he believed that Richmond purposefully interfered with incoming mail in order to exert more complete control over soldiers' impressions of life on the home front. "Deprive me of hearing from [my family] and you will deprive me of my all," he complained. When government authorities heaped such "abuses and oppressions" on its citizens, Lee's reasons for fighting for that government grew cloudy.[16] Meanwhile, men of the Third Battalion of North Carolina State Troops wrote to ask Governor Vance to allow them to go home right in the middle of the battle campaigns of the summer of 1863 so that they could harvest their wheat. How could fathers with "large familys of little children," one man demanded to know, "go into a battle with all this on our minds and fight," no matter how strategically critical a battle might be?[17]

Zebulon Vance recognized these tensions. From the time of his election in 1862, many white Tar Heels loved the governor for his ability to intercede between North Carolinians and a Confederacy that seemed prone to harming individuals' interests and threatening civil liberties. He regularly ran interference, for example, between the Confederate cavalry and the North Carolina civilians from whom cavalry officers tried to impress feed for horses.[18] Noting the concern the governor took in citizens' affairs, individuals wrote to Vance with their troubles. When a group of Salisbury women who stormed warehouses and helped themselves to flour, molasses, and money faced prosecution as rioters, they wrote to the governor "with perfect confidence" that Vance would be "able and willing to do something for us."[19] As the war's toll mounted, Vance even took the case of his constituents to President Davis, advising the president in late 1863 to remove North Carolinians' "sources of discontent" in any honorable way he could, up to and including negotiations with the Federal government.[20]

Despite Vance's efforts, he could not always resolve conflicts to his constituents' satisfaction. Believing peace negotiations to be beneath the dignity of the Confederacy and doomed to failure, Davis declined to approach Federal authorities as Vance advised, while hardship steadily worsened for North Carolinians. The Federal blockade obstructed the importation of household goods, the war itself impeded production of necessities like salt, and natural forces like drought, wheat rust, and hog cholera exacerbated supply shortages.[21] Inflation drove prices beyond the reach of ordinary North Carolinians, causing both soldiers and civilians to search for ways to get by without basic food and clothing.[22] Facing a long, cold winter without proper supplies, Private E. D. Mothey demanded in January 1864 to know if the governor was "goin to let us suffer ore not." Forced to stand picket duty on "frosend" ground without shoes, Mothey asked Vance to "send me new shues," or at the very least, "send me your old wans," because without some form of relief, "the Boys will knot stand it much longer . . . and by the spring they won't be nary of them here."[23]

Every state, not just North Carolina, faced conflicts between citizens' needs and interests and the demands of the Confederacy, and in every state, white southerners' attitudes toward slavery and race proved instrumental in how they handled the conflict. Whenever the gap between expectation and experience threatened to pry Confederate patriotism apart along the fault line created by its central tensions, the aspect that reliably proved strong enough to resolve, or at least manage, inherent tensions was the fear and conviction that no matter how bad the Confederacy was, the Union was worse because it meant abolition, and abolition meant the worst disaster of all for white southern families. When one new wife, lonely and worried about the impending arrival of her first child, asked her non-slaveholding Texas husband how he could justify the war or his participation in it when his own family needed him, he sternly reminded her that it was far preferable to "sacrifice the endearments of home for a season rather than lie supinely upon our backs and wait till we are all bound hand and foot & the fair daughters of the south reduced to a level with the flat-footed thick-liped negro."[24] North Carolinians similarly reasoned that even a disappointing Confederacy was better than the Union because the Union would free slaves and unleash them on the South, and that logic tamped down discontent and renewed waning resolve among North Carolina soldiers. Exhausted by the fierce fighting of the Seven Days' Battles, "anxious to see ... fond ones at Home," and eager to "prepare ourselves for a more appropriate station in life," Private William Bellamy nonetheless continued to believe that Confederate victory was absolutely vital, because surrendering to the Union would mean "the Negro population set free and the white population bound by fetters."[25] Hit hard by shortage, inflation, and the absence of men to farm the land, the mountain people of Macon County also found themselves pushed almost to the breaking point. It was hard for a soldier to fight when he heard grim reports from "a home where the helpless are perishing for want of his hand to provide." Yet no matter how bad things got, a local leader assured Vance, people in Macon County were "opposed to negro equality" and "to prevent this we are willing to spare the last man." Women and children suffering "for food and clothing" were hard to take, but "rather than see them equalized with an inferior race we will die with them," he promised.[26]

In 1863 and 1864, dissatisfaction in North Carolina coalesced into a peace movement led by *Weekly Standard* editor William Woods Holden. Especially after the discouraging defeats at Gettysburg and Vicksburg, Holden determined (and printed in the *Standard*) that "what the great mass of our people desire is a cessation of hostilities, and negotiations" leading to a "settlement . . . which would leave them in the future in the enjoyment of 'life, liberty, and happiness.'"[27] Since the people were sovereign and the people wanted peace, Holden argued, it was the duty of the Confederate government to serve the people by negotiating for that peace with Federal authorities, but if it refused, North Carolina should assert its state sovereignty and conduct its own negotiations, which would in turn inspire other states to do likewise, until a settlement could be reached. Sparked by Holden, communities throughout the state held mass meetings where they passed resolutions calling for negotiations to end the war, ideally between Confederate and Federal authorities, but through separate state action if necessary.[28]

Peace meetings and resolutions from the tidewater to the mountains clearly signaled that North Carolinians were not satisfied with the Confederacy as it was and that they were tired of the depredations of war, but those meetings and resolutions did not necessarily mean that North Carolinians wished to go back into the Union.[29] In fact, when editors of newspapers that supported his political rivals charged Holden with having "strained every nerve to render [the war] odious to the people" while working "to bring about the reconstruction of the Union," Holden expressly denied the charges, arguing that despotic Confederate practices and the neglect of North Carolina, not his defense of his home state, were responsible for North Carolinians' growing bitterness.[30] Cabarrus County, a hotbed of peace sentiment, illustrates the limits within which the peace movement usually stayed. Resolutions passed at a February 6 meeting began with the preamble shared by numerous sets of resolutions statewide: "Whereas a crisis has reached the point in our national affairs, in which it behooves North Carolina, ever jealous and watchful of the rights and liberties of her people, to rouse from her lethargy, rise in her might and say whether her flag . . . shall wave over her sons as freemen or slaves; therefore be it resolved that the war has lasted long enough, and that the people of North Carolina, in their sovereign capacity, should propose a cessation of hostilities until an effort is made through a Convention for an honorable peace." The resolutions went on to denounce measures, such as the suspension of habeas corpus, which were "threatening to sweep from the state the last vestige of civil and political liberty." Following the announcement "that the people of North Carolina are able and competent to manage their own affairs," the resolutions culminated with a call for residents of the entire state to "make 'a long pull, a strong pull, and a pull all together' until we have an honorable and lasting peace." Yet strident as the resolutions were, they did not call for a return to the Union.[31] Meanwhile, resolutions passed two days later in Caldwell County reasoned that overtures toward peace would actually shore up the Confederate war effort, because if they did not work, they at least would "restore harmony & unite the people" by quieting "dissatisfaction."[32]

Furthermore, the peace movement in no way rejected slavery but rather assumed the preservation of slavery to be part of securing an honorable peace. While resolutions revealed little timidity in listing all the failings of the Confederacy, they did not question any aspect of slavery, not even the twenty-slave law. A local lawyer who drafted resolutions at a meeting in Rockingham, North Carolina, even "put in a clause on the Slavery Question," just to make clear that local residents remained unwilling to countenance the "Revolution" that abolition would constitute, no matter how tired of war they might be.[33] Some prominent peace men even argued that the peace movement was the only way to *save* slavery, since if the war continued to the bitter end, the institution would surely be destroyed. "If the war should be continued twelve months longer," Holden warned in January 1864, "negro slavery will be utterly and finally destroyed in these States. . . . Its sudden destruction would involve the whole social structure in ruin."[34] On the other hand, if North Carolina could negotiate a settlement immediately, with slavery still intact, chattel bondage would survive, at least for a while.[35] The *Raleigh Daily Progress*, a pro-peace newspaper, announced, "We favor peace because we believe that peace now would save slavery, while we very much fear that a prolongation of the war will obliterate the last vestige of it." Holden agreed, arguing that the "worst befalling our people" would be "the condition of provincial dependence on the federal government, . . . and the emancipation and arming of our slaves," which, "if the war continues," were both "likely" to happen. The only way to prevent that fate, he told readers of the *Weekly Standard*, was to "close the war."[36]

Yet while the peace movement was not necessarily anti-Confederate, and while it certainly did not question the rectitude or necessity of slavery, it still posed logistical problems for the successful waging of the war, since supplies and manpower were harder to reap from a populace intent on demonstrating its discontent. Private Marcus Hefner, for example, instructed his wife to resist Confederate efforts to collect tax-in-kind, telling her "to keep your grain and baken close and don't pay no tax or rent atal." In the army, Colonel Robert Hill of the Forty-eighth North Carolina attributed the actions of "some 30 or 40 deserters" to "the Holden excitement."[37] Private William Wagner did not desert, but at a regimental meeting he and his comrades conducted a straw poll in which "most of the solegers voted for peese" on Holden's terms.[38] Even when the peace movement did not attract the outright enthusiasm of soldiers, it could still cause divisions among them, which became clear in September 1863 when Army of Northern Virginia soldiers passing through the state wrecked the *Weekly Standard* office and chased off Holden, sending the hapless editor fleeing to Vance for protection. "Verry much pleased to hear of the soldiers making a raid upon old Holden's office," Private Jacob Hanes wished troops had gone further and "pitched old Holden into the Streets and broke his neck instead of his press," but others were outraged at military interference with a civil liberty like freedom of the press.[39]

Reluctant at first to overreact to the peace movement, Governor Vance eventually saw the meetings and resolutions as threats to Confederate independence. In September 1863, he issued a proclamation "commanding all such persons" leading the public peace meetings "to renounce such evil intentions."[40] Holden, meanwhile, persisted in his calls for an end to the war, which led Vance to distort Holden's position by calling it "a fixed policy . . . to call a convention . . . to take N.C. back to the United States."[41]

And so the stage was set for the North Carolina gubernatorial race of 1864 between Vance, who remained committed to the war, and Holden, who promised to end it. At the outset, Holden's calls for peace negotiations proved so popular that even Vance thought that opposition to Holden's suggested course of action placed him on the "precipice of [his] own career." He understood the source of Holden's popularity: "Our people will not pay this price," meaning sacrifice of their own self-interest, "for their national independence!" Vance wrote. Holden seemed to offer a quicker end to the sacrifices.[42]

Many soldiers preferred Holden to Vance because they were tired of fighting, their families were suffering, and Holden seemed to offer the best chance for ending the conflict that brought so much misery. In fact, army officers grew so concerned about the groundswell of support for Holden among enlisted men that they staged elaborate meetings to denounce the *Weekly Standard* editor. One soldier in Major C. G. Wright's battalion wrote that Major Wright called a meeting where he made a speech against Holden and the peace movement, then asked the men to endorse his resolutions, at which "at least two-thirds of the battalion shouted no!" Displeased with the outcome, the major called for the vote again, with similar results, until finally he and other officers "ignored the evidence of their own ears" and declared the resolutions passed, in direct contradiction to the wishes of the men.[43] Private Daniel Abernethy supported Holden because after all the "talk of N.C. doing something for pease," Abernethy was tired of "people at home [who] keepe bloing and don't' strike." Holden looked like someone who might do something about ending the fighting, at least for North Carolinians.[44] Private Adelphos Burns felt sure that "Holden will beat Vance in the Army" because soldiers would rather be "without a Confederacy" than to keep "fighting this war out."[45] Even Private James Morris, who personally favored Vance, feared that the rest of his regiment would go overwhelmingly for Holden because several of Morris's fellow enlisted men were receiving letters from hungry wives frightened by Confederate cavalrymen who barged into homes and barns in the middle of the night to help themselves to crops, livestock, and whiskey. "If you wish to be elected governor," Morris warned, "you should try to put and [sic] end to those depredations." Unless Vance could convince soldiers that he would do something about families' problems, his reelection bid could be in trouble.[46]

But while personal and familial interests constituted integral aspects of Confederate patriotism for North Carolinians, Vance also recognized that one issue could trump material hardships: fears of the disaster that would befall white southerners if slavery were abolished. While the peace movement did not openly challenge slavery, and while Holden even claimed that peace offered the only hope for slavery's survival, the Emancipation Proclamation made that argument nothing more than a wishful pipe dream. Any end to the war short of outright military victory would require Confederate submission to abolition, and therein, realized Vance, lay the peace movement's—and Holden's—greatest vulnerability. To a peace sympathizer who asked for clear reasons why the governor opposed negotiation, Vance acknowledged citizens' "sufferings under the desolating scourge of civil war," but current suffering was nothing compared to the "result of submission," which would mean "with absolute certainty the abolition of slavery and the turning loose of four million blacks in our midst."[47] If Vance could expose the peace movement's inability to guarantee the survival of slavery while still continuing to express his own sympathy for the troubles that made Holden's peace platform attractive to North Carolinians, then he could win. He resolved to "take the stump early" so he could "spend all my time and strength trying to warn and harmonize the people."[48]

He began that task on February 22, 1864, at Wilkesboro, smack in the heart of the western mountains, where peace sentiment flourished. Taking the stump at Wilkesboro as strains of lively music from the Johnny Reb band wafted through the air, Governor Vance delivered a speech that he would repeat around North Carolina and to soldiers encamped in Virginia all spring and summer. Vance assured audiences that he, too, sought an end to the conflict, but most of all he invigorated them with his own resolute

insistence on achieving it without submitting to Lincoln and the abolitionists. The speech acknowledged the hardships facing North Carolinians.
"Gallant boys have been slaughtered," Vance recognized, and women and
children "pine for the presence and support of their natural protector." It
was understandable for war-weary people to flirt with ideas of negotiation,
just as "all are liable to reach out, with the spirit of a drowning man, to
grasp any passing straw." Yet North Carolinians must resist such temp-
tations, he urged. While it might look like the Confederacy was harming
rather than advancing families' best interests, the welfare of the Confederacy was inseparable from that of individual families. "In its destiny are
involved the welfare of State, community, home, wife, children, self," Vance
argued. Separate state negotiations amounted to secession from the Confederacy, and seceding had brought about warfare in the first place, so
seceding again could only result in more bloodshed.

Even more important, Vance continued in his Wilkesboro speech, North
Carolinians had better remember that putting their state "into the arms of
Lincoln" would destroy the racial order. If the state came to its own agreement with the Union, North Carolina men of arms-bearing age would not
be freed from military obligation but rather would be forced to join "the
service of Uncle Sam, to fight alongside of his Negro troops in exterminating the white men, women, and children of the South." They would have
to "take an oath to support [Lincoln's] proclamation abolishing slavery,
his proclamation inciting the slaves of our State to burn your homes and
murder your families!" Meanwhile, black slaves "are all to be turned loose
upon us." North Carolina would look like Beaufort, South Carolina, where
blacks owned land confiscated from whites. Every "Southern youth" would
have to watch meekly while "he saw a Negro officer walking the streets and
making his sister give way for him or insulting her." Any white southerners willing to endure such conditions deserved "the fate of dogs," Vance
thundered.[49]

As newspapers printed Vance's speech throughout the state, the governor's words worked marvels on the electorate.[50] According to the *Fayetteville Observer*, everybody "in the Confederacy thought it a great speech,
a patriotic speech, a speech that cheered both people and soldiers and
brought to the speaker numberless invitations from counties at home and
Brigades in the field to come speak to them."[51] Responses from around the
state confirmed the *Observer*'s report. "Some two months since our county
would have given a overwhelming majority in favor of W. W. Holden for
Governor," a Rutherford County man wrote from his mountain home, but
"since that time your speech at Wilkesborough has been published in the

papers . . . there are many citizens that have given up their notions of Convention and will support you in the coming Election."[52] Meanwhile, from the coastal plain, "Many Citizens" of Lenoir County sent their own letter advising Vance, "Your speech, in Wilkesboro, has done wonders in that county and we hope you will make it convenient to make one in our Town this spring."[53]

Word of the speech made it into the army and worked its magic there, too. When Colonel G. C. Moses "brought down with me 100 copies of your *speech*" for distribution among soldiers and civilians in Goldsboro, company officers enthusiastically requested additional copies. "They say send your speech to their army—it will carry the *county* for you," Moses informed Vance.[54] Some Confederate prisoners of war, the men who would seem to have the most reason to want the war to end in any way possible, were so exhilarated when they read Vance's speech that they formed a committee to draft a letter of praise. The governor was exactly right, the prisoners agreed: reunion would be just the excuse Lincoln's Republican administration desired "to confiscate the property of our people, both real and person, and to apportion it among their soldiers and freedmen (slaves whom they have liberated.)" Worse, "they propose to take the arms from the whites and put them in the hands of the negros, they propose to extend the right of suffrage to the blacks; while among the whites it is to be restricted." In short, "the order of nature would be reversed," and the South would become "one vast ruin," groaning under "a tyranny more revolting than the visage of death." The longest war imaginable was preferable to that.[55]

Vance's choice of the horrors of abolition as a topic to unite and reinvigorate North Carolinians posed risks, less because non-slaveholders might turn against a war for slavery (from the outset, non-slaveholders had demonstrated powerful convictions that the destruction of slavery amounted to a disaster for themselves and their families, even if they did not own slaves) than because the war itself destabilized the institution of slavery. War-weary soldiers and civilians might conclude that slavery had been weakened beyond repair anyway and question the wisdom of continuing to fight to prevent its destruction. Such a risk was less apparent in North Carolina than in other states with higher rates of Union occupation, where the presence of the Federal army undermined white southern control and encouraged enslaved men and women to claim their own freedom. In fact, in the western part of the state, the institution of slavery actually strengthened, as slave owners from elsewhere escaped to the relative safety of the mountains while more local non-slaveholders than ever suddenly found themselves able to obtain human property.[56] Yet the risk existed even in the Old North State, and a very few North Carolinians did begin to question the institution in ways they never had before the war. John Killian, a nonslaveholding North Carolinian who had gone to California in the 1850s, returned to his native state at the outbreak of war to help prevent abolition. As the war dragged on, Killian realized that the combination of his Christian faith and his years in California forced him to look at slavery with new eyes. In March 1864, he confessed to his sister, "I some times think that this is rong to one [own] a slave for the Bible ses that man shal eat bred by the swet of his brough." Further, he even entertained the notion that "if it is the wil of the Lord for the negro to be fre, this ma be the apointed time of their being made so." Yet even Killian, who proved far more willing to question the institution of bondage than the vast majority of his fellow enlisted men, could not quite face the prospect that "we wil aul be on an equaliety." In the end, he concluded that "the worse is to come yet if the Yanks whip us" and resigned himself to continuing to "fite for [slaveholders'] property."[57] The consequences of abolition remained too difficult for white southerners to face, which was why Vance's strategy proved so effective despite its risks.

For a brief time in the early spring, the familiar combination of war-weariness, resentment, and worries about home dampened the support for Vance that early reports of his speech had sparked among North Carolina troops. Compounding matters, President Davis secured congressional passage of a bill to suspend the writ of habeas corpus in the case of any person resisting Confederate authority or encouraging others to do likewise, and many citizens of North Carolina suspected that the move was aimed especially in the direction of their state.[58] The apparent advance of military despotism coupled with continued suffering dimmed the appeal of a governor committed to continuing the war, at least for some soldiers. One "barefooted and bare headed" North Carolinian who had professed himself "a Vance man last year" now "says that two thirds of his Brigade," including him, "will vote for Holden," a distressed Vance supporter wrote to warn the governor.[59]

Noting their men's waning enthusiasm, officers in North Carolina regiments stationed as far away as Virginia and Georgia appealed to the governor to come to camp to inspire the troops in person.[60] From March 26 to April 3, Vance visited North Carolina brigades camped along or near the Rapidan River in Virginia, methodically working his way along Brigadier General Stephen Ramseur's men on the right and Brigadier General James Henry Lane's men on the left. Wherever he went, the governor drew a crowd, including soldiers from other states and local civilians. His visits inspired the martial pomp of military reviews, but the focal point remained Vance's speech.[61] As he had at Wilkesboro, Vance acknowledged soldiers' grievances but reminded them that current suffering paled compared to the catastrophe that would befall them, their material interests, and their wives and daughters if slaves were freed. He also added new climaxes to the speech aimed specifically at soldiers, sometimes instructing troops to fight until hell froze over and then to cut the ice and fight on, and at other times varying the refrain by urging army men to fill hell so full of Yankees that their feet stuck out the windows.[62]

Some men remained unmoved by the governor's spirited exhortations. One wounded soldier who eventually made it home on furlough wrote that he and others were actually put off by Vance's flamboyant style. The governor's "great fuss of speaking and saying so much has set the people at variance with him," he claimed, because soldiers wanted "*action*, and not words."[63] Resistant to Vance's electrifying presence, Adelphos Burns remarked, "Governor Vance told us up at Orange to fight until Hell freezes over. That's rather longer than I care to fight."[64] George Williams shared Burns's disinclination to fight on the ice of hell.[65] For men like Burns and Williams, not even the governor's fabled dramatic streak could mask the growing hopelessness of the Confederate cause or disguise the pressing hardships faced by soldiers and their families.

Yet for many others, hearing the speech in person served as a booster shot, steeling their defenses and strengthening their commitment. When Private David Thompson's brother described Vance's speech after the governor visited his brigade, David could hardly wait for "next Tuesday," when Vance was scheduled to speak to his regiment. "I wouldent miss his speech for nothing," Thompson vowed.[66] Another sergeant who heard Vance at Orange Court House admitted that he remained "as tired of the War as enny man, but to support Holden I cant." Furthermore, he predicted, "Vance will make a clean sweep in the Armey." However badly he and his fellow enlisted men wanted the war to end, Vance reminded them that an end to slavery was too big a price to pay.[67]

Holden's election efforts proved no match for Vance's heroics. At first, Holden's campaign strategy consisted of doing nothing, on the grounds that his "principles and views" were already "well known to the people of the State." An ineffective public speaker, Holden opted not to campaign in person because he lacked much talent on the stump, although he tried to couch that decision in the patriotic language of one who was "not disposed, at a time like this, to invite the people from their employments, and add to the excitement which prevails in the public mind, by haranguing them for their votes."[68] To make matters worse, he also suspended publication of the *Weekly Standard* to protest the suspension of habeas corpus, telling a friend, "I felt that if I could not continue to print as a freeman I would not print at all."[69] Initially, many voters might have admired his principled stance, but the result was that he lacked a vehicle for placing his views before the public, just as Vance traveled around (and even outside) the state promoting his own candidacy with vigor and flair.

Too late, Holden recognized the damage that Vance's speech did to Holden's own chances. On April 6, days after Vance completed his speaking tour among soldiers in Virginia, Holden published a special edition of the *Weekly Standard* to try to curtail the governor's gains. Much of the issue reprinted carefully chosen selections from Vance's Wilkesboro speech and pointed out differences between the Conservative platform on which Vance had been elected in 1862 and the immovable prowar stance to which Vance committed himself at Wilkesboro and in all the locales in which he repeated the speech.[70] Neither the April 6 issue nor any of the regular editions Holden issued once he resumed publication on May 18 took on the slavery issue.[71] Instead, from May through the election, Holden worked diligently to keep readers focused on civil liberties, the sovereign right of North Carolina to act as it pleased without coercion from the Confederate government, and the material hardships faced by North Carolinians.[72] Yet despite Holden's efforts, the damage had been done; once Vance introduced the specter of abolition into the campaign, there was no taking it out again, no matter how hard Holden tried to refocus voters' attention.

As the election neared, both Holden and Vance launched and fended off personal attacks. Holden accused Vance of turning into a "Destructive," a pejorative term for the Fire-Eaters who embraced secession early and who continued to proclaim (if not personally exhibit) an unending willingness to fight. The Wilkesboro speech was "a war speech of the most ultra character," Holden complained. In effect, it validated every despotic move made by the Confederate government, including the suspension of the writ of habeas corpus, and it betrayed the Conservative constituency that had elected Vance in 1862.[73] Vance struck back by trying to tie Holden to a secret organization known as the "Heroes of America," or the "Red Strings," a clandestine, oath-bound society of Unionists dedicated to returning North Carolina to the United States by fair means or foul.[74] The accusations forced Holden to use valuable column space in the July 9, 1864, edition of the *Standard* to print: "We know nothing of the scarlet string or of secret political associations. We belong to no secret association, nor do we believe that any such association of a treasonable character exists in this State."[75]

As effective a campaigner as Zebulon Vance undoubtedly was, his bid for reelection received its biggest boon in April 1864 not from a speech or a newspaper but from the Battle of Plymouth, North Carolina, which boosted morale and, more important, reinforced the potency of Vance's racial exhortations by giving soldiers the opportunity to act on them. Located where Albemarle Sound met the Roanoke River, Plymouth was one of few places in the state to experience Federal occupation. From the time of its occupation in 1862, the town served as a supply depot for Union troops in eastern North Carolina, and it also contained a large community of escaped slaves who had begun to build new lives and institutions for themselves by 1864. Among the Union troops fortifying Plymouth was a company of locally recruited African American soldiers who had served in General Edward Wild's Brigade.[76] In mid-April, Confederate brigadier generals Robert Hoke and Matt Ransom, together with North Carolina troops pulled from elsewhere in the state and from Virginia, began to move on Plymouth. Backed up by an ironclad ram called the *Albemarle*, Confederates began the attack on April 17. When Union general Henry Walton Wessells surrendered on the morning of April 20, the Confederate soldiers who captured the town suddenly found themselves in possession of more than five hundred black Union soldiers and a whole town of former slaves. Suddenly, they had the opportunity to lash out at the black slaves whose emancipation they feared and blamed for causing the war. They pillaged the town and unleashed their rage and violence on captured black Union troops. Samuel Johnson of the Second U.S. Colored Cavalry managed to save his own life only by pulling off his Union uniform and passing as a local slave. No "negros found in blue uniform or with any outward marks of a Union soldier" were so lucky. Some soldiers were "taken into the woods and hung," Johnson reported, while others were stripped, lined up along a riverbank, and shot. Still others "were killed by having their brains beaten out by the butt end of the muskets in the hands of the Rebels." White officers and some of the black soldiers were kept alive for one day, only to be dragged through town with ropes around their necks the following morning. After that humiliation, the "remainder of the black soldiers were killed."[77]

Plymouth reinvigorated many North Carolina men's commitment to the war, partly because military victories generally elevated morale, but Plymouth meant more than that. In that Roanoke River town, former black slaves occupying property once enjoyed by white southerners, protected in their right to do so by armed black Union soldiers imposing Union rule, literally embodied the threats that Vance's Wilkesboro and subsequent speeches insisted that the end of slavery would pose.[78] Savaging such a town allowed white Confederate soldiers whose world was in upheaval to vent their fear and resentment of blacks released from slavery. Captain Henry Chambers, who took part in the Battle of Plymouth as a member of the Forty-ninth North Carolina, had noticed the previous month that attacks on black civilians in Suffolk, Virginia, could produce a notably salutary effect on morale. "We were nearly exhausted," Chambers recorded in his diary, and initially objected when the regiment received the unwelcome order to march at a "double quick" pace, "but when told that the hated negroes had been encountered, we received as it were renewed vigor and on we pushed." Although the black soldiers got away, black civilians were not so lucky. The men of the Forty-ninth noticed a house that "had Negroes in it" and set fire to the structure "before the negroes could be gotten out," killing the African Americans trapped inside.[79] Opportunities to use violence against blacks at Plymouth further allowed soldiers to strike at the embodiment of their racial fears, while the military success at Plymouth proved that fighting really could prevent those fears from coming to pass. As the newspapers put it, "Repeat Plymouth a few times and we shall bring the Yankees to their senses."[80]

The victory at Plymouth occurred in the context of a general brightening of Confederate military and political fortunes, all of which aided Vance. By the time soldiers voted in July, the Army of the Potomac's overland campaign had come to grief at places like the Wilderness and Cold Harbor, while in the West, Union attempts to capture Atlanta stalled. Moreover, odds in the upcoming Union presidential contest seemed to favor the Democratic candidate, George McClellan, who would be much less likely than Lincoln to insist on emancipation as a condition for peace. With neither Union military triumph nor the reelection of Lincoln looking probable, negotiations with the Lincoln administration to end the war seemed less necessary, and the risks that stopping short of Confederate battlefield victory posed to the preservation of slavery seemed needless. Timing, in other words, helped create an environment that increased Vance's chances, but it was the governor's strategy that most influenced the outcome of the election.

Aided by the Battle of Plymouth, Vance's election strategy of reminding soldiers that the horrors of abolition outweighed wartime deprivations paid off. Despite Holden's apparent popularity in the first weeks of 1864, and despite the temporary swoon in Vance support among soldiers in the early spring, Vance handily defeated his opponent. Even Sergeant Garland Ferguson, initially suspicious of Vance, grew convinced that Holden was "unsound." Ferguson wanted peace, "but I want that peace to be better than war," he told his brother, and that was why he was for Vance.[81] Ferguson's companions seemed to agree; on election day, seventy-four soldiers in his company voted for Vance, while not one cast a Holden ballot.[82] Vance also swept Private R. P. Allen's cavalry company, Captain Henry Chambers's infantry regiment, and even several wayside hospitals where North Carolina invalids cast votes for the sitting governor.[83] As election returns rolled in, Private Henry Patrick claimed that Holden's "stock" had fallen "so far below par that it is impossible to express its present status in figures."[84] When it came down to it, Vance successfully persuaded soldiers and voters that peace Holden's way would mean surrender and emancipation, and North Carolina troops were not yet prepared to confront, let alone concede, either prospect.

Vance's campaign and election matter because they highlight the role of racial fear in suppressing disaffection, in smoothing the tensions inherent in Confederate patriotism, and in keeping enlisted men committed to the war when the Confederacy violated some of its very reasons for being.[85] Running on a platform that admitted the unsatisfactory nature of the Confederate government, Vance reminded voters and soldiers that a faulty Confederacy was still better than reunion, because the Union would destroy the racial order that protected soldiers' families and defined their identities as white men. The election also provided soldiers with the opportunity to affirm their commitment to a racial hierarchy that helped manage their fears and frustrations and that they believed was vital to life in the South.

Moreover, Vance's campaign matters because it forces us to look carefully at exactly *how* Confederate soldiers' attitudes toward race influenced the war. Often, invoking racial fear or racism in explaining Confederate motivation claps a discussion closed, either because the suggestion that racism is at work alienates readers and listeners who reject that explanation and tune out, or because Confederate racism is assumed to be self-evident and leaves nothing else to say. Neither approach sheds much light on how and why race would seem so important, so emotional, and so personal to the white non-slaveholding men who made up the bulk of the Confederate army. Furthermore, neither approach does much to explain the 1864 North Carolina gubernatorial election, a contest that turned on racial fear, as demonstrated by Vance's campaign speeches and by the Battle of Plymouth. Vance won partly because the election took place in July 1864 when Union military prospects hit their nadir, but most of all, he won because he reminded voters that the need to preserve slavery and white supremacy outweighed wartime material hardships; the survival of slavery rested right at the heart of white southerners' prosperity and well-being, as well as at the heart of the Confederate nation. Close examination of how troops responded to Vance's election can at least help to begin a discussion of precisely what race meant to Confederates, what part it played in Confederate patriotism, and how it helped to define the relationship between Confederates and their new nation.

Notes

1. Vance to "Dear Sir" (probably David Swain), January 2, 1864, Raleigh, N.C., Zebulon Baird Vance Papers, Private Collections, North Carolina Department of Archives and History, Raleigh (hereafter NCDAH).

2. Pvt. George Williams, Seventh NC, to "Parents," April 5, 1864, near Gordonsville, Va., Williams-Womble Papers, NCDAH. Sgt. Martin Malone Gash of the Sixty-fifth NC similarly predicted that the majority of North Carolina soldiers stationed in Georgia would vote for Holden. See Gash to "Sister," June 18, 1864, Kinston, Ga., Gash Family Papers, NCDAH.

3. For election results, see Marc W. Kruman, *Parties and Politics in North Carolina, 1836–1865* (Baton Rouge: Louisiana State University Press, 1983), 265.

4. By Confederate patriotism, I mean individual white southerners' felt connection to the Confederacy and commitment to a war for its independence.

5. For analyses that emphasize Confederate class conflict, see Wayne K. Durrill, *War of Another Kind: A Southern Community in the Great Rebellion* (New York: Oxford University Press, 1990); Paul D. Escott, *After Secession: Jefferson Davis and the Failure of Confederate Nationalism* (Baton Rouge: Louisiana State University Press, 1978); and Armstead L. Robinson, *Bitter Fruits of Bondage: The Demise of Slavery and the Collapse of the Confederacy, 1861–1865* (Charlottesville: University Press of Virginia, 2005).

6. A voluminous literature on Confederate patriotism exists. The works that argue for the existence of genuine Confederate patriotism (as opposed to those that argue that internal divisions precluded patriotism from developing) can be usefully (if a little over simplistically) divided into three main strains represented respectively by Drew Gilpin Faust, *The Creation of Confederate Nationalism: Ideology and Identity in the Confederate South* (Baton Rouge: Louisiana State University Press, 1988); Gary Gallagher, *The Confederate War* (Cambridge, Mass.: Harvard University Press, 1997); and Anne Sarah Rubin, *A Shattered Nation: The Rise and Fall of the Confederacy, 1861–1868* (Chapel Hill: University of North Carolina Press, 2005). Faust stresses ideological factors, Gallagher argues for the centrality of the success of the Army of Northern Virginia (which did not exist until 1862), and Rubin emphasizes the desire for white southern independence. The addition here of the idea that many

white southerners' felt connection to the Confederacy was based on the belief that an independent Confederacy would better promote the interests, aspirations, and well-beings of themselves and their own families is not to deny the importance of ideology emphasized by other analyses of Confederation nationalism; in fact, the ways in which the Confederacy was better for individuals and families had to do with much more than materialism and were profoundly ideological. But for other explanations, self-interested behavior becomes a problem that needs explaining away as a contradiction or, for Rubin, temporary and regretted aberration on the part of white southerners who really wanted to be "better Confederates." In my view, self-interest was really central to Confederate patriotism and not a swerving away from it. Difficulties arose, then, not when Confederates temporarily swooned in their patriotism but rather when they acted in ways that self-interest-based patriotism dictated by its own internal logic. The problems, in other words, came less from individuals' inconstancy in their patriotism than from the very nature of the patriotism and could be most effectively managed for most of the war by the fear that the abolition of black slavery was the very worst thing that could befall white southerners, whether or not they owned slaves.

7. This interpretation of ordinary Confederate soldiers' perceptions of the relationship between slavery, individuals' and families' interests, white manhood, and soldiers' perceptions of the war arises from my own research in the personal letters and diaries of more than five hundred Confederate soldiers, soldiers' letters to civilian newspapers, and Confederate soldiers' regimental newspapers (see Chandra Manning, *What This Cruel War Was Over: Soldiers, Slavery and the Civil War* (New York: Knopf, 2007), but the work of several other historians also explores the relationship among (with varying emphases) the existence of slavery, the idea of mastery, attitudes toward women, and the manhood of white southern men. See, for example, Stephen W. Berry II, *All That Makes a Man: Love and Ambition in the Civil War South* (New York: Oxford University Press, 2003); Stephanie McCurry, *Masters of Small Worlds: Yeoman Households, Gender Relations, and the Political Culture of the Antebellum South Carolina Low Country* (New York: Oxford University Press, 1995); Nicholas W. Proctor, *Bathed in Blood: Hunting and Mastery in the Old South* (Charlottesville: University Press of Virginia, 2002); and Lee Ann Whites, *The Civil War as a Crisis in Gender: Augusta, Georgia, 1860–1890* (Athens: University of Georgia Press, 1995).

8. Lt. Macon Bonner, Co. B, NC Artillery (attached to Thirty-first NC Infantry), to "Wife," January 8, 1864, Fort Fisher, N.C., Macon Bonner Papers, Southern Historical Collection, University of North Carolina, Chapel Hill (hereafter SHC). For examples of accounts that minimize early support for Holden in the first place, see W. Buck Yearns and John G. Barrett's contention in *North Carolina Civil War Documentary* (Chapel Hill: University of North Carolina Press, 1980) that "the devotion of Holden's followers deceived many about the extent of his support," (317), and Robin E. Baker, "Class Conflict and Political Upheaval: The Transformation of North Carolina Politics during the Civil War," *North Carolina Historical Review* 69 (April 1992), which concludes from election results that "Holden stirred little enthusiasm for his candidacy among any significant portion of the electorate" (175).

9. See, for example, "The Vote of the Army," *Weekly Standard*, August 5, 1864,

3, in which Holden claimed, "It is our deliberate opinion, formed after hearing from various points, that not many more than one-third of the North Carolina soldiers voted at the late election. All the Vance men voted, and no doubt many who were opposed to him were induced in various ways to cast ballots for him; but the remainder, comprising a large majority of the army, either voted for Holden against influences never before brought to bear on elections in this country, or did not vote [at] all. *The army is beyond all question against Vance*, but unfortunately it was not in the power of the soldier so to declare by their votes."

10. On coercion in the Confederate army, see Gordon B. McKinney, *Zeb Vance: North Carolina's Civil War Governor and Gilded Age Political Leader* (Chapel Hill: University of North Carolina Press, 2004), 228–29. For General Hancock's observation about two North Carolinians deserting because they were not allowed to vote, see U.S. War Department, *The War of the Rebellion: A Compilation of the Official Records of the Union and Confederate Armies*, 128 vols. (Washington, D.C.: Government Printing Office, 1892), ser. 1, vol. 40, pt. 3, 598 (also available on-line through Cornell University's *Making of America* Web site).

11. Pvt. Henry Patrick, Forty-first NC, to "Wife," August 13, 1864, near Petersburg, Va., Henry Machen Patrick Letters, NCDAH.

12. Female sect of Rutherfordton, N.C., to Governor Vance, June 15, 1863, Rutherfordton, N.C., Zebulon Baird Vance Papers, Governor's Papers, box 5, NCDAH.

13. For more on the Confederate draft, see Albert Burton Moore, *Conscription and Conflict in the Confederacy* (Columbia: University of South Carolina Press, 1996), especially chap. 2. Later drafts eventually extended the age of enlistment from seventeen to fifty-five. The twenty-slave exemption grew into the most controversial part of the draft, but it did not turn soldiers against slavery, as historians such as Armstead Robinson (*Bitter Fruits of Bondage*) and others have argued. It did excite resentment against large slaveholders, but that is not the same thing as a desire or even willingness for the institution to go away.

14. James Hemby to Governor Vance, September 4, 1863, Green County, N.C., Zebulon Baird Vance Papers, Governor's Papers, box 6, NCDAH.

15. Pvt. James Zimmerman, Fifty-seventh NC, to "Wife," August 16, 1863, Orange Court House, Va., James Zimmerman Papers, Special Collections, Perkins Library, Duke University. See Pvt. J. Marcus Hefner, Fifty-seventh NC, to "Wife," March 4, 1864, Goldsboro, N.C., Marcus Hefner Papers, NCDAH.

16. Sgt. John Lee, Thirty-fourth NC, to Governor Vance, September 1, 1863, Zebulon Baird Vance Papers, Governor's Papers, box 6, NCDAH.

17. Company C, Third Battalion NC State Troops, to Governor Vance, June 9, 1863, Zebulon Baird Vance Papers, Governor's Papers, box 5, folder 2, NCDAH.

18. In February 1863, Vance wrote to tell Confederate brigadier general A. G. Jenkins that because of "the duty I owe my own people," who needed their crops for their own use, he could not grant Jenkins's request "to impress Corn & forage for the use of a number of Calvary horses." Furthermore, Governor Vance advised Brigadier General Jenkins to reign in his unruly troops, who were "making themselves a terror to the whole population." Vance to Brig. Genl. A. J. Jenkins, February 2, 1863, Executive Department, Raleigh, N.C., in Joe A. Mobley, ed., *The Papers of Zebulon Baird*

Vance, vol. 2 (Raleigh: Division of Archives and History, North Carolina Department of Cultural Resources, 1995), 40–41 (hereafter *Vance Papers*). When cavalry depredations against North Carolinians continued, Vance went over General Jenkins's head to the War Department. On February 25, he explained to Secretary of War Seddon that he had to impede impressment for "the existence of my own people" and warned that unless Jenkins's cavalry were removed from western North Carolina soon, "I shall be under the painful necessity of calling out the Militia of the adjoining Counties and driving them from the state" (ibid., 2:65–66)

19. Soldiers' Wives to "His Excellencey the Gov of the State of NC," March 21, 1863, Salisbury, N.C., *Vance Papers*, 2:92–93.

20. For Vance's correspondence with Davis about trying to organize peace negotiations in 1863 and 1864, see Zebulon Baird Vance Papers, Governor's Papers, especially boxes 9 and 10, NCDAH.

21. See John C. Inscoe and Gordon B. McKinney, *The Heart of Confederate Appalachia: Western North Carolina in the Civil War* (Chapel Hill: University of North Carolina Press, 2000), chap. 7, esp. 166–69.

22. Even in the mountains, supposedly the part of the state least dependent on cash exchange and a market economy, inflation skyrocketed. According to Philip Davis, in the western mountain counties, the price of eggs rose 1,666 percent, the price of bacon rose 2,272 percent, the price of flour rose 2,777 percent, and the price of corn and potatoes rose 3,000 percent. See Phillip G. Davis, "Mountain Heritage, Mountain Promise: The Origin and Devastation of Confederate Sympathy in the North Carolina Mountains during the Civil War" (M.A. thesis, Wake Forest University, 1994), cited in Inscoe and McKinney, *Heart of Confederate Appalachia*, 175.

23. Pvt. E. D. Mothey, Forty-seventh NC, to Governor Vance, January 18, 1864, Orange Court House, Va., Zebulon Baird Vance Papers, Governor's Papers, box 10, NCDAH.

24. Pvt. John Street, Eighth TX, to "Wife," February 25, 1862, Tishomingo Co., Miss., John K. and Melinda East Street Papers, SHC.

25. Pvt. William Bellamy, Eighteenth NC, diary, July 1862, near Richmond, Va., and July 16, 1862, Charles City Road, Va., William James Bellamy Papers, SHC.

26. D. W. Siler to Governor Vance, November 3, 1862, near Franklin, N.C., in Frontis W. Johnston, ed., *The Papers of Zebulon Baird Vance*, vol. 1 (Raleigh: State Department of Archives and History, 1963), 301–3. For western North Carolinians' commitment to slavery, which many historians have underestimated, see John C. Inscoe, "Mountain Masters: Slaveholding in Western North Carolina," *North Carolina Historical Review* 61 (April 1984): 143–73; and Inscoe and McKinney, *Heart of Confederate Appalachia*.

27. "Peace—When shall we have Peace?" *Weekly Standard*, July 22, 1863, 1.

28. The Zebulon Baird Vance Papers, Governor's Papers, box 10, and Private Collections, volume 3, both NCDAH, contain peace resolutions from many locations, including the North Carolina counties of Henderson, Forsyth, Rutherford, Cabarrus, Caldwell, and others. The *Weekly Standard* also includes several sets of peace resolutions. The issue of August 5, 1863, for example, includes on pages 1–3 resolutions from public meetings held in Wake, Moore, Gaston, Iredell, Buncombe, and Samp-

son counties. For more on *Standard* editor William Woods Holden and his role in the peace movement, see William C. Harris, *William Woods Holden: Firebrand of North Carolina Politics* (Baton Rouge: Louisiana Sate University Press, 1987), esp. chaps. 6 and 7.

29. While most resolutions did not express willingness to go back to the Union, there were a few exceptions. A "Humble Citizen" of Forsyth County, for example, wrote to tell Governor Vance that "the people of Bethania, Salem, and the surrounding country are riding about with petitions getting every person they can to sign them, deceiving the ignorant by telling them just sign it, the Governor will call a convention, we will send delegates that will vote us back into the Union, and we will have peace in less than three months." See Humble Citizen to Governor Vance, February 1, 1864, Forsyth Co., N.C., Zebulon Baird Vance Papers, Governor's Papers, box 10, NCDAH. This citizen's letter about peace meeting rumors he had heard suggests that some meetings discussed or even supported reentry into the Union, but the resolutions in Governor Vance's papers and published in North Carolina newspapers generally do not explicitly endorse returning to the Union.

30. *Weekly Standard*, July 29, 1863, 1. Holden was specifically replying to charges printed in the *Raleigh Register*.

31. Proceedings of Cabarrus County Meeting Sent to Governor Vance, February 6, 1864, John Heilman's Mill, Cabarrus Co., N.C., Zebulon Baird Vance Papers, Governor's Papers, box 10, NCDAH. Similar resolutions were passed at meetings throughout the state and were often published in the *Weekly Standard* and the *Raleigh Daily Progress*, two newspapers associated with the peace movement. The frequent repetition of near-identical resolutions at several meetings suggests a high degree of coordination rather than a grassroots upswelling. Caldwell County, for example, published a set with a first clause that repeated Cabarrus County's almost word for word. Yet despite similarities, resolutions did vary from meeting to meeting. The Cabarrus County set's statement that North Carolinians were most capable of managing their own affairs was unusual, for example.

32. Proceedings of Caldwell County Meeting, February 8, 1864, Caldwell Co., N.C., Zebulon Baird Vance Papers, Governor's Papers, box 10, NCDAH.

33. Walter Steele to Governor Vance, July 4, 1863, Rockingham, N.C., Zebulon Baird Vance Papers, Governor's Papers, box 5, NCDAH. The Rockingham meeting about which Steele wrote had initially been called by a former lieutenant colonel in the Confederate army and the lawyer who drafted the resolutions. The lieutenant colonel stated that he *was* willing to go back into the Union under the old Constitution, but the lawyer and the rest of the meeting repudiated that sentiment, hence the lawyer's "clause on the Slavery Question."

34. "The Fayetteville Observer and the Proposition to call a State Convention," *Weekly Standard*, January 20, 1864, 3.

35. For example, Henderson County Conservative Party leader Leander Gash argued, "The sooner Peace is made consentably, the longer slavery may be enjoyed by a gradual extinction. But prolong the war indefinitely and all must go together and end at the same time." See Gash to Vance, June 1, 1863, Zebulon Baird Vance Papers, Governor's Papers, box 5, NCDAH. Jonathan Worth, a prominent Whig (and later

postwar governor of North Carolina), also maintained that "a continuance of the war will result in universal emancipation" but that by negotiation, Confederates "could make peace on the basis of the Constitution of the U.S. whereby we would preserve our slaves, and save the further effusion of blood and destruction of every thing." See Worth to Daniel L. Russell, February 16, 1864, Raleigh, N.C., in J. G. D. Hamilton, ed., *The Correspondence of Jonathan Worth* (Raleigh: Edwards and Broughton Printing Company, 1909), 1:297.

36. The *Weekly Standard* of July 22, 1863, reprints the *Raleigh Daily Progress* editorial of July 15, 1863, on page 1 and follows it with Holden's commentary, also on page 1.

37. Pvt. J. Marcus Hefner, Fifty-seventh NC, to "Wife," March 4, 1864, Goldsboro, N.C., Marcus Hefner Papers, NCDAH; Col. Robert C. Hill, Forty-eighth NC, to Governor Vance, September 8, 1863, Taylorsville, Va., Zebulon Baird Vance Papers, Governor's Papers, box 6, NCDAH.

38. Pvt. William Wagner, Fifty-seventh NC, to "Wife," August 15, 1863, near Orange Court House, Va., in Joe M. Hatley and Linda B. Huffman, eds., *Letters of William F. Wagner, Confederate Soldier* (Wendell, N.C.: Broadfoot's Bookmark, 1983), 65. Wagner further noted the outrage of the men when the "Big men," meaning the senior officers, reported to the newspapers that the men had voted to carry on the war. "We never voted that a way we voted to have pease on some terms," the angry Wagner told his wife. See also Pvt. Francis Poteet, Forty-ninth NC, to "Family," November 22, 1863, Kinston, N.C., Poteet-Dickson Letters, NCDAH.

39. Pvt. Jacob Hanes, Fourth NC, to "Brother," September 16, 1863, near Rapidan River, Va., Catherine Hanes Papers, SHC.

40. "By the Governor of North Carolina: A Proclamation," September 7, 1863, *Vance Papers*, 2:268–69.

41. Vance to "Dear Sir" (probably David Swain), January 2, 1864, Raleigh, N.C., Zebulon Baird Vance Papers, Private Collections, NCDAH.

42. Ibid. For another example of Vance's recognition of the strength of support for Holden's platform, see Vance to his good friend E. J. Hale in which Vance confided, "The convention question is to be my test and I am to be beaten if I oppose it," December 30, 1863, Raleigh, N.C., *Vance Papers*, 2:359.

43. Included in "The Sentiments of the Soldiers," *Weekly Standard*, September 2, 1863, 1. The same article also included excerpts telling similar stories purporting to be from soldiers in the Thirty-first, Forty-second, Forty-ninth, Fifty-seventh, and Sixty-third NC regiments.

44. Pvt. Daniel Abernethy, Eleventh NC, to "Wife," February 25, 1864, and to "Father," February 25, 1864, near Orange Court House, Va., Daniel Abernethy Papers, Duke University. Abernethy was illiterate; he dictated letters to a messmate.

45. Pvt. Adelphos Burns, Forty-eighth NC, to "Father," July 17, 1864, Petersburg, Va., Adelphos J. Burns Letters, NCDAH.

46. Pvt. James M. Morris, Fifty-seventh NC, to Governor Vance, April 27, 1864, near Kinston, N.C., Zebulon Baird Vance Papers, Governor's Papers, box 11, NCDAH.

47. Vance to John H. Haughton, August 17, 1863, Raleigh, N.C., *Vance Papers*, 2:243.

48. Vance to "Dear Sir" (probably David Swain), January 2, 1864, Raleigh, N.C., Zebulon Baird Vance Papers, Private Collections, NCDAH.

49. Governor Zebulon Vance, "Address of Gov. Vance on the Condition of the Country," delivered in Wilkesboro, N.C., February 22, 1864, reprinted in the *Raleigh Daily Conservative*, April 16, 1864, 1, from the shorthand report of G. Clinton Stedman, NCDAH.

50. Some peace proponents remained unconvinced, and in a few cases, public meetings convened for the express purpose of denouncing Vance's speech, but for the most part, Vance's earnest words at Wilkesboro produced remarkable results. For an example of a community meeting unconvinced by Vance's Wilkesboro speech, see Gordon McKinney's discussion of a Wake County meeting that criticized the speech for containing "*all war, and no propositions for peace*" in *Zeb Vance*, 213–14.

51. *Fayetteville Observer*, April 11, 1864, 1.

52. T. Davis to Governor Vance, April 4, 1864, Rutherford County, N.C., Zebulon Baird Vance Papers, Governor's Papers, box 11, NCDAH.

53. "Many Citizens," Lenoir, N.C., March 9, 1864, Zebulon Baird Vance Papers, Governor's Papers, box 10 NCDAH.

54. Col. G. C. Moses to Governor Vance, March 4, 1864, Goldsboro, N.C., ibid.

55. Petition signed by "North Carolinians in prison at Johnson's Island, 231 in all," March 30, 1864, Johnson's Island, Ohio, Thomas Jefferson Green Papers, SHC.

56. For the effect of Union occupation on slavery, see Ira Berlin et al., eds., *Freedom: A Documentary History of Emancipation, 1861–1867*, series 1, *The Destruction of Slavery* (New York: Cambridge University Press, 1985). For the strengthening of slavery in the North Carolina mountains during the war, see Inscoe, "Mountain Masters"; and Inscoe and McKinney, *Heart of Confederate Appalachia*, chap. 9.

57. Pvt. John Killian, Twenty-third NC, to sister Eliza, March 5, 1864, Talersville [Taylorsville] Station, Va., Eliza C. Killian Papers, SHC.

58. See Harris, *William Woods Holden*, 143–44; and Escott, *After Secession*, 202.

59. Surgeon Thomas Boykin to Vance, April 12, 1864, Zebulon Baird Vance Papers, Private Collections, vol. 4, NCDAH. Surgeon Boykin personally supported Vance but wrote to tell him about a conversation he had with a Private Oates, who had once endorsed Vance but now did not. Deprivation had worn down Oates's support for Vance, but the final straw, as Oates told Boykin, came when Vance met Oates on the streets of Raleigh and treated Oates and another enlisted man rudely. More evidence that Vance was losing his momentum came when in a special election for Congress, pro-Vance candidate Alfred G. Foster lost decisively to peace candidate James M. Leach, who captured a comfortable majority of votes among soldiers and citizens alike. Leach, despite his peace stance, took pains to separate himself from Holden. See McKinney, *Zeb Vance*, 214.

60. See, for example, Resolutions of Cooke's Brigade to Governor Vance, March 14, 1864, near Orange Court House, Va.; Seaton Gales to Governor Vance, March 16, 1864, Headquarters, Ramseur's Brigade; Officers of the Fifty-eighth and Sixtieth NC

Infantry to Governor Vance, March 24, 1864, near Dalton, Ga., all in Zebulon Baird Vance Papers, Governor's Papers, box 11, NCDAH.

61. For accounts of Vance's visits to North Carolina troops in Virginia, see *Fayetteville Observer*, April 11, 1864, 2, and April 18, 1864, 1; and Max R. Williams, "The General and the Governor: Robert E. Lee and Zebulon B. Vance," in *Audacity Personified: The Generalship of Robert E. Lee*, ed. Peter S. Carmichael (Baton Rouge: Louisiana State University Press, 2004), 108–11.

62. Holden featured several "Specimens of Gubernatorial Literature," including Vance's exclamation to soldiers that "you must fight till you fill hell so full of Yankees that their feet will stick out of the windows," *Weekly Standard*, May 18, 1864, 1. Private George Williams noted that in Vance's speech, the governor said "he wants to fighte until hell freases over and then fight on the ice." See Pvt. George Williams, Seventh NC, to "Father and mother," April 5, 1864, near Gordonsville, Va., Williams-Womble Papers, NCDAH.

63. Wounded Soldier, Co. K, Eighteenth NCST, to Holden, July 4, 1864, Kitrellas, N.C., in *Weekly Standard*, July 13, 1864, 1.

64. Pvt. Adelphos Burns, Forty-eighth NC, to "Father," July 17, 1864, Petersburg, Va., Adelphos J. Burns Letters, NCDAH.

65. Pvt. George Williams, Seventh NC, to "Father and mother," April 5, 1864, near Gordonsville, Va., Williams-Womble Papers, NCDAH. Interestingly, neither Burns, Williams, nor any other soldier who opposed Vance brought up the speech's sections on slavery or racial disorder.

66. Pvt. David Thompson, Twenty-seventh NC, to "Mother," March 27, 1864, near Orange Court House, Va., Samuel Thompson Papers, SHC.

67. Sgt. Isaac LeFevers, Forty-sixth NC, to "Relatives at home," April 29, 1864, near Orange Court House, Va., Isaac LeFevers Papers, NCDAH.

68. "To the People of North Carolina," *Weekly Standard*, April 6, 1864, 3.

69. Holden to Calvin J. Cowles, March 18, 1864, quoted in Harris, *William Woods Holden*, 142.

70. *Weekly Standard*, April 6, 1864.

71. The closest the *Weekly Standard* came to answering explicit and implicit charges that peace negotiations were tantamount to abolition appeared on page 2 of the May 18, 1864, issue in an article signed "Patriota," which briefly acknowledged the accusation by writing, "It is said that none but the poor and illiterate are Conservatives," and then immediately answering, "Many of the 28,000 slaveholders in this State are true Conservatives, and even if this were not so, 'The poor have rights, if they be all, / And these the patriot will defend.'"

72. See, for example, *Weekly Standard*, May 18, 1864, 1, 3, and May 25, 1864, 1, 2.

73. Ibid., May 25, 1864, 1.

74. See McKinney, *Zeb Vance*, 224–25; and Harris, *William Woods Holden*, 150–51.

75. *Weekly Standard*, July 9, 1864, 1.

76. On Union occupation of and black settlement in Plymouth, see Durrill, *War of Another Kind*, 181–83.

77. Affidavit of Sgt. Samuel Johnson, Second U.S. Colored Cavalry, in the field, Va., July 11, 1864, in Ira Berlin et al., eds., *Freedom: A Documentary History of Emancipation, 1861–1867*, series 2, *The Black Military Experience* (New York: Cambridge University Press, 1982), 588–89. For more on Confederate killing of black Union prisoners and violence against the town of Plymouth, see Durrill, *War of Another Kind*, 204–8.

78. In fact, Vance made sure to make reference to North Carolina troops' captures of Plymouth, a town listeners knew to be occupied by former slaves, when he traveled to Fayetteville on April 21, 1864, to repeat his famous campaign speech. See the *Fayetteville Observer*, April 25, 1864, 3.

79. Capt. Henry Chambers, Forty-ninth NC, diary entry dated March 9, 1864, Suffolk, Va., Henry Chambers Papers, NCDAH.

80. *Richmond Examiner*, April 28, 1864, repeated in the *North Carolina Times* (New Bern), May 21, 1864, as quoted in Durrill, *War of Another Kind*, 208. The *Weekly Standard* was not publishing at the time of the Battle of Plymouth, but even when it resumed in May, it did not take the same triumphant tone. In fact, it barely mentioned Plymouth at all. One short article in the May 18, 1864, edition confines itself to describing the military maneuvers of the *Albemarle* and of General Hoke's brigade and then to commending the "highly praiseworthy" conduct of the North Carolina troops involved.

81. Sgt. Garland Ferguson, Twenty-fifth NC, to "Brother," July 13, 1864, between Chattahoochee River and Atlanta, Ga., Evelyn McInstosh Hyatt Collection, NCDAH.

82. Ibid., July 28, 1864.

83. See Pvt. R. P. Allen, Fourth NC Cavalry, to "Wife," July 28, 1864, near Petersburg, Va., R. P. Allen Letters, Museum of the Confederacy, Richmond, Va.; Capt. Henry Chambers, Forty-ninth NC, diary, July (n.d.), 1864, Suffolk, Va., Henry Chambers Papers, NCDAH; Richmond Mumford Pearson Papers, Duke University. The Richmond Mumford Pearson Papers contain not only election returns from numerous hospitals (General Hospital No. 5, Wilmington, N.C., and Tarboro Wayside Hospital, for instance) but also the returns for the First NC Battalion of Sharpshooters and the returns for Yadkin County soldiers stationed at Salisbury, N.C., on July 28, the day of the vote. In each case, Vance defeated Holden.

84. Pvt. Henry Patrick, Forty-first NC, to "Wife," August 13, 1864, near Petersburg, Va., Henry Machen Patrick Letters, NCDAH. Patrick admitted that one member of his regiment had voted for Holden but explained the anomaly by pointing out that the man had spent part of his life in the abolition stronghold of Boston.

85. Vance ran for a state rather than Confederate office, and the state in which he ran was atypical in that it contained a larger and more organized peace movement than any other Confederate state. Nonetheless, soldiers from other states watched the contest eagerly. South Carolina private William Templeton, for instance, heard Vance speak at Orange Court House, Virginia, and called the speech the best he ever heard. See Pvt. William Templeton, Twelfth SC, to "Sister," April 4, 1864, near Orange Court House, Va., Joseph and William Templeton Papers, South Carolina Library, University of South Carolina. Georgia cavalryman Noble John Brooks noted that

North Carolina seemed to be "in better spirits" in April than it had been the previous September, and he attributed the improvement to "the salutary effect" that "Gov. Vance's speech" exerted "on the public mind." See Pvt. Noble John Brooks, Cobb's Legion of Georgia Cavalry, diary, April 21, 1864, Hillsboro, N.C., Noble John Brooks Papers, Georgia Department of Archives and History, Atlanta. Men from outside North Carolina, in other words, considered Vance and his platform to be worthy of their attention.

JOHN C. INSCOE

To Do Justice to North Carolina

*The War's End according to Cornelia Phillips
Spencer, Zebulon B. Vance, and David L. Swain*

At the beginning of *Patriotic Gore*, his classic study of the literature of the Civil War, Edmund Wilson asked, "Has there ever been another historical crisis of the magnitude of 1861–65 in which so many people were so articulate?" He went on to muse that "the drama has already been staged by characters who have written their own parts; and the peculiar fascination of this literature which leads one to go on and on reading it is rather like that of [Robert] Browning's *The Ring and the Book*, in which the same story is told from the points of view of nine different persons."[1]

Although Cornelia Phillips Spencer was not one of the authors on whom Wilson focused, her postwar narrative, *The Last Ninety Days of the War in North Carolina*, published in serial form in the fall of 1865 and as a book the following year, represents a prime example of varied agendas at play—her own and those of others. If she herself never emerged as one of her own "characters," she did allow other characters to write their own parts, in effect. There is indeed a "peculiar fascination" in the story of how she came to produce this first substantive "history" of North Carolina's role in the war and of the various factors—personal, political, and patriotic—that shaped her telling of it. Spencer would later join other North Carolinians and southerners as outspoken critics of Reconstruction and proponents of the "Lost Cause." But in writing her history of the war so soon after the fact, she established a significant precedent for numerous other southern women in the postwar decades who in a variety of venues would come to serve as interpreters of the war, defenders of the South and the Confederacy, and hagiographers of its leadership.

The legacy of the Civil War in North Carolina would have been far different had the conflict been brought to an end only a month or so earlier than it was. For it was only during the final throes of Confederate resistance that William T. Sherman's army marched into the state from the south.[2] Nearly sixty thousand Union forces crossed the border from South Carolina between March 6 and March 8, 1865. Sherman's first major target was Goldsboro, a key railroad juncture where he planned to join forces with General John M. Schofield, who commanded occupying forces in eastern North Carolina and would provide new resources and supply lines to Sherman's men. En route, Sherman's columns moved through Fayetteville, where they destroyed an armory and a substantial stash of grain and foodstuffs, along with several public buildings. Joseph E. Johnston, recently renamed as the commander of forces opposing Sherman, mounted far more military resistance than Union troops had faced since Atlanta. A skirmish at Monroe's Cross-Roads on March 10 and a day-long clash at Averasboro on March 16 only briefly delayed the Union thrust; far more serious was the battle of Bentonville, just west of Goldsboro, where Johnston's concentrated forces caught Federal troops off guard on March 19 and nearly crushed them. Sherman responded quickly enough to send reinforcements, who over the course of the next two days thoroughly outnumbered the Confederates and sent them into retreat.[3]

These upheavals, along with the constant activity of "bummers," Union raiders who took advantage of orders to forage for food and supplies and to pillage and destroy civilian property far more wantonly than authorized, proved as traumatic and as disruptive as anything North Carolina's civilians had faced over the course of the four-year conflict.[4] Yet perhaps because of the relative brevity of Sherman's presence in the state, there was a sense among North Carolinians at war's end that neither their suffering nor their efforts at resistance were fully appreciated by other southerners at the time or since. The pervasive peace movement in the state, the high level of desertion by Tar Heels, and the rampant internal dissension in several sections of the state, from the mountains to the coast, all suggested that, from the war's midpoint on, North Carolina had not pulled its weight in its support of the southern cause or in staving off Confederate defeat. Even Union troops moving into the state at war's end presumed that they were entering far friendlier territory than that they were leaving behind in South Carolina.[5] It was these impressions that many North Carolinians felt were unfair and needed to be challenged.

Among those who felt these slights to their home state most acutely was Cornelia Phillips Spencer. Certainly no one else articulated that frustration more often and more fully than she did, though she was rather ambivalent as to where the blame for these slights lay. In October 1865, she vented in her diary: "I feel ashamed of N. Carolina in some respects. She seems to lack some element of greatness." But she was quick to absolve the state itself of its poor standing and shifted the blame clearly onto those who refused to give North Carolinians their full due: "No state in the Confederacy did more for the cause than she, no state acted more handsomely, no state was more abused. N.C. was systematically insulted by the general Government of the Confederacy as unloyal, unreliable, and was suspected and accused of being secretly disposed toward reconstruction—this in the face of her efforts and her sacrifices in the Southern cause."[6] To counter these indignities, Spencer responded in the most substantive manner possible: she wrote a history of North Carolina's war, focusing on its final weeks, when its residents experienced its full fury, a story she felt many people—North and South—needed to know.

Spencer had plenty of encouragement to produce her history from other like-minded Tar Heel citizens. Two men in particular, both former governors, were influential not only in encouraging her to write but in shaping the narrative that she ultimately produced. Both David L. Swain and Zebulon B. Vance, close colleagues themselves, felt a crying need for Spencer's story to reach a broad readership. If their prime motives were, like Spencer's, to provide a corrective to the way in which North Carolina's sacrifices and trauma had been overlooked by those outside the state, they also had in Spencer a close friend who could be counted on to use this history to restore their own reputations that, for very different reasons, had been greatly damaged at the war's end.

It was Swain, president of the University of North Carolina and Spencer's longtime mentor and confidante, who first urged her to produce such a history. Sometime in the summer of 1865, he proposed that she write a narrative of recent events. "He wished a record made that might be published of North Carolina's position at the close of the war," Spencer informed Vance in sharing the finished manuscript with him in late October. "After some consultation it was decided that the article should be extended so as to include a slight sketch, also of the few months immediately preceding the *finale*."[7]

Governor Vance had been, in the war's last month, "obsessed with the fear that he and his state would become scapegoats for the failure of the Confederacy," as Gordon B. McKinney, his most recent biographer, has put it.[8] Thus Vance too was particularly eager to see Spencer chronicle just how fully the state had suffered. "Withhold nothing of the truth of the outrages of Sherman's army," he instructed her when he learned of her intention to produce such a narrative. In what quickly became an impassioned harangue, he told her that "it would be an outrage to suppress the truth of history under such circumstances." The fact that the South had lost the war made it all the more imperative that its story be told by southerners.

"History," the former governor insisted, "the nemesis of the oppressed, personating the righteous anger of the gods, is to avenge us with the scorn of posterity upon our despoiled memories; and I pray that no Southern pen may help to turn its consuming fierceness from its legitimate prey."[9]

Such were the impulses that drove Spencer to tell that story and shaped the means by which she did so. She consulted with both Swain and Vance, along with other prominent participants and not-so-prominent eyewitnesses to the war's final days, to produce what is by turns an oral history, a compilation of correspondence and official documentation, a reflective essay on the nature of war and what it does to those who wage it, and, first and foremost, a vigorous defense of North Carolina and its leadership.

But if the impact of Sherman's devastation of the Old North State remained the primary impetus for Spencer's narrative, equally obvious was her impulse to provide that rehabilitation for prominent friends and acquaintances who found themselves or their actions at war's end either misunderstood or unappreciated, particularly Vance and Swain. In defending them, Spencer's agenda became closely entwined with theirs; together, their story tells us much about the very conscious attempts of certain southerners to control their own memories and interpretations of the war for themselves, for posterity, and, in this particular case, for their state. The fact that these men relied so heavily on the ability and the credibility of a woman to salvage their reputations and establish their places in history is at one level quite extraordinary; and yet it foreshadows the roles later undertaken by many other women, through other means and in other guises, in rehabilitating their Confederate men, both individually and collectively, over the course of the "Lost Cause" era.

In some respects, Cornelia Spencer seems an unlikely historian of the war. Certainly other southern women wrote about the war, though only recently have scholars given serious attention to their role in creating a written record of the conflict and its legacy.[10] But most of their writings were far more personal—the publication of their journals, diaries, or memoirs of the war as they and their families had experienced it—or more literary, in the form of novels, short stories, or even poetry.

As Sarah E. Gardner notes in *Blood and Irony*, her recent study of southern women's Civil War narratives, most women writers did not see the writing of "history," in the traditional sense of the term, within their purview. Georgia novelist Augusta Evans, perhaps the most successful of wartime authors, informed Alexander Stephens that she was not sure a woman could write critically on "military matters." She admitted that sentimentality and even hero worship would compromise any claims to objectivity, noting that "my heart vetoes the verdict of my judgment."[11] Sarah Dorsey, who wrote a biography of Louisiana's wartime governor, also expressed reservations about the prospects of those of her gender taking on the role of historian. "It is an ambitious venture for women with her feminine mind," Dorsey wrote in 1866, "which is too entirely *subjective* to attempt in any way *the* writing of history." General history, she felt, was far too "panoramic" for women to undertake, requiring instead "the broad, objective grasps of the masculine soul."[12]

Spencer seemed to have no such qualms. Although she had been an ardent diarist and correspondent from her early adulthood, nothing else in her background suggested that she had any aspirations or talents for more conventional historical narrative. In fact, given that the vast majority of nonfictional published writings by southern women after the war were their journals, diaries, and memoirs, it is particularly striking how little of her own experience found its way into her narrative. And yet, from the beginning, she had the enthusiastic support and encouragement of two former governors who never indicated any doubt as to her abilities in taking on this decidedly unconventional task. Vance confided to Swain, "The more Miss Corny has to do with scheme and the less anyone else, the better."[13]

Born in 1826 in Harlem (not yet a part of New York City) to James Phillips, a British-born mathematician, and Judith, his New Jersey–born wife, Cornelia was still an infant when her father accepted a faculty position at the University of North Carolina and moved south with his family, which included Cornelia's two older brothers. She spent most of the rest of her life in Chapel Hill, where the Phillipses made themselves integral parts of both university and village life. In 1851, she met a third-year student from Alabama, James Munroe Spencer, and married him four years later. They moved to Clinton, Alabama, where Spencer had already established a law practice, and in 1859, Cornelia gave birth to their only child, Julia. James suffered from poor health throughout the marriage and in June 1861 died at a mere thirty-four years of age.[14]

By early 1862, the grieving widow and her young daughter returned to her parents' home in Chapel Hill. Although she continued to make regular diary entries, few make any mention of the Civil War during its first two years. Preoccupied with her widowhood and some hearing loss, she bemoaned in June 1862, "My hearing is going and with it my youth and hope and love. . . . God in His Providence has brought me back here to sit among the ruins of my happiness, to *sit here*, and *look on*, and *remember*."[15]

Spencer struggled with bouts of depression throughout the rest of the war, and it took the president of the university to provide her with at least one therapeutic outlet for her personal woes. Sometime in the summer of 1865, Swain suggested that she write an account of recent events.

Spencer had known David Lowery Swain for most of her life. In 1836, the Asheville native and former governor (1833–35) accepted an offer to become the president of the still young university. He would serve in that role for the next thirty-three years, until his death in 1868, and during the antebellum years, he oversaw a dramatic growth spurt in both physical facilities and personnel that gave UNC the highest student enrollment of any southern college and made it among the most prosperous by the eve of the war.[16] Upon their arrival in 1836, Swain and his family moved into a house on East Franklin Street, just across the street from the Phillips home. For an impressionable ten-year-old girl, this distinguished new neighbor quickly became a father figure, and as she grew to adulthood, Swain remained a mentor and close confidante.

It was as a college student that a twenty-one-year-old Zeb Vance also came to know both Swain and Spencer. President Swain was an acquaintance of the Baird family, including Margaret, Vance's mother, and he generously offered her son a personal loan of three hundred dollars in order to attend the university. During Vance's one year as a student, 1851–52, Swain became a friend and mentor to this fellow Buncombe County native. At the same time, the Phillips family befriended Vance, and he seemed to have formed a particularly close relationship with Cornelia, who was five years his senior.[17]

When at war's end Swain suggested that Spencer undertake a history of recent events, he had nothing as ambitious as a book in mind, nor did she. As noted earlier, he had proposed an article, to which she decided to add "a slight sketch" of the war's final months. Only as the writing process got underway did that article turn into a series of articles published at weekly intervals that, by year's end, would be compiled into book form.[18]

Other factors figured heavily as influences on Spencer's historical narrative. Yet another acquaintance and former university faculty member provided her with the venue to publish her work. Charles F. Deems had been recruited by President Swain to come to UNC in 1842, where he served as a professor of logic and rhetoric for several years. He then moved on to other southern institutions before abandoning academia for the ministry in New York City. At the war's end, Deems edited a religious newspaper, the *Watchman*, and to promote sectional reconciliation by giving northern readers access to southern voices, he offered to publish what became a series of articles by his old acquaintance from Chapel Hill.[19]

A very different impetus for Spencer's determination to write came in the form of another chronicle of the war's latter days in North Carolina. General Sherman's aide-de-camp, Major George Ward Nichols, kept a daily journal of the army's experiences from the Atlanta campaign through Johnston's surrender. He moved quickly after the war's end to publish it by July 1865 as a celebratory—and to southerners, quite smug—book entitled *The Story of the Great March*. "Sherman's army rests upon the laurels it has bravely won," Nichols wrote in a preface. "Its heroes are now in other fields of duty, and a grateful Nation thanks them for their gallant deeds."[20]

That self-congratulatory tone much offended Spencer and many other southerners, offenses compounded by the fact that Nichols's book was so well received in the North and sold remarkably well as one of the first of many military memoirs that would eventually find their way into print. Swain had presented a copy to Cornelia Spencer, who declared with disgust in her journal: "I cannot read the Yankee glorifications with any coolness. It is like enveloping oneself in a blister. How I do hate the whole Yankee nation when I put such a book down."[21] Edward J. Hale, the editor of the *Fayetteville Observer* whose office was burned down by Sherman's men, reflected the sentiments of many when he declared to Spencer: "A fellow named Nichols, of Sherman's staff, has written a book to glorify the 'Great March' & to excuse or conceal its villainies."[22]

Spencer found particularly irksome Nichols's denial of any atrocities committed by Sherman's troops in North Carolina, and she went out of her way to refute him directly and repeatedly in her narrative. To cite merely one example, she concludes a detailed description of the plunder of Fayetteville homes and farms with a quote from *The Great March*: "Private property in Fayetteville has been respected to a degree which is remarkable." Her quick retort: "It is just possible that Major Nichols did not know the truth; that, being very evidently of an easy and credulous temper, and too busy making up his little book for sale, he allowed himself to be imposed upon by wicked jokers." She continued: "He was evidently hard of hearing besides; for he says 'I have yet to hear of a single outrage offered to a woman by a soldier of our army,'" which she refuted with several examples to the contrary. Ultimately, Spencer said, the only reason for "prolonging these painful memories" was that northerners should know that "the career of the grand army in the Great March, brilliant as was the design, masterly as was the execution, and triumphant as was the issue, is yet, in its details, a story of which they have no reason to be proud." If the full truth were revealed to them, she claimed, "their bitterness toward the South would turn into tender pity, their exultation over her into a manly regret and remorse."[23]

Equally offensive to Spencer was Nichols's claim that her state was more Unionist in sentiment than that from which he entered it. She wrote: "It is very evident that General Sherman entered North Carolina with the confident expectation of receiving a welcome from its Union-loving citizens." Nichols had claimed a perceptible difference in the conduct of his men— no sign of plundering, or of fire and smoke, which had been so evident in their wake in South Carolina. "Our men seem to understand," he wrote, "that they are entering a State which has suffered for its Union sentiment, and whose inhabitants would gladly embrace the old flag again if they can have the opportunity, which we mean to give them." Such assumptions, Spencer noted, were quickly corrected, and "their amiable dispositions were speedily corrected and abandoned."[24] With great satisfaction, she was able to quote Nichols's own retraction of his preconceptions about the Old North State. "Thus far," he wrote after a full week within its bounds, "we have been painfully disappointed in looking for the Union sentiment in North Carolina, about which so much has been said. Our experience is decidedly in favor of its sister State." In fact, he concluded, "the rebels have shown more pluck at Averasboro and at Bentonville than we have encountered since leaving Atlanta."[25]

Spencer admitted that the need to refute Nichols had much to do with prompting her to put pen to paper, and she felt that nothing would bring about reconciliation more effectively than southerners being allowed to set the record straight for northern readers. In a remarkable letter to an old friend in Connecticut (the sister-in-law of UNC professor Elisha Mitchell), Spencer herself confided that the war had created a "great gulf" between northerners and southerners, one that she very much hoped "may be filled up some time or other, in God's own good time." She wrote that "words which passed from North to South, and back again, did more to set us against each other than the bullets." She acknowledged that misconceptions were mutual—"I look back aghast now to think what lies we swallowed about you, and . . . what lies you swallowed about us"—but went on to implore, "Now dear friend, cannot you get rid of some of your prejudices and try to understand that the South was sinned against, as well as sinning?"[26]

Yet her true intent was hardly a two-way corrective, nor as conciliatory as her letter to Connecticut suggested. Spencer never abandoned her own charges of misbehavior by Union troops; indeed, their atrocities would become a major theme in her book. She also suggested that they were alone in committing such acts. "Our pastime in war," she informed her Connecticut correspondent, "was not in burning houses and ravaging open country, or stripping or starving women and children. We fought honestly, we planned no assassinations, nor wholesale murders, such as the Northern press complimented us by ascribing to us."[27]

If it was the depredations of Sherman's March that provided the most obvious impetus for Spencer's narrative, her devotion to her two close friends seems to have been equally as strong a motivating factor. Spencer sent the manuscript of her first article to Vance, then living in Statesville, on October 30 and explained that Swain had proposed that the narrative be given "value and dignity by inserting certain individuals and interesting letters . . . by various distinguished gentlemen during that time." She went on to confide that Swain's "main object however in the enterprise appears to me to have honor due and justice done to *Gov. Vance*," an object she made clear was one she fully embraced as well.[28]

In part, she was asking the governor for permission to include some of his private correspondence in her history. Swain had shared with Spencer letters he had received from Vance, and she assured the latter that "I have seen no letter of yours that does not do you honor, and which would not if published still further enhance your reputation." Her admiration was unequivocal, and she gushed to Vance that, having read his letters, she was "glad to know that North Carolina was even more right than we had supposed when she chose you for her leader. We will have you in that chair again Governor, or in one still higher, for I know that I am only one of the many thousands in our State whose hearts throb warmly with admiration and affectionate regret for *our own* Governor."[29]

Vance expressed his thanks and surprise at Spencer's efforts on his behalf. "I am truly gratified, not so much at the handsome things said about myself, but at the fact that in my checkered career I have been able notwithstanding my follies and short-comings, to inspire such disinterested and sincere friendship in your breast & the Governor's [Swain]." He offered only minor corrections to her account but did ask that one of his letters—a diatribe against Jefferson Davis—be deleted. In September 1864, Vance had confided to Swain his pessimism as to the Confederacy's future and blamed Davis. "By the time the President . . . displays again his obstinacy in defying public opinion and his ignorance of men," Vance vented, "the ruin will be complete."[30] In reference to those remarks, Vance told Spencer, "I confess some repugnance to making public my remarks on Mr. Davis in the letter you copy. When they were written he was in power, and backed by great armies; now he is in chains and a mean mob is clamoring of his blood." Vance claimed no regrets in having made such "fair criticism of public men" but insisted that he would never stoop to "countenance that basest and most cowardly of all human frailties—the striking of a fallen foe."[31]

Spencer responded that she appreciated his feelings and "had more than a dim sense while I was copying your letter that perhaps it ought to be omitted." But she did not let the issue rest. She told Vance that she felt sure President Davis would no longer be in prison—"I have an idea that Pres. Johnson means to make a general *jail delivery* on his Thanksgiving day," she confided. In addition, she reasoned, "It will be another valuable testimony of your good judgment and insights. . . . [A]mong other things it will be well for *some* people to know that you were no blind follower of President Davis."[32]

Despite his recognition of what an opportunity Spencer's history offered, both as a response to his critics and as a chance to rehabilitate a faltering postwar reputation, Vance was also politically savvy enough to fear that perhaps her chronicle had become too blatantly a paean to him and his administration. In a later letter, he gingerly suggested to her that perhaps the whole in its present form was a bit too transparent and that it might achieve more credibility if the positive spin were a bit more subtle. It "seemed to impress the reader with the idea of something as the lawyers say 'dehors the record' interpolated to prejudice the case in favor of Gov. Vance." In its present form, he noted, the title of the work could be "A Vindication of Gov. Vance" instead of "The Last Ninety Days of the War in N Ca." Hammering the point, he continued: "The latter title is the best one, both to make a readable work, and to vindicate me, provided that the said 'Vindication' doesn't stick out too plainly." Applying the lessons of history, Vance concluded: "Half the world learned to regard Charles I as a sainted Martyr from [British philosopher and historian David] Hume's 'History of England,' whereas his 'Vindication of Charles 1st' would have been set down as the zeal of a partisan. Do you take my idea?"[33]

On the other hand, Vance admitted to Spencer that "perhaps my greatest desire [is] to be vindicated before my countrymen."[34] It was only after the success of the series of *Watchman* articles, as she began to expand those articles into a book-length manuscript, that Spencer confronted him with the most serious allegations behind his great desire for vindication—his behavior in the face of Sherman's invasion of Raleigh, actions that had raised doubts among both his critics and his allies as to his sense of duty and honor and even his courage. In April 1866, she first broached what she called "the delicate point regarding your movements after leaving Raleigh." She explained to Vance that "I am (in my book) now closing up the last few desperate days of the Confederacy, when the bottom fell out so unexpectedly." She hoped that he would think it advisable to "let on" about the reasons he was hindered from returning. She was very forthright in stating that "many of your friends, Gov. S. among them, have always regretted your leaving Raleigh." Swain, she said, "thinks you should be our Gov now — & never have been deposed." Others, it seems, recognized why Vance left but felt that his failure to return was his ultimate offense.[35]

As Union forces advanced on Raleigh, the governor left the city on April 12 and made his way first to Chapel Hill, to seek out Swain, and then to Hillsborough, to see William A. Graham. The governor had consulted closely with both of these former governors in the weeks leading up to Sherman's arrival at the capital and the collapse of the Confederacy. Finding neither man at home — ironically, both were in Raleigh — Vance proceeded on to Greensboro, where he had been summoned for a consultation with Jefferson Davis, as Davis fled south from Virginia after Richmond's fall, only to find that he had missed the Confederate president, who had moved on to Charlotte a day earlier. But the fact that Vance did not return to Raleigh led his opponents, William W. Holden, editor and political figure, chief among them, to accuse him of abandoning his office and his duties and even of undercutting the Confederacy by not being present when Sherman ultimately arrived in the city and the terms of North Carolina's surrender were worked out between the Union commander and General Johnston with no input from the state's governor.[36]

A related point of contention was Vance's decision nearly three weeks earlier not to call the legislature into session as Sherman began his advance on Raleigh from Goldsboro. In late March, William Graham, just returning home from the dissolved Confederate Congress in Richmond, urged such a move in order that the state General Assembly could issue a resolution declaring North Carolina's readiness to make peace and invite other states to do likewise, or merely negotiate the state's own peace with Sherman himself. Vance remained reluctant to take that step, and Graham in a later letter to Swain claimed that the governor had missed an opportunity to end the war several weeks earlier and thus spare the state the damage it suffered in those final days. Swain had shared that letter with Spencer, and she had included it in the sixth of her *Watchman* articles.[37]

Spencer admitted to Vance that that letter had "made an unfavorable impression on me." "Not calling the Gen Ass. & doing something to avert our ruin," she wrote, along with his failure to return to Raleigh, "really did lead me to suppose that your wisdom was under some temporary eclipse at that time & that you preferred to hold on to some wild & visionary hopes for the Confederacy." But once she read his recent "account of your journey from Raleigh & *why* — & why also you never returned, did I understand enough to do you justice."[38]

Vance welcomed the chance to set the record straight and in a series of letters provided Spencer with a detailed account of his actions of the previous year and the rationales behind them. On April 11, on the advice of General Johnston, the governor had sent both Swain and Graham as commissioners by special train with a "flag of truce" and a letter for Sherman, then stationed fourteen miles south of the capital city. His delegates were instructed to "learn verbally upon what terms I could remain & exercise the functions of my office, &c." Late that day he learned that the train had been captured and Swain and Graham detained. At that point, he determined that he should leave the city himself. "I made all my arrangements for leaving, wrote letters to Sherman for the Mayor of the city, asking protection for its inhabitants, the Asylums, public buildings &c and lingered until midnight still hoping the Commissioners might return."[39]

Assuming they had been purposefully detained or even captured, and "not being willing to trust myself in their (Yankee) hands without terms so long as 8,000 N.C. soldiers under Gen. Hoke remained under arms, I got on my horse and rode out of town to Hoke's camp." While some of his friends thought Vance had made a mistake in leaving the city, he insisted that "whilst there was a soldier in the field I stood with him, and it saved me the humiliation of being afterwards thrust out of my office and treated with personal indignity as Gen. Schofield intimated to me at Greensboro would have been the case."[40]

That merely answered the question of why Vance left Raleigh. As to why he didn't return, it was another letter altogether in which he provided Spencer with an explanation. Once he failed to locate either Swain or Graham and missed finding Jefferson Davis in Greensboro, Vance followed him to Charlotte, where they met briefly on April 19. In the meantime, Sherman and Johnston had met on April 18 and negotiated a treaty, the terms of which were sent on to Washington for governmental approval. Given that development, Vance claimed that meeting with Davis was fruitless, in that he talked "wildly about rallying Lee's scattered men around Johnston, appealing to the people forming another army sufficient to prolong the war &c.," which Vance merely termed Davis's "imperfectly constituted genius . . . extremely stubborn in adherence to his own opinions, and absolutely blind to those things which his prejudices or hopes did not desire to see."[41]

Vance returned almost immediately to Greensboro and learned there that the first treaty between Sherman and Johnston had been disapproved and negotiations were to resume. "I demanded & rec'd permission for Mr. Worth [Jonathan Worth, the state treasurer] to go to Raleigh bearing a letter to Sherman." But once it became apparent that Sherman was no longer in the city, Vance explained that General Schofield, himself en route to Greensboro, "declined to permit my return to Raleigh." He waited for Schofield to arrive "to surrender myself or learn the pleasure of the Govt. towards me."[42]

As for Graham's charges as to the opportunities missed by Vance's failure to call the legislature into session, Vance stated simply that he did not want North Carolina to become the first state to initiate a plea for peace. Graham, who had been a member of the Confederate Congress when it disbanded, had tried to convince him that "the matter had been settled in Richmond that the war was to be closed by the backing down of individual states, one by one" and that now, quoting Graham, 'N.C. not hampered by former committals, false pride of opinion,' &c., was selected to *lead* the roll of infamy as she had been made to *follow* in the struggle for independence." This honor, Vance concluded, "I felt inclined to deny my native state. I told [Graham] that if S.C. or Ala. were whipped, it was *their* duty to say so, and that by saying it for them, thought they would doubtless gladly take the benefit for it, yet five generations would not have the end of their denunciations."[43]

It was thus posterity—his own and that of his state—that Vance insisted was his prime concern in not bringing the legislature together to initiate the peace process. He and his fellow North Carolinians "would never cease to hear of our defection as the cause of our failure," he insisted. "I asked [Graham] why *they* (the men with whom he consulted & who advised him) did not take steps to move their own states & people and provide for their own salvation? They were afraid of the *odium of history*!" As if that alone were not reason enough for Vance to have disregarded Graham's proposal, he equivocated by drawing on a legal technicality. Even if he had wanted to do so, he claimed, his Council of State, whose authorization was required to call the General Assembly into session, had split evenly on the matter, so that "I could not call it unless by consent of a majority of a quorum."[44] But of course, far more significant is the fact that his first line of defense was one that linked his own postwar legacy with that of North Carolina itself.

Spencer responded to Vance's explanations with enthusiasm and assured the governor that she would make sure that she would use her final entries in the *Watchman* series to set the record straight. "In the summing up the last No, I wish to say something of the State's action or rather *in*action at the close—show that it *could not* have done otherwise than it did through our Executive—(namely do nothing at all)—say this & say it so well & say it so undeniably that it *will never need to be said over again!*"[45]

In her book, Spencer limited her coverage of the exchange between Vance and Graham to their own words, though she made it clear that she gave Vance the full benefit of the doubt in terms of the wisdom of his restraint in acting upon Graham's advice. She stated that she was "assured of [Vance's] inaction in this momentous crisis, deprecated as it was at the time, by one party as evincing too little energy in behalf of peace . . . ; and reviled by the other as indicative of a disposition toward inglorious surrender and reconstruction, was in effect, *masterly*, that masterly inactivity with which he who surveys the tumult of conflict from an eminence, may foresee and calmly await the approaching and inevitable end."[46]

By the same token, Spencer echoed Vance's self-defense in terms of why he failed to return to Raleigh but, again, avoided the explicit explanation that he had recently provided her. She simply stated: "While Generals Johnston and Sherman were engaged in their negotiations, Governor Vance found that having obeyed President Davis's summons to Greensboro before accepting General Sherman's invitation to Raleigh, he was effectually precluded from all further participation in the affairs of the State." More evasively, she noted in her next sentence: "I am not at liberty to say why or how this was; but it is probable that the Governor himself does not very deeply regret it, since it is not likely he would have been permitted by the Federal authorities to retain his office, even if had returned to Raleigh and resumed the reins."[47]

She argued further that as "matters have since turned out," it was for the best that Vance was not in Raleigh, reasoning that "he and his noble State were equally incapable of any attempt to make terms for themselves, even had it been likely that any terms would have been granted. Our fortunes were to be those of our sister States whom we had joined deliberately, fought for, and suffered with," the latter obviously a reflection of Vance's own argument as to the pitfalls of any attempt at unilateral action on the behalf of North Carolina or its governor. Having established that nothing was lost by the governor's absence from the state capital, she then confirmed that General Schofield had denied him permission to return to

Raleigh when the two met in Greensboro following Vance's meeting with Davis in Charlotte.[48]

Even more challenging for Spencer than having to explain Vance's flight from Raleigh was dealing with the awkward fact that Swain found himself the father-in-law of one of Sherman's officers, Brigadier General Smith Atkins of Illinois. Atkins had led four thousand Michigan cavalry into Chapel Hill on April 17, hot on the heels of Confederate general Joseph Wheeler's cavalry, which had been encamped in the university town for three days until they retreated upon word of Atkins's advance. Two days after his arrival, Atkins made a courtesy call on the college president, where he met Swain's twenty-one-year-old daughter, Eleanor. It seemed to have been love at first sight, for when the Union general left Chapel Hill two weeks later, Ellie Swain announced to her parents that they were engaged.[49]

Spencer of course knew Ellie Swain well, and the romantic in her reveled in her young friend's whirlwind courtship. Yet she was troubled by the impact of this romance and wedding—only four months after the couple met—on the father of the bride. Within a week of the wedding, she recorded in her diary: "This marriage was of ill omen to Governor Swain. The blight that immediately fell upon the University was directly attributable to the fact that he not only permitted his daughter to marry an invader, but that he gave her a fine wedding." It seriously divided the residents of Chapel Hill, with very few attending the ceremony in August. "Invitations were *spit upon*" in one or two houses, she wrote.[50] According to a student diary, feelings were so strong that on the day of the wedding, students tried to disrupt the ceremony by loudly tolling the college bell for over three hours, then hanging Swain and Atkins in effigy. Spencer confided in her journal that rumors abounded statewide that Ellie Swain departed for her groom's home in Illinois "loaded with finery and jewels stolen from women of states farther south, and given to her by her husband."[51]

Swain found it hard to shake the stigma of the marriage, and his continued leadership of the university remained in doubt for as much as a year later, as it still struggled to get underway again. In September 1866, Spencer reported to a friend that "General and Mrs. Atkins came home this week. Most persons think it a great pity she should come home at all in such a crisis in our affairs." Local residents, she noted, "were all full of the general talk and excitement against Governor Swain" and that the Atkinses' appearance in Chapel Hill "has increased the bitterness. Everyone agrees that the Governor must resign, or the University is doomed, yet nobody will tell him so. I think he has no idea of resigning. He thinks he will live it down."[52] Cornelia obviously sympathized with her close friend and mentor, and his vindication was at least as important to her as that of the governor, though she struggled with how to do so through her narrative.

Early on in the undertaking of her history, she confided to Vance: "That very business of Gen. Atkins has worried me no little in connection with the 'last 90 days.'" Atkins's behavior in overseeing the Union occupation of Chapel Hill was not, in itself, the root of the problem, although he was not blameless in that regard. Swain, well before he realized that Atkins would soon be a part of his family, wrote an assessment of him to Sherman on April 19: "While he manifests a disposition to execute his orders with as much forbearance as he deems compatible with the proper discharge of his duty . . . nevertheless, many worthy families have been stripped by his soldiers of the necessary means of subsistence."[53]

Far more serious were stories of the ruthless treatment of Goldsboro and Fayetteville residents by Atkins's troops. How was Spencer to confront these atrocities in her narrative without doing further damage to the Swain family? "I have heard so much about his spoliations," she wrote to Vance. "In fact every man or woman in the State who lost a teaspoon by the Yankee raiders, is ready to swear it was stolen by '*Gen. Atkins & his staff.*' Especially down in Sampson [County] about the Faison neighborhood [near Clinton], the most awful stories are told. What's a body to do about it?"[54]

Indeed, reports from those towns and elsewhere confirmed the disruption and destruction of troops under Atkins's command, whether they implicated him directly or not in the atrocities they described. Charles P. Mallet produced a written statement of what took place in Fayetteville only days afterward and later provided Spencer with a copy of his report. "The whole town was swarming with yankees," Mallet testified. "Every house and store was entered, and except when guards were promptly obtained, were robbed of everything valuable or fit to eat." He detailed the havoc wreaked by this wholesale plunder but admitted that "no personal violence was offered in town, except divesting two or three gentlemen of their pants and boots and taking the watches and money of nearly every one." Far worse was what Sherman's men inflicted on the surrounding countryside, where "the outrages were hellish" and several men were physically tortured or shot. "At night, and every night for a week," Mallet wrote from his in-town perspective, "the horizon was brilliant with the flames of burning dwellings." Few houses were burned "where the Ladies staid at home, but nearly every Lady who did stay at home was grossly insulted; and fearing this, many preferred the burning to the insulting."[55]

Mallet never referred to Atkins by name but made it clear that the Union officers were fully complicit in the rampages of those under their command. "The officers say that such things are not allowed, and are contrary to orders," he stated, "but this is a lie. The whole thing is authorized and encouraged. One of the rascals was overheard reporting to a Colonel of a Reg't how he had been out robbing and plundering, at which the Colonel laughed heartily, told him it was all right, and to go ahead." He laid the blame for the "horrors of Sherman's visitation" right at the top: "It is the universal opinion that in the whole army there are not ten godly or pious men. Gen. Sherman has no use for any such. He is a fit chief for such an army—has no respect for God or man, or fear of the devil. . . . He is a perfect fanatic and will hear no reason, self-conceited, puffed up, and very profane."[56]

If Atkins was implicated merely by association with the atrocities in and around Fayetteville, reports from Clinton, a smaller community thirty miles to the east, were more explicit in singling him out for blame. On March 24, just after the battle of Bentonville nearby, Atkins led a brigade of cavalry back to Clinton to acquire supplies, knowing the town to be a base of Confederate storehouses. In response to an inquiry from Spencer regarding Atkins's behavior in particular, a local resident, H. A. Bizzell, provided her with the most specific and most damning testimony regarding Swain's new son-in-law.

Atkins, according to Bizzell, set up headquarters and watched as his men "entered every private residence in Clinton and carried off whatever they chose, chiefly whatever was most valuable and easily transportable. A great many families were left without any thing to eat." Bizzell claimed that they took the last of the meat from his own smokehouse, along with chickens, eggs, flour and meal, and other foodstuffs. As for Atkins's role in this wholesale theft, Bizzell wrote: "I only know this—the men for two days galloped up and down the road . . . carrying their plunder in the most public manner. I saw them carrying chairs, buggies, carriages and indeed whatever they fancied. . . . I never heard or saw any effort to restrain or even remonstrate with the men."[57]

More specifically, Bizzell told Spencer of Atkins's treatment of the families in whose homes he established his own headquarters. The first was a widow's farmhouse where he ordered that all the fencing around both her yard and garden be pulled down and burned. When his troops' horses then trampled the plants, "the old lady or one of her daughters requested Gen Atkins to spare it. He replied that he guessed the horses wouldn't hurt it much." According to the widow's later testimony, Atkins made no attempt to restrain his men, and when other local residents approached him about providing a guard or some protection against his unruly troops, he responded that "he guessed his men would not take more than they needed." Others testified that Atkins's cook carried with him "a large quantity of jewelry in a basket which he said he had taken from ladies South, and others on his staff were seen hauling mirrors, lamps, and large trunks of fine clothing in Atkins' own wagon."[58]

David Swain was eager to see such reports refuted and eagerly clung to Atkins's own denials. Spencer confided to Vance that she and Swain had spent many hours discussing "his son-in-law's character." "Gov. Swain is convinced that these stories have no foundation in fact," she informed the governor. "He has often talked the subject of plundering over with A . . . & A has repeatedly asserted that *his* hands were clean." Atkins seemed equally intent on convincing Cornelia Spencer of his innocence. He denied any such collusion with those who inflicted such damage on civilians in any of the communities through which he and his men passed and told her that "let who would in the Federal army enrich themselves, he left the South as poor as he entered it." He insisted to Spencer that "he would be willing to go into any house where he was quartered in N.C. & wd be sure of receiving a warm welcome." "I was very frank," she said, "& told him all I had ever heard of him. . . . He met it all quietly, good-naturedly & with a point blank denial, & declared himself willing to [undergo] any sort of investigation."[59]

It is clear that Spencer fell under his spell over the course of that discussion, for she concluded her letter to Vance by saying, "I am inclined to believe him," and then, tellingly, only a few lines later, "I am *willing* to believe him." Yet she remained perplexed as to how to deal with Atkins in print, with probably more concern for her publication's impact on Swain's reputation than on Atkins's. "I am thinking there are plenty of people who when the '90 days' comes out will charge me with 'suppressio veri,' and say that I & the Gov [Swain] & Dr. D [Charles Deems] do not tell all we ought to, or all we know."[60]

Vance responded to her dilemma by offering some very practical advice. "I appreciate your embarrassment on the Atkins question," he replied to her letter three days later. "Don't mention him at all, but withhold nothing of the truth of the outrages of Sherman's army, generally speaking." He ranted: "They would *all* like to dodge, but they are *all* responsible, whether their individual hands are stained with the plunder of women & children, or whether they served and associated without protest or comment with those who gorged upon the spoils of the helpless." Nevertheless, he concluded, "I can not see that you are called upon to particularize him [Atkins]."[61]

Spencer did just as the governor suggested. In her book, she provided vivid descriptions of the harsh treatment of civilians and their property by Sherman's troops in Fayetteville, Goldsboro, and other communities along their route. Yet she avoided naming individual officers in those passages and never mentioned Atkins in connection with any of them. She even avoided mention of Clinton altogether, thus ignoring the richly detailed eyewitness accounts accumulated and provided her by Bizzell.[62]

Shrewdly, Spencer made her only real reference to Atkins's military leadership in *The Last Ninety Days* through Swain's own words. She reproduced his April 19 comment to Sherman (cited above), which in very measured tones suggested that his son-in-law showed appropriate restraint in his occupation of Chapel Hill while nevertheless acknowledging that some households had been robbed and/or ransacked by his men.[63] In limiting her commentary on Atkins to this assessment by Swain, written only two days after Atkins and his men arrived in town (and ironically on the day on which Atkins met his future wife), Spencer not only absolved her close friend of any complicity in the Union occupation and in Atkins's behavior but also avoided any reference to accusations of Atkins's treatment of civilians elsewhere along Sherman's route that Chapel Hill residents would only later bring to the fore.

On the surface, Spencer's narrative of the war appears to be unique. It must be among the only factually based accounts of the war by a woman in which her personal experiences are subsumed so completely to the actions of men, both known and unknown. Not only are her own thoughts and actions not central to her account; they are practically nonexistent. In only a very few instances, primarily in describing the early occupation of Chapel Hill, does she ever lapse into the first person, with phrases like "I remember" or, in plural form, "a day to be remembered by us all" and "for the first time in four years we saw the old flag," to express reactions and experiences she shared with local residents at large. Even in those few passages, a comparison of her published account and that recorded in her journal at the time reveals how restrained she was in the latter, deleting from the book nearly all of the emotional intensity she and others felt as Union troops marched into town.[64]

And yet, such an impression of objective distance from her subject is deceptive, for personal friendships were always central in the creation of Spencer's narrative and a vital part of the agenda she set for herself in writing it. She admitted to Vance that those considerations had made her task far more difficult than she had anticipated. "I used to wonder why intelligent men who had lived and acted through important eras in history did not oftener have their experience and knowledge of facts and events on record," she wrote to the governor in May 1866, as she was still struggling with how to depict his actions in particular. "I see now that it is one of the hardest things to write clearly while the actors' minds are still heated and a thousand contradictory reports and views continually presented."[65]

But she was ultimately rewarded by an extraordinary assessment of the final product from Vance, especially in his acknowledgment of the qualities that he felt only a woman could have brought to the book. "The real value of these sketches does not consist in stringing together the prominent events of the War, in order," he told her in August 1866, "but in the graphic setting forth of the feelings and sufferings of our own people. This you have performed with such peculiar and womanly happiness that wherever you have turned from it to the recital of mere historical details, I have felt like I had got off the cars at Durham and had started in a miserable hack for Chapel Hill."[66]

There is hidden in this vivid, if odd, analogy a strong sense of gratitude for the personal vindication that Spencer provided Vance himself.[67] But perhaps more important is the governor's conclusion that it took a woman to capture the very human dimension of the war that rendered her account so effective and so powerful. "I am jealous of any masculine intervention in the matter," he confided. "The truth is it is a woman's task, & I know of but one woman who could do it!"[68]

Women would take a significant lead in determining how white southerners would come to understand, interpret, and commemorate the Civil War and its outcome. Always central to the "Lost Cause" were their efforts to protect, define, and rehabilitate the reputations of their men—either individually, as LaSalle Pickett, Helen Dortches Longstreet, and Varina Davis felt compelled to do for their late husbands, or collectively, as thousands of women did through the United Daughters of the Confederacy and other organized attempts to shape and control the war's legacy for postwar generations.[69]

In her own way, and long before most had entered the fray, Cornelia Phillips Spencer did both and, in so doing, became among the first of a long line of female agents who, as Sarah Gardner has put it, "participated directly and influentially in this conscious effort to fashion a distinctly southern story of the war."[70] Yet Spencer did so unlike any other woman. She became neither a novelist, autobiographer, memoirist, diarist, nor journal-keeper. She became a historian. If Vance and Swain were crucial elements of what Spencer found herself defending, it was also her state that she perceived to be sorely in need of rehabilitation, and Vance recognized and lauded that emphasis in her work. "I am sure it will be greedily read by North Carolina," he assured her. "For my own part I can only confess that I shed tears freely over some parts of it . . . whenever the suffering and heroism of our people for the last four years are forcibly brought home to my mind." By "our people" it was obvious to Spencer that he referred only to their fellow Tar Heels, but he himself clarified the reference a sentence later: "North Carolina is a glorious old State—well worthy of our love."[71]

Like her beloved governor, and unlike most proponents of the "Lost Cause," Cornelia Spencer was never inspired by the Confederacy or the South as a whole. She identified herself first and foremost as a North Carolinian, and it was her state and its leadership to whom she remained most committed in her vigorous historical defense of what they had suffered and how they had endured in the war's final days. When "posterity shall sit in judgment on the past four years in the South," she wrote in her preface to *The Last Ninety Days*, "history can have no more invaluable and irrefragable witnesses for the truth" than the private sources of "prominent and influential men who either acted in, or were compelled to remain quiet observers of, the events to their day." And if this be true of the South in general, she insisted, "more especially and with tenfold emphasis is it true of the State of North Carolina."[72]

Notes

1. Edmund Wilson, *Patriotic Gore: Studies in the Literature of the American Civil War* (New York: Farrar, Straus and Giroux, 1962), ix–x.

2. Simultaneous with Sherman's march through the southeastern part of North Carolina was a raid by General George Stoneman through western North Carolina (March 28–April 26). Given its greater relevance in this essay, the focus will remain on Sherman's March rather than Stoneman's Raid, although Cornelia Spencer gives the latter equal coverage in her book. For accounts of Stoneman's Raid, see Ina Van Noppen, "The Significance of Stoneman's Last Raid," *North Carolina Historical Review* 38 (January, April, July, October 1961); William R. Trotter, *Bushwhackers! The Mountains*, vol. 2 of *The Civil War in North Carolina* (Greensboro, N.C.: Signal Research, 1988), part 5; John C. Inscoe and Gordon B. McKinney, *The Heart of Confederate Appalachia: Western North Carolina in the Civil War* (Chapel Hill: University of North Carolina Press, 2000), chap. 10; and Inscoe, "Talking Heroines:

Elite Mountain Women as Chroniclers of Stoneman's Raid, April 1865," in *Inside the Confederate Nation: Essays in Honor of Emory M. Thomas*, ed. Lesley J. Gordon and John C. Inscoe (Baton Rouge: Louisiana State University Press, 2005), 230–50.

3. The most thorough accounts of Sherman's campaign in North Carolina include John G. Barrett, *The Civil War in North Carolina* (Chapel Hill: University of North Carolina Press, 1963), chaps. 14–16; W. Buck Yearns and John G. Barrett, eds., *North Carolina Civil War Documentary* (Chapel Hill: University of North Carolina Press, 1980), chapter 20; Wilson Angley, Jerry L. Cross, and Michael Hill, *Sherman's March through North Carolina: A Chronology* (Raleigh: North Carolina Division of Archives and History, 1995); and Jacqueline Campbell, *When Sherman Marched North from the Sea: Resistance on the Civil War Home Front* (Chapel Hill: University of North Carolina Press, 2003).

4. Joseph T. Glatthaar, *The March to the Sea and Beyond: Sherman's Troops in the Savannah and Carolinas Campaign* (New York: New York University Press, 1985); and Campbell, *When Sherman Marched North from the Sea*, provide the fullest treatments of the treatment of civilians and property along Sherman's route.

5. Campbell, *When Sherman Marched North from the Sea*, 76–78; see also Steven E. Nash's essay in this volume for further elaboration of this view.

6. Journal entry, October 28, 1865, volume 3 (1854–1868), Cornelia Phillips Spencer Papers (hereafter Spencer Papers), Southern Historical Collection (hereafter SHC), University of North Carolina, Chapel Hill.

7. Cornelia Phillips Spencer (CPS) to Zebulon B. Vance (ZBV), October 30, 1865, Spencer Papers, SHC. Most of what we know of the discussions that led to her commitment comes through such exchanges with Vance and others, since Swain and Spencer were neighbors and spoke almost every day, rarely having to communicate in writing.

8. Gordon B. McKinney, "Zebulon Vance and His Reconstruction of the Civil War in North Carolina," *North Carolina Historical Review* 75 (January 1998): 72; see also McKinney, *Zeb Vance: North Carolina's Civil War Governor and Gilded Age Political Leader* (Chapel Hill: University of North Carolina Press, 2004), 245–46.

9. ZBV to CPS, October 14, 1865, Spencer Papers, SHC.

10. Two works in particular have focused on women's postwar writings about the war: Sarah E. Gardner, *Blood and Irony: Southern White Women's Narratives of the Civil War, 1861–1937* (Chapel Hill: University of North Carolina Press, 2004); and Jane Turner Censer, *The Reconstruction of White Southern Womanhood, 1865–1895* (Baton Rouge: Louisiana State University Press, 2003), particularly chap. 7, "Becoming an Author in the Post-War South," and chap. 8, "Women Writing about the North and South."

11. Evans quoted in Gardner, *Blood and Irony*, 43.

12. Dorsey quoted in ibid., 47.

13. Quoted in Hope Summerell Chamberlain, *Old Days in Chapel Hill: Being the Life and Letters of Cornelia Phillips Spencer* (Chapel Hill: University of North Carolina Press, 1926), 103.

14. There are two full biographical works on Cornelia Spencer: Chamberlain, *Old*

Days in Chapel Hill; and Phillips Russell, The Woman Who Rang the Bell: The Story of Cornelia Phillips Spencer (Chapel Hill: University of North Carolina Press, 1949). Both provide thorough accounts of Spencer's early life.

15. Russell, Woman Who Rang the Bell, 43.

16. Carolyn Wallace, David Lowery Swain: The First Whig Governor of North Carolina, James Sprunt Studies in History and Political Science, vol. 39 (Chapel Hill: University of North Carolina Press, 1957); Archibald Henderson, The Campus of the First State University (Chapel Hill: University of North Carolina Press, 1949), 148–49.

17. McKinney, Zeb Vance, 20–22.

18. CPS to ZBV, October 30, 1865, Spencer Papers, SHC.

19. Russell, Woman Who Rang the Bell, 88, 90–91; Chamberlain, Old Days in Chapel Hill, 103.

20. George Ward Nichols, The Story of the Great March (New York: Harper and Brothers, 1865), preface to the twenty-second edition, an expanded version of the book, published in November 1865.

21. Quoted in Russell, Woman Who Rang the Bell, 79.

22. E. J. Hale to CPS, January 11, 1866, Spencer Papers, SHC.

23. Cornelia Phillips Spencer, The Last Ninety Days of the War in North Carolina (New York: Watchman Publishing, 1866), 68–70.

24. Nichols quoted in ibid., 96–97.

25. Nichols quoted in ibid., 97, 99.

26. CPS to Eliza Mitchell North in New London, Conn., March 7, 1877, reproduced in Chamberlain, Old Days in Chapel Hill, 127–31. Spencer had come to know Miss North from numerous visits the latter made to visit the Mitchells before the war.

27. Ibid., 129.

28. CPS to ZBV, October 30, 1865, Spencer Papers, SHC.

29. Ibid.

30. ZBV to David L. Swain, September 22, 1864, David Lowery Swain Papers, SHC. See Joe A. Mobley, "War Governor of the South": North Carolina's Zeb Vance in the Confederacy (Gainesville: University Press of Florida, 2005), 2–11, for a historiographical discussion of the relationship between Davis and Vance. Mobley himself downplays the tensions between the two leaders.

31. ZBV to CPS, November 1, 1865, Spencer Papers, SHC.

32. CPS to ZBV, November 11, 1865, Spencer Papers, SHC. Spencer was wrong in this hunch. Jefferson Davis was not released from Fort Monroe, Virginia, until May 10, 1867, exactly two full years after his arrest.

33. ZBV to CPS, November 15, 1865, Spencer Papers, SHC.

34. Ibid.

35. CPS to ZBV, April 25, 1866, Spencer Papers, SHC.

36. For full accounts of Vance's actions in the final days before Johnston's surrender to Sherman and the criticism they inspired, see McKinney, Zeb Vance, 245–52; and Mobley, "War Governor of the South," chap. 9.

37. McKinney, *Zeb Vance*, 249; William A. Graham to ZBV, March 12 and March 26, 1865, in Spencer, *Last Ninety Days*, 128–31; ZBV to CPS, April 27, 1866, Spencer Papers, SHC.

38. CPS to ZBV, May 4, 1866, Spencer Papers, SHC.

39. ZBV to CPS, February 17, 1866, Spencer Papers, SHC.

40. Ibid.

41. ZBV to CPS, April 27, 1866, Spencer Papers, SHC; McKinney, *Zeb Vance*, 249; Mobley, *"War Governor of the South,"* 208–9.

42. ZBV to CPS, April 7, 1866, Spencer Papers, SHC.

43. Ibid.

44. Ibid.

45. CPS to ZBV, May 4, 1866, Spencer Papers, SHC.

46. Spencer, *Last Ninety Days*, 128.

47. Ibid., 182–83.

48. Ibid., 183, 185.

49. The fullest accounts of the Atkins-Swain romance are found in Henderson, *Campus of the First State University*, 185–87; Chamberlain, *Old Days in Chapel Hill*, chap. 8; and Russell, *Woman Who Rang the Bell*, chap. 6 and appendix: "A Note on Eleanor Swain's Marriage," 283–86.

50. Journal entry, August 23, 1865, vol. 3, Spencer Papers, SHC.

51. Ibid., August 30, 1865. The student diary is quoted anonymously in Henderson, *Campus of the First State University*, 186. For another perspective on the wedding, see Mena Webb, *Jule Carr: General without an Army* (Chapel Hill: University of North Carolina Press, 1987), 24–25.

52. CPS to Mrs. J. J. Summerell, September 30, 1866, reprinted in Chamberlain, *Old Days in Chapel Hill*, 131–32.

53. David L. Swain to William T. Sherman, April 19, 1865, reprinted in Spencer, *Last Ninety Days*, 178–79.

54. CPS to ZBV, October 11, 1865, Spencer Papers, SHC.

55. "Extracts from a statement by Ch. P. Mallet, Esq., March 22, 1865," in Spencer Papers, SHC.

56. Ibid.

57. H. A. Bizzell to CPS, October 25, 1866, Spencer Papers, SHC.

58. Ibid.

59. CPS to ZBV, October 11, 1866, Spencer Papers, SHC.

60. Ibid.

61. ZBV to CPS, October 14, 1866, Spencer Papers, SHC.

62. For Spencer's account of Union troops' behavior in Fayetteville and Goldsboro, see Spencer, *Last Ninety Days*, 66–70, 94–96. In Spencer's defense, Bizzell's letter is dated both October 25, 1866, at its end and, in a different hand, January 1, 1867, at its beginning. That, plus Bizzell's lengthy apology for having taken so long to respond to her request for information, suggests that his letter arrived too late for Spencer to incorporate it into her narrative, though she made it clear in a letter of October 14 that she was fully aware of Atkins's role in depredations in the "Faison neighborhood."

63. Spencer, *Last Ninety Days*, 178–79.

64. Ibid., 166–71, passim. Compare with journal entries from March 20 through May 4, 1865, vol. 3, Spencer Papers, SHC.

65. CPS to ZBV, May 4, 1866, Vance Microfilm, North Carolina Division of Archives and History, Raleigh.

66. ZBV to CPS, August 31, 1866, Vance Microfilm.

67. For a thorough account of the lifelong quest of Vance to win vindication for his wartime leadership, see McKinney, "Zebulon Vance and His Reconstruction of the Civil War"; and Steven E. Nash, "The Immortal Vance: The Political Commemoration of North Carolina's War Governor," in this volume.

68. ZBV to CPS, August 31, 1866, Vance Microfilm.

69. On Pickett, see Lesley J. Gordon, *George E. Pickett in Life and Legend* (Chapel Hill: University of North Carolina Press, 1998), and "'Cupid Does Not Give Way to Mars': The Marriage of LaSalle Corbell and George E. Pickett," in *Intimate Strategies: Military Commanders and Their Wives*, ed. Carol K. Bleser and Lesley J. Gordon (New York: Oxford University Press, 2001), 69–81. On Davis, see Carol K. Bleser, "The Marriage of Varina Howell and Jefferson Davis: A Portrait of the President and First Lady of the Confederacy," in *Intimate Strategies*, ed. Bleser and Gordon, 3–31. On Longstreet, see Gardner, *Blood and Irony*, 209–20. On organized women's activities, see Catherine Clinton, *Tara Revisited: Women, War, and the Plantation Legend* (New York: Abbeville Press, 2001); Karen L. Cox, *Dixie's Daughters: The United Daughters of the Confederacy and the Preservation of Confederate Culture* (Gainesville: University Press of Florida, 2003); and Tara McPherson, *Reconstructing Dixie: Race, Gender, and Nostalgia in the Imagined South* (Durham: Duke University Press, 2003).

70. Gardner, *Blood and Irony*, 5.

71. ZBV to CPS, November 15, 1865, Spencer Papers, SHC.

72. Spencer, *Last Ninety Days*, 14.

LAURA F. EDWARDS

Reconstruction and North Carolina Women's Tangled History with Law and Governance

Women were no strangers to North Carolina courts during Reconstruction. They had little choice but to appear when they were the ones charged with crimes. That had always been the case, even before the upheaval of war and emancipation. But women—even African American women—regularly initiated complaints themselves during the Reconstruction era with the expectation that they would be heard and their concerns resolved. These cases surprised me when I began research on the political culture of Reconstruction. The presence of African American women was particularly unexpected because of all the legal barriers that stood in their way. These women nonetheless persevered, seeking out the assistance of the legal system—through the Federal army, the Freedmen's Bureau, and then state courts—even before they were formally emancipated or granted civil rights. Their stories challenged me to think about the period differently by highlighting connections between the "private" domestic realm and "public" matters of labor, government policy, and party politics.[1]

Maybe it was because their presence was so unexpected that I interpreted these women's actions as unique to the period, a break with the past. That presumption found support in both historical events and historiographical debates. It is hard to overstate the dramatic impact of emancipation on Reconstruction-era policy changes, particularly the extension of civil and political rights to African Americans. Why would women's legal actions not be part of those upheavals? Yet the emphasis on discontinuity raises other questions: If there was so little in the experience of women—particularly enslaved women—to encourage faith in the legal system, why would they seek its assistance during Reconstruction? What of white women's use of the legal system? And what of all these women's apparent familiarity with the process? These questions percolate beneath the surface of other recent scholarship, including my own, which explores freedpeople's use of the legal system but not the reasons for it. Although historians connect such actions with changes in federal or state policies, they also emphasize that African Americans' efforts to use the legal system preceded changes in federal or state policy. Such top-down change also provides a less compelling explanation for freedwomen's legal actions, since Reconstruction-era legislation did not extend civil and political rights to them.[2] I never thought I would find answers to those questions in North Carolina's slave past, although recent scholarship does root freedpeople's activism in the period before the Civil War.[3] Building on that literature, this essay argues that North Carolina's legal culture before the Civil War is crucial in understanding women's use of law afterward. The point is not to discount or dismiss the dramatic effects of top-down Reconstruction-era initiatives. Rather, the essay highlights understudied aspects of the existing legal culture that shaped how North Carolinians experienced those changes. The procedural practices and the conceptual logic of that legal culture have much to tell us, particularly in the area of law that dealt with public matters. In the parlance of the times, such matters concerned the maintenance of the peace, not the protection of individual rights. In this area of law, nuisances such as wandering livestock or redolent latrines shared quarters with violent neighbors, abusive husbands, recalcitrant slaves, and those accused of felonies, such as rape and murder. North Carolinians had regular, direct contact with such matters, because the legal process was so localized that it involved people—including women of both races—who did not have the rights necessary for participation in other legal matters and at other levels of the legal system. Even if they were never directly involved in a case themselves, most North Carolinians, black and white, witnessed such hearings and trials on a regular basis.[4]

This localized legal culture provides the context for understanding the post-emancipation period. Like other North Carolinians, women were familiar with the legal process and viewed the system in terms of the maintenance of the peace, not just the protection of individual rights. Those expectations explain why they thought that they could make use of the legal system after the Civil War, even when they could not claim the individual rights that historians now identify as its basic foundation. The essay is divided into three parts. The first section explores women's relationship to the daily process of localized law in the decades between the Revolution and the Civil War. The second section steps back to consider the guiding principles of this legal system, which integrated women into its workings by incorporating personal issues and relationships—what we would label "private"—within the rubric of "public" law. The conclusion then considers how women's legal presence in this earlier period alters our understanding of the changes in the rights of North Carolinians, white and black, during Reconstruction.

Women's Physical and Imaginative Proximity to the Legal Process

The U.S. South seems an unlikely place to look for a legal culture that included women, particularly African American women. The region has a well-deserved reputation for its profoundly hierarchical legal order. In their statutes and appellate decisions, southern states not only denied individual rights to all enslaved men and women but also restricted the civil and political rights of free black and poor white men as well as all free women. From this perspective, the system was rigid and exclusionary, disciplining those on the margins while prohibiting them from using law in their own interests. Statutes and appellate decisions, however, provide only a partial view of southern legal culture. Those texts tend to emphasize individual rights, in their most abstract form, as the law's primary fulcrum, thereby obscuring key elements of what was, in fact, a highly localized system that rooted legal culture directly and concretely in daily life.[5]

The legal system operated in close physical proximity to ordinary North Carolinians because the basic institutional structures of state government in this period were so localized. During the Revolution, lawmakers decentralized North Carolina's government, drawing equally on Revolutionary ideology, established elements of Anglo-American law, and undercurrents of political unrest within the new state. The results displayed a blatant disregard for distinctions that would later become so important within state government, not only allowing local custom, politics, and law to mingle freely but also blurring the demarcation between "local administration" and "the state." In its basic design and daily operations, the state located its authority in local institutions, directed political matters to legal venues, and gave these local legal venues considerable autonomy over a wide range of public matters. As a result, the state level was largely dependent on local jurisdictions, particularly in the period between 1787 and 1840. Statutes, for instance, often responded to individual and local concerns and frequently had limited effect beyond the specific issue or area. Similarly, appellate decisions resolved issues in particular cases without necessarily establishing an authoritative guide for other cases elsewhere in the state. Legislation and appellate decisions then accumulated piecemeal, full of inconsistencies and contradictions, without constituting a systematic body of state law.[6]

Not all North Carolinians, however, were happy with legal localism. Between the Revolution and the Civil War, a dedicated group of reform-minded legislators worked to change that situation. These reformers—including such prominent names as James Iredell Sr., Joseph Gales, John Haywood, Thomas Ruffin, William Gaston, Paul Cameron, and David Swain—were actually part of a national network that sought to rationalize law and centralize the operations of state governments. By the 1840s, Carolina reformers had made significant progress in creating unified bodies of law intended to apply throughout their state. The effort included not only the organization of statutes and the creation of stronger appellate courts with the power to set precedent but also the elevation of the state level over the local level as the place where a uniform body of law was created and interpreted. In the resulting statute collections and appellate decisions, lawmakers relied heavily on the rubric of individual rights, taking the legal principles that had governed civil matters involving property since the Revolution and applying them to areas of law that had been left to local areas, namely criminal matters and other public issues. These legal texts, however, did not necessarily describe or govern practice in the area of public law, even in the 1840s and 1850s. In fact, reformers were most successful at the ideological level, particularly in their efforts to legitimize the concept of a unified body of state law as desirable and even inevitable. In terms of actual institutional change, their accomplishments were uneven. Local areas retained considerable authority throughout the antebellum period. On the eve of the Civil War, counties and districts or municipalities remained important loci of government authority: major questions about the public welfare were still aired and decided at the local level.[7]

Within this localized system, a large portion of government business was handled in what are now considered "legal" venues. The most visible were the circuit courts, which met on a regular schedule in county seats or court towns and which held jury trials. Not only did circuit courts provide obvious symbols of government authority, but their grand juries also made recommendations for the enforcement and modification of laws at the local, state, and even national levels. Grand juries interpreted their authority broadly: they issued pronouncements on foreign policy, trade, and federal legislation; they advised legislatures to pass statutes on a range of issues, usually related to local concerns about slavery, transportation, crime, and family relations; and they also dispatched local officials to investigate abused apprentices, unreported births, distributions to the deserving poor, unkempt roads, and other suspicious situations, such as "disorderly" houses, which usually involved some combination of noise, sex, liquor, violence, and gambling. But circuit courts were only the most conspicuous part of a system dominated by even more localized legal proceedings, including magistrates' hearings and trials, inquests, and other ad hoc legal forums. Magistrates not only screened cases and tried minor offenses but also kept tabs on the orphaned, ill, and poor as well as on matters involving markets, health, and morals. It was in all these informal, nominally legal arenas that North Carolinians did the business of "keeping the peace," a well-established concept in Anglo-American law that expressed the ideal order of the metaphorical public body, subordinating everyone (in varying ways) within a hierarchical system and emphasizing social order over individual rights.[8]

This legal system was everywhere and nowhere. There was no single location for localized law or the government authority it represented. Towns where circuit courts met were likely to have courthouses, although that was not always the case. The practice of law was not associated exclusively with courthouses anyway, because most legal matters were conducted elsewhere.[9] The legal system moved around promiscuously, following the officials who oversaw it and the people it served. When people had a complaint, they initiated the legal process by going to find a magistrate—the official who presided at the first, busiest level of the legal system. A magistrate heard complaints when and where he received them: in the fields where he had been working or even from the bed where he had been sleeping. Then he held hearings and trials in convenient spots that could accommodate a crowd—taverns, country stores, front porches, a room in the magistrate's house if large enough or, if not, under a canopy of trees outside.[10] Legal reformers cringed, seeing disrespect in the informality of these proceedings. "The places of trial," wrote one observer through gritted teeth, "are usually some tavern or some such place, where such scenes are sometimes exhibited, as justice never before witnessed."[11]

That was the point. Such locations pushed law physically into the community and into the lives of the people there. As a result, the bulk of legal business was conducted in those places where ordinary North Carolinians were most likely to be: in houses, yards, fields, or other community meeting places. Legal forums, for instance, often crystallized at community gatherings, emerging from the interactions of those there. Inquests provide excellent examples. When a death occurred, those in the neighborhood gathered to pay their respects, to clean and dress the body, and to grieve. That process also could reveal evidence of wrongdoing. Sometimes the signs were easily spotted by those who first saw the body. Sometimes they were uncovered by the women whose job it was to ready the body for burial. And sometimes they emerged through the mourners' conversations, as information was shared and the pieces began to form ominous patterns. When doubts acquired critical mass, the coroner—or someone designated to act as one—was called, if he was not already there. The gathering then reconstituted itself as a legal hearing: a jury was formed, often from among those in attendance, and mourners became witnesses. One by one, they offered their observations, repeating for the record what had already been said. And so law arrived at the wake, at the invitation of no one and everyone.[12]

The physical proximity of the legal system did not mean that individuals had equal access to it or enjoyed equal treatment within it. To the contrary, the system was designed to maintain a rigid social order based in stark inequalities. The distribution of individual rights fell out along that same hierarchy, simultaneously reflecting and buttressing status within the social order. Many of those individual rights involved private property or were related in some way to private property: in addition to the rights to buy, sell, and own were rights to one's body and the products of one's labor as well as rights to contract. Other procedural rights—including those to trial, to face one's accusers, to know the charges against one, to bring charges, and to testify—also had strong associations with private property, in the sense that they provided predictable processes for its protection. Legal officials scrupulously safeguarded such rights in civil suits involving private property in its various forms, whether real estate, moveable goods, perishable items, other people's bodies, or one's own body. These matters were "private" in the sense that they involved the private property of specific individuals and were thus titled with the names of those individuals, such as "*John Smith v. William Brown.*" Individual rights, particularly those involving procedure, also applied in criminal cases and other public matters, where they were an important component, even at the local level, providing crucial avenues of access and influence within the system. The difference was that individual rights were not the only consideration in this body of law. In theory, public matters involved offenses against the peace, the metaphorical public body—a fact signaled in the cases' titles, such as "*State v. Mary Jones.*" In practice, public offenses encompassed everything but civil suits involving private property and included all criminal matters as well as a range of ill-classified infractions that were judged to disturb the peace in some way. The interests of the peace, which made the cases public, provided other points of entry and standards of evaluation.

Given the acknowledged place of individual rights in public law, though, it is not surprising that white men from the middling ranks of society were most likely to summon the legal system to resolve their problems. Their rights gave them access to it, while their social status brought the process within easy reach. White women from that social stratum also tended to approach law with an air of proprietary familiarity, based more in their status than in their formal legal rights, which were few. They routinely called on legal officials for aid and provided information about the problems of others. By contrast, the legal experiences of slaves, free blacks, and poor whites—both men and women—were likely to affirm their subordination, precisely because it was crucial to the maintenance of social order as it was defined in this system. In general, slaves' and free blacks' participation in law was not voluntary: they were summoned by the legal system; they did not summon it. Brute force often characterized their legal encounters, as they were yanked out of their daily routines, tried, and sentenced by white people with whom they worked and worshiped. The process then transformed familiar domestic settings into menacing sites of interrogation and punishment. Poor whites often met up with law on unfavorable terms as well. When neighbors arrived at Elizabeth Adcock's Orange County house in 1813, for instance, it was not for a social visit but to search for bacon she was alleged to have stolen.[13] Some poor whites and African Americans nonetheless mobilized the legal system on occasion. When they did, though, it was not because their rights had been violated but because legal officials considered their problems a threat to the larger social order.

The legal system's proximity nonetheless familiarized North Carolinians with the practice of law by weaving it into the fabric of daily life. The emphasis on social order also had the effect of combining formal law with local custom, particularly in the area of law that dealt with public matters. Lawyers had not yet claimed this legal terrain and professionalized it—unlike the situation in civil matters involving private property, a lucrative area that constituted the bulk of lawyers' incomes.[14] Public offenses still were governed by common law in its traditional sense as a flexible, customary collection of principles rooted in local practice. In most issues, the parties represented themselves. If lawyers entered into the picture, it was in the very final stages, if the case went to a jury trial, which was unlikely. Public law thus had deep cultural roots. As an institution, a process, and a body of knowledge, this area of law existed as an extension of those mechanisms through which communities maintained social order.[15]

That was exactly how North Carolinians, white and black, used this area of law. In fact, a wide range of people expected the legal system to enforce their notions of the public order, which were usually defined in terms of their own needs and interests. Those expectations produced an endless stream of complaints to magistrates and grand juries about threats to com-munity health, welfare, and order. Depending on the informants' predilec-tions, these ran the gamut from the absurd to the serious: from dilapidated fences and ill-kept roads to neighbors with a penchant for late nights, drinking, or pilfering to threats or actual instances of physical violence. Among those offenses worthy of legal intervention were domestic issues. Masters filed charges against hired servants and slaves whom they could not control; white and free black wives filed charges against husbands; and free children informed on their parents. Free families brought their feuds to court for resolution, with wives, husbands, parents, children, siblings, aunts, uncles, and cousins all lining up to air their dirty laundry. Neighbors routinely involved legal officials in their quarrels, sometimes using the system in combination with insults, threats, and violence as yet another weapon in an ongoing conflict. In all these instances, North Carolinians marched off to magistrates, certain that the legal system would cure what ailed them: legal action could keep a lazy man at work, a philanderer from tempting young girls, a bully from terrorizing his neighbors, a husband from beating his wife, or a drunk from his whiskey bottle. Those expecta-tions represent a remarkable leap of faith.[16]

The influential literature on southern honor has pointed historians in another direction, leading many to assume all southerners' distance from legal institutions and their disdain for law. This culture of honor suppos-edly encouraged white men to prefer individual acts of retribution to legal action. While claiming rights for themselves, these men questioned a sys-tem of law that limited their actions by recognizing those rights in others, even other white men. They also excluded African Americans, granting them neither honor nor rights in an underdeveloped legal system that was clearly subordinate to the whims of elite white men. The result was African Americans' deep alienation from the law. Yet Bertram Wyatt-Brown, the historian most closely associated with the scholarship on southern honor, does not actually posit an irreconcilable contradiction between honor and law.[17] That is partly because his analysis of the legal system includes local-ized legal proceedings. At this level, unlike appellate courts, the process was not just about the protection of individual rights and universalizing legal abstractions, the elements of law that other scholars characterize as foreign to southern culture and at odds with honor. The scholarship, notably that of Ariela Gross, has further reduced the distance between the mechanisms of law and the dynamics of daily life in southern society, showing how honor and law comfortably coexisted.[18] Moreover, the denial of rights to slaves and free blacks did not necessarily result in their rejection of law as a conceptual system of rule. In fact, many of those on the system's margins still had faith that the system could work for them, under the proper circumstances.

If anything, though, law was more deeply embedded in southern culture than even recent scholarship suggests, because the difference between local legal venues and other means of governing misconduct was not always evident or meaningful. Magistrates and local courts, for instance, handled the same kinds of offenses as church disciplinary hearings—drunkenness, sexual impropriety, and conflicts within families and among neighbors. In fact, most offenses in local courts emerged out of otherwise ordinary encounters involving otherwise ordinary people who knew each other well. The most common criminal cases involved fights, usually among men— white and black, slave and free—who had been socializing. Women also got caught up in this sort of violence and the legal cases that inevitably resulted. Although fights among men were about male culture, women became involved when their menfolk brought both their friends and their bad habits home with them. Women also became active participants in those situations when everyday forms of sociability went awry or when they needed to defend their interests or those of their families. Free women, white and black, filed complaints against their husbands when they thought domestic discipline had gone too far. They initiated proceedings on behalf of children or friends and family members who had experienced violence but were too young, too old, or too ill to act for themselves.[19]

Women also became involved in the legal system when disagreements with neighbors got out of hand. Such matters tended to involve a mob, usually composed of multiple household members, often including slaves. Violence was rarely random, although the source of the conflict was not always identified in the records. Most cases involved ongoing feuds between families, usually over property. Violence went back and forth, with one side making a raid and the other side retaliating. That pattern explains the Orange County case against John Howes and his wife and Jordan Gilliam and his wife, who all marched over to Leonard Barrow's house. After threatening him, they then went out to the kitchen garden where his wife, Sarah, was working and "proceeded to cut to peaces & dig up and destroy all the grothe in said garden." It was later disclosed that the source of the conflict was "the right of possession to a certain tenement," subsequently settled through arbitration.[20]

In theory, calling in the magistrate represented a significant escalation of an issue, transforming it into a formal legal matter. In practice, however, the results were not always distinguishable from the services offered by churches or the mediation of neighbors or family members. Magistrates usually handed out nothing more than sympathy or censure. When they took action, they were likely to issue a peace warrant, which labeled the perpetrator's actions a potential yet unrealized public offense. The errant individual then secured a bond for good behavior for a specified period of time but did not incur any criminal penalty unless he or she broke the peace thereafter.[21]

This approach to crime derived from a cultural milieu that accepted misconduct as a part of everyday life rather than as a deviation from it. Disorderly behavior was a regrettable but inescapable aspect of the human condition, because original sin made all human beings susceptible to evil. What distinguished crime from other forms of disorder was the venue in which it was handled: it became crime when it met the legal system.[22] Criminal behavior, moreover, did not necessarily make the offender into a criminal. All those guilty of misconduct—criminal or otherwise—could be forgiven, even excused, as long as they confessed and repented. Then community members could receive them back into the fold. That last step was crucial, because the remedy for individual offenders was integration back into the community, not expulsion from it. That logic, for instance, underlay peace bonds, which threw enforcement back on the community, summoning family, friends, and neighbors to police troublemakers. Bonds required one or more other people to put up part of the amount, making them liable if the accused broke the peace again. That economic obligation represented the signers' promise to keep the offender in line. Peace bonds put everyone else on notice as well, investing them with the responsibility to monitor the situation and make sure the offender was successfully re-integrated into community life.[23] Even capital punishment, which had the result of severing the offender's social ties permanently, did not have that intent: death was punishment for the offense, not a means of eliminating a dangerous criminal from society.[24]

The detection and prosecution of crime also required community par-ticipation. Because the legal system construed the maintenance of order as a public responsibility, it gave police power to ordinary people in local communities as well. They, not legal professionals, identified wrongdoing, investigated the crimes, and conducted prosecutions. Knowledge about legal procedure was so widely diffused that North Carolinians knew exactly what to do when they encountered a suspicious event. The first step was to announce the crime—to give "information" about it to a legal official. "Information" was a recognized legal term that covered complaints about offenses as well as facts that supported those charges, including physical evidence and other details about the crime and those involved. People assumed that the discovery of a crime entailed the responsibility to investigate and gather evidence—all part of "information." They followed through, doing what was necessary: pursuing tracks, hunting down witnesses, searching houses for stolen items, sorting through burnt coals for the charred remains of missing livestock, measuring footprints against the shoes of suspects, and reconstructing fights to gauge the order, reach, and severity of participants' blows. The formal use of community policing also tended to legitimize customary forms of discipline. In fact, the difference between unsanctioned customary action and sanctioned forms of community policing was not always clear.[25]

The legal system rested on the initiative of local people in less direct, but no less important, ways as well. Hearings and trials turned on local gossip networks that produced knowledge about individuals. That knowledge occupied a formal place in the legal system known as "common reports"—information that was widely held to be true, even though positive proof was lacking. The mechanisms of gossip that produced "common reports" were so efficient and influential that evangelical Protestant churches regularly disciplined their members for spreading false rumors.[26] True rumors were an altogether different matter, although the distinction between a true rumor and a false one was less about verifiable facts and more about the extent to which others believed the story. The true rumors lodged in local information exchanges, where they circulated until they became common reports. In this way, the gossip produced and conducted through community networks became the information that provided an evidentiary basis for legal decisions.[27]

Because information was different from sworn testimony, people who could not legally testify could supply it. Not only did they bring crimes to the attention of legal authorities, but they also found and provided the information necessary in determining cases. Slaves occasionally provided information—as distinct from testimony—in cases involving whites, bypassing restrictions against their sworn testimony. It was more common, though, for information to reach the courtroom through the testimony of whites in ways akin to those described by other historians for civil cases. Slaves nonetheless played crucial roles in cases that involved offenses against them and other African Americans, where their information framed how and whether the issues would go forward in law.[28]

For legal proceedings to have the desired effect of restoring order, a range of community members needed to be there to fill the role of a classical chorus, witnessing and commenting on events. Women turned out for this phase of the legal process as well, which began at magistrates' hearings where information was aired and evaluated. Sometimes people brought others with them when they filed complaints. Cases also could acquire quite a crowd as they moved from complaint to hearing. If the magistrate acted on a complaint, he compiled a list of witnesses and then summoned them to give information on the matter. Those lists could be extensive, although the ability to give sworn testimony depended on the race of the accused. But an invitation was not always necessary, as people insinuated themselves into the process at all levels of the system. They did not "participate" in the sense of taking out time from their daily lives to perform a civic duty. Rather, involvement in the legal process was part and parcel of established community dynamics in which people made it a point to keep tabs on everyone else because they assumed that it was their duty to do so. They showed up at hearings, whether summoned or not, expecting to say their piece, even if the information was hearsay or irrelevant or duplicated what others had said. The repetition and accumulation of details were central to the process, which was as much about airing the conflict, repairing a rift, and establishing order as it was about determining the facts of the crime.[29]

The close connection between cultural knowledge and legal practice thus drew a range of North Carolinians into the system, allowing them to influence the terms through which conflicts were interpreted, even when they could not participate directly in institutional arenas where such issues reached a formal resolution. In this context, women—enslaved and free of both races—figured into a wide range of legal matters, because they created and passed on information that ultimately shaped legal cases. Ordinary white women were particularly influential in this regard because they were so central to the community networks that informed the legal process. The dynamics of race and slavery placed African American women at a further remove in this localized legal system. Although they exercised considerable influence in their own social circles, they were relegated to the margins of the local networks, largely dominated by whites, that were so influential in shaping the legal process. Their legal status as slaves or free blacks then placed formal limits on their participation in law, beyond those imposed on white women. As a result, African American women could rarely have the effect on legal matters that white women did. They nonetheless shaped the trajectory of specific cases, leaving a discernible imprint on the proceedings. Particularly compelling are two rape cases from Chowan County, prosecuted on behalf of Annis and Juno, both slaves. It is hard to imagine how their owners would have known about the attacks unless the two women had said something. Knowledge of the sexual component certainly would seem to require Annis's and Juno's input. Most suggestive of all is the fact that the offenses were prosecuted as rape. It is hard to imagine either the women's owners or white court officials leaping to this conclusion without at least some prompting. After all, many white southerners believed that African American women were always willing sexual partners and thus could not experience rape. Nor were such cases easily prosecuted within existing law. To be sure, there is any number of reasons why these particular offenses were prosecuted, none of which necessarily had anything to do with Annis and Juno per se. In those scenarios, though, prosecution could have gone forward as assault rather than rape. That the charge was rape speaks volumes about the influence of Annis and Juno.[30]

Like other people without individual rights, women usually left their imprint at the very early stages of the process, when records were less likely to be kept. Their presence became less obvious as cases moved through the legal system and away from the localized proceedings in their communities. By the time those cases reached trial in North Carolina superior courts, the influence of women over the proceedings could be difficult to discern, as propertied white men took over the process at that stage. Yet at that point, the cases usually had already been all but decided anyway. Both white and black women who could not testify at trials were crucial in laying the groundwork for them, providing the context for defining the charges and interpreting the evidence. Having set the stage, they sat back and watched the results, knowing that it was their input that turned a fight into assault—or rape.[31]

Superior courts were more formal and more distant from daily life, particularly from the lives of women. At this level, the possession of individual rights became more important to the legal process, circumscribing their participation. Courtrooms were also noisy, opinionated places, which some historians have associated with the distinctly masculine culture of white southern men. But the swirl of activity surrounding court sessions was not limited to white men.[32] Criminal trials spiced up the dull routines of rural life, and people followed the proceedings with the same addictive attention now reserved for television soap operas. White women, for instance, routinely attended criminal trials for that reason. Court also provided an excuse to come to town to relax, shop, trade, visit, or gawk—the crowds included slaves and free blacks as well as white women and children. There was always conversation to be had about the cases, the guilt or innocence of the accused, the evidence presented, and the performance of the lawyers and judges. Gossip permeated the parlors of respectable households, where white matrons entertained friends and relatives in town for court. Similar conversations could be overheard down the street in modest houses and shanties as well as in the backrooms and kitchens of the wealthy, where slaves worked and visited. The discussions then extended beyond the town's boundaries, involving people in the countryside who could not be in town for court but who eagerly awaited the latest grist to put into the gossip mill.[33]

White and black North Carolinians also knew enough about the circuit court to appreciate its limits. The gossipy crowds on court days had a distinct role in the legal culture, shaping the reception of trials' outcomes. In fact, a trial did not necessarily mark the end of the case. Pardons constituted an alternative appeals process: like cases presented in appellate courts, pardon petitions contested a trial's outcome, although they did so by skipping over legal points and going directly either to the facts of the case or to its social context. Petitioners constructed these appeals as if they were making extraordinary requests: they described the situations as singular, emotional, and urgent, which was why they were begging the governor to intercede with mercy. The language, however, can be misleading. Petitions circulated after every court session in a routine as predictable as clockwork. They followed specific rhetorical conventions, resulting in something akin to a handwritten legal form, in which the petitioners themselves churned out the appropriate boilerplate and then filled in the necessary details.[34]

Although white male property owners signed these petitions, their names did not represent their interests and opinions alone. Petitions also reflected currents of gossip that had coalesced into something more tangible as community members evaluated the reputations of both the guilty offender and the victims. In these calculations, everything mattered: age, personality, family responsibilities, demeanor, church attendance, work habits, family ties, and community connections. Other people's opinions on these issues concerned the elite white men who usually made out pardon petitions, because their own reputations depended on the same gossip networks that produced common reports about the people involved in criminal cases. For those outside these tight circles of local knowledge, the conclusions can seem arbitrary: Why did communities rally around one convicted murderer but not another? Why did whites occasionally rally to the defense of certain slaves? Why did they ignore the offenses against certain white men? The answers lie less in the abstractions of race, gender, class, or rights and more in the networks of personalized information produced about specific individuals by the people who knew—or thought they knew—them.[35] In this legal culture, neither the process nor its outcomes were confined to the boundaries of the courtroom or delimited by the interests and concerns of white propertied men.

The Law's Reach

The point of North Carolina's localized legal system was neither the protection of women's interests nor the recognition of their rights. Yet it still incorporated women of both races into its basic workings because they were part of the social order that the legal process was charged with maintaining. One result was that women had intimate knowledge of the legal system: they not only knew the process but also understood its underlying logic, in which individual rights provided access and privileges but which nonetheless elevated the maintenance of social order over the interests of individuals. Another result was that a wide range of issues, including those of direct interest to women, could acquire "public" resonance.

In theory, the peace was both hierarchical and inclusive. While the term was common in post-Revolutionary legal culture, it was based in a long-standing, highly gendered construction of government authority, which subordinated everyone to a sovereign body, just as all individual dependents were subordinated to specific male heads of household. That metaphorical body was represented first through the king and then, after the Revolution, through "the people" via the agency of the state—although the state's form was still an open question in the post-Revolutionary decades, a situation that made it possible to locate so much governing authority at the local level. The sovereign body, though, was always a patriarch, whatever its location or physical embodiment. That remained the same, whether sovereignty resided in local jurisdictions or centralized institutions or whether it took the form of a male king, a female queen, or a combination of men and women from different social ranks as "the people."[36]

The peace was inclusive only in the sense that it was an equal-opportunity enforcer, enclosing everyone in its patriarchal embrace and raising its collective interests over those of any given individual. Typical was John Haywood's North Carolina magistrates' manual, published in 1808, which identified the "peace" as "a quiet and harmless behavior towards the government, and all the citizens under its protection." The substitution of "citizen" for "subject" was more a Revolutionary flourish than a substantive change, since the manual explicitly included domestic dependents and other subordinate groups, including free blacks and slaves, within the peace: not only were they accountable to law, but they were also under its protection. Separate entries in justices' manuals covered every conceivable legal category of people, including wives, widows, women, children, wards, students, free blacks, slaves, Indians, and servants. While including all those people within the peace, the entries also made the hierarchical structure abundantly clear by focusing on the restrictions unique to those in each legal category. The combination underscored the importance of coercion in this system: individuals in every category had a place, and force was necessary to keep them there.[37]

Yet, it was precisely because the patriarchal peace combined rigid hierarchy with coercive inclusion that subordinates, even slaves, could play active roles in the system. They could trump the authority of their immediate patriarchs by appealing to the higher patriarchal authority of the peace. Slaves, free blacks, and white wives and children who could not testify, for instance, regularly gave information that initiated cases and shaped their outcome. Even when they could not prosecute cases in their own names, they made complaints that resulted in prosecutions and convictions for their injuries. In such instances, subordinates did not use the law in their own right. When legal officials acted on such information and complaints, they did so by invoking the larger interests of the peace. The source of the information was irrelevant if the peace was threatened. Those dynamics were particularly evident in cases involving injured subordinates, who were unable to prosecute in their own names: although the injury was to a specific individual, officials prosecuted by making the legal offense the theoretical damage to the peace in its guise as the metaphorical public body. The injured peace thus replaced the actual victim and prosecuted the case. At issue was who could act in law. The metaphorical public body could do so when the actual, corporal bodies of subordinates could not. This legal form erased injured subordinates only in theory. In practice, they still remained central because the damage to the public body was done through their flesh and blood. Always present yet unacknowledged—this convenient legal fiction allowed subordinates a central role in the legal order without disturbing the hierarchies that also defined it.[38]

Local officials routinely invoked the interests of the peace when they confronted offenses against subordinates—white women, free blacks, slaves, and free children of both races. The concept accounts for the otherwise mystifying array of cases in local courts, such as incest, child abuse, wife-beating, and violence by masters against slaves. At least, that is the best explanation for what local officials did, a conclusion based in the distillation of ideas from action, since magistrates, sheriffs, and circuit court judges did not stop to record what they were doing or why. A liberal application of the peace, for instance, likely explains the two separate rape cases of the enslaved women Annis and Juno, discussed in the previous section. By casting the offenses as against the public order, it was legally possible to prosecute the rapes. In this legal logic, of course, Annis's and Juno's injuries were not the basis of the prosecution. The crime consisted in the virtual violence done to the metaphorical public body through these two women's injuries. That framework nonetheless assumed these enslaved women's place within the peace and made their experiences visible as public crimes.[39]

Those cases, however, did not alter Annis's and Juno's legal status or the status of slaves generally. Local officials considered complaints on a case-by-case basis, righting specific wrongs done to the metaphorical public body without extending or denying rights to any category of individuals. The interests of the peace thus drew unique boundaries around each case, circumscribing the legal implications for the rights and status of the people involved. The individual rights of those involved were not at issue; it was the good order of the peace that governed the cases. Acting on behalf of the peace, local officials could follow up on the complaints of one white wife or one enslaved woman. They could undercut the domestic authority of one husband or one master. But those circumstantial assessments did not translate into universal statements about the rights of all wives, all slaves, all husbands, or all masters in all like conditions. That was because such cases were about the peace, not the rights of the individuals involved. The logic emphasized the collective order rather than specific individuals within it. In the name of the peace, subordinates could move out from under the legal purview of their household heads and acquire a direct, if momentary, relationship to law and government.[40]

It was possible for anyone's personal problems—even those that we would expect to be private—to emerge and assume public significance, given the right circumstances, because localized legal culture subsumed everything within the public order. Personal matters were always present within the public order, although not always legally relevant to it. In the localized legal system, people established and expressed legal relevance through the categories "private" and "public." The concepts were a means rather than an end. They provided useful tools to establish and to rank the seriousness of problems, determining how they would be treated within the legal process: private issues either remained with those immediately involved or became civil matters; public matters, which affected the good order of the peace, had wider ramifications and merited collective intervention of some kind. Beyond that, the consensus broke down, because North Carolinians invariably disagreed about what, exactly, should be private and public in any given situation. In local legal practice and common parlance, then, the terms did not refer to normative principles or specific categories of people (such as domestic dependents) or places (domestic spaces) that were inherently private or public. Any given matter could be either one or the other, depending on the circumstances. In the context of localized law, a domestic matter was not, by its nature, private. What made it private was the decision that outside intervention was inappropriate or unnecessary. Those determinations were part of a dynamic process—the ongoing negotiations necessary in maintaining order within communities. In fact, the terms "private" and "public" themselves expressed conflict rather than consensus. It was at those moments when the distinction between private and public was the most unclear that people tended to invoke the concepts the most forcefully: they appeared when there was the least agreement about them.

That construction of "private" and "public" is more apparent in people's use of localized law than it is in the legal texts produced at the state level, on which historians usually rely. North Carolinians used the legal system with the assumption that all personal matters were potentially public. That immanent connection explains why free North Carolinians felt so comfortable moving their own problems—what later would be private—into the legal system without any sense that they were challenging the social order. That is also why they peppered their legislatures with requests for new laws to resolve individual problems and local issues. The challenge lay in convincing legal officials that the issue would go forward in the system, which usually meant categorizing it as a public issue, not a private one.[41]

This conception of private and public is different from the one now current in the historiography of the nineteenth-century South. This scholarship, including my own, tends to construe the interests of domestic dependents and the dynamics involving dependents within households— including wife-beating, child abuse, incest, and violence against slaves—as inherently private, insofar as they were separate and excluded from the public realm of law and politics. As a result, one tendency in the scholarship is to assume that the legal system either did not handle such issues or gave them cursory attention. The other is to assume that they represented either a disruption or challenge to the public order when they did appear. In the context of the slave South, historians explain that situation in terms of the concept of dependency, which incorporates race and class as well as gender. Only those who could be independent—that is, white men with property or the capacity to acquire it—could claim the civil and political rights necessary to participate directly in matters on the public side of the line. Excluded from public participation were all those people—slaves, white women, free blacks, and even propertyless white men—whose gender, race, and class marked them with dependency, which signaled the incapacity for self-governance and, by extension, for the governance of others.[42]

In fact, domestic dependents and domestic issues are categorized as private in the legal texts on which nineteenth-century historians have tended to rely—appellate decisions, statutes, and the writings of those reformers who favored changes that would elevate those bodies of law. But those sources are limited in their representation of southern legal culture. At issue is the fact that appellate courts and legislatures were not the only or even the primary locus of legal authority in the South for much of the period between the Revolution and the Civil War. Nor did the statutes and decisions produced in these arenas define a comprehensive body of law applicable throughout the entire state, although they held more sway in property issues than they did over criminal matters and other public legal issues. While appellate decisions and statutes did acquire more legal authority in all areas of law by the 1840s, they did not assume their place at the top of the legal hierarchy until Reconstruction. Indeed, recent scholarship that includes local court records provides a very different picture of the legal process.[43]

Even in the late antebellum period, when statutes and appellate decisions did become more authoritative, they still underscored the continued importance of localized law, particularly in the broad area of public matters. Specifically, appellate cases and statutes settled conflicts that could not be resolved at the local level. In the resulting texts, appellate cases and statutes tended to use the terms "private" and "public" as if they were settled, mutually exclusive abstractions. In fact, though, lawmakers had to use "private" and "public" in that way because the point was to impose order on local conflicts, generated because some people thought their concerns rose to the level of public issues and others did not. Regardless of what statutes advised and what appellate courts ruled in any particular case, the peace still made it possible for similar kinds of private problems to become public in other cases. All those private issues were already part of the peace; it was just a question of whether they were problematic enough to become a public concern: that included petty disputes (that might be considered private because of their seeming insignificance) as well as the complaints of domestic dependents and even problems associated with private property. Such private matters routinely became public—including legal issues that historians either assumed to be private because they did not appear at all in statutes or appellate cases or that were explicitly labeled private in these legal texts. In localized law between the Revolution and the Civil War, the public realm of the peace was littered with issues that many historians have considered outside its bounds. If anything, those matters were the defining element of public law rather than exceptions to it.

The peace was as capricious as it was capacious. Enfolding the entire range of conflicts that characterized community life in North Carolina's slave society, it was contradictory and conflicted, just like the people who composed it. Even as it reflected and enforced rigid hierarchies, the peace was never defined solely in terms of the rights or interests of individual patriarchs. Of course, the interests of the peace and rights of individual patriarchs often coincided, because elite white men were the ones who wielded public authority, oversaw the interests of the peace, and played an influential role in defining the public order. But at this particular histori-cal moment, those men held that position, at least in part, at the behest of the public order; they did not yet possess patriarchal authority solely by individual right, at least not in public matters as they were adjudicated in localized law. In fact, individual white men acquired their status through their own particular form of subordination to the peace: their domestic authority was necessary to the maintenance of order, just as dependents' submission was. Yet the peace encompassed them, like everyone else, and demanded their acquiescence as well. As such, the peace could never be defined solely in terms of individual patriarchs' interests, whatever they might be.

By contrast, historians often describe post-Revolutionary North Caro-lina in terms of an individualized version of patriarchy, one in which the interests of propertied white men and the goals of law and government were the same. Such men, it is assumed, could label the concerns of "their" dependents and other subordinates "private" and exclude them from the realms of law and politics. To be sure, many North Carolinians at this time saw white men's authority in exactly those terms. Some of the region's most prominent and prolific residents expounded on such views at great length. Many more expressed them through their daily interactions with each other. White men habitually acted as if their domestic authority was an individual right, one among many that their government was bound to uphold. Their aspirations found support in certain areas of law and political theory. Between the Revolution and the Civil War, for instance, property law emphasized the protection of individual rights—rights fully claimed only by those white men with the resources to support dependents. Some Revolutionary-era political principles went a step further, identifying the protection of individual rights as the central purpose of law and government. From there it was a short leap to a public order defined exclusively in terms of the interests of propertied white men, since they were the only ones who could claim the full range of rights as legally recognized individuals.

Given the popularity of this individualized version of patriarchy among those North Carolinians who left most of the records, it is no wonder that it now takes up so much space in the historiography. But rhetoric and desire were not sufficient to make it so, no matter how forcefully expressed. Within the institutional structures of law and government, individualized forms of patriarchy occupied only certain, limited spaces. Before the Civil War, they shared legal quarters with other conceptions, including the one that emphasized everyone's subordination to the peace of the public body and, by extension, the notion that the legal system was about the maintenance of a social order more broadly defined than just the protection of individual rights. Even if the system did not always acknowledge everyone's claims on it, the logic still obtained. It was difficult for even the most subordinated people within this system not to see themselves as part of this public order, if only because it was so difficult for them to escape it. For them, familiarity with this legal order was a product of coercion—but familiarity is often acquired in that way.

That familiarity is what is so striking about legal culture in the slave South: even those on its margins *assumed* that they were part of it, whether for good or for ill. White women and even free blacks regularly tried to use the system, sometimes with surprising success, despite the denial of rights that limited their access. Enslaved men and women did not so much use law as survive legal proceedings they had no choice but to endure. Their acceptance of the system might better be termed resignation. Although they knew the legal system was capricious, they nonetheless lived with its processes and understood it as a means to regulate the communities in which they lived. They had to, because legal practice was so thoroughly integrated into the rhythms of daily life. Ordinary problems were legal because the localized legal system was supposed to maintain peace by resolving all the ordinary problems generated within it. Within the localized system, legal questions involved concrete relations within households and communities, not abstract concepts that existed outside of people's lives. The legal adjudication of all these issues rested on local knowledge created through informal community networks. As a result, women of both races contributed regularly to southern legal culture: they were integral to the base of local knowledge on which localized law depended.

Reconstruction

This backdrop is crucial for understanding North Carolina women's use of law during Reconstruction. During and after the Civil War, women continued to use the legal system to address questions of public order. White women fired off missives to local, state, and Confederate officials during the war with every expectation that the government would deal with their personal problems. After the war, they continued to bring a range of issues in their own lives and those of their families and communities to local courts. If viewed in isolation, severed from the antebellum past, such cases might appear novel, the result of disruptions that pushed women into new realms. White women's actions, however, had deep roots in the past.

African American women's use of antebellum legal culture took more dramatic forms. Black women and men both seized the opportunities created by the Civil War and emancipation to use the system in new ways, initiating cases and mobilizing it on their own behalf. They did so even before emancipation, during the Civil War, with refugees and black soldiers directing letters and complaints to Federal officers and agencies. They continued after the Civil War, before the passage of the Fourteenth Amendment and under the notorious state Black Codes, which limited freedpeople's individual rights and barred them from using local and state courts in most instances. Freedpeople nonetheless brought complaints to federal Freedmen's Bureau officials, turning them into legal intermediaries. After the passage of the Fourteenth Amendment and democratic restructuring of southern state governments, freedpeople made valiant efforts to use all the new legal arenas open to them at the local, state, and federal levels. As recent scholarship suggests, freedpeople made substantive claims about the postemancipation social order in these legal arenas that went beyond their individual rights: they made powerful statements about economic justice, racial equality, and political democracy.[44] Freedpeople turned to the legal system because of the dramatic policy changes of the era, which not only granted them individual rights that allowed new kinds of access but also encouraged them to think that the system could now be a more reliable ally. As important as those changes were, however, they constitute only part of the story. African Americans' past experiences also encouraged them to look to the legal system. Like other North Carolinians, they were familiar with the system's workings. More than that, they had experienced law as a system designed to protect community order. After emancipation, African Americans had every reason to think that they could assume more active roles in defining the public order, even when their claims to individual rights were tenuous.

Those expectations are particularly pronounced in the actions of freedwomen, who did not acquire the full range of rights that freedmen did. In fact, African American women shed the legal bonds of slavery only to acquire all the legal disabilities of other free women. Yet, as records indicate, freedwomen used courts not just to assert civil and political rights but also to address a range of domestic issues: they filed for divorces, brought charges against their husbands for neglect and abuse, informed on annoying neighbors, testified in cases involving community conflicts, and prosecuted neighbors and even family members on behalf of their children. These uses of the legal system were strikingly similar to those of white southern women of poor to modest means who had expected the legal system to resolve such problems before the Civil War and continued to bring such cases afterward.[45]

Women's use of the legal system is important, given the trajectory of Reconstruction. The same Reconstruction-era lawmakers who extended civil and political rights to African Americans also made other changes that were not as democratic. Legislation in the late nineteenth century centralized state authority and systematized a body of state law around the concept of individual rights. Those changes built on trends from the late antebellum period, spearheaded by reform-minded southern lawmakers who tried to move governing authority away from local jurisdictions and create a uniform body of state law that slotted individuals into generic categories. Ironically, the efforts of these southern statesmen were not fully realized until after the Civil War, as part of the systematic reform of the region under the terms of the congressional Reconstruction plan and the dramatic revision of state constitutions under Republican rule. The institution of capitalist labor relations and the extension of individual rights to former slaves required a hierarchical legal system, which construed law as a set of universal rules, consistently applied within defined categories. Although most southern legal reformers who lived through the Reconstruction era bitterly opposed the abolition of slavery, the Fourteenth and Fifteenth Amendments, and other changes that came with Republican rule, their basic vision of the legal system was similar to that of Reconstruction-era Republicans. It is no coincidence that Democrats left these changes in place when they took over after Reconstruction.[46]

Within the political context of the post-Reconstruction era, this new version of state authority did not necessarily work to the benefit of most North Carolinians. Consider the experience of African American men during and after Reconstruction. The extension of civil and political rights to them also formally linked possession of those rights with citizenship—in the broader sense that civil and political rights were considered essential markers of citizenship and, more than that, prerequisites to participation as full members in the polity, whether at the state or national level. That link between individual rights and citizenship actually redefined the basis of participation in law and governance. As Redemption and Jim Crow rolled back the legal changes of the Reconstruction era, the subsequent denial of those individual rights had devastating effects for men, denying them what had become the only entry to law and governance. That outcome highlights the problems of relying on the conventional, theoretical legal subject—a (masculine) individual with an unrestricted array of civil and political rights—as the historical standard against which to measure historical change. In legal practice, most men—even white men—were more like women, in the sense that they never enjoyed the full array of rights associated with that theoretical individual. Assessing change in those terms—that is, the acquisition or loss of individual rights—fails to capture the complexities of most Americans' legal status and the radical changes they experienced in that regard. Moreover, the trajectory of change in the Reconstruction-era South suggests the limits inherent within legal changes that emphasized individual rights and that usually are associated with democracy and political progress. Although individual rights held great promise, they arrived with new legal institutions that undermined other forms of access to law that had existed within a localized system. In that localized system, a person's subordination and lack of rights were not always a barrier either to making claims on the community or to participation in the basic processes of community governance.

The emphasis on southern legal culture and women's position within it thus reveals an important historical counternarrative for the Reconstruction era, one in which individual rights were only one way to imagine and produce claims on the state. Women's persistent use of the legal system reveals not just the fight to obtain individual rights but also the presence of a broader legal culture in which citizenship and participation in governance were not defined exclusively in those terms. Local court records indicate that many North Carolinians approached the legal system and other institutions of state governance before and after the Civil War laden with the same expectations. Of course, North Carolinians differed radically in their conceptions of what that public order should look like. But the *way* they viewed the process of achieving that order—however it might be defined—was strikingly similar. Turning our attention to people at these local levels provides a different understanding of legal and political history of Reconstruction. In this history, ordinary men and women without civil and political rights would have more substantive roles. This history also would be based in a different narrative of political development, one defined through expansive historical contests over the content of the public order instead of through the acquisition of individual rights.

Notes

I would like to thank the American Historical Association for permission to reprint this piece; it appeared in slightly different form as "Status without Rights: African Americans and the Tangled History of Law and Governance in the Nineteenth-Century U.S. South," *American Historical Review* (April 2007): 365–93. I also thank Priscilla Wald, Dylan Penningroth, Giovanna Benadusi, Joe Miller, Chris Tomlins, Adrienne Davis, Gunther Peck, Jolie Olcott, the audience at the Jean Gimbel Lane Humanities Lecture at Northwestern University (2006), and the participants at the Political History Workshop at University of Chicago (2006) for their invaluable comments. The biggest debts are to Jacquelyn Hall, who read innumerable drafts and whose insights on writing and history have been an inspiration, and to John McAlliser, whose thoughts were crucial in shaping this piece. I also thank Kelly Kennington and Alisa Harrison for research assistance. A postdoctoral fellowship from the National Endowment for the Humanities, a Mellon Foundation Fellowship in the Humanities at the Newberry Library, a Rockefeller Foundation Fellowship at the National Humanities Center, and leave time from Duke University provided time to research and write.

1. Laura F. Edwards, *Gendered Strife and Confusion: The Political Culture of Reconstruction* (Urbana: University of Illinois Press, 1997). Also see Edwards, *Scarlett Doesn't Live Here Anymore: Southern Women in the Civil War Era* (Urbana: University of Illinois Press, 2000).

2. African Americans' use of law—at all levels—is a common theme in the literature on the Civil War and Reconstruction. The series *Freedom: A Documentary History of Emancipation, 1861–1867* emphasizes African Americans' involvement with various government institutions and legal forums at the federal, state, and local levels. See, for instance, Ira Berlin, Joseph P. Reidy, and Leslie S. Rowland, eds., *The Black Military Experience* (New York: Cambridge University Press, 1982); and Ira Berlin, Thavolia Glymph, Steven F. Miller, Joseph P. Reidy, Leslie S. Rowland, and Julie Saville, eds., *The Wartime Genesis of Free Labor: The Lower South* (New York: Cambridge University Press, 1991). Also see Ira Berlin, Stephen F. Miller, and Leslie S. Rowland, "Afro-American Families in the Transition from Slavery to Freedom," *Radical History Review* 42 (1988): 89–121. Subsequent scholarship also has relied extensively on legal materials produced at various levels of government; see,

for instance, Nancy D. Bercaw, *Gendered Freedoms: Race, Rights, and the Politics of Household in the Delta, 1861–1875* (Gainesville: University Press of Florida, 2003); Edwards, *Gendered Strife and Confusion*; Barbara J. Fields, *Slavery and Freedom on the Middle Ground: Maryland during the Nineteenth Century* (New Haven: Yale University Press, 1985); Noralee Frankel, *Freedom's Women: Black Women and Families in Civil War Era Mississippi* (Bloomington: Indiana University Press, 1999); Susan E. O'Donovan, *Becoming Free in the Cotton South* (Cambridge, Mass.: Harvard University Press, 2007); Dylan Penningroth, *The Claims of Kinfolk: African American Property and Community in the Nineteenth-Century South* (Chapel Hill: University of North Carolina Press, 2003); Julie Saville, *The Work of Reconstruction: From Slave to Wage Laborer in South Carolina, 1860–1870* (New York: Cambridge University Press, 1994); Leslie A. Schwalm, *A Hard Fight for We: Women's Transition from Slavery to Freedom in South Carolina* (Urbana: University of Illinois Press, 1997); Diane Miller Sommerville, *Rape and Race in the Nineteenth-Century South* (Chapel Hill: University of North Carolina Press, 2004); and Christopher Waldrep, "Substituting Law for the Lash: Emancipation and Legal Formalism in a Mississippi County Court," *Journal of American History* 82 (March 1996): 1425–51.

3. See, in particular, Steven Hahn, *A Nation under Our Feet: Black Political Struggles in the Rural South from Slavery to the Great Migration* (Cambridge, Mass.: Harvard University Press, 2003). Also see Stephanie M. H. Camp, *Enslaved Women and the Geography of Everyday Resistance in the Plantation South, 1830–1865* (Chapel Hill: University of North Carolina Press, 2004); Penningroth, *Claims of Kinfolk*; William A. Link, *Roots of Secession: Slavery and Politics in Antebellum Virginia* (Chapel Hill: University of North Carolina Press, 2003); Joseph P. Reidy, *From Slavery to Agrarian Capitalism in the Cotton Plantation South: Central Georgia, 1800–1880* (Chapel Hill: University of North Carolina press, 1992); and Heather Williams, *Self-Taught: African American Education in Slavery and Freedom* (Chapel Hill: University of North Carolina Press, 2005).

4. This essay is based on legal records and a range of other sources from both the local and state levels, 1787 to 1840. Materials from the local level focus on three counties—Orange, Granville, and Chowan—and include extensive runs of court documents from those areas. Unlike sampling, which abstracts cases from context, an intensive approach reveals the information that is so essential in understanding the underlying conflicts and their resolutions. Such an approach also allows insight into the ways that people defined rights and justice, on the ground, in the years following the Revolution. That perspective is particularly important, since so many areas of law were left to local discretion in this period. The research then extends outward to other counties to include divorce, apprenticeship, poorhouse, and church records. At the state level, the materials cover statutes, appellate decisions, and various published legal sources; state government documents such as governors' correspondence, legislative committee reports, pardons, and petitions; newspapers; and the diaries and letter collections of various leaders in state law and politics. Although the essay focuses on particular examples, they are representative of larger patterns within the research more generally.

5. Laura F. Edwards, "Enslaved Women and the Law: The Paradoxes of Subordi-

nation in the Post-Revolutionary Carolinas," *Slavery and Abolition* 26 (August 2005): 305–23.

6. Recent scholarship has emphasized the localized character of law and government in the post-Revolutionary decades; see William J. Novak, *The People's Welfare: Law and Regulation in Nineteenth-Century America* (Chapel Hill: University of North Carolina Press, 1998). In North Carolina, localism persisted in the half-century following the Revolution; see William J. Adams, "Evolution of Law in North Carolina," *North Carolina Law Review* 2 (1923-24): 133–45; Atwell Campbell McIntosh, "The Jurisdiction of the North Carolina Supreme Court," *North Carolina Law Review* 5 (1926-27): 5–29; Walter Parker Stacy, "Brief Review of the Supreme Court of North Carolina," *North Carolina Law Review* 4 (1925-1926): 115–17; and George Stevenson, "Higher Court Records," in *North Carolina Research: Genealogy and Local History*, ed. Helen F. M. Leary (Raleigh: North Carolina Genealogical Society, 1996), 331–44. The trend embraced a unique blend of Revolutionary ideology, the Anglo-American legal tradition, and the politics of the 1760s Regulator Movement. For these points, see Lars C. Golumbic, "Who Shall Dictate the Law? Political Wrangling between 'Whig' Lawyers and Backcountry Farmers in Revolutionary Era North Carolina," *North Carolina Historical Review* 72 (January 1996): 56–82; Walter F. Pratt Jr., "The Struggle for Judicial Independence in Antebellum North Carolina: The Story of Two Judges," *Law and History Review* 4 (1986): 129–59; and James P. Whittenburg, "Planters, Merchants, and Lawyers: Social Change and the Origins of the North Carolina Regulation," *William and Mary Quarterly* 34 (April 1977): 215–38. Also see F. Thornton Miller, *Juries and Judges versus the Law: Virginia's Provincial Legal Perspective, 1783–1829* (Charlottesville: University of Virginia Press, 1994); and Christopher M. Curtis, "Jefferson's Chosen People: Legal and Political Conceptions of the Freehold in the Old Dominion from Revolution to Reform" (Ph.D. diss., Emory University, 2002).

7. See Adams, "Evolution of Law," 133–45; McIntosh, "Jurisdiction," 5–29; Pratt, "Struggle for Judicial Independence," 129–59; Stacy, "Brief Review," 115–17; and G. Stevenson, "Higher Court Records," 331–44. The larger point draws on scholarship that questions the centrality and inevitability of the nation-state's development; see Benedict Anderson, *Imagined Communities: Reflections on the Origins and Spread of Nationalism* (London: Verso, 1983); and Etienne Balibar, "The Nation Form: History and Ideology," in *Race, Nation, Class: Ambiguous Identities*, by Etienne Balibar and Immanuel Wallerstein (London: Verso, 1991), 86–106. Also see James Vernon, ed., *Re-reading the Constitution: New Narratives in the Political History of England's Long Nineteenth Century* (New York: Cambridge University Press, 1996); and Bonnie Smith, *The Gender of History: Men, Women, and Historical Practice* (Cambridge, Mass.: Harvard University Press, 1998).

8. For the overlap between law and politics in this period, see Novak, *People's Welfare*.

9. Many districts and counties had neither courthouses nor other public buildings, such as jails, in the first decades of their existence. Courts met in whatever available buildings were large enough. If there was a courthouse, the buildings were modest structures, replaced only later by more imposing ones, in the wave of courthouse

building that took place in the last decades of the antebellum period. Even when there were courthouses, they were not always the imposing symbols of state authority that they later came to be. See Robert Paschal Burns, *100 Courthouses: A Report on North Carolina Judicial Facilities*, 2 vols. (Raleigh, N.C.: Administrative Office of the Courts, 1978), 1:243–44, 435. Vernon, *Politics and the People*, makes a similar point about nineteenth-century England, noting that town halls and other such formal government buildings were linked to changes that formalized the political process.

10. The statute collections and codes of both states summarize the duties of the local courts and local officers. See the appropriate headings in *Laws of the State of North-Carolina*, 2 vols. (Raleigh, 1821), and *The Revised Statutes of the State of North Carolina*, 2 vols. (Raleigh, 1837). The actual dynamics emerge from the local court records. The descriptions of local courts in the following paragraphs are drawn from records in Criminal Action Papers, Granville County, 1790–1840; Criminal Actions Concerning Slaves and Free Persons of Color, Granville County, 1800–1839; Superior Court Minutes, Granville County, 1790–1840; Criminal Action Papers, 1787–1808, Orange County; Superior Court Minutes, Orange County, 1787–1840; all in North Carolina Department of Archives and History (hereafter NCDAH).

11. *Raleigh Register*, October 25, 1822.

12. These patterns are drawn from coroners' reports attached to murder cases in the court records listed in note 10 above.

13. *State v. London Adcock and Elizabeth Adcock*, 1813, box 11, Criminal Action Papers, Granville County, NCDAH. These patterns are drawn from the records listed in note 10 above. The compulsory and brutal qualities of law are obvious in cases with slave defendants. Those inequalities are well documented in the scholarship as well; see, for instance, Edward L. Ayers, *Vengeance and Justice: Crime and Punishment in the Nineteenth-Century American South* (New York: Oxford University Press, 1984); Michael Hindus, *Prison and Plantation: Crime, Justice and Authority in Massachusetts and South Carolina, 1767–1878* (Chapel Hill: University of North Carolina Press, 1980); Thomas D. Morris, *Southern Slavery and the Law, 1619–1860* (Chapel Hill: University of North Carolina Press, 1996); and Christopher Waldrep, *Roots of Disorder: Race and Criminal Justice in the American South, 1817–80* (Urbana: University of Illinois Press, 1998). For a haunting description of these dynamics, although in the realm between culture and law, see Walter Johnson, *Soul by Soul: Life inside the Antebellum Slave Market* (Cambridge, Mass.: Harvard University Press, 1999).

14. Civil suits, involving property, constituted the great bulk of court business in most southern jurisdictions. Ayers, *Vengeance and Justice*, 32, estimates that there were about three or four civil cases for every criminal case in a typical southern court. Also see Ariela Gross, *Double Character: Slavery and Mastery in the Antebellum Southern Courtroom* (Princeton: Princeton University Press, 2000), 23. The preponderance of civil cases, however, actually reflected property law's relative inaccessibility. Property law had been professionalized before the Revolution, which was one of the North Carolina Regulators' chief complaints; see Whittenburg, "Planters, Merchants, and Lawyers." Lawyers then solidified their hold on economic matters in the decades following the Revolution, given the unsettled state of the economy, the scarcity of cash and credit, and the uncertainty of land titles in the Carolinas. The

situation continued into the nineteenth century, largely because of the widespread use of notes, mortgages, and other instruments of debt as the primary means of economic exchange and capital formation. As a result, property law became even more elaborated and professionalized than it already was. The place of lawyers in a wide-range economic exchange was also apparent in their practices, which were composed largely of property matters; see, for instance, letter book, William Gaston Papers, #272, box 7; Cameron Family Papers, #133, subseries 1.2, boxes 4-28 (business-related correspondence); both in the SHC.

15. Robert W. Gordon, "Critical Legal Histories," *Stanford Law Review* 36 (January 1984): 57-125. For the customary nature of criminal law as well as its professionalization in the early nineteenth century, see Lawrence M. Friedman, *A History of American Law*, 2nd ed. (New York: Simon and Schuster, 1985), 280-94; Michael Meranze, *Laboratories of Virtue: Punishment, Revolution, and Authority in Philadelphia, 1760-1835* (Chapel Hill: University of North Carolina Press, 1996); and Allen Steinberg, *The Transformation of Criminal Justice: Philadelphia, 1800-1880* (Chapel Hill: University of North Carolina Press, 1989).

16. This analysis is based on the local court records listed in note 10. North Carolinians' embrace of the legal system as a mechanism of social control also echoes Christopher L. Tomlins's emphasis on a broad construction of police power and his characterization of law as a "primary modality of rule" in the early Republic; see *Law, Labor, and Ideology in the Early American Republic* (New York: Cambridge University Press, 1993).

17. Bertram Wyatt-Brown, *Southern Honor: Ethics and Behavior in the Old South* (New York: Oxford University Press, 1982), esp. 401. Traditionally, southern historians have tended to link honor to premodern culture and approaches to justice and, thus, to posit a conflict between honor and a modern, institutionalized legal system. The same presumptions that emphasize white men's preoccupation with honor also imply African Americans' exclusion from honor and southern law (except as criminal defendants): Ayers, *Vengeance and Justice*; Kenneth Greenberg, *Honor and Slavery: Lies, Duels, Noses, Masks, Dressing as a Woman, Gifts, Strangers, Humanitarianism, Death, Slave Rebellions, the Proslavery Argument, Baseball, Hunting, and Gambling in the Old South* (Princeton: Princeton University Press, 1996); Hindus, *Prison and Plantation*; Peter Kolchin, *American Slavery, 1619-1877* (New York: Hill and Wang, 1993). Scholarship that focuses on the blatant inequalities in slave law does not always deal with African Americans' view of law, but, given the nature of the sources, the analyses understandably tend to assume that such inequalities resulted in African Americans' alienation from the system. In addition to the above, see Peter W. Bardaglio, *Reconstructing the Household: Families, Sex, and the Law in the Nineteenth-Century South* (Chapel Hill: University of North Carolina Press, 1995); Victoria E. Bynum, *Unruly Women: The Politics of Social and Sexual Control in the Old South* (Chapel Hill: University of North Carolina Press, 1992); Melton A. McLaurin, *Celia, a Slave* (Athens: University of Georgia Press, 1991); Morris, *Southern Slavery and the Law*; Mark Tushnet, *The American Law of Slavery, 1810-1860: Considerations of Humanity and Interest* (Princeton: Princeton University Press, 1981); and Waldrep, *Roots of Disorder*.

18. For the compatibility of honor and law in the South, see Gross, *Double Character*, esp. 53–37. Also see Sharon Block, *Rape and Sexual Power in Early America* (Chapel Hill: University of North Carolina Press, 2006); Joshua D. Rothman, *Notorious in the Neighborhood: Sex and Families across the Color Line in Virginia, 1787–1867* (Chapel Hill: University of North Carolina Press, 2003); and Sommerville, *Rape and Race*. For work that links honor to institutions and practices associated with the modern nation-state, including legal systems that dispense impersonal forms of justice, see William M. Reddy, *The Invisible Code: Honor and Sentiment in Postrevolutionary France, 1814–1848* (Berkeley: University of California Press, 1997); and Joanne Freeman, *Affairs of Honor: National Politics in the New Republic* (New Haven: Yale University Press, 2001).

19. These observations are based on the local court records explained in note 10.

20. *State v. John Howes and wife and Jordan Gilliam and wife*, 1800, box 6, Criminal Action Papers, Orange County, NCDAH.

21. These generalizations are based on the local court records explained in note 10.

22. These ideas, common in the Christian tradition, were accepted parts of legal culture that were so obvious that they needed no explanation. This analysis also is based on the minutes of evangelical Protestant churches in North Carolina, from the collections at the SHC and NCDAH. They include Baptist, Primitive Baptist, Methodist, and Presbyterian, although the majority are Baptist and Primitive Baptist. Also see John B. Boles, *The Great Revival, 1787–1805* (Lexington: University of Kentucky Press, 1972); Donald G. Matthews, *Religion in the Old South* (Chicago: University of Chicago Press, 1977); Jean E. Friedman, *The Enclosed Garden: Women and Community in the Evangelical South, 1830–1900* (Chapel Hill: University of North Carolina Press, 1985); Rachel H. Klein, *Unification of a Slave State: The Rise of the Planter Class in the South Carolina Backcountry, 1760–1808* (Chapel Hill: University of North Carolina Press, 1990), 269–302; and Lacy K. Ford Jr., *Origins of Southern Radicalism: The South Carolina Upcountry, 1800–1860* (New York: Oxford University Press, 1988), 19–43.

23. In North Carolina, peace bonds are mixed in with the other court documents: Criminal Action Papers, Orange County; Criminal Action Papers, Granville County; Criminal Actions Concerning Slaves and Free Persons of Color, Granville County; all in NCDAH.

24. North Carolina's John Clary, for instance, was treated to a pointed visit from the extended family of the young woman whom he impregnated, an action that many historians would designate "extralegal." Although Clary prosecuted the mob and they were convicted for riot, the entire group was later pardoned by the governor. The pardon owed, partly, to the nature of Clary's offense. It also reflected the ambiguity between extralegal violence and legally sanctioned policing—and, in a larger sense, the legal system's deep customary roots within local communities. David Stone, Pardon of Nixon, White, Copeland, Copeland, Townsend, and Jordan, October 31, 1809, vol. 17, 115, Governor's Letter Book, NCDAH. The point is similar to but not the same as the one made by Wyatt-Brown, *Southern Honor*, 366, that extralegal sanctions replaced

legal punishments within the southern criminal justice system without undermining the integrity of law. In contrast to Wyatt-Brown, I am arguing that the distinction between "legal" and "extralegal" was less meaningful because of the institutional structures of law.

25. The process of private detection was similar to that described by Cynthia Herrup, *The Common Peace: Participation and the Criminal Law in Seventeenth-Century England* (New York: Cambridge University Press, 1987), 67–92. Also see Steinberg, *Transformation of Criminal Justice*, who describes the process of private prosecution and community-based policing in Philadelphia in the early Republic. These generalizations about the process are based on the local court records explained in note 10.

26. The term "report" figured prominently in church hearings, suggesting the influence of legal culture on religious practice: members reported on themselves and others; church members investigated those reports to find out whether they were true or false; they also charged people with false reports or false swearing. For particularly illustrative examples, see New Hope Baptist Church, Purlear, Wilkes County, Church Minutes, 1830–1930; Cane Creek Baptist Church, Minutes and Membership Roll, 1829–1941, Orange County; Brassfield Baptist Church, History and Minutes, 1823–1948, 1 vol., Creedmore, Granville County; Wheeley's Primitive Baptist Church, Roxboro, Session Minutes and Roll Book, 1790–1898, Person County; all in NCDAH.

27. Recent scholarship on the nineteenth-century South, in particular, has emphasized the importance of local custom in the legal process. See, in particular, Ariela Gross, "Beyond Black and White: Cultural Approaches to Race and Slavery," 101 *Columbia Law Review* 640 (2001): 640–89. Also see Block, *Rape and Sexual Power*; Gross, *Double Character*; Johnson, *Soul by Soul*; Penningroth, *Claims of Kinfolk*; Rothman, *Notorious in the Neighborhood*; and Sommerville, *Rape and Race*. As other legal historians have emphasized, custom continued to play a central role in local venues; see Michael Willrich, *City of Courts: Socializing Justice in Progressive Era Chicago* (New York: Cambridge University Press, 2003). The implications for law's content, however, were different in the late nineteenth and twentieth centuries because local courts occupied a different place within the institutional structures of law.

28. Magistrates and grand juries both identified community problems that required legal action based on "information" that had been given to them. An "information" was one of the ways to establish a criminal charge in British law. In its strict sense, "information" was the charge brought by one individual against another. That information was then investigated by the magistrate, who determined whether the case would go forward. In practice, in the post-Revolutionary Carolinas, "information" acquired a broader definition, encompassing all the evidence given at the investigatory hearing. See Arthur P. Scott, *Criminal Law in Colonial Virginia* (Chicago: University of Chicago Press, 1930), 72–75. For a brilliant analysis of the way that slaves' words entered court in civil cases despite restrictions on their testimony, see Gross, *Double Character*.

29. These observations are based on local court records explained in note 10. For

similar dynamics, see Block, *Rape and Sexual Power*; and Rothman, *Notorious in the Neighborhood*. The process also was similar to the kind of social witnessing that slaves used to claim property that Penningroth describes in *Claims of Kinfolk*, 91–109.

30. *State v. George*, 1826; *State v. Tom*, 1824; both in Criminal Action Papers, Chowan County, NCDAH. Many scholars have noted the acceptance of rape and the idea of the sexual accessibility of black women among whites. Recently, however, historians have gone further, showing its place within the basic structures of power within the slave South; see Edward E. Baptist, "'Cuffy,' 'Fancy Maids,' and 'One-Eyed Men': Rape, Commodification, and the Domestic Slave Trade in the United States," *American Historical Review* 106 (December 2001): 1619–50; Kathleen M. Brown, *Good Wives, "Nasty Wenches," and Anxious Patriarchs: Gender, Race, and Power in Colonial Virginia* (Chapel Hill: University of North Carolina Press, 1996); Adrienne D. Davis, "The Private Law of Race and Sex: An Antebellum Perspective," *Stanford Law Review* 51 (January 1999): 221–88; and Kirsten Fischer, *Suspect Relations: Sex, Race, and Resistance in Colonial North Carolina* (Ithaca: Cornell University Press, 2001). For African American women and sexual violence, see Adele Logan Alexander, *Ambiguous Lives: Free Women of Color in Rural Georgia, 1789–1879* (Fayetteville: University of Arkansas Press, 1991); Victoria E. Bynum, "Misshapen Identity: Memory, Folklore, and the Legend of Rachel Knight," in *Discovering the Women in Slavery: Emancipating Perspectives on the American Past*, ed. Patricia Morton (Athens: University of Georgia Press, 1996), 29–46; Catherine Clinton, "Caught in the Web of the Big House: Women and Slavery," in *The Web of Southern Social Relations: Women, Family, and Education*, ed. Walter J. Fraser Jr., R. Frank Saunders Jr., and John L. Wakelyn (Athens: University of Georgia Press, 1985), 19–34; Angela Davis, "Reflections on the Black Woman's Role in the Community of Slaves," *Black Scholar* 3 (December 1981): 3–15; Harriet Jacobs, *Incidents in the Life of a Slave Girl, Written by Herself*, ed. Jean Fagan Yellin, (Cambridge, Mass.: Harvard University Press, 1987); Jennings, "'Us Colored Women Had to Go Through a Plenty': Sexual Exploitation of African American Slave Women," *Journal of Women's History* 1 (Winter 1990): 45–74; Johnson, *Soul by Soul*; McLaurin, *Celia, a Slave*; Nell Irvin Painter, "Soul Murder and Slavery: Toward a Fully Loaded Cost Accounting," in *U.S. History as Women's History: New Feminist Essays*, ed. Linda K. Kerber, Alice Kessler-Harris, and Kathryn Kish Sklar (Chapel Hill: University of North Carolina Press, 1995), 125–46; Brenda E. Stevenson, *Life in Black and White: Family and Community in the Slave South* (New York: Oxford University Press, 1996), 236–38; and Deborah G. White, *Ar'n't I a Woman? Female Slaves in the Plantation South* (New York: Norton, 1985), 27–46.

31. Edwards, "Enslaved Women and the Law."

32. Diaries of David Schenck and William D. Valentine contain descriptions of trials and courtrooms; see David Schenck Papers, #652, Diaries, ser. 1, folder 2, vol. 1, particularly 7–8, 33, 80–82, 137–40, 151, SHC; and William D. Valentine Diaries, #2148, April 14, 1837, August 16, 1837, September 21, 1837, March 23, 1838, May 16, 1838, September 21, 1838, SHC. The patterns echo those in colonial Virginia described so well by A. G. Roeber, "Authority, Law, and Custom: The Rituals of Court Day in Tidewater Virginia, 1720-1750," *William and Mary Quarterly* 37 (January

1980): 29–52, although early national and antebellum courts seemed to be less decorous. Also see Gross, *Double Character*, 22–46; and Rhys Isaac, *The Transformation of Virginia, 1740–1790* (Chapel Hill: University of North Carolina Press, 1982).

33. For court day as a place to exchange gossip and for gossip about court cases and court officials, see John Hill Wheeler to David S. Reid, in Lindley S. Butler, ed., *The Papers of David Settle Reid* (Raleigh: Division of Archives and History, 1993), 1:207–10, 222–24, 229–30; William Henry Hoyt, ed., *The Papers of Archibald D. Murphey* (Raleigh: Publications of the North Carolina Historical Commission, 1914), 1:93–95, 168–70; and David Schenck Papers, #652, Diaries, ser. 1, folder 2, vol. 1, p. 151, SHC. *Raleigh Register*, July 14, 1808, contains a suggestive article regarding the governor's attempts to gauge public opinion through circuit judges' and their contact with people and gossip at court. Newspapers also reported on notorious cases in a way that suggested the larger swirl of gossip that surrounded them. Even out-of-state cases, republished in local papers, indicate the way trials functioned as local entertainment. See, for instance, *Raleigh Register*, July 12, 1810, October 11, 1810, February 22, 1822, April 9, 1824, April 12, 1825, November 12, 1829, April 8, 1830, May 20, 1830, and October 7, 1830. William Valentine's evaluations of judges' and lawyers' abilities also suggest the entertainment value of court dynamics; see, for instance, William D. Valentine Diaries, #2148, August 16, 1837, September 21, 1837, August 18, 1837, May 16, 1838, September 21, 1838, October 29, 1841, September 27, 1845, March 18, 1846, October 12, 1846, March 26, 1847, June 1, 1848, June 6, 1848, and December 20, 1848, SHC.

34. This analysis is based on about 650 letters and petitions related to pardon requests to North Carolina governors from 1787 through 1845. This correspondence is in two different record groups, Governors' Papers and the Governors' Letter Books, vols. 6–36, NCDAH.

35. The concept of credit was crucial to deliberations about who would receive pardons and who would not. External indices of social status—such as gender, race, age, and property—all figured prominently in establishing credit, just as they had for centuries in the legal culture of both England and continental Europe. But they provided only the starting point. What determined any given individual's credit was specific knowledge about that person, disseminated through the exchange of gossip among those who knew that person. The personal and impersonal aspects of credit worked together, creating a unique balance in each instance. That was why local courts routinely included testimony about the reputations of witnesses as well as of defendants and victims, if their information was crucial to the case. Such character witnesses were believed necessary to establish the reliability of key accounts, a practice that suggests the personal connotations of credit: who someone was, at a very personal level, was essential in evaluating what they said in court—and determining the implications and consequences of what they were judged to have done. See, in particular, Craig Muldrew, *The Economy of Obligation: The Culture of Credit and Social Relations in Early Modern England* (London: St. Martin's Press, 1998). Credit, then, carried over into the legal evaluation of other kinds of information; see Laura Gowing, *Domestic Dangers: Women, Words, and Sex in Early Modern London* (Oxford: Clarendon Press, 1996), 50–52, 232–62; and Cynthia B. Herrup, *A House*

in Gross Disorder: Sex, Law, and the 2nd Earl of Castlehaven (New York: Oxford University Press, 1999). Also see Barbara Shapiro, *"Beyond Reasonable Doubt" and "Probable Cause": Historical Perspectives on the Anglo-American Law of Evidence* (Berkeley: University of California Press, 1991), 6–12, 114–85.

36. This summary draws on the scholarship that uses gender to illuminate women's status and their relation to government in the early modern period and the age of Revolution. See, for instance, Susan Dwyer Amussen, *An Ordered Society: Gender and Class in Early Modern England* (Oxford: Blackwell, 1988); Brown, *Good Wives, "Nasty Wenches," and Anxious Patriarchs*; Nancy Fraser and Linda Gordon, "A Genealogy of Dependency: Tracing a Keyword of the U.S. Welfare State," *Signs* 19 (Winter 1994): 309–36; Carol Karlsen, *The Devil in the Shape of a Woman: Witchcraft in Colonial New England* (1987; repr., New York: Vintage Books, 1989); Linda K. Kerber, *Women of the Republic: Intellect and Ideology in Revolutionary America* (Chapel Hill: University of North Carolina Press, 1980); and Joan B. Landes, *Women and Public Sphere in the Age of the French Revolution* (Ithaca: Cornell University Press, 1988). Also see Edwards, "Enslaved Women and the Law."

37. John Haywood, *The Duty and Office of Justices of the Peace, Sheriffs, Coroners, Constables, &c. According to the Laws of the State of North Carolina* (Raleigh, 1808); quotation from 191. Haywood's was the standard guide in North Carolina. Throughout the South, such manuals were based in either Michael Dalton, *The Countrey Justice*, or Richard Burn, *The Justice of the Peace, and Parish Officer*. They also duplicated earlier colonial guides. By contrast, the guidelines in Blackstone were much less detailed; see Sir William Blackstone, *Commentaries on the Laws of England*, 4 vols. (reprint; Chicago: University of Chicago Press, 1979), vol. 3, on private wrongs, and vol. 4, on public wrongs. Also see Scott, *Criminal Law in Colonial Virginia*, which describes procedural elements that continued to guide the process between the Revolution and the Civil War in North Carolina.

38. The logic was laid out clearly in contemporary justices' manuals, which drew on rules from the earlier British guides. See note 37 above. Also see Laura F. Edwards, "Law, Domestic Violence, and the Limits of Patriarchal Authority in the Antebellum South," *Journal of Southern History* 65 (November 1999): 733–70.

39. *State v. George*, 1826; *State v. Tom*, 1824; both in Criminal Action Papers, Chowan County, NCDAH. These rape cases are just one example of prosecutions at the local level, which seem legally marginal, if not altogether impossible, given the status of the victim and the accused. In the mid-1820s, when charges were filed, North Carolina statutes and case law remained silent as to the criminal status of the rape of an enslaved woman by an enslaved man, although existing elements of slave law militated against such prosecutions. Prosecuting the cases as offenses against the peace bypassed those issues. Morris, *Southern Slavery and the Law*, 305–7, notes the loopholes in rape laws that allowed for such prosecutions and discusses several cases, including an 1859 Mississippi case, in which the Mississippi State Supreme Court overturned a local judge's ruling, which allowed for the trial and conviction of an enslaved man for the rape of an enslaved child under ten years old, on the basis that statute and common law did not apply to slaves; and six Virginia cases, between 1790 and 1833, in which enslaved men were tried for raping free black women. Morris

characterizes all the Virginia cases as exceptions and the Mississippi State Supreme Court decision as the rule. Given the changes in the court structure, however, another interpretation would be that local jurisdictions retained the ability to define and prosecute such incidents as rapes until the appellate courts (1) acquired the power to say they could not and (2) heard cases relating to the matter and rendered decisions, like the Mississippi State Supreme Court, that specifically disallowed prosecution. Within a year from the Mississippi court's decision, the legislature passed a statute that established as a crime the rape of all African American females under twelve by an African American man. Given their assumptions about the structure and logic of the legal system, Morris and other historians concluded that this statute extended new rights. For a discussion of the Mississippi statute, also see Bardaglio, *Reconstructing the Household*, 67–68. An alternate explanation is that the statute codified local practice and framed it in the language of rights. Sommerville, *Rape and Race*, 64–68, notes rape cases involving African American females, although she emphasizes the age of the victims and attributes prosecution to social proscriptions that categorized the rape of children as a different, particularly heinous offense.

40. This analysis is based not only on local court records, cited in note 10 above, but also on the relationship between those cases and state appellate decisions. The legal implications of local cases were confined to the cases at hand, a situation that reform-minded state lawmakers tried to remedy throughout the period between the Revolution and the Civil War in a number of ways: abolishing the Court of Conference, which reviewed problematic cases, offered suggestions, and then returned them to the district courts; replacing it with an appellate court; strengthening the appellate court's power to set precedent; and elevating both appellate decisions and statutes as a single consistent, authoritative body of law that applied throughout the state.

41. Individual requests for laws took up most of the state legislatures' business. Petitioners identified problems that they considered of public import and requested action in the form of new laws. If successful, those requests usually resulted in statutes labeled as "private" acts, which far outnumbered public ones. Private acts ranged as widely as complaints brought to magistrates and included the incorporation of voluntary organizations, the chartering of businesses, grants of manumission, divorce, legitimization of children, and suspensions of existing laws in particular instances. But the categorization of "private acts" and "public acts" was imposed after the fact by the lawmakers, by the terms of an existing process, or by those publishing and organizing the statutes. The terminology was not that of the petitioners. As such, it can be misleading, because it implies a clear dichotomy that did not always exist in practice. In theory, the terms attempted to define the implications of legislation, along the same lines that distinguished private issues from public ones in other areas of law: "private" referred to the scope of enforcement, which applied only to those named rather than to everyone in the state, as did "public" acts. But the line between private acts and public acts was not always well maintained. Public acts were initiated in the same way as private ones, through local initiative, usually petitions and grand jury presentments. The difference was that the sources of public law usually came through a request authored by a group—rather than by an individual—which claimed to represent the interests of a particular area or constituency. Yet many public acts, like pri-

vate ones, addressed specific, highly localized problems. The *Raleigh Register*, which provided day-by-day updates of the assembly's business, only started separating out "private acts" from "public acts" around 1809. Until then, it mixed them together, even when it listed the new laws published at the end of each legislative session. It is easy to see why the *Register* did not bother to make the distinction, considering the nature of so many "public acts." Whether labeled public or private, statutes resulted from a process similar to that in the localized legal system. Individuals or small groups requested outside legal intervention in personal or highly localized matters by linking them to the maintenance of the peace.

42. Nineteenth-century historians once assumed that "public" and "private" were separate realms, configured in a hierarchical arrangement, much like that posited by liberal political theorists, notably John Locke: the "private" realm of the household was distinct from and subordinate to the "public" world of politics and commerce. The influence was apparent within southern history, where the traditional focus on political history and the men who figured in law and party politics centered on the "public" side of the equation. Later work on social history moved in the other direction, back toward the "private" sphere, although broadly conceived to include matters such as economic production, labor, and the slave system as well as the daily lives of all those enmeshed in that system, particularly slaves and their white mistresses. Where earlier scholarship on the South accepted that distinction as a given, recent work in the field has used the analytical lens of gender to explain its presence, the resulting dynamics, and their wider implications. These historians construe private and public as products of politics and culture rather than as expressions of nature, distinct spheres, or actual physical space. As a result, they have focused on the ideological assumptions that underlay the concepts, how they changed, and how they were used. In the context of the slave South, historians have linked the dynamics of private and public to the concept of dependency, which incorporates race and class as well as gender. Yet the scholarship still tends to assume that the legal system in the slave South treated all problems of domestic dependents as "private" and thereby either excluded them or did its best to ignore or limit them when they did appear, a situation that did not change until after Reconstruction. See, in particular, Bardaglio, *Reconstructing the Household*. Also see Bercaw, *Gendered Freedoms*; Brown, *Good Wives, "Nasty Wenches," and Anxious Patriarchs*; Bynum, *Unruly Women*; Jane Dailey, *Before Jim Crow: The Politics of Race in Postemancipation Virginia* (Chapel Hill: University of North Carolina Press, 2000); Edwards, *Gendered Strife and Confusion*; Elizabeth Fox-Genovese, *Within the Plantation Household: Women in the Old South* (Chapel Hill: University of North Carolina Press, 1988); Frankel, *Freedom's Women*; Glenda Elizabeth Gilmore, *Gender and Jim Crow: Women and the Politics of White Supremacy in North Carolina, 1896–1920* (Chapel Hill: University of North Carolina Press, 1998); Stephanie McCurry, *Masters of Small Worlds: Yeoman Households, Gender Relations, and the Political Culture of the Antebellum South Carolina Low Country* (New York: Oxford University Press, 1995); Schwalm, *Hard Fight for We*; Amy Dru Stanley, *From Bondage to Contract: Wage Labor, Marriage, and the Market in the Age of Slave Emancipation* (New York: Cambridge University Press,

1998); and Lee Ann Whites, *The Civil War as a Crisis in Gender: Augusta, Georgia, 1860–1890* (Athens: University of Georgia Press, 1992).

43. Gross, "Beyond Black and White." Also see Block, *Rape and Sexual Power*; Stephanie Cole, "Keeping the Peace: Domestic Assault and Private Prosecution in Antebellum Baltimore," in *Over the Threshold: Intimate Violence in Early America*, ed. Christine Daniels and Michael V. Kennedy (New York: New York University Press, 1999), 148–69; Gross, *Double Character*; Johnson, *Soul by Soul*; Penningroth, *Claims of Kinfolk*; Rothman, *Notorious in the Neighborhood*; and Sommerville, *Rape and Race*.

44. Berlin et al., *The Black Military Experience*, *The Destruction of Slavery* (New York: Cambridge University Press, 1985), and *The Wartime Genesis of Free Labor*. Also see Bercaw, *Gendered Freedoms*; Edwards, *Gendered Strife and Confusion*; Fields, *Slavery and Freedom on the Middle Ground*; Eric Foner, *Nothing but Freedom: Emancipation and Its Legacy* (Baton Rouge: Louisiana State University Press, 1983); Hahn, *Nation under Our Feet*; Thomas C. Holt, *Black over White: Negro Political Leadership in South Carolina during Reconstruction* (Urbana: University of Illinois Press, 1977); John C. Rodrigue, *Reconstruction in the Cane Fields: From Slavery to Free Labor in Louisiana's Sugar Parishes, 1862–1880* (Baton Rouge: Louisiana State University Press, 2001); Saville, *Work of Reconstruction*; Schwalm, *Hard Fight for We*.

45. Berlin et al., "Afro-American Families"; Bercaw, *Gendered Freedoms*; Victoria Bynum, "Reshaping the Bonds of Womanhood: Divorce in Reconstruction North Carolina," in *Divided Houses: Gender and the Civil War*, ed. Catherine Clinton and Nina Silver (New York: Oxford University Press, 1992), 320–33; Edwards, *Gendered Strife and Confusion*; Frankel, *Freedom's Women*; O'Donovan, *Becoming Free in the Cotton South*; Elizabeth Regosin, *Freedom's Promise: Ex-slave Families and Citizenship in the Age of Emancipation* (Charlottesville: University of Virginia Press, 2002); Hannah Rosen, "'Not That Sort of Women': Race, Gender, and Sexual Violence during the Memphis Riot of 1866," in *Sex, Love, Race: Crossing Boundaries in North American History*, ed. Martha Hodes (New York: New York University Press, 1999), 267–93; Sommerville, *Rape and Race*, 147–75; Schwalm, *Hard Fight for We*, 147–268; Karin L. Zipf, *Labor of Innocents: Forced Apprenticeship in North Carolina, 1715–1919* (Baton Rouge: Louisiana State University, 2005). For white women, see Drew Faust, *Mothers of Invention: Women of the Slaveholding South in the American Civil War* (Chapel Hill: University of North Carolina Press, 1996); and George C. Rable, *Civil Wars: Women and the Crisis of Southern Nationalism* (Urbana: University of Illinois Press, 1989).

46. Accounts focusing on the development of the state's courts usually note this point. See, for instance: Adams, "Evolution of Law"; McIntosh, "Jurisdiction"; and John V. Orth, "North Carolina Constitutional History," *North Carolina Law Review* 70 (1991–92): 1759–87.

No Longer under Cover(ture)

Marriage, Divorce, and Gender in the
1868 Constitutional Convention

Eighteen-year-old Martha A. Hopkins suffered a broken heart during the Civil War. Her husband of only one year, William T. Hopkins, deserted her in February 1864. She had married Hopkins against the will of her father, Robert D. Hart, who later came to suspect that Hopkins was a fraud. Hopkins claimed that he was the son of a Louisville, Kentucky, judge and that the Confederate army had discharged him on ill health. Martha and William had met in 1862 when Martha's father offered to board Hopkins at their home. Within months, Martha and William married. Almost immediately, William's demeanor changed, which led Martha and her family and friends to doubt his identity. Upon learning that Martha's father had begun to investigate his background, William disappeared. His departure came one year after his marriage and shortly after the birth of his child. Shortly thereafter, Martha's father hired a friend in the community to investigate Hopkins's origins in an effort to find him. After "making diligent inquiries and publications" in Kentucky, the investigator, Charles E. Landis, came to believe that no such person named William T. Hopkins existed. By 1868, the family had no further word from Hopkins. Martha desperately hoped to end her marriage to this "person of low and depraved character and an imposter." Unfortunately for Martha, North Carolina divorce laws restricted courts from granting divorces to abandoned wives. Unless Martha could prove the fraud, her best hope for relief from the courts was a "separation from bed and board," a status that might grant Martha certain property rights but would not end the marriage. Given the restrictions by the courts, Martha opted to petition for a divorce with the North Carolina Constitutional Convention of 1868. Armed with her own testimony and those of her father, Charles Landis, and another community member named William S. Skinner, who had suspected that Hopkins's discharge papers were forgeries, Martha hoped that the convention would disregard the law and grant her a full divorce.[1]

She was not the only North Carolinian in such desperate straits. During the convention proceedings, delegates considered the Hopkins petition and twenty-six others from across the state. By including these petitions in their proceedings, delegates sparked unprecedented debates on divorce, marriage, husband and wife relations, and prescriptions of manhood and womanhood that spelled a larger significance not only for divorce but also for the question of gender relations and the marriage contract. This article argues several key points. First, these divorce debates, carried on among ordinary men and women, lawmakers and jurists, upset long-held legal and political traditions—defined as "coverture"—that presumed women's inability to serve as contractual agents within marriage. Coverture, an English and North Carolina common law tradition, subsumed a married woman's legal identity and property under her husband's and assumed her incapacity to reason and consent independent of her husband. While the 1868 debates about divorce never resulted in a rallying cry for women's rights or widespread demands for the franchise, they nonetheless represent an important shift in views about women and dependency as lawmakers and ordinary people expressed beliefs that defied traditional principles of coverture and marriage. Second, these debates illuminate both legalistic and vernacular discussions about married women's rational abilities to contract and, in turn, to break contracts, a crucial component of Lockean principles of republican government and social contract theory. Finally, this article will demonstrate that the divorce petitions provoked a conflict between prominent white Republicans and their African American counterparts who appeared more sympathetic to women's rights.[2]

When the North Carolina Constitutional Convention assembled in January 1868, delegates had little reason to suspect that divorce petitions would consume a significant portion of the docket. Delegates, elected by the state's registered voters in November 1867, gathered in Raleigh on January 14, 1868, to discharge their obligations under the Reconstruction Acts. The Reconstruction Acts divided all former Confederate states into military districts and required elections for delegates who would become responsible for drafting new state constitutions that would bring the states in line with the requirements of Congress. In North Carolina, the vote to hold a constitutional convention passed easily, as the Reconstruction Acts had disfranchised former Confederates in punishment both for their traitorous behavior during the Civil War and for their deep antagonism toward racial equality when they briefly resumed political control in 1865. Republican delegates outnumbered Conservatives, a party that first emerged during the Civil War and was populated mostly by former Confederates,

107 to 13. At least thirteen delegates were African American. Thus, the purpose of the convention was to redraft the state's social compact to reflect more accurately the responsibilities and rights of North Carolina's male citizenry, both black and white, rich and poor. When the convention finally adjourned on March 14, William B. Rodman and George W. Gahagan offered a closing address that boldly celebrated this accomplishment: "Just men must admit," they pronounced, "that all who are expected to bear their share of the manifold burdens of the government at all times, and to expose their lives for its defence in war, should be allowed a full participation in its direction."[3]

Yet numerous North Carolina men and women envisioned other purposes for the convention. In divorce petitions sent to delegates across the state, ordinary people endeavored to shift the convention's priorities toward private matters that many lawmakers typically characterized as outside the bounds of government. Numerous North Carolinians across the social spectrum carefully drafted divorce petitions that detailed their most intimate lives and personal frustrations. Some petitioners were brief, such as James and Nancy Brady, who desired an absolute divorce because "owing to some unfortunate difficulties," their marriage had "ripened into a total estrangement." But others, such as Martha Hopkins, used graphic detail as evidence of their despair. More than a few petitions include testimony and signatures of community and family members, indicating the very public dimensions of their private lives. The twenty-seven petitions flustered some delegates, who found them a nuisance and beyond the purview of the convention. Nonetheless, divorce petitions constituted a significant portion of the work of the convention. Fifteen of the total of fifty-eight ordinances that the convention passed sanctioned individual divorces.[4]

In historical terms, petitioning for divorce was not uncommon. The very act of petitioning a lawmaking body to grant a divorce was rooted in North Carolina and English common law. In England, the ecclesiastical courts controlled matrimonial matters. Thus, there was no provision for divorce unless by legislative enactment. The ecclesiastical courts allowed legal separations, known as divorce *a mensa et thoro*, for two causes, cruelty or adultery. However, absolute divorce that would allow both parties to remarry did not exist. As North Carolina lacked ecclesiastical courts, the legislature served as the only body to grant divorces prior to 1814, and no record even of legislative divorce exists until 1794. After the Revolution, the General Assembly received numerous divorce petitions but granted few. As a result of the legislature's unwillingness and in response to the great need for relief, the equity courts invented an action of alimony without divorce, a sharp departure from English common law that considered a husband's control of his wife's property as absolute. By the time that the legislature passed its first general divorce statute in 1814, North Carolina equity courts already offered alimony and restored limited property rights to women whose husbands did "wilfully fail and refuse" support. The legislature offered an absolute divorce, *a vinculo matrimonii*, but only by private enactment.[5]

In response to growing numbers of divorce petitions flooding the legislature, the General Assembly transferred jurisdiction to the state's superior courts in 1814. The 1814 act authorized the courts to decree both forms of divorce, absolute divorce and bed and board separations, at the judges' discretion. A court might consider an absolute divorce, the form sought by Martha Hopkins and James and Nancy Brady, but only in very limited circumstances. The law required proof of "natural impotence" or that one party had physically separated from the other and lived in a continual state of adultery. This form of divorce prevented the offending party from remarrying and, by 1816, restored the wife's right to any property that she might afterward obtain. For estranged couples who failed to meet the strict conditions of an absolute divorce, courts could grant divorces from bed and board, a decree that amounted to a modern-day separation agreement. Jurists hesitant to decree an absolute divorce might choose a separation by bed and board instead. Courts also granted bed and board divorces in cases of cruelty or abandonment or where a husband "maliciously turns his wife out of doors" or "offers intolerable indignities to her person." While the code lay silent on the specifics of those indignities, judges often demanded hard evidence that the offending party had committed the indignities maliciously and willfully. Bed and board divorces might restore a wife's property rights and grant her alimony, but neither party could remarry. Furthermore, if the couple should reconcile and end their separation, the wife's coverture status would resume. In 1814, divorces were final only upon the General Assembly's ratification, but the legislature removed this provision in 1818. By 1827, the legislature, overwhelmed by divorce petitions, vested the superior courts with "sole and original jurisdiction in all cases of application for divorce." Nonetheless, the General Assembly continued to grant divorces by legislative enactment until the 1835 Constitutional Convention permanently removed the General Assembly's "power to grant a divorce or secure alimony in any individual case."[6]

Scholars have argued that judicial discretion and legislative reforms led to a liberalization of divorce laws not only in North Carolina but also in the South and across the nation. Jane Turner Censer has argued that except in

South Carolina, where divorce was unavailable, southern judges expanded the definition of cruelty and expressed sympathy for women, particularly affluent ones who appeared well-bred and ladylike. Women deemed respectable and of good character, rather than poorer women, appealed to judges' sentiments and were more likely to possess the resources to pursue a divorce. According to Censer, judicial discretion could work in favor of or against women, but "the enlargement of the concept of cruelty, decisions decreeing alimony and property settlements necessary, and changes in custody all were modifications favoring women." From 1814 to 1860, judges and legislators expanded the definition of cruelty and personal indignities so as not to require physical violence. Most often, judges ruled that a bed and board divorce required evidence that a husband had made vindictive acts and utterances that included unfounded charges of a wife's infidelity, an act that could permanently besmirch her reputation. While cruelty sometimes warranted a bed and board divorce, the supreme court consistently refused to allow absolute divorces in cases of violence and abuse. The court rejected women's petitions for divorce even in the most extreme cases. When a husband horsewhipped and beat his wife, Chief Justice Richmond Pearson refused to allow the wife a divorce. "The law," he stated, "gives the husband power to use such a degree of force necessary to make the wife behave and know her place." By 1852, judges and legislators recognized as many as fifteen causes for separation or divorce, including the following: desertion, adultery, separation with division of property, wife living with another in husband's absence, wife in love with another, family feud, and where petitioner received property rights by legislative enactment and believed she had the right to remarry.[7]

Despite their sympathies, North Carolina judges agonized over the prospect that their judicial opinions might undermine the sanctity of the marriage contract. Judges at once defended the judicial discretion granted by the statute but took pains to explain that courts must restrain themselves from exercising discretion loosely. In 1832, the courts denied Marville Scroggins a divorce when his wife, Lucretia, bore a "mulatto child" just five months after their marriage. Chief Justice Thomas Ruffin praised the lower court for dismissing the petition because it did not meet the grounds of fraud. Had Lucretia Scroggins defrauded her husband, the courts could nullify the marriage contract. But Lucretia was pregnant when they married and, Ruffin argued, her concealment of the child's father was not true fraud. For fraud to exist, Ruffin continued, Marville Scroggins "must appear not to have been voluntarily blind, but to have been the victim of a deception which would have beguiled a person of ordinary prudence."

Although Ruffin certainly did not condone Lucretia Scroggins's actions, he worried that to sanction her husband's grounds for fraud would lead to petitions for other "idle" causes such as "faults of temper," "idleness," or "extravagance." In marriage, Ruffin stated, couples agree to take each other "*as they are*." As for Marville Scroggins, Ruffin added, "We think him criminally accessory to his own dishonor, in marrying a woman whom he knew to be lewd." The marriage contract, Ruffin concluded, must remain binding. The Scrogginses' indiscretions were a mere inconvenience compared to the radical precedent the case would set on grounds for divorce.[8]

Many North Carolinians nonetheless pressed for divorces. Before the passage of the 1814 divorce law, twenty-three petitioners successfully obtained legislative divorces. Even after the courts assumed jurisdiction, the legislature continued to receive petitions. In 1821, the legislature resumed granting petitions. More petitions appeared, though none passed, after the meeting of the 1835 Constitutional Convention, which ratified an amendment that explicitly banned the legislature from such action. In total, North Carolinians filed 1,171 divorce petitions with the legislature between 1784 and 1837. Yet the legislature passed only a few. One scholar has argued that the legislature passed at least sixty-two divorces from 1794 to 1835. In fact, only a small fraction of divorce petitions were granted in any given year. For example, in 1810, the legislature granted one of twenty petitions, and in 1813, it passed four of twenty-two. According to studies of antebellum divorce, petitioners sought legislative relief because they claimed grounds outside the narrow confines of the statute or could not expend the costs and time required of a judicial divorce. As the numbers attest, only a few petitioners triumphed.[9]

The men and women who petitioned the 1868 North Carolina Constitutional Convention thus drew upon traditional processes to obtain their divorces. The backlog in the courts, the expense of pursuing a decree, and the narrow statutory ground that the law allowed propelled distraught men and women to request their representatives to present their petitions. While there is no available record of all requests made to convention delegates, it is clear that delegates presented at least twenty-seven petitions during the course of the convention. Fifteen passed. Like their antebellum counterparts, petitioners begged for relief that courts would not avail. Harmon Merritt claimed that the expense of a court case was too great and that the court would not hear his case because of its large docket that put it 250 cases behind. James and Nancy Brady argued that court costs prevented them from seeking local redress, and James Overton stated that the combined effects on his ill health and the onset of war prevented him from seeking divorce in the Bertie County courts.[10]

Exercising their sovereign power, the convention delegates granted most divorce ordinances for causes outside the narrow bounds of the statute. In the petitions that have survived, petitioners cited numerous causes, most of which did not meet the criteria of the statute. Six women and one man petitioned on the grounds of abandonment. One of these women also charged her husband with impotence. Five men claimed adultery, and three petitioners cited incompatibility as a reason for estrangement. One man claimed that his wife was mentally incompetent; another argued that his wife never showed him affection and refused to perform her household duties. Sometimes the convention followed the statutes when granting divorces, but mostly it did not. Among the grounds petitioners claimed, only two, adultery and impotence, warranted absolute divorces. All other claims were grounds for bed and board separations. Thus, the law allowed absolute divorces in only six of the aforementioned cases and only if the petitioners presented adequate proof. However, the convention approved only two of these six cases. Instead, the convention granted numerous absolute divorces for causes that the law would recognize only as warranting bed and board separations. For example, abandonment was grounds for a bed and board separation, but the convention granted full divorces to all six women who petitioned on this charge. John Crutchfield, the lone man who made this charge, was denied. Delegates also granted two divorces where petitioners claimed incompatibility or loss of affection and one divorce where a wife refused to perform her household duties. Often, legislators' liberal attitudes benefited women petitioners. The court granted divorces to nine individual women, more than half of the petitions that resulted in private divorce ordinances.[11]

Though convention delegates appeared to show disproportionate sympathy to women, men received a generous application of the law. The convention issued ordinances to five individual men and one spousal couple that filed jointly. As in the women's petitions, successful petitions by men did not always meet the strict scrutiny of the law. Edward Shroyer fully realized that no state court would accept his grounds for divorcing his wife, Mary. Shroyer's marriage to Mary had never fully met his expectations. When the Confederate army conscripted Shroyer into service, Mary moved to her married sister's home. At the war's end, Shroyer planned a move to Warrenton, North Carolina, where he expected to resume his trade as a tinner. However, Mary refused to follow. Despite his requests for her "to go with him to live in said town and to manage his household affairs for him, as it was her duty to do," she "absolutely" refused to leave her sister until he forcibly brought her home. Eventually, Mary returned to her sister's while Edward was away on business. According to Edward's petition, Mary not only abandoned him but, worse, "never manifested, (after a short period immediately succeeding their marriage) that affection which should be the basis of the marital relation." Nor did she perform for him "the most trifling yet most necessary offices" that apparently she had performed for her brother-in-law without request. Shroyer pleaded for a divorce to relieve him of his impudent wife. The convention was his only hope, as he admitted that he had "no grounds to impugn the chastity of his wife" on charges of adultery. Having framed his marital troubles in terms of contractual relations, Shroyer apparently convinced delegates that his wife had broken the nuptial contract by failing to fulfill her obligations. Delegates passed an ordinance authorizing Shroyer's absolute divorce on the last day of the convention.[12]

In 1868, no one would dispute the logic that impelled Shroyer to bypass the courts and seek redress from the convention. Antebellum and post-bellum jurists did not accept the premise upon which Shroyer founded his interpretation of the marriage contract. Judges would have rejected Shroyer's complaint unless, perhaps, he had requested a bed and board separation on charges of abandonment. Shroyer had argued that Mary simply had not fulfilled her contractual obligations and thus the contract was broken. For Shroyer, marriage was a contract like any other. Parties consented, provided consideration, and pledged their obligations. Broken contracts indicated the failure of one party to meet those obligations. But judges argued that although marriage followed certain contractual rules, it was a form of contract sui generis, an institution unlike any other. Under the terms of marital contracts, significant political and natural inequalities prevailed. Therefore, common law and equity courts scrutinized divorce cases with great care. To treat marriage like other contracts ran the risk of undermining the marital institution and overturning gender conventions by confirming a wife's full political and natural equality to her husband. In 1864, one attorney aptly summarized the legal profession's characterization of marriage. Marriage, he said, "is a contract *sui generis*, and unlike any other. So soon as this status is established it falls under the control of the public and ceases to be the creature of the parties. Neither, nor both together, are authorized to annul the status." Close reading of antebellum and postbellum judicial opinions explain the exclusivity of the marriage contract and the profound social and gendered implications of divorce.[13]

In many ways, marriage operated like other contracts. At the heart of any contract, including marriage, lay the concepts of reason and consent. In 1864, Justice Matthias Evans Manly defined a contract as "an agreement upon sufficient consideration to do, or not to do, a particular thing, between parties able to contract, willing to contract, and actually contracting." Both parties' ability to reason was central to a marriage contract's validity. Judges assumed that single women and men both possessed clear mental abilities to reason and consent. If one party lacked the power of reason, the marriage was null and void. Indeed, judges had applied similar interpretations of contracts to the marital relation well before the Civil War. Twice in 1843 the North Carolina Supreme Court ruled that courts must void marriages if either party is proved to be a "lunatic" at the time of marriage. The court nullified Ann Kincade's marriage to Reese Johnson, a proclaimed "idiot . . . from his birth," when relatives claimed that she had married him only to gain access to his small but significant property holdings. Supreme court justice Thomas Ruffin confirmed Reese Johnson's mental incapacities and stated that evidence showed that Johnson "was incompetent to make any contract, and especially, one of such great importance as marriage." Johnson's inability to reason thus protected him from Ann Kincade's scurrilous intent. "A competent share of reason is necessary to the validity of the matrimonial contract, for that it, as every other, depends on the consent of the parties, and, without understanding, consent cannot be given." As such, the marriage never legally existed and required no divorce decree, an act that dissolved a valid marriage on judicial discretion.[14]

The courts presumed that single women possessed ample abilities to reason, a necessity because marriage required a dramatic change in a woman's legal status. To engage in a marriage contract, a woman must exhibit understanding of her changing role. In the term following the Reese Johnson case, the North Carolina Supreme Court declared null and void the marriage of Letitia M. Crump to Henry Morgan. Ruffin argued that though evidence demonstrated that Crump experienced "lucid intervals," including the day of her marriage, "she was considered and treated by all as an insane person, and she acted as if she was always insane." Because the law of coverture passed control and ownership of wives' property to their husbands, women must exhibit reason and understanding about their new status. Ruffin stated that the marriage contract operated like other contracts that transferred property from one party to another. If one "party is incapable of understanding the nature of the contract itself," Ruffin argued, "and incapable, from mental imbecility, to take care of his or her person and property, such a one cannot dispose of his or her person or property by the matrimonial contract, any more than by any other contract."[15]

Yet the law refused to recognize a woman's ability to contract once she married. The law of coverture, a common law dictum accepted in North Carolina and throughout most of the United States, stipulated that upon marriage, a woman's identity merged with her husband's. Married women could not sue or be sued, contract, hold custody of their children, or maintain separate property outside of their husband's interests and control. Judges upheld these traditions in reference to oft-cited words of Sir William Blackstone, an English treatise writer, who argued that "by marriage, the husband and wife are one person in law: that is, the very being or legal existence of the woman is suspended during the marriage, or at least is incorporated and consolidated into that of the husband; under whose wing, protection, and *cover*, she performs everything." In other words, the patriarchal conditions of coverture presumed that a husband's identity so pervaded a wife's that the law viewed her as unable to exercise consent to contract independently and without undue influence from her husband. Only if she and her husband had mutually agreed to establish a separate estate for her property, had contracted the agreement before marriage, and had provided that the property remain with a trustee would the law recognize her as having any control of her property.[16]

North Carolina Supreme Court justice Thomas Ruffin upheld these conditions in an 1840 dispute between a wife's trustee and a husband's creditor. In that case, the creditor, John L. Ferrill, successfully won a judgment that voided a couple's postnuptial settlement intended to secure a wife's property from her husband's creditors. While the couple had signed a valid antenuptial settlement, the agreement lacked full protections against the husband's debts. The postnuptial contract, however, was invalid. In defense of his opinion, Ruffin referenced an Elizabethan-era statute that firmly established that no postnuptial settlement between a husband and wife could change the conditions of a premarital agreement. Ruffin's views of marital relations depict the marriage contract as unique because it signified a sacred family bond that emphasized a husband's domestic authority as master of his dependents, including his wife, children, and slaves. In cases involving marital disputes, Ruffin believed that the welfare of the community should prevail over the wishes of one or both married partners. Thus, Ruffin depicted marriage as a unique civil contract that necessitated special scrutiny.[17]

Postwar judges firmly defended these precedents as the Constitutional Convention assembled in 1868. But their opinions drew more upon ideas of marriage as a natural state than as a civil union. One postwar justice used the language of John Locke to describe marriage. Chief Justice Edwin Reade, a former Unionist and prominent Republican, wrote numerous opinions between 1867 and 1872 on marriage. Reade embraced a characterization of marriage as profoundly unique, as did Ruffin. However, he depicted marriage as a natural state in which the husband not only exercised legal authority as master of his dependents but also possessed a natural superiority that his wife lacked. To Reade, the marriage contract was more than a unique civil contract, a contract sui generis. In his view, it represented a divine institution that could exist outside of civil society. The marriage contract, Reade believed, operated according to natural laws, not man-made ones. In a Lockean state of nature, where chaos reigned, marriage operated spontaneously between a man and a woman to balance sex-based characteristics of a husband's independence and strength and a wife's dependence and weakness. Reade's predecessor, Thomas Ruffin, had argued that the marriage contract required government formalities to make it binding. But Reade, who emphasized the divine nature of marriage, argued that government recognition of marriage was unnecessary. "The substance of marriage," he said, rested in the consent of the parties, not in government recognition. Even a mere verbal consent between a man and woman secured this "most endeared relation which nature makes or society forms." Reade denoted a mystical quality to marital relations that placed the institution beyond the bounds of civil society. "Little legislation is necessary to define and regulate it," he argued; "we know it by intuition." Marriage, "formed in perfect freedom" without constraints of parents, customs, or laws, existed "in perfect simplicity and preserved in religious purity." Ruffin, who depended upon statutory and common laws to define a masters' dominion over his dependents, likely would have disapproved of Reade's purely natural characterization of marriage.[18]

Reade's Lockean view of the marriage contract rested upon his beliefs about gender relations. For Reade, the state's most powerful justice, men and women achieved their most natural state upon marriage. Propelled by "ardent and mutual" love, husband and wife assume their most perfect roles. "The husband is the stronger, and rules as of right," Reade argued; "the wife is the weaker, and submits in gentleness." Any condition that violates these natural duties fundamentally undermines the natural state of marriage. Separation and divorce, Reade believed, reduced marriage to a capricious experiment that created "the anomalous condition of a husband without a wife, a wife without a husband, parents without children, and children without parents." Judges' willingness to recognize wives' separate estates or to grant married women rights as "free traders" so that they may keep their earnings, principles upheld not in law but in some equity courts, violated the natural principles that govern marriage. The recognition by equity courts of married women's limited rights, Reade argued, "tends to produce an artificial and complicated state of things; so that, while at law the wife's existence is considered as merged in that of her husband, her earnings are his, she can not contract or sue and be sued; in equity she is entitled to her earnings, may act as a free trader, acquire property, sue and be sued in respect thereto."[19]

Reade's belief in married women's natural weakness and dependence rested upon his assumption that married women lacked the capacity to reason and were unable to articulate any self-interest separate from their husbands. Reade clearly presented his views in an 1867 opinion in the case *Collins v. Collins*. In 1863, Elizabeth Collins and her husband, Mark L. Collins, mutually agreed to formalize their separation by drafting an agreement that immediately granted Elizabeth rights to one-third of her husband's estate. In return, she would rescind her dower rights (her right to one-third of his estate upon his death for her life only), a principle that normally would take effect upon his death. In other words, Mark Collins agreed to give his wife one-third of his estate for her separate use (the amount normally reserved as a widow's dower) but prior to his death. Reade declared the agreement invalid. "Parties are not allowed to be the judges" in divorce and separation matters, Reade stated, and must apply to the courts for such remedies. Voluntary and mutual separation agreements "make the relation of husband and wife a mere trade or bargain, dependent upon their caprice." Furthermore, such agreements presumed a wife's capacity to act in her own self-interest, an unnatural state for a dependent wife. Mutual agreements between husbands and wives were, by definition, unequal, and "open[ed] the door to fraud," Reade opined, where an "imperious husband" could "compel a separation" from his "faultless" wife and "she, to buy her peace, would take such terms as he might offer" and less than the law might allow. Most likely, Reade concluded, Mark Collins had defrauded Elizabeth of her dower rights because as a wife she had no will of her own to sign a valid contract with him.[20]

As the *Collins* case demonstrates, Reade abhorred any contract, agreement, or court decree that suggested a married woman's independence and ability to contract. To Reade, marriage was a natural state that served as the "nursery of morality and piety, and the bulwarks of society." In marriage, men and women assumed their natural states of superiority and "gentleness." Divorce and separation agreements that pretended to serve married women's self-interests, Reade argued, introduced great "evil" that trained children "to hate one parent or both" and exposed society to the "nuisance" of a couple's "infidelities." And, Reade suggested, these agreements undermined the natural authority of a husband over his wife. Reade dismissed divorce cases where husbands committed malicious assault and battery upon their wives, even when there was no provocation. In marriage, Reade argued that husbands and wives formed domestic governments "suited to their own peculiar conditions, and that those governments are supreme, and from them there is no appeal except in cases of great importance requiring the strong arm of the law, and that to those governments they must submit themselves." Even equity courts that recognized women's limited independence threatened the very foundation of the patriarchal social order. Granted a will of her own, a wife violated the natural principles of marriage and gender relations, thus presenting a threat to social harmony.[21]

With such restrictive views of divorce dominating Reade's opinions, it is not surprising that North Carolinians such as James and Nancy Brady and Edward Shroyer opted to bypass the courts and, instead, petition the Constitutional Convention for divorce. In fact, three petitions, including James and Nancy Brady's, requested full divorces by couples in mutual agreement. By Reade's understanding, these petitions represented a fundamental threat to the "bulwarks" of society by falsely presuming married women's capacity to choose their fate without undue influence by their husbands.[22]

Reade's line of thinking is consistent with early social contract theorists such as Locke and Immanuel Kant, who viewed marriage as an important contractual agreement that granted men rights to women's bodies. The marriage contract featured prominently in early theorists' writings about social contract theory, the heart of nineteenth-century American republicanism. Carole Pateman, who has studied Locke, Kant, and other social theorists, argues that social contract theory, the belief that free social relations represent a contract among men, is also a sexual contract. "It is sexual in the sense of patriarchal," Pateman states. The social contract establishes men's shared political rights, and it is "also sexual in the sense of establishing orderly access by men to women's bodies." According to Pateman, social contract theory is premised upon assumptions that men share political obligations and responsibilities as independent and rational citizens, characteristics that women lack. Thus, men participated in contractual relations, both at the ballot box and in civil society, because they possessed the power to consent and contract. Women did not. "Women in general," Kant once stated, "have no civil personality, and their existence is, so to speak, purely inherent." Marriage served as the safest refuge for women who by nature lacked full capacity to consent and contract. Because married women were unable to consent and contract, the safety of society rested upon men's control of them in marriage. In her analysis, Pateman exposes the deep contradictions latent in the belief that all contracts, including nuptial ones, depend upon assumptions of individuals' natural powers to reason and consent. Marriage contracts also assign these same values to women, enabling them to join the nuptial contract, and then strips them of their civil personality once married. "How," Pateman muses, "can beings who lack the capacities to make contracts nevertheless be supposed always to enter into this contract?" In *Collins*, *Susan Cooke v. Henry L. Cooke*, and *State v. A. B. Rhodes*, Reade fails to explain, except to suggest that women's rationality is truly imperfect and may be exercised only in limited form.[23]

While Reade held fast to early interpretations of marriage and social contract theory, 1868 convention delegates broke away from these traditional beliefs. They assessed petitions on a case-by-case basis and dissolved those marriages that appeared entirely irreconcilable. When considering petitions, delegates accepted testimonies from across the community. For most common people, family matters involved extended relatives, neighbors, and sometimes whole communities. Husbands and wives found their actions scrutinized by church members, neighbors, coworkers, boarders, employees, and former slaves. James Overton submitted the testimony of a former slave, Dolly Mayo, to support his case for a divorce from his wife, Charlotte Overton. As a slave, Dolly had witnessed Charlotte Overton and W. W. Hathaway sleeping together "at least twelve times." Hathaway and Overton had threatened to whip Mayo and sell members of her family if she informed anyone about their carnal activities. Neighbor James Norman testified that he had seen men entering Charlotte Overton's house during her husband's absence. Apparently, gossip buzzed through the community as neighbors speculated about Overton's male visitors. "The Common and general sound opinion in this vicinity," argued Norman, "is that she is nothing more or less than a common prostitute is ready and willing to receive in her wonton embrace any man that will visit her." Convention delegates, persuaded by these depositions that Charlotte Overton had conducted herself wrongly, granted the divorce in favor of her husband, James.[24]

Convention delegates accepted grounds of impotence and abandonment even where evidence was slim. Eliza Wagner's petition was among the first considered at the convention. Wagner hoped to divorce her foreign-born husband, Herman Wagner, when she "learned that he was destitute of One of the most essential qualities that constituted a man and the marriage vow." Though Wagner failed to cite specifically the qualities of manhood that her husband lacked, she nonetheless asked that the state dissolve her marriage because her husband failed to meet his responsibilities toward her. For similar reasons, Josephine Parks requested a divorce from her husband, James M. Emanuel, who had abandoned her, moved to South Carolina, and forged his brother's name on a five thousand dollar loan. "I as a victim upon the alter [sic] of his sacrifice," pleaded Parks, "appeal to your clemency for redress."[25]

At first, divorce petitions stymied the delegates because procedures seemed unclear. On February 1, 1868, William B. Rodman, chair of the Committee on the Judicial Department, presented a recommendation for the case of Dewitt C. Willson and Nancy C. Willson. The convention president, Calvin Cowles, had designated the judiciary committee to handle the case because no other committee seemed appropriate. The new responsibility perplexed members of the judiciary committee. Members argued that the committee had no jurisdiction of "private matters." Rodman diplomatically reported "that if the Convention determines to legislate on private matters, they recommend a favorable consideration of the case."[26]

Three days later, the convention still had not determined how to handle the divorce petitions. Clear differences among Republican delegates emerged. African American delegates actively pressed for consideration of the petitions despite firm opposition from prominent white Republicans who argued that divorce was outside the bounds of the convention and wished to refer the petitioners to the courts. On February 4, the judiciary committee recommended that the convention pass an ordinance granting a divorce to Martha Hopkins. Several delegates immediately attempted to block any additional discussion of divorce issues in the convention. Richard W. King of Lenoir moved to table the vote, and Albion Tourgee, a former Greensboro Unionist born in Ohio, argued that he opposed "on principle to granting divorces by legislation." Other delegates demanded to hear the case. James Walker Hood, an African American minister who represented Cumberland County, wanted more details about Hopkins's case. The vote was tabled, though eleven of the thirteen African American delegates voted against the postponement. Clearly, most of the African Americans, including Hood, found divorce a public matter worthy of consideration by the convention.[27]

African American delegates, dissatisfied with the convention's treatment of Hopkins's case, strongly urged delegates to hear divorce cases.

Two days after the convention had tabled Hopkins's case, James Henry Harris, perhaps the convention's most prominent African American delegate, presented the divorce petition of Ann Underdue, an African American woman born free before the Civil War. Cowles, hoping to prevent another stalemate, appointed a "committee of three," headed by Harris, to consider Underdue's petition. Within a week, Harris's committee had accumulated several more petitions and earned the name "Special Committee on Divorce." As divorce petitions poured into the convention hall, Cowles apportioned most to the new committee. But as Harris's docket became swamped, Cowles sent some petitions to the judiciary committee and others to a "committee of seventeen" in order to alleviate the divorce committee's heavy load.[28]

It is possible that African Americans fought for the divorce petitioners because their view of gender relations differed from those of some of the prominent white Republicans at the convention. Some African Americans actively campaigned for women's rights. Abram Galloway, an African American delegate and former slave from New Hanover County, worked tirelessly to secure rights for African Americans and women. Like his counterparts James Walker Hood and James Henry Harris, Galloway voted in favor of considering the divorce petitions. Furthermore, he continued his work for women's rights as a North Carolina state senator. In 1869 and again in 1870, Galloway introduced two separate bills to North Carolina's senate that proposed an amendment to grant women's suffrage. In addition, he pushed for legislation to secure women's rights to property and to fight domestic abuse. Galloway's effort to pursue gender equality was extremely rare among North Carolina legislators. By these actions, Galloway demonstrated that he believed, to some degree, that women possessed self-interests separate from their husbands. Unable to accept the idea that husbands' authority should remain unquestioned, Galloway campaigned for women's franchise, property rights, and autonomy over their bodies. Although Galloway left no lasting evidence of direct statements about his views of gender roles, his efforts to secure women's political, economic, and social rights to consent and contract lie documented in the bills that he presented.[29]

Despite African American efforts to make divorce an issue at the convention, prominent white Republicans strongly dissented. Most vocal was Samuel S. Ashley, formerly of Rhode Island and employed as a Freedmen's Bureau agent and minister in the American Missionary Association. Ashley joined Albion Tourgee in his opposition to the convention as a forum for divorce matters. When Harris presented Ann Underdue's petition, Tourgee moved to table it. His motion lost, and Harris proceeded to state Underdue's case. Before long, Ashley requested that the convention refer divorce issues to the legislature. "No doubt it [is] a case of hardship," he argued, "but let the whole affair, with all similar cases, pass over to the Legislature . . . where such provisions could be made in the law as would be liberal and just." Richard W. King agreed and argued that the convention should discard the divorce petitions and concentrate upon performing its "legitimate duties." He claimed that "if one divorce [is] granted, twenty thousand would pour in." Discussion of divorce at the convention, he asserted, "was out of the question." King's hyperbolic prediction did not come to pass. The convention granted fifteen divorces, but delegates presented a mere twenty-seven petitions.[30]

Yet neither Ashley, Tourgee, nor King could deter Harris from presenting petitions. Eventually, delegates came to a compromise. The convention would consider only cases of "extreme hardship"—those unusual cases for which the law did not provide. County courts, they decreed, must settle all cases regarding "ordinary" matters, such as adultery. The convention would grant divorces in egregious cases where the law did not otherwise allow for relief. Thus, Harris's committee of three recommended that the convention grant Ann Underdue a divorce because her husband had abandoned her and left the state. However, this committee refused to consider Harmon Merritt's petition because it appeared to be a cut-and-dry matter of adultery. "The petitioner," Rodman argued, "is fully entitled to a remedy in the Courts and they see no reason for giving him any special relief." Sometimes the convention granted divorces despite a committee's unfavorable recommendation. The judiciary committee refused to grant a divorce to Jethro Morgan, a farmer who claimed that his wife possessed an "ungovernable temper" and "spent everything . . . in the most foolish manner." Rodman argued that Morgan presented a weak case. Apparently, the convention found Morgan's case a compelling one and granted him relief, anyway.[31]

By the convention's end, delegates had granted fifteen divorces. By doing so, they had largely rejected the state's statutory and case precedent on divorce. In numerous cases such as Morgan's, delegates accepted far broader grounds and relied upon much less evidence than the courts would have allowed. Some delegates found extremely troubling the convention's loose construction of divorce laws. Prominent white Republicans balked at the possibility that divorce might once again become a legislative matter. Immediately after the convention had decreed the last divorce, Calvin Cowles and J. Q. A. Bryan entered an official dissent against the ordinances. "Being of the opinion that all cases of divorce properly belongs to the Courts," they protested, "we dissent from granting the same otherwise." To prevent North Carolinians from petitioning the legislature for divorces as they had petitioned the convention, Tourgee and Rodman drafted a measure, ratified on March 13, 1868, limiting the General Assembly's power over divorce issues. The measure stated that "the General Assembly shall have power to pass general laws regulating divorce and alimony, but shall not have power to grant a divorce or secure alimony in any individual case." Just as Ashley and Tourgee had wished, divorce once again had become a matter for the courts.[32]

Yet most delegates favored consideration of the divorce petitions. Their favorable votes indicate that unlike the judges' opinions, North Carolinians' views of marriage had evolved to reflect some of the principles advocated by northern feminists such as Elizabeth Cady Stanton, Julia Ward Howe, and Lydia Maria Child. Northern feminists argued that marriage resembled other contracts at law. Stanton attacked traditionalists' views of marriage as a status that enforced gender inequalities and reduced women to a state of slavery by dispossessing them of their property and bodies. The state, she contended, should recognize marriage as equivalent to other free contracts. "Let the State be logical," she proposed; "if marriage is a civil contract, it should be subject to the laws of all other contracts." She condoned divorce as a necessary freedom for women "to sunder a yoke she has freely bound." Most feminists embraced Stanton's view of the marriage contract and its implication for equal rights within marriage, though fewer accepted her view of divorce. Feminists did not believe that the marriage contract should resemble marketplace contracts of sale. Women were not to be bought and sold, which to some was the implication of unrestricted divorce laws. However, feminists, those who had matured in the age of abolition and emancipation, equated marriage with bondage and slavery. By recognizing women's equal contract rights in marriage, American courts and legislatures would emancipate women as the Civil War had emancipated slaves. The divorce ordinances at the 1868 North Carolina Constitutional Convention suggest that convention delegates shared views with many feminists. By dissolving fifteen of twenty-seven divorces, delegates demonstrated that they believed that marriage should resemble other contracts and enforce equalities between husband and wife. But by rejecting nearly half of the petitions, they also indicated that divorce should not reduce the relationship between husband and wife to a marketplace transaction.[33]

Indeed, convention delegates sought other reforms for married women.

A measure to grant married women full property rights passed a committee, though members of the convention floor diluted the proposal. What passed nonetheless amounted to a fairly significant reform in married women's property rights. The fight for married women's property rights originated as the "Majority Report of the Committee on Homesteads." In its report, the committee proposed that married women would possess full and separate control of their property and be able to control, dispose, or bequeath it at will. "All real and personal property that any female in the state should acquire before and during marriage," the committee maintained in the report submitted by chairman C. C. Jones, would "remain [her] sole and separate estate . . . as if she were a *femme sole.*" Delegates on the floor rejected the language. The amended version maintained married women's separate ownership, but control rested upon husbands' assent. The final version appeared as Section 6 of Article 10, "Homesteads and Exemptions." It granted married women a small measure of control of their real and personal property "acquired before and during marriage." The difference between this provision and the law before 1868 rested upon the husband's legal claim to the property. Before 1868, he claimed fee simple possession of his wife's property. The constitutional provision, legislated by the General Assembly in 1868–69, endowed him with control only as if he were a trustee.[34]

Perhaps the most significant property reform for married women rested not in Section 6 of the homestead article but in Section 8, the "privy examination." The "privy examination" operated fully at odds with the common law because it presumed married women's ability to consent independent of their husbands' influence. This measure, proposed by James Walker Hood, required married women's consent when husbands conveyed property. In a "private examination," a county official secured the wife's consent in a private interrogation. The "privy examination" first passed the legislature in 1866–67 as a law that required married women's consent in a "private examination" when husbands conveyed the homestead and certain adjacent lands. Hood's provision added the "privy examination" to the constitution. One year later, the General Assembly extended the "privy examination" to all lands owned by the husband "at any time during coverture." The language had vast consequences to husbands' property rights. Prior to 1868–69, the law allowed a wife to claim dower (life interest to one-third of the estate) only to the lands that her husband owned upon his death. The 1868–69 legislation redefined dower to extend to all the lands he owned during the marriage. Thus, the new law required married women's consent to any sale or debt secured against the property. The new dower and privy exam laws also bore significance for gender relations. The state presumed that a wife could freely exercise her consent in a private exam that her husband could not attend. For good or ill, the privy exam presumed married women's capacity to reason and consent independent of their husbands.[35]

Some historians have maintained that antebellum and Reconstruction-era legislators passed reforms in married women's property laws primarily to benefit men. Suzanne Lebsock and Angela Boswell have argued that property reform acts worked to protect family property from a man's debts. "There was something in them for men," Lebsock asserts, "and they had nothing to do with feminism." Boswell adds that husbands used the laws not only to provide for their families but also to extend their household authority. But Nancy Bercaw argues that this interpretation of married women's property reforms disregards the importance of married women's consent. Under the new laws, both wives and husbands were required to seek spousal consent. Once empowered, married women withheld consent in order to secure property for themselves and their children. The laws produced conflicts but also forced couples to come to agreements. As a result, Bercaw notes that these reforms partially subjected husbands to their wives. "Manly authority," Bercaw states, "became dependent, in part, on the partial emancipation of married women."[36]

It seems that Chief Justice Edwin Reade interpreted the new reforms as endowing married women with unnecessary contractual freedoms, for he registered his dismay at the new dower law. In *Sutton v. Askew* (1872), Reade forbade women who had married prior to passage of the new dower law from claiming its protections. In every other respect, he upheld the law, but not without deep criticism of the legislature's action. He argued that dower was part of the marriage contract, and thus the legislature had no power to control it. Legislative meddling, he argued, threatened to abuse the institution by introducing language that was untested and vulnerable to exploitation. "And so, we see, that this great right, favored like life and liberty, instead of being as it ought to be, and as until lately it has been, so plain, that he that runs may read, is now involved in much confusion, by inconsiderate legislation and conflicting adjudications." Reade further argued that the 1868–69 dower law impaired husbands' vested rights in their wives' property as granted by the marriage contract. *Sutton* upheld the new dower law but nonetheless weakened it. Legislatures could not retroactively forbid husbands married before the act's passage from selling or conveying their property without their wives' consent. The new dower law, he argued, violated husbands' constitutionally protected property rights. By taking his property from him, Reade intoned, "and giving it to another, under the notion, as is said, of the 'paramount public good,' without compensation, then we cannot understand what would be an instance of such a violation of the rights of property." Former slaveholders had referenced the same constitutional principles in regard to their property in slaves. It is ironic that Reade, a prominent Republican jurist and defender of African American rights, did not make this connection in terms of gender relations. Nor did he recognize the constitutional problem in coverture laws that divested a woman from all of her property in the first place.[37]

While Reade vociferously denounced the new dower law, his colleague Justice Robert P. Dick heartily embraced it. Dick was a former loyalist Unionist who had served in the state legislature during the Confederacy and had helped form the state's Republican Party in 1867. He offered a weighty dissent in *Sutton* that demonstrates an alternative to Reade's Lockean opinion of gender relations and the marriage contract. In *Sutton*, Dick argued, Reade had failed to consider the true nature of marriage. Reade had asserted that the new dower law requiring a privy exam violated a husband's contractual rights in marriage. In three points, Dick argued otherwise. First, he maintained, dower rights derived from equity courts and statutory law and thus remained outside the bounds of the marriage contract. Second, he declared, marriage is not only a contract but a status regulated by law. "It would be a very narrow view, in times like those through which we have passed, to regard it merely as an individual agreement, governed entirely, by the strict technical rules of ordinary contracts." Finally, Dick added, the constitution empowered the legislature to restrict property rights when in the interest of the general public good. Dick, concerned about married women's desperate economic straits due to the losses of war and indebtedness, favored married women's expanded rights. "Surely," he pleaded, "there has never been a time in the history of this country, more appropriate than the present, for a liberal exercise of the remedial powers of legislation for the general public good." Furthermore, he added, a woman's rights under the new dower law did not conflict with a husband's constitutional rights to her property. Although the expanded dower law restricted his rights, it did not deprive "him of his property within the meaning of the Constitution" because the wife's rights would take effect only after his death and were part of a husband's legal and moral obligation to "make suitable provision for her support and comfort after his death."[38]

Although Dick made no reference to his views of women's character, his dissent offers some interesting insight to show that, unlike Reade, he accepted women's abilities to reason, if only nominally. In his dissent, Dick affirmed the view of women's dependence upon men by stating that husbands had obligations to support their wives. Yet he indicates that this dependence derived from man-made laws, not natural characteristics. Marriage, he said, is an institution regulated by legislative authority, not by any express contract between the parties. "The common law," he stated, "declares that the effect of a marriage shall be to vest in the husband certain rights as to the wife's personal property in possession, the rents and profits of her real estate, and her chattels real and choses [that is, personal] in action; and in consideration of these benefits, he is required to take care of his wife, and if he is able, supply her with such things as may be necessary to her comfort in her condition in society." Given this definition, married women's status did not derive from women's natural weakness, as Reade had argued in *Collins*, but upon "positive law adopted by the legislative authority." Thus, married women's status derived from their political dependence only and not from any natural inability to reason. Therefore, the new dower laws and the privy exam that required women's consent were perfectly constitutional.[39]

Dick's dissent, lawmakers' reforms, and convention delegates' ordinances reflected the Reconstruction-era sea change in gender relations that had occurred in the law. The Constitutional Convention had undermined common-law coverture laws that bound women's identity and self-will. Lawmakers willingly recognized, albeit with certain limitations, married women's contractual abilities and capacity to reason independent of their husbands. Divorce petitions and ordinances passed during the 1868 convention demonstrate that some petitioners and delegates viewed marriage as a contract, an agreement where both men and women acted as rational agents who could break the contract or dissolve it at will. Convention delegates and lawmakers extended these liberal views of divorce only toward petitions received during its tenure and not in the general law. But married women's property rights fared differently. Both in the convention and in the subsequent session of the General Assembly, lawmakers acknowledged married women's rational abilities to consent, in the form of private examinations, to their husbands' sales, conveyances, and transfers of property. To be sure, these gains did not place women on the same footing as men in regard to citizenship and economic independence. Yet the issues raised in the 1868 Constitutional Convention marked a watershed for women's political status. Once considered in the same legal category as minors, women's status had grown in the eyes of lawmakers who increasingly accepted the belief in women's abilities to reason. Thus, masters of households suffered two defeats during Reconstruction. Although emancipation and enfranchisement of African American men represented a spectacular change in the nation's political development, legal reforms for women had a more quiet effect. By acknowledging married women's ability to reason and contract, these reforms significantly undermined husbands' legal authority in unprecedented fashion.

Notes

1. Petition of Martha H. Hopkins; Deposition of Robert D. Hart; Deposition of Charles E. Landis; Deposition of William S. Skinner; all dated January 15, 1868, and maintained in a folder entitled "Ordinances, etc." in the Records of the Constitutional Convention, 1868, box 295, Secretary of State Documents, North Carolina State Archives (hereafter NCSA), Raleigh.

2. Recent studies of gender and marriage contracts in Reconstruction primarily emphasize degrees of women's dependency and men's authority in household relations. See Laura F. Edwards, *Gendered Strife and Confusion: The Political Culture of Reconstruction* (Urbana: University of Illinois Press, 1997); and Nancy Bercaw, *Gendered Freedoms: Race, Rights, and the Politics of Household in the Delta, 1861–1875* (Gainesville: University Press of Florida, 2003). While I accept the framework of household relations as presented in current scholarship, the argument here examines the marriage contract and gender relations in the context of social contract theory. On gender and social contract theory, see Carole Pateman, *The Sexual Contract* (Stanford: Stanford University Press, 1988), 90–91; and Amy Dru Stanley, *From Bondage to Contract: Wage Labor, Marriage, and the Market in the Age of Slave Emancipation* (New York: Cambridge University Press, 1998), 56–59. I explain coverture in North Carolina in *Labor of Innocents: Forced Apprenticeship in North Carolina* (Baton Rouge: Louisiana State University Press, 2005), 20, 21, 85–86. See also Peter Bardaglio, *Reconstructing the Household: Families, Sex, and the Law in the Nineteenth-Century South* (Chapel Hill: University of North Carolina Press, 1995), 31; Victoria E. Bynum, *Unruly Women: The Politics of Social and Sexual Control in the Old South* (Chapel Hill: University of North Carolina Press, 1992), 60; and Suzanne Lebsock, *The Free Women of Petersburg: Status and Culture in a Southern Town, 1784–1860* (New York: W. W. Norton, 1984), 23. Marylynn Salmon describes coverture in the terms of "unity of person" in *Women and the Law of Property in Early America* (Chapel Hill: University of North Carolina Press, 1986), 14, 200n1.

3. Eric Foner, *America's Unfinished Revolution, 1863–1877* (New York: Harper and Row, 1988), 276–77; Horace Raper, *William W. Holden: North Carolina's Political Enigma* (Chapel Hill: University of North Carolina Press, 1985), 55, 98; William C. Harris, *William Woods Holden: Firebrand of North Carolina Politics* (Baton Rouge: Louisiana State University Press, 1987), 232, 234; Paul D. Escott, *Many Excellent People: Power and Privilege in North Carolina, 1850–1900* (Chapel Hill: University of North Carolina Press, 1985), 142; Karin L. Zipf, "'The WHITES shall rule the land or die': Gender, Race, and Class in North Carolina Reconstruction Politics," *Journal*

of Southern History 65 (August 1999): 503-6. The quote appears in the *Journal of the Constitutional Convention of the state of North- Carolina, at its session 1868* (Raleigh: J. W. Holden, 1868), 484 (microform). While other scholars have noted that fifteen African American delegates participated in the convention, Leonard Bernstein definitively identified only thirteen. For Bernstein's comments on this matter, see "The Participation of Negro Delegates in the Constitutional Convention of 1868 in North Carolina," *Journal of Negro History* 34 (1949): 391.

4. For petitions, see "Ordinances, etc.," box 295, NCSA; for ordinances, see *Constitution of the State of North Carolina, together with the Ordinances and Resolutions of the Constitutional Convention, Assembled in the City of Raleigh, Jan. 14th, 1868* (Raleigh: Joseph W. Holden, Convention Printer, 1868); and for a chronology of events of the convention, see *Journal of the Constitutional Convention . . . 1868.*

5. Pateman, *Sexual Contract*, 183; Joseph S. Ferrell, "Early Statutory and Common Law of Divorce in North Carolina," *North Carolina Law Review* 14 (1963): 604-9, quotation on 608.

6. For specific historical references to the legislative acts regarding divorce, see *The Revised Statutes of the State of North Carolina, Passed by the General Assembly at the Session of 1836-7* (Raleigh: Turner and Hughes, 1837), 1:238-39; Jane Turner Censer, "'Smiling through Her Tears': Ante-Bellum Southern Women and Divorce," *American Journal of Legal History* 25 (January 1982): 31-32; and Ferrell, "Early Statutory and Common Law of Divorce," 610-12.

7. In 1822, the court specified grounds for an absolute divorce and established that malicious intent was necessary in cruelty cases in *Long v. Long*, from Washington 9 N.C. 189 (1822). On grounds for divorce, see Censer, "'Smiling through Her Tears,'" 33, 37-38; Guion Griffis Johnson, *Ante-Bellum North Carolina: A Social History* (Chapel Hill: University of North Carolina Press, 1937), 221-22; *Andrew Whittington v. Lucy Whittington*, 19 N.C. 64 (1836) and *Rebecca J. Wood v. Lorenzo Wood*, 27 N.C. 674 (1845); and *Ruthey Ann Hansley v. Samuel G. Hansley*, 32 N.C. 506 (1849). On divorce in the antebellum United States, see chapter 2 in Norma Basch, *Framing American Divorce: From the Revolutionary Generation to the Victorians* (Berkeley: University of California Press, 1999), 43-67; and Nancy Isenberg, *Sex and Citizenship in Antebellum America* (Chapel Hill: University of North Carolina Press, 1998), 161-67. Bardaglio discusses divorce laws in the South generally in *Reconstructing the Household*, 32-34. Quotation is from Bynum, *Unruly Women*, 61. On divorce in antebellum Virginia, see Lebsock, *Free Women of Petersburg*, 68-72.

8. *Marville Scroggins v. Lucretia Scroggins*, 14 N.C. 535 (1832); Bynum examines antebellum North Carolina justices' attitudes toward divorce in *Unruly Women*, 68-77.

9. Ferrell, "Early Statutory and Common Law of Divorce," 609-10; Ransom McBride, "Divorces and Separations from Petitions to the North Carolina General Assembly from 1779 (Part 26 and Last)," *North Carolina Genealogical Society Journal* 30, no. 1 (February 2004): 86-88; Johnson, *Ante-Bellum North Carolina*, 217.

10. Petition of Harmon Merritt, February 26, 1868; "Application to Divorce James Brady and Nancy Brady," n.d.; Petition of James Overton, February 13, 1868; all in "Ordinances, etc.," box 295, NCSA.

11. Data drawn from "Ordinances, etc.," box 295, NCSA; and *Constitution of the State of North Carolina, . . . 1868.*

12. Petition of Edward Shroyer, February 11, 1868, and entry dated March 14, *Journal of the Constitutional Convention . . . 1868,* 482.

13. *T. H. Gatlin v. Edward S. Walton,* 60 N.C. 333 (1864). On divorce and gender relations, see Bardaglio, *Reconstructing the Household,* 34. Basch explains the unusual contractual nature of marriage in *Framing American Divorce,* 25–28; Pateman provides an analysis of the marriage contract in *Sexual Contract,* 182–84.

14. *Reese Johnson by his Guardian v. Ann Kincade,* 37 N.C. 470 (1843).

15. See ibid. and *Letitia M. Crump by her Guardian v. Henry Morgan,* 38 N.C. 91 (1843). Postbellum courts affirmed Ruffin's view of single women's capacity to contract in *Susan Cooke v. Henry L. Cooke and others,* 61 N.C. 583 (1868) and *State v. Wesley Hairston and Puss Williams,* 63 N.C. 451 (1869).

16. Quoted in Bynum, *Unruly Women,* 60; and Pateman, *Sexual Contract,* 91. Emphasis in original.

17. *Edward Saunders v. John L. Ferrill,* 23 N.C. 97 (1840). Other cases where Ruffin specified the nature of the marriage contract include *The State v. Samuel, A Slave,* 19 N.C. 177 (1836); *Marville Scroggins v. Lucretia Scroggins,* 14 N.C. 535 (1832); and *William Irby et al. v. William J. Wilson et al.,* 21 N.C. 568 (1837). The court upheld a man's right to beat his wife as in the best interests of the community, despite the state's code on assault and battery. According to the court, "We know that a slap on the cheek, let it be as light as it may, indeed any touching of the person of another in a rude or angry manner—is in law an assault and battery. In the nature of things it cannot apply to persons in the marriage state, it would break down the great principle of mutual confidence and dependence; throw open the bedroom to the gaze of the public; and spread discord and misery, contention and strife, where peace and concord ought to reign. It must be remembered that rules of law are intended to act in all classes of society." See *State v. William Hussey,* 44 N.C. 123 (1852).

18. Quotes from *Elizabeth Collins v. John M. Collins,* 62 N.C. 153 (1867). See also *State v. Young Harris,* 63 N.C. 1 (1868). Yet Reade later argued that under certain conditions, the state can regulate marriage. Reade departs from his views of the state's role in marriage in *State v. Wesley Hairston and Puss Williams.* The state, he argues, can intervene and should in the case of intermarriage between the races. In this decision, he states that the substance of marriage—consent of the parties—precedes the law but that the state nonetheless can regulate the institution. Thus, a white woman and black man conceivably could consent to a marriage contract, but the state has the power to prevent them from fulfilling that contract. On Reade, see Buck Yearns, "Edwin Godwin Reade," in *Dictionary of North Carolina Biography,* ed. William S. Powell (Chapel Hill: University of North Carolina, 1979–96), 5:183–84.

19. *Elizabeth Collins v. John M. Collins.*

20. Ibid. The husband, Mark Collins, had died, and the case arose because his nearest living relation, John M. Collins, filed suit over the estate.

21. *State v. A. B. Rhodes,* 61 N.C. 453 (1868). Edwards explains how the marriage contract defined household relations in Reconstruction North Carolina in *Gendered Strife and Confusion,* 24–45. Bercaw examines alternative definitions of marriage

contracts in Reconstruction Mississippi in *Gendered Freedoms*, 110–20. Stanley examines freedmen's and freedwomen's views of the marriage contract, generally, in *From Bondage to Contract*, 44–50.

22. Petition of James Brady and Nancy Brady, n.d.; Petition of Henry G. Wood and Elizabeth Wood, February 11, 1868; and Petition of Dewitt C. Willson and Nancy C. Willson, January 29, 1868; all in "Ordinances, etc.," box 295, NCSA.

23. Pateman, *Sexual Contract*, 1–6, 168–70.

24. Deposition of Dolly Mayo, circa February 1, 1868; Deposition of Joseph Norman, February 1, 1868; and Petition of James Overton, February 13, 1868; all in Records of the Constitutional Convention, 1868, box 295, Secretary of State Documents, NCSA.

25. Petition of Eliza Wagner, January 21, 1868; and Petition of Josephine Parks, March 9, 1868; both in Records of the Constitutional Convention, 1868, box 295, Secretary of State Documents, NCSA.

26. See entry dated February 1, 1868, in *Journal of the Constitutional Convention . . . 1868*, 119–20.

27. See entry dated February 4, 1868, in ibid., 127–28; and the *Raleigh Standard* "Supplement," February 12, 1868. I located this copy of the "Supplement" in Letters to the Commissioner, Records of the Bureau of Refugees, Freedmen, and Abandoned Lands, RG 105, Reel 54, National Archives, Washington, D.C. See Otto H. Olsen, "Albion Winegar Tourgee," in *Dictionary of North Carolina Biography*, ed. Powell, 5:47–48; and John L. Bell Jr., "James Walker Hood," ibid., 3:195–96.

28. See entries dated February 7, 1868, February 14, 1868, and March 14, 1868, in *Journal of the Constitutional Convention . . . 1868*, 153, 225, 465. On Harris, see Roberta Sue Alexander, "James Henry Harris," in *Dictionary of North Carolina Biography*, ed. Powell, 3:53.

29. Galloway's views of the marriage contract reflected those of northern feminists such as Elizabeth Cady Stanton, who argued that society should recognize the contractual nature of marriage and sanction divorce. See Stanley, *From Bondage to Contract*, 184–86. Edwards explains that African Americans asserted alternative views to gender relations and the marriage contract in *Gendered Strife and Confusion*, 45–54, 54–65. Galloway's bills did not survive committee. In 1869, Conservative John Graham, chair of the judiciary committee, reported an unfavorable recommendation of the women's suffrage bill and asked that the assembly discharge the committee from further consideration of the matter. Upon Galloway's death in 1870, the female suffrage bill received no further mention from the General Assembly. Entries dated February 1, 1869, and February 24, 1869, in *Journal of the Senate of the General Assembly of the State of North Carolina at its Session of 1868–1869* (Raleigh: M. S. Littlefield, State Printer and Binder, 1869), 223, 343; and entries dated January 31, 1870, and March 1, 1870, in *Journal of the Senate of the General Assembly of the State of North Carolina at its Session of 1869–1870* (Raleigh: M. S. Littlefield, State Printer and Binder, 1870), 264, 466. On Galloway, see William R. Titchener, "Abram H. Galloway," in *Dictionary of North Carolina Biography*, ed. Powell, 2:271–72; and William Still, "Blood Flowed Freely," *The Underground Rail Road* (Philadelphia: William Still, 1883), 150–52. Two articles provide exhaustive information on the

African American politicians who served North Carolina during Reconstruction. See Bernstein, "The Participation of Negro Delegates," 391–409; and Elizabeth Balanoff, "Negro Legislators in the North Carolina General Assembly, July, 1868–February, 1872," *North Carolina Historical Review* 49 (1972): 22–55.

30. *Raleigh Standard* "Supplement," February 12, 1868. On Ashley, see John L. Bell Jr., "Samuel Stanford Ashley," in *Dictionary of North Carolina Biography*, ed. Powell, 1:58–59.

31. Petition of Jethro Morgan, January 14, 1868; Petition of Ann Underdue, circa February 1, 1868; and Petition of Harmon Merritt, February 26, 1868; all in "Ordinances, etc.," box 295, NCSA.

32. For Cowles's and Bryan's dissent, see March 13, 1868, *Journal of the Constitutional Convention . . . 1868*, 446. See Article 2, Section 12, *Constitution of the State of North Carolina, . . . 1868*, 11.

33. Stanley, *From Bondage to Contract*, 184–86.

34. See Article 10, "Homesteads and Exemptions," Section 12, *Constitution of the State of North Carolina, . . . 1868*, 34–35; *Journal of the Constitutional Convention . . . 1868*, 230, 277–79.

35. See Article 10, "Homesteads and Exemptions," Section 12, *Constitution of the State of North Carolina, . . . 1868*, 34–35; *Journal of the Constitutional Convention . . . 1868*, 230, 277–79; *Public Laws of the State of North Carolina, Passed by the General Assembly at its Session 1866–1867* (Raleigh: Wm. E. Pell, State Printer, 1867), 83; *Public Laws of the State of North Carolina, Passed by the General Assembly at its Session 1868–1869* (Raleigh: M. S. Littlefield, State Printer and Binder, 1869), 213–14. Prior history of married women's dower rights is provided in *W. M. Sutton and Wife v. J. A. J. Askew, et al.*, 66 N.C. 172 (1872).

36. Suzanne Lebsock, "Radical Reconstruction and the Property Rights of Southern Women," *Journal of Southern History* 43 (May 1977): 197; Angela Boswell, "Married Women's Property Rights and the Challenge to Patriarchal Order: Colorado County, Texas," in *Negotiating Boundaries of Southern Womanhood: Dealing With the Powers That Be*, ed. Janet L. Coryell et al. (Columbia: University of Missouri Press, 2000), 99; Bercaw, *Gendered Freedoms*, 141–43, quotation on 141; on gender and legal reforms, see 171–74. Stanley examines the implications of "earnings laws" on women's contractual rights; see Stanley, *From Bondage to Contract*, 175.

37. *W. M. Sutton and Wife v. J. A. J. Askew, et al.* On dower rights, see Salmon, *Women and the Law of Property in Early America*, 139–47. Lebsock discusses dower and the "privy examination" in *Free Women of Petersburg*, 24–25.

38. *W. M. Sutton and Wife v. J. A. J. Askew, et al.* On Dick, see Horace W. Raper, "Robert Paine Dick," in *Dictionary of North Carolina Biography*, ed. Powell, 2:63.

39. *W. M. Sutton and Wife v. J. A. J. Askew, et al.*

PAUL YANDLE

Different Colored Currents of the Sea

Reconstruction North Carolina, Mutuality, and
the Political Roots of Jim Crow, 1872–1875

In his work *The New South Creed*, Paul Gaston notes the
unanimity with which white southerners saw themselves as the protectors
of African Americans in a segregated society after the postwar amendments to the Constitution provided the slaves with freedom and United
States citizenship. Gaston's work is probably the most recognizable of those
covering the development of a "New South" philosophy in newspaper and
magazine articles and lectures written and given between the 1860s and
1890s. Gaston presents an array of newspaper editors and southern men
of letters who provided the public with pictures of an industrialized, self-
sufficient, segregated South that allowed politicians and jurists to undo the
gains African Americans had made during Reconstruction and to move
toward Jim Crow. These "New South" proponents, Gaston argues, began
promoting a plan for race relations soon after the Civil War and ultimately
won victory when Booker T. Washington emerged as an African American
spokesman for their segregationist program after his famous speech at the
Atlanta Cotton States Exposition in 1895.[1]

Washington did take a step toward accommodation that year by denying that African Americans sought to give integration, or what was then
loosely known as "social equality," legal sanction. His statement that "in all
things that are purely social we [African Americans and whites] can be as
separate as the fingers, yet one as the hand in all things essential to mutual
progress" has long been quoted—with some justification—as an African
American sellout to Jim Crow.[2] But despite the depth of discussions held
about Washington's speech for more than a century, it remains unclear just
what Washington meant by such terms as "separate as the fingers" and
"mutual progress."

Historians observe that Washington used a similar premise for race
relations that Henry W. Grady used in his editorials and his famous "New
South" speech, given in New York in the 1880s. Whites, including Grady,

were almost unanimous in their view that white landowners directed and benefited from African American labor and that African Americans depended upon landowners and the fruit of their labor for economic survival. Louis Harlan, Washington's biographer, refers to this premise by the term "mutuality" and argues that it was the theme of Washington's speech (although it should be noted that Washington also allowed for the existence of black professionals in a segregated setting).[3]

Washington may have endorsed a form of "mutuality," but unlike many pieces written by whites in the post–Civil War nineteenth century, Washington's speech never explicitly pairs "mutuality" with legalized Jim Crow as a permanent institution.[4] Washington's speech presents some acceptance of African American and white relationships as they existed in the South but as a social, not a legal, matter.[5] Historians from Harlan to August Meier have noted that Washington's concession to "mutual progress" "was more subtle than it seemed to be."[6]

Southern whites, however, seemed to have no questions about the meaning of Washington's words. By pairing "mutual progress" with racial separation in any form, voluntary or otherwise, Washington was pointing whites to terminology they had associated with legalized segregation years before Washington or even Grady discussed "mutuality" for national audiences. Parlance similar to Washington's had been used at the state and local level ever since the days following emancipation. Equally important, that parlance, though vaguely defined, had been used by whites in conjunction with increasingly clear, direct actions that began to entrench segregation legally in states as early as the 1870s. The use of such words as "mutual progress" and the consequences of their use at the state and local level enabled white southerners all the more to see Washington's speech in the most segregationist terms possible.[7]

During Reconstruction, the "mutuality" theme seems to have been used much more by whites than by African Americans. However, southerners black and white were accustomed to hearing some form of the theme. On New Year's Day, 1875, Edward Cantwell, a white Republican who served in North Carolina's state senate, gave an obscure speech discussing race relations to an audience of African Americans observing the anniversary of their emancipation in the coastal port city Wilmington. Cantwell, one of the few whites in the state who publicly supported federal civil rights legislation then under consideration in Washington, D.C., also supported segregation, and he did so with words quite similar to those used by Washington almost a generation later. "On the basis of our mutual interests and common grievances, we will learn to live together as the Saxons and Normans did," reads a published version of Cantwell's speech. "Separated in our social organizations, separated in our schools, separated in places of public amusement, but joined in political destiny and associations, each equally free to pursue happiness in the sphere God has severally allotted. Both equal in every priviledge conferred by the laws of the Union to citizens elsewhere; and therefore equal to all in the sight of the law."[8]

In this portion of the speech, Cantwell seems to stand with Washington on the malleable nature of segregation. However, Cantwell seems to give racial separation a more permanent basis by using a simile to compare race relations to the Atlantic Ocean just east of the town where he spoke: "Like those twin and different colored currents of the sea, which, within sight of the eastern coasts of Carolina, run side by side for a hundred miles, without intermixture, and towards opposite hemispheres."[9] Unlike Washington, Cantwell presents segregation as an unchanging fixture in the South. But even Cantwell is a little vague. He never tells his audience that segregation should be legally required; he simply suggests that it was the natural course for race relations to follow.

The distinction is important. Cantwell had tried in the state senate to behave as a bridge between African Americans and whites by endorsing both federal civil rights legislation and a form of states' rights. He would be unsuccessful—whites would reject civil rights legislation, and by the end of 1875, North Carolinians would draft a new state constitution requiring segregated schools. When North Carolina voters ratified the constitution in 1876, they established even further the premise for race relations that whites and African Americans had settled into a permanent relationship in which interdependence meant racial and economic domination of African Americans by whites, not social interaction.

Cantwell's speech is only one of a number of pieces on integration and segregation published in newspapers by white and black North Carolinians in the early to mid-1870s. Many of those pieces use some variation on the "mutuality" theme. A look at these pieces and the context in which they were written suggests that Washington's vagueness about "mutuality" in the 1890s was far from unique or attributable to some slipperiness in his character. In the 1870s, whites were often unclear about whether "mutuality" was simply a custom, an arrangement necessitated by racism, or a permanent necessity. Strict segregationists usually left nothing to interpretation, but other whites, including Cantwell, usually did. White Republicans whose constituents or audiences included African Americans usually stopped short of calling segregation a permanent necessity. However, white Republicans with few African American constituents, usually in the western piedmont and mountains, were often more racist in their speech and votes. The wording surrounding such terms as Cantwell's "mutual interests" may have remained vague, but it was clear by the latter half of the 1870s that even Republicans were tying it to legalized segregation. A look at speeches by Cantwell and other whites given in the 1870s suggests that when whites used wording similar to that used later by Washington, they were doing so as they moved to make segregation a permanent arrangement. In the midst of this atmosphere, African American politicians rarely if ever explicitly endorsed "mutuality" or even used terminology to describe a mutual relationship between African Americans and whites. They did, however, assure whites that they did not seek to force integration. A look at speeches by African Americans and whites from statehouse politicians during Reconstruction can help inform our view of Washington's speeches, because he seems to have combined ideas discussed vaguely for decades.

The speeches and actions of Cantwell and other nineteenth-century politicians at the state level also hold importance to those seeking to assess Washington, because scholars have claimed that orators' words were very important to southerners in the post–Civil War South.[10] If it is assumed that southern white politicians espoused states' rights because they wanted states to control race relations, it should follow that the words and votes of state politicians, as well as those of U.S. congressmen and senators spoken in part for their home constituencies, deserve close, side-by-side examination. It was at the local and state levels, after all, that Jim Crow came into existence. Unfortunately, most intellectual and social histories have paid little attention to political oratory or the mechanics of politics at the state level and have relegated statehouse debates and votes to a vague backdrop hovering behind such prominent figures as Washington. By doing so, they have left largely undetected the relationship between political argument and the actual behavior of politicians. Political editorials and speeches such as Cantwell's, given at the state and even the local level, helped define the New South's rhetorical path long before Washington's imprecise comments on both "mutual progress" and "social equality." At the same time, the votes of obscure local and state politicians helped institutionalize the New South vision that more prominent politicians and editors described for larger audiences.

Cantwell's speech can be a first step toward clarifying the white interpretation of "mutuality" at the state level. A look at speeches and politics in Cantwell's state, North Carolina, offers us the opportunity to trace the usage of such terms as "mutual interests" among the two sides vying for control of North Carolina during Reconstruction: Republicans and the coalition of former Whigs and Democrats known in the state then as the Conservative Party. By looking at how "mutuality" was defined *in action* by whites as Reconstruction was being overthrown and Jim Crow institutionalized in the state, we can get a clue regarding what whites heard when Washington spoke of "mutual progress" a generation later. We can also see how African American politicians within North Carolina's Republican Party tried to negotiate race relations in the 1870s as the usage of such terms as "mutual interests" was becoming hardened.

The years between 1872 and 1875 are a natural period to try to observe how North Carolinians discussed—and voted on—matters regarding race relations. Debate over segregation was fierce then, largely because southern whites were beginning to react to efforts by U.S. senator Charles Sumner in the final years of his life to have a new civil rights bill passed with a provision for integrated schools to supplement the federal Civil Rights Act of 1866. Debate over the supplemental bill, under consideration in Congress in the early to mid-1870s, intensified in North Carolina between 1873 and 1875 and led to a demand for school segregation in the North Carolina Constitutional Convention of 1875. Conservatives, who unequivocally espoused segregation, chided white Republicans for Republican support of the bill in Washington. As white Republicans were forced to comment on the civil rights bill, they backed away from integration. At the convention, they signed on to the idea of segregated schools as a constitutional requirement. African Americans saw that they faced a losing battle against the rising tide of racism, and many of them saw little choice but to go along with it themselves in an attempt to preserve the rights they had.

The course of this battle reveals how white Republicans geared their words and their votes concerning race relations to their different audiences and constituencies. Conservatives were usually unanimous in their opposition to any civil rights legislation in any form. White Republicans varied according to where they lived. Racism was strong in every section of the state, but within the Republican Party, it often found its strongest expression among officeholders from the mountains. Republicans from the western part of the state proved more overtly contemptuous toward black aspirations than their eastern counterparts because they did not depend on black votes. In the statehouse, they seem to have spoken with African

American and white peers in mind. However, when accused of acting in concert with African Americans, they voted with their largely white constituencies. Examining the regional mix of audiences also helps show the many uses of the "mutuality" theme in white politicians' speeches, even as their actions moved the state toward Jim Crow.

In North Carolina, the most common terms used to describe African American and white interaction in society were "mutual interests" and "mutual dependence." In North Carolina, the "mutuality" premise for race relations was visible by the mid-1870s. It began with two basic variations, a white Conservative variation and a white Republican variation. White Conservatives, opposing federal intervention and speaking almost exclusively to white voters, concentrated on white dominance when presenting their picture of "mutuality." When white Republicans discussed race relations, they had to keep both African Americans and whites in their party united. For white audiences, they emphasized what they called the "mutual dependence" of African Americans and whites as an attempt to remind Conservatives that African Americans and whites were interdependent and that it worked against the interests of whites to harass African Americans. At the same time, white Republicans emphasized to African Americans that segregation was necessary because the entrenched prejudices of whites required it. White Republicans combined the ideas of interdependence and segregation for two reasons: they wanted to prevent Conservatives from committing violent acts against black and white Republicans, and they wanted to keep African Americans from abandoning their party. But despite the variations on their arguments, white Conservatives and Republicans agreed that African Americans and whites were to work together when they could but remain separate in the public sphere. In their unanimity, white politicians eventually enacted statute and fundamental law consistent with "mutual dependence."

In North Carolina, "mutual dependence" themes coincided with discussions of federal civil rights legislation. Detailed, urgent, and bipartisan calls for a segregated society came after the introduction of the supplemental civil rights bill with an integrated schools provision in 1872. When the federal government began to look as if it might challenge the segregation of schools nationwide, it created a racist backlash throughout the state that placed Republican legislators in peril.[11] As early as 1869, a Republican newspaper from Rutherford County, on the eastern edge of the Blue Ridge, pointed out that no legislator who supported integrated schools could survive politically in western North Carolina, and in mountain counties, white Republicans tolerated African Americans only as much as was politically expedient.[12] Members of the Conservative Party, regardless of where they lived, fought the Republican Party as the "negro party," warning that African Americans trying to integrate public facilities would precipitate a "race war" they were destined to lose. White Republicans in the coastal plain, the piedmont, and the mountain counties tended to support segregation with varying degrees of bluntness, claiming that it was necessary to prevent the violence that they hinted would come from Conservatives if the civil rights bill passed. In the east, this claim was made in a genteel fashion. In the west, with smaller African American audiences and constituencies, warnings of violence were set in a more racist context. African American Republicans tended to strive toward the unity of the Republican Party, knowing that with it lay their better hopes for political survival. Arguments concerning race relations in North Carolina took on a regional as well as a party component because different regions had different audiences.

A good place to begin an examination of the different uses of the "mutual dependence" argument by white Conservatives and white Republicans is western North Carolina. If it is true that Republicans in the west saw less need than their eastern counterparts to cater to an African American electorate, then a look at mountain Republican words and behavior toward civil rights legislation can show their approaches to two different audiences: their biracial audience in the statehouse at Raleigh and their largely white audience at home.[13]

Conservatives from the mountains, speaking only to whites, promptly attacked any new civil rights legislation. In May 1872, Conservative James C. Harper, a North Carolinian who represented a mountain district in Congress, printed in the *Congressional Globe* a speech opposing an unsuccessful version of the supplemental civil rights bill introduced in the House of Representatives by William Frye, a congressman from Maine.[14] Harper gave his opposition to the legislation a specifically mountain flavor:

I have the honor to represent the mountaineers of western North Carolina, a hardy and intelligent people, who, like their mountain brethren of Switzerland, have always kept alive among their forests and on their hill-tops the sacred fires of liberty. They are men who, born free, wish so to live and so to die. They have the instincts of their Caucasian race more strongly, if possible, than the dwellers on the plains; and what I have to say of their manner of treating the negroes, therefore, and of their relations with a class whom they will always believe to be their inferiors, can be applied in a less rather than in a greater degree to the inhabitants of my whole State.

Harper's speech suggests that North Carolina's postwar political leadership in its mountain counties saw the mountains as being ideally southern and white. He saw race relations in the mountains as already having settled into a good, mutual arrangement, adding later:

We live together, the old masters and the old slaves, side by side, in perfect peace, in perfect civil equality before the law, in the equal enjoyment of civil, moral, educational, and religious privileges. And so we should continue to live, each race helping the other, the whites teaching the blacks economy of time, improved methods of labor, and the cultivation of those qualities which give a man self-respect and the good will of his fellows. And the colored race, lending to the whites their strong arms and trained muscles, giving their labor for wages to support themselves and their families.[15]

Harper was confident in the propriety of this arrangement, and his speech included a pronouncement that it was permanent along with a vague warning to those who would challenge it. "Generations hence," he continued,

should the negro exist that long, will see no change in the relations between the races, the whites acknowledging the civil equality of the blacks, and habituated to it; the blacks equally cognizant of and believing in their social and intellectual inferiority to the whites. To disturb this state of things will cause, not a civil war, but a strife equally distressing—a social war. These bills, if passed into law and enforced, contain the fire-brands destined to kindle the fires of social discord and hatred.[16]

Harper was not alone in pronouncing the permanence of this arrangement. In early 1874, another mountain Conservative, Robert B. Vance, decried the civil rights bill after it again became a matter of controversy nationwide with a new effort by Senator Sumner to get it passed. Vance, who followed James Harper into Congress after the election of 1872, gave a lengthy speech against the bill on the House floor that was published in the *Congressional Record* as well as in the *North Carolina Citizen*, a Conservative newspaper in Asheville.[17]

According to the *Citizen*'s version of the speech, Vance began by tracing his interest in the welfare of African Americans back to his grandfather and by denying that southerners opposed the civil rights bill because of race prejudice. Insisting that southerners were glad that slaves had been emancipated, he argued that slavery was brought into southern culture from outside the region and had become so entrenched that only war could have ended it. After the Civil War, Vance said, white southerners "went to work and secured the colored man in all his civil rights. The people there consented that he should vote; they consented he should hold office; they consented he should serve upon juries; they consented that he should hold property, and that he should be a witness in court."[18]

However, Vance differentiated between "civil rights" and "social rights," arguing that the civil rights bill was designed to provide the latter to a group of citizens who already had the former. Vance showed his disapproval of a desegregated society, pointing out that if the bill passed, an African American could do more than simply enter the same hotel as a white person; he might actually keep company with whites once he got in. "Even if he is allowed to go into the dining-room, and is placed at a separate table because of his color it will be a violation of this law," Vance argued. Likewise, schools might be desegregated. Though African Americans had the right to public education, "this bill goes further, and provides that colored children shall go into the same school with white children, mixing the colored children and the white children in the same schools. I submit to the committee whether that is not a social right instead of a civil right."[19]

Anticipating the Republican Edward Cantwell, Vance spoke of "mutual interests" governing society, but he pictured a society based on overt white supremacy. Vance defended southern whites as worthy protectors of dependent African Americans by stressing the dependence he saw of African Americans on whites: "There are between four and five millions of colored people in the South, whose interests are intimately and closely connected with those of the white people," Vance wrote. "The one cannot do well without the other. Where does the colored man get his place to live, where does he obtain employment? In a great measure from the white men of the country, and almost entirely from those opposed to this bill." African Americans, Vance wrote, "do not want to be brought into apparent antagonism to the white people, because their interests are closely connected together. The colored man cannot do well in the South, he cannot prosper, unless he has the kind care, of the white man extended to him."[20]

That "care" was to be provided in a structure under which whites would provide menial jobs and African Americans would provide the labor. Vance assured his colleagues that whites were ready to defend that structure, arguing that passage of the civil rights bill could spark a race war that whites were sure to win. "I submit it in good faith, that if the question is ever presented in the South, Shall this country be ruled by white men or ruled by colored men? the colored man is not able to stand any such an antagonist as that; he will necessarily sir, go down." The structure was as inviolable to Vance as it was to Harper; in fact, he argued that the bill gave African Americans false aspirations by challenging it. "It begets hopes and raises an ambition in the minds of the colord [sic] man that can never be realized," Vance said.[21]

Vance's view of race relations created a bar that was impossible for African Americans to clear because he also insisted that African Americans should raise themselves by their own bootstraps to an equal footing with white Americans. Vance argued that if he were an African American, "I would not stand here and ask the passage of a law to force me into what are termed my civil rights. If I belonged to the colored race I would come up by my own merit. I would wait for time and opportunity, and I would not ask any help from Congress." Yet Vance was asking African Americans to pull themselves to a level that he did not believe they were capable of reaching. "[I]t is absurd for gentlemen to talk about the equality of the races," Vance told Congress.[22]

A variation on Harper's and Vance's positions was shared by mountain white Republicans in North Carolina.[23] Their variation, however, was a bit harder to interpret. When speaking to African Americans and whites, they were less overtly white supremacist than their Conservative counterparts, and they spoke with greater respect for the postwar amendments to the Constitution. They also tended to put greater emphasis on the point that African Americans and whites needed each other for society to prosper. But unlike Conservatives, they often shied away from presenting this mutual economic arrangement or social segregation as necessarily permanent. During his gubernatorial administration, Tod Caldwell, whose home was in mountainous Burke County, offered a succinct summary of the Republican version of the "mutual dependence" argument. Caldwell had shown a strong willingness in 1871 to cooperate with the federal government in its fight against the Ku Klux Klan, a willingness that had angered Conservatives and pleased Republicans.[24] "I feel it my duty as it is my pleasure to see full justice done to the colored people as well as to the white people of North Carolina," Caldwell later wrote.[25] Nonetheless, Caldwell saw a structure for race relations similar to that presented by Harper and Vance. Responding to fears that African Americans were starting to leave the state, Caldwell made a public appeal that was published in the *Raleigh Weekly Era*, the chief Republican newspaper in the state, months before James Harper gave his speech in Congress.[26] "I feel well satisfied that there is no better place under the sun for the honest, industrious colored man and woman," Caldwell argued. African Americans and whites should realize that they needed each other:

> Let the white and colored people of North Carolina strike hands and become friends. The white man's land needs the colored man's labor; the colored man's labor needs the white man's land. Let a truce be made and a bargain struck—each is dependent upon the other, and each will do the other good if a proper understanding can be arrived at, and good faith maintained between the contracting parties. Is there any reason why this shall not be done? None whatever that I am able to see, but on the contrary everything in North Carolina seems to conspire to so interweave the interests of the races as to make *the success of the one almost entirely dependent upon the prosperity of the other.*[27]

Caldwell's position, published for African Americans and whites, sounds similar to the Conservative position, but it leaves indefinite how permanent or strongly enforced a "mutual dependence" arrangement should be.

Problems that the vagueness presented for African Americans started to become clear during the 1873–74 session of the North Carolina General Assembly, when discussion of Sumner's civil rights bill pitted Republicans in the state House against each other. The flap among Republicans was prompted by the introduction of a resolution by Conservative piedmont legislator R. B. B. Houston decrying Sumner's bill. To the glee of Conservatives, several white Republicans supported the resolution. "Nearly all the white Radicals voted against tabling [the resolution], which led to some bitter recrimination by the colored members, and charges of treachery to their race, and infidelity to promises," gloated a Conservative paper in the piedmont without giving details.[28] In Asheville, the Conservative *Citizen* was more specific. One of the "charges of treachery" came from Edward Dudley, a Republican from coastal-plain Craven County and one of a small number of African American state legislators who had tried, unsuccessfully, to introduce civil rights legislation and resolutions in November and December.[29] Dudley was paraphrased in the *Citizen* as saying that "he did not expect anything from Conservative members, but he did think he had a right to expect the support of all those who were elected by Rebublican [*sic*] votes."[30]

Possibly because they had less to lose politically than their eastern counterparts, white mountain Republicans were quick to respond to him. Republican James Blythe, who represented Henderson County, counseled Dudley that African Americans "had better let well enough alone, and await the development of the future." Pushing for more rights than they had would alienate "their present white friends," leaving them "in such a hopeless minority that they would be powerless to promote their future prosperity." Blythe added that African Americans "could not control the west as they did some portions of the east." Soon after, Mitchell County Republican Jacob Bowman, also from the mountains, revealed in an exchange with another African American Republican, Wake County's Stewart Ellison, that he was against integrating schools. Squire Trivett, a white Republican from Ashe County, also gave his views on the matter: "Trivett said," according to the *Citizen*, that "he was a true Republican, and had all the time advocated giving to the colored people equal rights before the law, but he was not prepared to go any further. He did not like to see this exemplification of the old saying, 'give an inch and an ell will be taken.'"[31]

The *Citizen* report tends to align Trivett's views with those of Vance and Harper. Fortunately, however, a more detailed version of his views that was printed in the *Raleigh Weekly Era* reveals important nuances of difference between his position and Vance's. On January 29, 1874, the *Era* quoted Trivett as saying that African Americans "have guaranteed to them the same rights and civil liberties that is [*sic*] conferred upon their former owners, so far as freedom and protection is concerned — conferred upon them by the Constitution and laws of the National Government. For one, I am ever ready to stand by them in their rights before the law — by the enforcement of all laws that would tend to that end."[32]

Trivett's words, unlike those of Conservatives, suggest enthusiastic support for the postwar amendments to the U.S. Constitution. His speech also implies approval of such legislation as the Enforcement Act of 1870 and the Ku Klux Klan Act of 1871, used by the federal government to prosecute defendants in the federal Klan trials in North Carolina in 1871.[33] Trivett did go on to say, like Vance, that African Americans were asking for too much with the civil rights bill and that they should bide their time "for extraordinary rights and privileges." However, there is a subtle difference between Vance and Trivett. Trivett saw white Republicans as the guarantors of African American civil rights against white Conservatives and suggested that African Americans be patient out of political as well as social concerns: "I say to our colored friends if they force this issue upon us, the republican party is divided, and the democratic party elevated to power, and before the next decade shall have passed, their condition will be reduced to a worse servitude than they ever experienced in the past."[34]

Like both Harper and Vance, Trivett upheld segregation under white supremacy, but he did not explicitly argue that white superiority was a fact of nature:

> The white people of this country have been ed-educated [sic] to believe them superior [in] every respect to the colored race and to this the colored race have assented until it has become a fixed principle in the two races, so much so that in my opinion no statute can make the white race of this generation feel that the colored race is their equal. . . . I feel that it is my duty as a friend of the colored race to warn them to beware how they run counter to the deep-rooted prejudices of generations, and attempt to force social equality with a race so vastly superior in numbers, so much higher in the scale of knowledge, and possessing such a large proportion of the wealth of the country.[35]

Trivett concluded with his picture of an interdependent, calm society: "Without it [the civil rights bill], but with laws protecting the colored man in all his rights of person and property, with separate churches and schools, I have every reason to hope for peace and good feeling between all our people, and that we will all, both white and colored, *give a helping hand to each other*."[36]

In all likelihood, Trivett hoped that his remarks would find some support from an African American audience. Caldwell had geared his own appeal toward African Americans and whites, and Trivett was speaking to African American as well as white colleagues. Trivett strongly hints that a challenge to segregation would lead to violence against African Americans, who were outnumbered. However, Trivett makes the hint from a defensive position, stating that white prejudice, not any inherent inferiority in African Americans, made necessary a mutual dependence arrangement that would leave African Americans in the inferior position for at least a generation. At best, Trivett was doing what August Meier notes that Booker T. Washington would later do, "put[ting] Negro equality off into a hazy future that did not disturb the 'practical' and prejudiced men of his generation."[37] Like Caldwell, Trivett thought that it was necessary for the good of society for African Americans and whites to live in a segregated arrangement much like the one that Harper and Vance had presented.

However, the two Republicans presented that arrangement more in terms of mutual need, downplaying (though not dismissing) the point that African Americans were to be permanently treated as the more needy group.

African American Republicans, then, had to face white Republican as well as white Conservative arguments in favor of segregation under "mutual dependence." In 1872, most of the African American contingent in the General Assembly had supported their party and endorsed Caldwell's appeal for African Americans to stay as laborers in North Carolina. In 1874, when Squire Trivett and James Blythe gave their warnings to African Americans to "let well enough alone," African American Republican legislators from the eastern piedmont and the coastal plain were caught in another difficult position. Most if not all African American legislators supported the civil rights bill. However, they were also afraid of Conservatives' using the bill to make a power play.[38]

John Williamson, an African American legislator for coastal plain Franklin County, was among Republicans who feared that Conservatives were trying to divide and conquer his party.[39] In his argument against the Houston resolution, Williamson contended that Houston's proposal would have no effect on Congress. The resolution was, instead, a trap for western Republicans. If they did not support it, Conservatives could say that western Republicans "voted for social eqality [sic]." Williamson took a conciliatory approach: "How could we stand as a party without the white republicans to stand with us? If we, by precipitate and inconsiderate action, drive them from us we shall regret it, for we hazard our chances for civil and all other rights. They have nothing to lose while we might fail to get what we claim. And further they are already in the possession of civil rights. Let us not act rashly but be patient."[40] Williamson believed that African American Republicans should choose their battles, and the battle over this resolution was one they could not win.

To aid his party, Williamson offered a substitute for the Houston resolution that called for "equal civil and political rights" but not any "tending to an enforcement of social equality."[41] The Williamson substitute failed, the press at the time noting that the vote fell largely on party lines. Mountain Republican Jacob Bowman was one of two Republicans cited in the press as recording a vote against it.[42] The Houston resolution then passed, 76-25, with an amendment from Conservative Edward Jones of Caldwell County that charged that Congress's civil rights bill would cause "the thorough demoralization of our society, and the cause of bitter strife between the two races."[43] Republicans James Blythe, Squire Trivett, and Jacob Bowman supported the resolution with their votes, as did three other mountain Republicans: Thomas Dula and Abraham C. Bryan, both from Wilkes County, and Eli Whisnant of Rutherford County.[44]

Clear patterns reveal themselves in votes involving the Williamson substitute and the Houston resolution. Most noticeable is the solid bloc of Conservative votes against tabling the Houston resolution, against the Williamson substitute, and in favor of the Houston resolution with Edward Jones's amendment. Every Conservative who voted in any of the three roll calls followed the party line, a fact that adds credibility to Williamson's argument that the Houston resolution was introduced as an attempt to embarrass Republicans.

Republican voting patterns were not so solid. Fifty Republicans, twelve of whom were African American, voted in one or both of the roll calls involving the Williamson substitute and the final passage of the Houston resolution. The vast majority of Republicans were willing to support the Williamson substitute. Of forty-eight who voted, only two—Jacob Bowman from the mountains and F. M. Godfrey, a coastal plain Republican— failed to support it. Five of the seven mountain Republican representatives supported the Williamson substitute, including four of the six mountain Republicans who ended up supporting the Houston resolution. (Representative Dula did not vote in the roll call on the Williamson substitute.)[45]

African American Republicans voted closely together. Eleven voted in both roll calls; ten of those supported the Williamson substitute but not the Houston resolution with the Jones amendment. The vast majority of African American Republicans wanted some version of the civil rights bill, even if they had to endorse a weaker version of it.

For the Houston resolution, forty-seven Republican legislators registered votes in the roll call; twenty-two of them supported it, including six of the seven mountain Republicans in the House. One African American, Stewart Ellison, supported it.[46] Of the fifteen white Republicans who voted against the Houston resolution, twelve were from coastal plain counties, many with relatively large African American populations. Only one came from the mountains and two from the piedmont. Of the two piedmont legislators, one was from Caswell County, of which African Americans made up 59 percent of the population in 1870.[47]

White Republican support for the Williamson substitute shows that almost all Republicans would accept at least nominal enforcement of civil rights as they saw them defined under the postwar amendments.[48] However, the debates and votes also show that mountain Republicans were willing to oppose additional civil rights legislation just as vehemently as Conservatives when pushed into a corner. The mountain Republican votes

Legislator	County	Party	Ethnicity	"Motion to Table" Houston Resolution (HJ 296) (Failed 29-65)[a]	Williamson Substitute (HJ 298) (Failed 46-55)[a]	Passage of Houston Resolution with Amendments, Second Reading (HJ 298-99) (Adopted 77-25)[a,b]
Coastal Plain						
Ballard	Gates	Conservative	White	N	N	Y
Bryan, W. H.	Sampson	Conservative	White	N	N	Y
Bullard	Cumberland	Conservative	White	Dnv	Dnv	Dnv
Carter	Hyde	Conservative	White	N	N	Y
Grady	Harnett	Conservative	White	N	N	Y
Hinnant	Johnston	Conservative	White	Dnv	Dnv	Dnv
Jones, B.	Tyrrell	Conservative	White	N	N	Y
Joyner	Johnston	Conservative	White	N	N	Y
Lindsay	Nash	Conservative	White	N	N	Y
Maxwell	Sampson	Conservative	White	N	N	Y
McNeill	Robeson	Conservative	White	N	N	Y
Moss	Wilson	Conservative	White	N	N	Y
Norment	Robeson	Conservative	White	N	N	Y
Outlaw	Duplin	Conservative	White	Dnv	Dnv	Dnv
Richardson	Columbus	Conservative	White	N	N	Y
Shackelford	Onslow	Conservative	White	N	N	Y
Stanford	Duplin	Conservative	White	N	N	Y
Webb	Carteret	Conservative	White	N	N	Y
Woodhouse	Currituck	Conservative	White	N	N	Y
Abbott	Craven	Republican	African American	Y	Y	N
Brooks	Brunswick	Republican	White	N	Y	Y
Bryan	Pitt	Republican	White	N	Y	Y
Bryant	Halifax	Republican	African American	Y	Y	N
Bunn	Edgecombe	Republican	African American	Y	Y	N
Cobb	Edgecombe	Republican	White	Y	Y	N
Copeland	Wayne	Republican	White	Dnv	Y	Dnv
Corson	Beaufort/ Pamlico	Republican	White	Y	Y	N
Cox	Pitt	Republican	White	N	Y	Y
Darden	Perquimans	Republican	White	Dnv	Dnv	Dnv
Davis	Lenoir	Republican	White	Dnv	Dnv	Dnv

TABLE 1 } *continued*

Legislator	County	Party	Ethnicity	"Motion to Table" Houston Resolution (HJ 296) (Failed 29-65)[a]	Williamson Substitute (HJ 298) (Failed 46-55)[a]	Passage of Houston Resolution with Amendments, Second Reading (HJ 298-99) (Adopted 77-25)[a,b]
Coastal Plain (continued)						
Dudley	Craven	Republican	African American	Y	Y	N
Ellison	Wake	Republican	African American	Y	Y	Y
Gilbert	Wake	Republican	White	Y	Y	N
Godfrey	Pasquotank	Republican	White	N	N	Y
Goodwyn	Halifax	Republican	White	Y	Y	N
Gorman	Wake	Republican	White	N	Y	N
Gray	Dare	Republican	White	Y	Dnv	N
Guyther	Washington	Republican	White	Y	Y	N
Heaton	New Hanover	Republican	White	Dnv	Dnv	Dnv
Hughes	Granville	Republican	African American	Y	Y	N
Jones	Camden	Republican	White	Dnv	Dnv	Dnv
Jones Burton	Northampton	Republican	White	Y	Y	N
King, G.	Warren	Republican	African American	Dnv	Dnv	Dnv
Lloyd	New Hanover	Republican	African American	Y	Y	N
Lutterloh	Cumberland	Republican	White	Y	Y	N
McLaurin	New Hanover	Republican	African American	Y	Y	N
Miller	Bertie	Republican	White	Y	Y	N
Mizell	Martin	Republican	White	Dnv	Y	Y
Paschall	Warren	Republican	African American	Y	Y	N
Patrick	Greene	Republican	White	Dnv	Y	Y
Perry	Bladen	Republican	White	Y	Y	Y
Perry, R.	Wake	Republican	White	Dnv	Y	Y
Rhodes	Wayne	Republican	White	Dnv	Y	Y
Scott	Jones	Republican	White	Dnv	Y	N
Sharp	Hertford	Republican	White	Y	Y	Y
Sneed	Granville	Republican	White	Y	Y	N
Williamson	Franklin	Republican	African American	Dnv	Y	N
Winslow	Chowan	Republican	White	Y	Y	Y

TABLE I } *continued*

Legislator	County	Party	Ethnicity	"Motion to Table" Houston Resolution (HJ 296) (Failed 29-65)[a]	Williamson Substitute (HJ 298) (Failed 46-55)[a]	Passage of Houston Resolution with Amendments, Second Reading (HJ 298-99) (Adopted 77-25)[a,b]
Piedmont						
Anderson	Davie	Conservative	White	N	N	Y
Bennett	Anson	Conservative	White	N	N	Y
Brown	Mecklenburg	Conservative	White	Dnv	Dnv	Dnv
Costner	Lincoln	Conservative	White	N	N	Y
Craige	Rowan	Conservative	White	N	N	Y
Gant	Alamance	Conservative	White	N	N	Y
Gidney	Cleveland	Conservative	White	Dnv	N	Y
Gilmer	Guilford	Conservative	White	N	N	Y
Hanner	Chatham	Conservative	White	Dnv	Dnv	Dnv
Houston	Catawba	Conservative	White	N	N	Y
Johns	Rockingham	Conservative	White	N	N	Y
Jones, P.	Orange	Conservative	White	N	Dnv	Dnv
Luckey	Rowan	Conservative	White	N	N	Y
Marler	Yadkin	Conservative	White	N	N	Y
McGehee	Person	Conservative	White	N	N	Y
Mitchell	Stokes	Conservative	White	N	N	Y
Moring	Chatham	Conservative	White	N	N	Y
Presson	Union	Conservative	White	N	N	Y
Reid	Mecklenburg	Conservative	White	N	N	Y
Settle	Rockingham	Conservative	White	N	N	Y
Shaw	Moore	Conservative	White	N	N	Y
Shinn, C. L.	Iredell	Conservative	White	N	N	Y
Shinn, T.	Cabarrus	Conservative	White	N	N	Y
Stowe	Gaston	Conservative	White	N	N	Y
Turner	Iredell	Conservative	White	N	N	Y
Waddill	Stanly	Conservative	White	N	N	Y
Watson	Orange	Conservative	White	N	N	Y
Waugh	Surry	Conservative	White	N	N	Y
Wiley	Guilford	Conservative	White	N	N	Y
Bean	Randolph	Republican	White	Y	Y	Y
Bowe	Caswell	Republican	African American	Y	Y	N
Brown	Davidson	Republican	White	Y	Y	Y
Fletcher	Richmond	Republican	African American	Dnv	Y	Dnv

TABLE I } *continued*

Legislator	County	Party	Ethnicity	"Motion to Table" Houston Resolution (HJ 296) (Failed 29-65)[a]	Williamson Substitute (HJ 298) (Failed 46-55)[a]	Passage of Houston Resolution with Amendments, Second Reading (HJ 298-99) (Adopted 77-25)[a,b]
Piedmont (continued)						
Foster	Caswell	Republican	White	Y	Y	N
Jordan	Montgomery	Republican	White	Y	Y	N
Michael	Davidson	Republican	White	Y	Y	Y
Reid	Randolph	Republican	White	Dnv	Y	Dnv
Wheeler	Forsyth	Republican	White	Dnv	Y	Y
Carson, J.	Alexander	Independent	White	Dnv	Dnv	Dnv
Mountains						
Anderson	Clay	Conservative	White	Dnv	Dnv	Dnv
Blackwell	Buncombe	Conservative	White	N	N	Y
Bryan	Alleghany	Conservative	White	N	N	Y
Bryson, J.	Jackson	Conservative	White	N	N	Y
Bryson, T. D.	Swain	Conservative	White	N	Dnv	Y
Byrd	Yancey	Conservative	White	Dnv	Dnv	Dnv
Dickey	Cherokee	Conservative	White	N	N	Y
Freeman	McDowell	Conservative	White	N	N	Y
Gudger, H.	Madison	Conservative	White	N	Dnv	Y
Haynes	Haywood	Conservative	White	N	N	Y
Johnston, T.	Buncombe	Conservative	White	N	N	Y
Jones, Ed.	Caldwell	Conservative	White	N	N	Y
Robinson, J.	Macon	Conservative	White	Dnv	Dnv	Dnv
Todd	Watauga	Conservative	White	N	N	Y
Warlick	Burke	Conservative	White	N	N	Y
Whitmire	Transylvania	Conservative	White	N	N	Y
Blythe	Henderson	Republican	White	N	Y	Y
Bowman	Mitchell	Republican	White	N	N	Y
Bryan, A.	Wilkes	Republican	White	N	Y	Y
Dula	Wilkes	Republican	White	N	Dnv	Y
Hampton	Polk	Republican	White	Y	Y	N
Trivett	Ashe	Republican	White	Dnv	Y	Y
Whisnant	Rutherford	Republican	White	N	Y	Y

Sources: Regions are from Thomas E. Jeffrey, *State Parties and National Politics, 1815–1861* (Athens: University of Georgia Press, 1989), 278 (map 4, "Change in the Democratic Vote, 1850–60"); and Gordon McKinney, "Women's Role in Civil War Western North Carolina," *North Carolina Historical Review* 69 (January 1992): 40 (map).

TABLE 1 } *continued*

Party affiliations are determined from "General Assembly," *Raleigh Weekly Era*, August 29, 1872; "General Assembly," *Carolina Watchman*; final roll call vote for U.S. senator, *Journal of the Senate of the General Assembly of the State of North Carolina, at its Session of 1872-'73* (Raleigh: Stone and Uzzell, State Printers and Binders, 1873), 7? (hereafter cited as *Senate Journal, 1872-73*); final vote for U.S. senator, *Journal of the House of Representatives of the General Assembly of the State of North Carolina, at its Session of 1872-'73* (Raleigh: Stone and Uzzell, State Printers and Binders, 1873), 108-9 (hereafter cited as *House Journal, 1872-73*); first roll call vote for U.S. senator, *Senate Journal, 1872-73*, 41; first vote for U.S. senator, *House Journal, 1872-73*, 77-78; roll call vote for state senate president, *Senate Journal, 1872-73*, 4-5; and roll call vote for state house speaker, *House Journal, 1872-73*, 4-5.

Ethnicities are found in Eric Anderson, *Race and Politics in North Carolina, 1872-1901* (Baton Rouge: Louisiana State University Press, 1981); "The Colored Members of the Legislature," *Raleigh Daily Era*, December 4, 187? (reprinted in *Raleigh Weekly Era*, December 12, 1872); "General Assembly," *Carolina Watchman*, October 17, 1872? J. G. de Roulhac Hamilton, *Reconstruction in North Carolina* (1914; Gloucester, Mass.: Peter Smith, 1964), 593n3 "Appendix G: Negro Members of the General Assembly for the Session of 1872-1874," in Elaine Joan Nowaczyk "The North Carolina Negro in Politics, 1865-1876" (M.A. thesis, University of North Carolina, 1957), 195; "Appendix: Negro Legislators in the North Carolina General Assembly, July, 1868-February, 1872," in Elizabeth Balanoff "Negro Legislators in the North Carolina General Assembly, July, 1868-February, 1872," *North Carolina Historical Review* 49 (January 1972): 55; and "Appendix: Biographical Sketches of the Thirteen Black House Members of the General Assembly of North Carolina, 1876-77," in Frenise A. Logan, "Black and Republican: Vicissitudes of a Minority Twice Over in the North Carolina House of Representatives, 1876-1877," *North Carolina Historical Review* 61 (July 1984): 344-46.

Votes from *Journal of the House of Representatives of the General Assembly of the State of North Carolina, at its Session of 1873-'74* (Raleigh: Josiah Turner, Jr., State Printer and Binder, 1874), 296, 298-300 (hereafter cited as *House Journal, 1873-74*).

ª Y = Yea; N = Nay; Dnv = Did not vote.

ᵇ The roll call for this vote is recorded in the *House Journal* as 75-25, but 76 names are listed there. One representative (Sharp) had his vote recorded after the roll call and counts as the 77th name. See *House Journal, 1873-74* 298-300.

helped show that E. R. Dudley's fears were well-based. White Republicans could not be counted on to stand by direct civil rights legislation. However, Republican votes as a whole show little about where they stood on segregation as a permanent arrangement, even if they did not support the civil rights bill.

Discussion of the civil rights bill by white Republicans carried a risk, for 1874 was a state election year.[49] Williamson and other African American legislators were well aware of the dilemma that Republicans in largely white counties and districts faced. John A. Hyman, an African American state senator, probably expressed the thoughts of African Americans in both houses when he wrote that he was sorry that the Houston resolution was introduced just months before voters would be going to the polls. Like Williamson, he believed that the resolution had been introduced simply to divide the Republican Party. "The democrats laughed in the sleeves and thought they had thrown a fire-brand into the ranks of the republican party, when they saw republicans for the resolution and others against. ...Vain hope! However strong the representative men of the colored race may advocate civil rights, they are not to be driven from their allegiance to the party of enfranchisement and popular liberty, because a few republican members of the legislature refused to vote as the colored representatives did upon this question."[50] A letter writer identified as "A Colored Republican" voiced similar sentiments in the *Raleigh Weekly Era*: "We did expect some of our white Republican friends to stand by us in opposition to Houston's resolution, who to our disappointment voted the other way; but we would be fools indeed if this disappointment were permitted to drive us from the party, which has secured to us so many high and inestimable privileges, and make us ally ourselves with a party which has vehemently, and persistently, endeavored at all times and in all places to deprive us of those privileges and reduce us again into a state of servitude and bondage."[51]

When speaking for themselves, neither Williamson, Hyman, nor "A Colored Republican" specifically endorsed a white version of "mutual dependence." All three, however, showed that they were concerned about Republican unity against the Conservative electoral threat. In Williamson's case, that meant endorsing a civil rights bill that allowed segregation to stand while remaining silent on its propriety. Hyman went even further than Williamson in explaining to whites that black support for the civil rights bill did not mean that they wanted integrated schools: "The colored man demands equal, civil and political rights. He does not want social equality—he would not be the social equal of the white man if he could be made so by the stroke of a pen."[52] This same desire for party unity had probably motivated the African American lawmakers who had endorsed Caldwell's appeal two years before. However, neither Williamson, Hyman, nor "A Colored Republican" speaking on their own—even to a white audience—presented a society in which African Americans were bound to be laborers.

Without overt complaints from African Americans in the General Assembly, the white "mutual dependence" view of race relations would hold going into the election of 1874. During the election, white Republicans would be sure to let voters know that they were committed to that view.

In the North Carolina mountains, the 1874 campaigns centered largely on Sumner's bill, and mountain Republicans suffered under fierce attack, despite party unity on "mutual dependence."[53] Republican newspapers, speaking to a predominantly white readership, would come out against the civil rights bill's school integration provision with no rhetorical varnish added for African Americans. They emphasized racism for their white readers at the expense of any African American readers they may have had.

In Asheville, the Conservative *North Carolina Citizen* had an easy task. All it had to do was present Conservatives as opponents of the bill, something that was unquestionably true. On May 23, Robert Vance was renominated for his Eighth District seat and endorsed by the *Citizen*.[54] Remaining in Washington, Vance announced that it was his duty to fight the civil rights bill, which had just passed the U.S. Senate and was being considered in the House.[55] The *Citizen* praised Vance's fight against the bill, and he did make it home in time to campaign in July.[56]

Mountain Conservatives similarly stressed the efforts of Senator Augustus S. Merrimon against the civil rights bill.[57] Next to former governor Zebulon Vance, his longtime political rival, Merrimon was the most prominent mountain North Carolinian of his generation, and he was chosen as a U.S. senator over Vance after losing the 1872 gubernatorial race to Tod Caldwell.[58] Late on the night of May 22, Merrimon delivered in the Senate a two-and-a-half-hour speech against Sumner's bill.[59]

Merrimon argued that Congress had no power to enact the supplemental civil rights bill because the states had retained their sovereignty despite the Civil War. Because of this, Merrimon argued, state citizenship and national citizenship remained separate, and the definition and protection of civil rights remained the responsibility of the states. To support his argument, Merrimon quoted extensively from the Supreme Court's treatment of national and state citizenship in its 1873 *Slaughterhouse Cases* decision.[60]

Merrimon went on, like his Conservative predecessors, to discuss what he saw as the impropriety of an integrated society and the necessity for African Americans in the South to live under white domination. Like Robert Vance in the House, Merrimon spoke of African Americans and whites having compatible goals while stressing the perceived need African Americans had for white supervision. "They [African Americans] need help from the white man in the South; they need his strong arm; they need the benefit of his advice and intelligence; they need his protecting guardianship," Merrimon told the Senate.[61]

Back in North Carolina, Conservative newspaper editors wrote editorials against the civil rights bill more noteworthy for their venom than for their logic. After the bill passed the Senate, rhetoric over the civil rights bill heated up in Asheville's newspapers. Most of the editorializing centered on the bill's provision for integrated schools. The *North Carolina Citizen* proclaimed that this was "a direct thrust at our poor people—an effort on the part of the radicals to not elevate the negro to social equality with them, but to force our poor white people down upon a level with the negro" and compel white children to "set [*sic*] by the side of the little ebony Sambos and Dinahs."[62] Reactions such as this across the South helped force Congress to put the bill on hold.[63]

Thrown on the defensive, mountain Republicans in North Carolina raced to distance themselves from the bill. During the summer of 1874, the *Asheville Weekly Pioneer*, a Republican paper, seemed to show as much disinclination toward the civil rights bill as Vance had in Congress months before. After the Senate passed its version of the bill, the *Pioneer* went out of its way to decry it.[64] Saying that its previous silence had been due to a conviction that Charles Sumner would have no success, the *Pioneer* now announced: "We are decidedly opposed to the bill *as it has passed the Senate*":

> We see no reason why such legislation should be had. The colored element of the South now enjoy all the privileges that they are entitled to, provided the laws are properly enforced. They have all the rights which a white man has, and why do they and a few fanatical friends of theirs clamor for such legislation as will force social equality, whether it be desired or not, by the majority of the white people? What do they expect to gain by it?
>
> We oppose the passage of any law by Congress, or any other legislative body, that attempts to regulate the social status of our people. Such questions can be regulated only by a congeniality existing between individuals. Any attempt to force the two races into schools together, or regulate any other matters of a social character, is bound to bring about a conflict that will inevitably prove dissastrous [*sic*] to the colored people of the country.[65]

Noticeably absent in the editorial was an appeal to "mutual dependence" and the reminders of Conservative prejudice that white Republicans made when speaking to African Americans as well as whites. But as strong as the *Pioneer* editorial sounds, a close reading of it shows that although it completely decries the civil rights bill as proposed by Sumner, it does not speak against any civil rights bill in any form. The *Pioneer* piece actually seems to offer the same fence-straddling that mountain representatives offered when they supported both Houston and Williamson months earlier. The blunt nature of the editorial simply shows that it was primarily written for whites on one side of the fence.

Nevertheless, Conservatives were successful in tying Republicans to "social equality"[66] both in Asheville and in the Seventh Congressional District, a combination of western piedmont and mountain counties that by this time including Ashe (Squire Trivett's home county), Alleghany, Watauga, and Wilkes. Trying to distance themselves from desegregation as they appealed to their largely white constituencies, Seventh District Republicans passed a resolution stating that they were "opposed to the provisions of the [civil rights] bill, believing that it is injurious and pernicious in its tendencies, not only to the peace of society and the well being of the country, but also to the success of the system of public schools."[67]

In the east, white Republicans were more concerned about African American voters. Eastern white Republicans were largely unwilling to endorse the civil rights bill as it existed, but they were more tactful than western white Republicans in their refusal to do so because they had to worry about African American constituencies. The Republican *Wilmington Evening Post* made a plea similar to Trivett's, endorsing segregation while urging African American Republicans not to let Conservatives divide the Republican Party over the civil rights bill:

> The laws of the land, faithfully administered, are a sufficient protection to every citizen of the United States. The arrogance of certain individuals, who insist upon still drawing a distinction between whites and blacks in regard to their treatment in hotels, conveyances, and other public places, only needs an appeal to the principles of the common law to be crushed. There is no honest man, whose opinions are not covered by a scale of prejudice thicker than an alligator's hide, who will deny that a colored man who pays his way is entitled to the same treatment in a hotel that a white man is. If, however, in deference to a sentiment or a prejudice which is as strong as the partiality a parent feels for his children, a hotel keeper spearates [*sic*] his white and colored guests, providing equal accommodations for those who pay alike, who can gainsay his right to do so? It is upon this principle that the Southern States have provided for separate schools for the races, in doing which the[y] exercised a sovereignty and a right which is incontestably theirs.[68]

The *Post* editorial fits more with the white Republican "mutual dependence" argument presented for African Americans and whites than does the less tactful *Pioneer* editorial against the civil rights bill. The *Post* was in agreement with the *Pioneer*—and even with the Conservative position of U.S. senator Augustus Merrimon—that states had the right to require separate schools. However, like Trivett during the 1873–74 session of the General Assembly, the *Post* made the seemingly milder assertion that segregation was required by white prejudice for the sake of party unity. Later, in June 1874, after the civil rights bill passed the Senate and stalled in the House, the *Evening Post* came out more directly against the bill's then-current version in a second editorial, arguing that the civil rights bill "would prove ruinous to the very class which its author hoped and designed it should benefit. It would be an irresistable [*sic*] ally of the Southern Democracy in drawing political lines by shades of color, and it would consign a minority of colored people into a helpless mass."[69]

In the east, commentary about the civil rights bill and race relations seems to have differed when white Republicans spoke for African Americans from when they spoke *in consultation with* African Americans. In Wilmington's congressional district, the Third, Republicans were not as clear as the *Post* about the civil rights bill or about the relationship between African Americans and whites in society. Portions of the set of resolutions Third District Republicans released for the election have the earmarks of wording hammered out in a compromise, and they open speculation on whether the African American presence in the district (and probably at the convention) kept white Republicans from describing race relations as specifically as did the press. Three of the Third District party resolutions dealt with segregation vaguely without explicitly condemning—or even mentioning—the civil rights bill. One of the resolutions endorsed public schools and "the education of all classes of our people, without regard to race or color." The resolution left unspoken whether those schools would be segregated. Another resolution was vague enough to require even more reading between the lines, proclaiming "that there is a *mutual dependence of our people upon one another*, and that the advancement of learning, the development of the resources of our State, and the promotion of the public good, can only be secured by an open acknowledgment of this fundamental principle regardless of race, color or previous condition."[70] In this appearance of "mutual dependence," details on how African Americans and whites would relate to each other in society were left unspecified. Such resolutions contrast strongly with the clear stand against the civil rights bill endorsed by Republicans of the western Seventh District. With white as well as African American Republicans, the source of a statement and the audience it addressed made a difference in its wording.

The arguments of the Republican press, good and bad, left a lot of voters unimpressed on Election Day, as Conservatives won seven of the state's eight congressional races and made significant strides in the state legislature. In mountain North Carolina, a few Republicans won election to the state House, but in the congressional races, Robert Vance won over 60 percent of the popular vote in the Eighth District, and Conservative W. M. Robbins defeated his Republican challenger, Columbus Cook, in the Seventh.[71]

The aftermath of the election of 1874 led directly to more rhetorical fencing in the statehouse. Conservatives used their success to renew attacks on the civil rights bill, which was again under consideration in Washington.[72] After the 1874–75 legislative session opened, they decided to use the opportunity to denounce not only the civil rights bill but also the Republican Party, and Republicans also felt the need to decry the bill by some form of resolution. On the third day of the session, Ashe County Republican Squire Trivett introduced a resolution that, according to coverage of the legislature in the *Weekly Era*, asked Congress not to give the civil rights bill its support. However, a joint committee ended up endorsing instead a Conservative substitute by Paul Means, whose resolution, said the *Era*, "is of a vindictive character and denounces the [Grant] Administration as oppressive towards the Southern people."[73]

The Means substitute was chosen over Trivett's resolution 76-29, and a final version of the resolution was adopted 81-20 after the vote was reconsidered. Both roll calls followed party lines very closely. In the vote on its final passage, not one Conservative voted against the resolution. Two of the five mountain Republicans—Trivett and Buncombe County's William G. Candler—voted for the Means substitute in the second of the two votes, signaling to their predominantly while constituencies their opposition to the civil rights bill. Interestingly, the only other Republican to vote yes was Edward H. Hill, an African American from Craven County.[74]

In the state senate, Republicans faced the same political pressures over the Means resolution. One white Republican, Edward Cantwell of New Hanover County, endorsed the civil rights bill throughout the fight for its passage. Cantwell, who in a matter of weeks would give his Emancipation Day speech comparing whites and African Americans to diverging currents in the Atlantic Ocean, offered his own substitute for the Means resolution, strongly supporting segregation by affirming the ability of a state to dictate its own citizens' rights and citing the U.S. Supreme Court's

Legislator	County	Party	Ethnicity	Adoption of Means Substitute (HJ 77-78) (Adopted 76-29)[a]	Final Adoption (Final Version) (HJ 79-80) (Adopted 81-20)[a]
Coastal Plain					
Ballard	Gates	Conservative	White	Y	Dnv
Barrett	Pitt	Conservative	White	Y	Y
Bennett	Brunswick	Conservative	White	Y	Y
Bizzell	Johnston	Conservative	White	Y	Y
Bryan	Sampson	Conservative	White	Y	Y
Dortch	Wayne	Conservative	White	Y	Y
Catman	Wilson	Conservative	White	Y	Y
Etheridge	Dare	Conservative	White	Y	Y
Griffin	Nash	Conservative	White	Y	Y
Holt	Johnston	Conservative	White	Y	Y
Hooker	Greene	Conservative	White	Dnv	Dnv
Isler	Wayne	Conservative	White	Y	Y
Jessup	Cumberland	Conservative	White	Y	Y
McCalop	Sampson	Conservative	White	Y	Y
McRae	Cumberland	Conservative	White	Y	Y
Mitchell	Franklin	Conservative	White	Dnv	Dnv
Mosely	Duplin	Conservative	White	Y	Y
Mullin	Camden	Conservative	White	Y	Y
Page	Wake	Conservative	White	Y	Y
Parrott	Lenoir	Conservative	White	Y	Dnv
Richardson	Columbus	Conservative	White	Y	Y
Shackelford	Onslow	Conservative	White	Dnv	Dnv
Spears	Harnett	Conservative	White	Y	Y
Staton	Pitt	Conservative	White	Y	Dnv
Stephenson	Wake	Conservative	White	Y	Y
Strong	Wake	Conservative	White	Y	Y
Thompson, W. H.	Beaufort	Conservative	White	Y	Y
Walker, W. W.	Tyrrell	Conservative	White	Y	Y
Wells	Duplin	Conservative	White	Y	Y
Whitley	Wake	Conservative	White	Y	Y
Wiley	Washington	Conservative	White	Y	Y
Woodhouse	Currituck	Conservative	White	Y	Y
Brewington	New Hanover	Republican	African American	Dnv	Dnv
Bunn	Edgecombe	Republican	African American	N	N

TABLE 2 } *continued*

Legislator	County	Party	Ethnicity	Adoption of Means Substitute (HJ 77-78) (Adopted 76-29)[a]	Final Adoption (Final Version) (HJ 79-80) (Adopted 81-20)
Coastal Plain (continued)					
Carter	Warren	Republican	African American	N	N
Crews	Granville	Republican	African American	N	N
Elliott	Chowan	Republican	African American	N	Dnv
Good	Craven	Republican	African American	N	N
Goodwyn	Edgecombe	Republican	White	Dnv	Dnv
Hill	Craven	Republican	African American	Dnv	Y
Hughes	Granville	Republican	African American	N	N
Jones	Halifax	Republican	African American	N	N
Lloyd	New Hanover	Republican	African American	N	N
Mizell	Martin	Republican	White	N	Dnv
Moore	New Hanover	Republican	African American	N	N
Munden	Pasquotank	Republican	White	Dnv	Dnv
Newell	Bladen	Republican	African American	N	N
Parker	Hertford	Republican	White	N	Dnv
Scott	Jones	Republican	White	Dnv	Dnv
Thorne	Warren	Republican	White	Dnv	Dnv
Walden	Northampton	Republican	White	N	Dnv
Ward	Bertie	Republican	White	N	N
White	Halifax	Republican	African American	N	N
Williams	Warren	Republican	African American	N	N
Wood	Perquimans	Republican	White	Dnv	N
McNeill	Robeson	Independent	White	Y	Y
Norment	Robeson	Independent	White	N	Y
Oaksmith	Carteret	Independent	White	Dnv	Y
Smith, A. J.	Hyde	Independent	White	Y	Y

TABLE 2 } *continued*

Legislator	County	Party	Ethnicity	Adoption of Means Substitute (HJ 77-78) (Adopted 76-29)[a]	Final Adoption (Final Version) (HJ 79-80) (Adopted 81-20)[a]
Piedmont					
Anderson	Davie	Conservative	White	Y	Y
Atwater	Orange	Conservative	White	Y	Y
Bernheardt	Rowan	Conservative	White	Y	Y
Bettis	Cleveland	Conservative	White	Y	Y
Finger	Catawba	Conservative	White	Y	Y
Freeman	Stanly	Conservative	White	Y	Y
Gaither	Iredell	Conservative	White	Y	Y
Hanner	Chatham	Conservative	White	Y	Y
Harrison[b]	Caswell	Conservative	White	Y	Y
Haymore	Surry	Conservative	White	Y	Y
Hurley	Montgomery	Conservative	White	Y	Y
Jetton	Mecklenburg	Conservative	White	Y	Y
Johnston	Rockingham	Conservative	White	Y	Y
Kendall	Randolph	Conservative	White	Y	Y
Latta	Orange	Conservative	White	Y	Y
Martin	Stokes	Conservative	White	Y	Y
McCubbins	Rowan	Conservative	White	Y	Y
McIver	Moore	Conservative	White	Y	Y
Means	Cabarrus	Conservative	White	Y	Y
Mebane	Rockingham	Conservative	White	Dnv	Dnv
Mendenhall	Guilford	Conservative	White	Y	Y
Mock	Davidson	Conservative	White	Y	Y
Moffitt	Randolph	Conservative	White	Y	Y
Moring	Chatham	Conservative	White	Y	Y
Pinnix	Davidson	Conservative	White	Y	Y
Presson	Union	Conservative	White	Y	Y
Reid	Mecklenburg	Conservative	White	Y	Y
Sharp	Iredell	Conservative	White	Y	Y
Smith, W. E.	Anson	Conservative	White	Y	Y
Staples	Guilford	Conservative	White	Y	Y
Stowe	Gaston	Conservative	White	Y	Y
Thompson, W. A.	Lincoln	Conservative	White	Y	Y
Walker, P. D.	Richmond	Conservative	White	Y	Y
Barnett	Person	Republican	White	N	N
Boyd	Alamance	Republican	White	N	N
Cary	Caswell	Republican	African American	N	N

TABLE 2 } *continued*

Legislator	County	Party	Ethnicity	Adoption of Means Substitute (HJ 77-78) (Adopted 76-29)[a]	Final Adoption (Final Version) (HJ 79-80) (Adopted 81-20)[a]
Piedmont (continued)					
Glenn[c]	Yadkin	Republican	White	Dnv	Dnv
Wheeler	Forsyth	Republican	White	N	N
Carson	Alexander	Independent	White	Y	Y
Mountains					
Barnhardt	Caldwell	Conservative	White	Y	Y
Bryson, T. D.	Swain	Conservative	White	N	Y
Davis, F. M.	Haywood	Conservative	White	Y	Y
Davis, E. D.	Jackson	Conservative	White	Y	Y
Erwin	McDowell	Conservative	White	Y	Y
Fields	Alleghany	Conservative	White	Y	Y
Gash	Transylvania	Conservative	White	N	Y
Greene	Watauga	Conservative	White	Y	Y
Gudger, H. A.	Madison	Conservative	White	Y	Y
Hicks	Clay	Conservative	White	Dnv	Y
King	Cherokee	Conservative	White	N	Y
Patton	Buncombe	Conservative	White	Y	Y
Proffitt	Yancey	Conservative	White	Y	Y
Robinson (Speaker)	Macon	Conservative	White	Dnv	Dnv
Tate	Burke	Conservative	White	Y	Y
Young	Mitchell	Conservative	White	Y	Dnv
Blythe	Henderson	Republican	White	N	N
Candler	Buncombe	Republican	White	N	Y
Dula	Wilkes	Republican	White	Dnv	Dnv
Foote[c]	Wilkes	Republican	White	N	N
Trivett	Ashe	Republican	White	N	Y
Whisnant	Rutherford	Republican	White	N	N
Garrison	Polk	Liberal Republican or Republican	White	Y	Y

Sources: Regions are from Thomas E. Jeffrey, *State Parties and National Politics, 1815–1861* (Athens: University of Georgia Press, 1989), 278 (map 4, "Change in the Democratic Vote, 1850–60"); and Gordon McKinney, "Women's Role in Civil War Western North Carolina," *North Carolina Historical Review* 69 (January 1992): 40 (map).

Party affiliations are determined from "Members-Elect to the General Assembly for 1874–75," *Rutherford Star and West-Carolina Record*, August 29, 1874 (a similar list also appears under "Members-Elect to the General Assembly for 1874–'75," *Raleigh Weekly Era*, August 20, September 3, 1874; and "Directory," *Raleigh Weekly Era*, January 14,

TABLE 2 } *continued*

875); House speaker roll call vote in *Journal of the House of Representatives of the General Assembly of the State of North Carolina, at its Session of 1874-'75* (Raleigh: Josiah Turner, Public Printer and Binder, 1875), 6 (hereafter cited as *House Journal, 1874-75*); "Convention!," *Citizen*, March 25, 1875; J. G. de Roulhac Hamilton, *Reconstruction in North Carolina* (1914; Gloucester, Mass.: Peter Smith, 1964), 606n2; Senate president roll call vote in *Journal of the Senate of the General Assembly of the State of North Carolina, at its Session of 1874-'75* (Raleigh: Josiah Turner, Public Printer and Binder, 1875), 4-5; "Mr. Norment's Speech," *Wilmington Weekly Post*, March 5, 1875; "Election Returns," *Raleigh Weekly Era*, August 13, 1874; "Republican Ticket," *Rutherford Star and Record*, July 25, 1874; and John Everett Huggins, "The Resurgence and Decline of the Republican Party in North Carolina, 1871-1876" (M.A. thesis, Wake Forest University, 1966).

Ethnicities are found in Eric Anderson, *Race and Politics in North Carolina, 1872-1901* (Baton Rouge: Louisiana State University Press, 1981); "The Colored Members of the Legislature," *Raleigh Daily Era*, December 4, 1872 (reprinted in *Raleigh Weekly Era*, December 12, 1872); "General Assembly," *Carolina Watchman*, October 17, 1872; Hamilton, *Reconstruction in North Carolina*, 593n3, 604nn3, 4; "Appendix G: Negro Members of the General Assembly for the Session of 1872-1874," in Elaine Joan Nowaczyk, "The North Carolina Negro in Politics, 1865-1876" (M.A. thesis, University of North Carolina, 1957), 195; "Appendix: Negro Legislators in the North Carolina General Assembly, July, 1868-February, 1872," in Elizabeth Balanoff, "Negro Legislators in the North Carolina General Assembly, July, 1868-February, 1872," *North Carolina Historical Review* 49 (January 1972): 55; "Appendix: Biographical Sketches of the Thirteen Black House Members of the General Assembly of North Carolina, 1876-77," in Frenise A. Logan, "Black and Republican: Vicissitudes of a Minority Twice Over in the North Carolina House of Representatives, 1876-1877," *North Carolina Historical Review* 61 (July 1984): 344-46; "Carter, Hawkins Wesley" card in "Legislators" file, drawer "A-C," Search Room stacks, North Carolina Division of Archives and History, Raleigh; R. A. Shotwell and Natt Atkinson, *Legislative Record, Giving the Acts Passed Session Ending March, 1877, Together with Sketches of the Lives and Public Acts of the Members of both Houses* (Raleigh: Edwards, Broughton and Co., 1877); and W. McKee Evans, *Ballots and Fence Rails: Reconstruction on the Lower Cape Fear* (New York: W. W. Norton, 1974).

Votes from *House Journal, 1874-75*, 77-78, 79-80.

ᵃ Y = Yea; N = Nay; Dnv = Did not vote.
ᵇ Some uncertainty exists about Harrison's party affiliation.
ᶜ Defected from the Republican Party.

decision to that effect in the *Slaughterhouse Cases*. Cantwell's substitute also praised the civil rights bill—but with the stipulation that it allowed for this prerogative of the states. The substitute described the bill meeting this requirement as "a measure of the wisest statesmanship and a final settlement of this dangerous and distracting question, which has already occupied its full share of the attention of the country, and ought to be forever put at rest."[75]

Cantwell must have known that his substitute would not pass. Of the five Republicans other than Cantwell himself who supported the substitute, four made up the entire African American contingent in the senate.[76] The ruling in the *Slaughterhouse Cases* had probably suggested to the African American senators that African Americans in North Carolina were to be left increasingly at the mercy of their state government whether they liked it or not, and they had little to lose by endorsing the ruling along with the civil rights bill.[77] White Republican senators, on the other hand, knew they had a lot to lose politically by supporting the civil rights bill in any form. The Senate approved the Means resolution 37-11.[78] Conservative senators were unanimous against the Cantwell substitute and for the Means resolution. White Republicans tended to vote against both the Means and Cantwell resolutions.[79]

Events in Washington, D.C., kept Conservative lawmakers on the attack even after the passage of the Means resolution. On February 4, a variation of the civil rights bill made it through the House of Representatives. In Asheville, the *Citizen* called on its Republican neighbor, the *Weekly Pioneer*, to "either denounce and repudiate its party, or endorse the . . . bill."[80] The *Citizen*'s call reflected what was already taking place in Raleigh. On February 8, the paper noted, Yadkin County Republican William B. Glenn repudiated his party on the House floor and introduced yet another resolution against the civil rights bill, one aimed even more squarely at Republicans.[81] Glenn was joined in his defection by another Seventh District Republican, Wilkes County's James H. Foote.[82] Curiously, Foote had been among Republicans who protested the Means substitute. The Glenn resolution was not adopted,[83] but so much partisan maneuvering, despite the clear lack of support of white Republicans for integrated schools, revealed that Conservatives were having success in tying Republicans to African Americans in the minds of North Carolina's white voters through the civil rights bill.

On March 1, soon after the state House's tousle, the U.S. Congress passed the civil rights bill without the integrated schools provision. However, Section 1 of the law did read "that all persons . . . shall be entitled to the full and equal enjoyment of the accommodations, advantages, facilities, and privileges of inns, public conveyances on land and water, theaters, and other places of public amusement." The bill gave federal courts jurisdiction in cases stemming from violations of the law, and it included a section meant to ensure that African Americans could serve on juries.[84]

The sections of the bill allowing African Americans the use of facilities seem to have caused great concern among white Republicans. Rumors spread in the east that African Americans were planning to use violence to assert their rights. In fact, African Americans were quick to make assurances through the Republican press that they did not pose a threat to peace. They did so with circumspection similar to that seen a year earlier. A letter in the *Raleigh Weekly Era*, signed "A Colored Citizen," questioned the motives of Conservatives: "They well know that the term civil rights

Senator	District	Party	Ethnicity	Cantwell Amendment to the Means Resolution (SJ 99) (Failed 6-42)[a,b]	Yeas and Nays on Concurring in the Means Resolution (SJ 100) (Concurred 37-11)[a]
Coastal Plain					
Bell	9	Conservative	White	N	Y
Boddie	7	Conservative	White	N	Y
Busbee	18	Conservative	White	N	Y
Cooke	7	Conservative	White	N	Y
Jernigan	1	Conservative	White	N	Y
Kerr	14	Conservative	White	N	Y
Latham	2	Conservative	White	N	Y
Pegram	16	Conservative	White	N	Dnv
Selby	2	Conservative	White	N	Y
Shaw	1	Conservative	White	N	Y
Smith	10	Conservative	White	N	Y
Stanford	10	Conservative	White	N	Y
Stickney	6	Conservative	White	N	Y
Sugg	11	Conservative	White	Dnv	Y
Waddell	17	Conservative	White	N	Y
Bryant	4	Republican	African American	Y	N
Cantwell	12	Republican	White	Y	N
Cashwell	13	Republican	White	N	N
Mabson	5	Republican	African American	Y	N
Paschall	19	Republican	African American	Y	N
Peebles	3	Republican	White	Y	N
Sneed	21	Republican	White	N	N
Tucker	8	Republican	African American	Y	N
French	15	Independent	White	Dnv	Dnv
Piedmont					
Albright	22	Conservative	White	N	Y
Anderson	28	Conservative	White	N	Y
Clement	30	Conservative	White	N	Y
Graham Jr.	37	Conservative	White	N	Y
Hargrave	31	Conservative	White	N	Y

TABLE 3 } *continued*

Senator	District	Party	Ethnicity	Cantwell Amendment to the Means Resolution (SJ 99) (Failed 6-42)[a,b]	Yeas and Nays on Concurring in the Means Resolution (SJ 100) (Concurred 37-11)[a]
Piedmont (continued)					
Irvin	23	Conservative	White	N	Y
LeGrand	26	Conservative	White	N	Y
Marler	33	Conservative	White	N	Y
McCauley	27	Conservative	White	N	Y
Morehead	24	Conservative	White	N	Y
Parish	20	Conservative	White	N	Y
Waring	29	Conservative	White	N	Y
Williamson	20	Conservative	White	N	Y
Worthy	25	Conservative	White	N	Y
Cook	32	Republican	White	N	N
Holton	24	Republican	White	N	N
Jenkins	38	Independent	White	N	Y
Mountains[c]					
Armfield (pres. of Senate)	M/34	Conservative	White	N	Y
Linney	M/34	Conservative	White	N	Y
Love	42	Conservative	White	N	Y
McElroy	40	Conservative	White	N	Y
McMillan	35	Conservative	White	N	Y
Mills	36	Conservative	White	N	Y
Young	36	Conservative	White	N	Y
Taylor[d]	41	Republican	White	N	Y
Walker	39	Republican	White	N	N

Sources: Regions are from Thomas E. Jeffrey, *State Parties and National Politics, 1815–1861* (Athens: University of Georgia Press, 1989), 278 (map 4, "Change in the Democratic Vote, 1850–60"); and Gordon McKinney, "Women's Role in Civil War Western North Carolina," *North Carolina Historical Review* 69 (January 1992): 40 (map).

Party affiliations are determined from "Members-Elect to the General Assembly for 1874–75," *Rutherford Star and West-Carolina Record*, August 29, 1874 (a simliar list also appears under "Members-Elect to the General Assembly for 1874–'75," *Raleigh Weekly Era*, August 20, September 3, 1874; and "Directory," *Raleigh Weekly Era*, January 14, 1875); House speaker roll call vote in *Journal of the House of Representatives of the General Assembly of the State of North Carolina, at its Session of 1874–'75* (Raleigh: Josiah Turner, Public Printer and Binder, 1875), 6; "Convention!," *Citizen*, March 25, 1875; J. G. de Roulhac Hamilton, *Reconstruction in North Carolina* (1914; Gloucester, Mass.: Peter Smith, 1964), 606n2; Senate president roll call vote in *Journal of the Senate of the General Assembly of*

TABLE 3 } *continued*

the State of North Carolina, at its Session of 1874-'75 (Raleigh: Josiah Turner, Public Printer and Binder, 1875), 4–5 (hereafter cited as *Senate Journal, 1874-75*); "Mr. Norment's Speech," *Wilmington Weekly Post*, March 5, 1875; "Election Returns," *Raleigh Weekly Era*, August 13, 1874; "Republican Ticket," *Rutherford Star and Record*, July 25, 1874; and John Everett Huggins, "The Resurgence and Decline of the Republican Party in North Carolina, 1871–1876" (M.A. thesis, Wake Forest University, 1966).

Ethnicities are found in Eric Anderson, *Race and Politics in North Carolina, 1872-1901* (Baton Rouge: Louisiana State University Press, 1981); "The Colored Members of the Legislature," *Raleigh Daily Era*, December 4, 1872 (reprinted in *Raleigh Weekly Era*, December 12, 1872); "General Assembly," *Carolina Watchman*, October 17, 1872; Hamilton, *Reconstruction in North Carolina*, 593n3, 604nn3, 4; "Appendix G: Negro Members of the General Assembly for the Session of 1872-1874," in Elaine Joan Nowaczyk, "The North Carolina Negro in Politics, 1865-1876" (M.A. thesis, University of North Carolina, 1957), 195; "Appendix: Negro Legislators in the North Carolina General Assembly, July, 1868-February, 1872," in Elizabeth Balanoff, "Negro Legislators in the North Carolina General Assembly, July, 1868-February, 1872," *North Carolina Historical Review* 49 (January 1972): 55; "Appendix: Biographical Sketches of the Thirteen Black House Members of the General Assembly of North Carolina, 1876-77," in Frenise A. Logan, "Black and Republican: Vicissitudes of a Minority Twice Over in the North Carolina House of Representatives, 1876-1877," *North Carolina Historical Review* 61 (July 1984): 344-46; "Carter, Hawkins Wesley" card in "Legislators" file, drawer "A–C," Search Room stacks, North Carolina Division of Archives and History, Raleigh; R. A. Shotwell and Natt Atkinson, *Legislative Record, Giving the Acts Passed Session Ending March, 1877, Together with Sketches of the Lives and Public Acts of the Members of both Houses* (Raleigh: Edwards, Broughton and Co., 1877); and W. McKee Evans, *Ballots and Fence Rails: Reconstruction on the Lower Cape Fear* (New York: W. W. Norton, 1974).

Votes from *Senate Journal, 1874-75*, 99, 100.

[a] Y = Yea; N = Nay; Dnv = Did not vote.
[b] Vote count is listed as 6-35 in SJ 99.
[c] District 34 includes a mountain county (Wilkes) and western piedmont counties.
[d] Some uncertainty exists about Taylor's party affiliation.

does not mean any such position or power as they have alleged and stuffed into the minds of the people in our last campaign. They only used it in that light as a political engine, because they were deprived of the Ku Klux."[85] John Paschall, one of the African American senators who had voted for Cantwell's amendment, also wrote a lengthy letter to the *Era* seemingly reassuring its white readers that race relations would take care of themselves:

> We [African Americans] should practice fidelity, deserve the benefit of this liberty, improve our minds, and become competent to aspire to positions of trust and honor. Then if we fit ourselves our false accusers will have misrepresented us and consequently will not be demoralized by us. It is highly essential on the part of ourselves that we give our hearts, our time and minds to the work of elevating ourselves as a people. Most

of us like to enjoy ourselves, and know we can best accomplish that with our equals, with whom we will be found according to *the general ruling of social equality, which has always regulated itself and always will*. That being true, let us first take care of our character and behave ourselves.[86]

Paschall's use of the term "social equality" was vague enough to satisfy whites that he didn't want integration legally enforced while it stopped short of viewing segregation as permanent and immutable. Booker T. Washington himself would be similarly elusive in 1895.

The 1874–75 session of the General Assembly, coupled with the immediate aftermath of the passage of the civil rights bill, showed that an increasingly confident Conservative majority had pushed white Republicans toward a more vehement stance on segregation than they had held before the 1874 election season. African Americans, meanwhile, continued to try to convince whites that they had no violent designs toward society. They espoused leaving the law out of "social equality," some even implying they wanted segregated facilities — though without espousing enforced segregation.[87] Soon, though, they would be faced with the possibility that segregation would indeed be legally and indefinitely forced upon them.

Before the 1874–75 General Assembly adjourned, plans were being made to call a convention to amend the state's constitution, ratified under congressional Reconstruction in 1868.[88] The convention convened on September 6, 1875, and wrapped up business on October 11, 1875. Despite calls by Conservatives — who by that time accepted the name "Democrats" — for a completely new constitution, the convention proposed amendments that rewrote the 1868 constitution in principle.[89] Many of the convention's ordinances — the measures on which the amendments would be based — were designed to ensure that white Conservatives would regain and maintain power in the state. Some of them were aimed directly at African Americans, and among the amendments was one requiring schools to be segregated.[90] The school amendment implied a new level of permanence, and it was a precursor to the establishment of long-term Jim Crow measures after Reconstruction.

At the Constitutional Convention, the subject of segregation took on a new urgency. Fights against the civil rights bill involved whether or not integration could be required. Now, the threat of permanent, statewide segregation stood directly in front of African Americans. One of the delegates to the convention, African American John H. Smyth, was keenly aware that the threat necessitated an end to African Americans' vagueness about segregation because it was not being endorsed or tacitly accepted but built into the state's fundamental law.[91] "If you pass this ordinance, if you incorporate this into, and make it a part of the Constitution of North Carolina, you determine—fix the status of the races as to education," Smyth told his colleagues about the separate schools proposal. "This the makers of the ordinance had in mind, this they purposed to accomplish by it,"[92] Smyth elaborated on the dangers of fixing segregation so firmly on the state, acknowledging the power of public opinion but noting that it might change. In the process, he gave a rare refutation of the argument that segregation was natural: "The sentiment of the people is opposed to the mixed schools, and so long as this sentiment exists the races will be separate by the sanction of the law which each race makes unto itself. An ordinance that would forbid a change of public sentiment, that would prohibit the people of the State from outgrowing a prejudice, is wrong *per se*. . . . Naturally there is no complexional barrier which separates the streams, and uninterrupted, they seek the [s]ame level, mingling and flowing on to the ocean of life."[93]

By 1875, statements like Smyth's were rare before statewide audiences. They also came too late. As scholars have long noted, Conservatives successfully used the civil rights bill to tie politics to race in North Carolina in their quest to sanction segregation legally.[94] Now, white Republicans could speak of legalizing segregation even as they remained vague about whether such legislation was permanently necessary.

Two days after Smyth gave his speech, Rufus Barringer, a white Republican delegate from Mecklenburg County in North Carolina's western piedmont, gave a speech published by the *Weekly Era*.[95] Barringer seems to have thought that keeping schools separate was a good way to stop the controversy over the issue.[96] "In my private opinion, sir, there is no real necessity for this provision," Barringer said. "But, looking to the public sentiment of the country, and recognizing the measure as only a prudent safeguard in the new and untried circumstances surrounding us, I strongly favor an organic requirement on the subject."[97]

Barringer decided that white fears that African Americans would assert a right to integration necessitated enforced segregation to keep the peace:

> Despite these private opinions of mine . . . we cannot disguise the fact that society [in the] South is still greatly unsettled, and that now and then rash and revengeful parties of both races are tempted and induced to intrude upon the rights and the presence of others, and it is against all such cases, and even the chances of wrong or outrage, that this provision

and similar laws are intended to guard. But above all, . . . there is in the hearts of our white people, and especially the Democratic masses—an honest, long cherished, deep seated sentiment on this subject, which it is prudent in law givers to respect.[98]

Though he did not use the term, Barringer also thought that segregation under a "mutual dependence" arrangement was good. "I have never doubted that the two races could dwell here on the same soil together in peace and harmony, acting and co-operating with each other in all public or political affairs, and without any disturbance in or interference with our admirable social system," he concluded.[99] White Republican vagueness on "mutual dependence" was allowing them to move in a direction increasingly unfavorable to African Americans—now the concept was being used explicitly to support enforced segregation. The separate schools ordinance passed with overwhelming support, even from African Americans. African American delegates were probably afraid that they would lose funding for schools entirely if they did not support the measure. Smyth did not vote.[100]

It would be hasty to be extremely critical of white Republicans, as it would be to malign African American Republicans, who seemed to accept race relations as they stood in 1874 and 1875. Many of them were trying to bring, sometimes at personal risk, unifying words to a state that had been riddled with war, vigilante violence, debt, and the most contentious of political battles when Conservatives and Democrats in neighboring states had resorted to virtual coups d'état to regain control. Whatever their motives in making the argument, white Republicans had every reason to believe they were correct when they suggested that the civil rights bill would prompt violence against African Americans. Moreover, their party was becoming increasingly weaker. In the 1876 elections, Zebulon Vance, Robert Vance's brother, won the governorship, the work of the Constitutional Convention was ratified, and the amended state constitution would read that "the children of the white race and the children of the colored race shall be taught in separate public schools."[101]

But white Republicans who remained vague about the permanence of "mutuality" generally assumed that African Americans were mainly to be manual laborers, whether or not they said so explicitly. They also had to know that the direction in which the state was moving was much more precise than their own words on the matter. North Carolina's actions in those years reflected fading interest in Reconstruction nationwide. In his 1874 speech, Conservative Augustus Merrimon made a prediction about the civil rights bill: "If this bill shall pass, I do not doubt that the court, when the appropriate time comes, will declare it void."[102] In 1883, the sections of the 1875 Civil Rights Act allowing African Americans freedom to use accommodations and transportation were declared unconstitutional.[103]

African Americans were in for harder times throughout the South. In 1886, three years after the U.S. Supreme Court's weakening of the civil rights bill, Henry Grady gave his own assessment of race relations in his famous "New South Speech." The South was presented by Grady as financially and socially successful. Some whites, such as Edward Cantwell, had recognized that African Americans were perfectly capable of being politicians. However, Grady's view of "mutuality" gave African Americans little room for negotiation. "To liberty and enfranchisement is as far as law can carry the negro," Grady asserted. "The rest must be left to conscience and common sense. It must be left to those among whom his lot is cast, with whom he is indissolubly connected, and whose prosperity depends upon their possessing his intelligent sympathy and confidence."[104] By praising the status quo, Grady was implying to his white audience that segregation was desired socially and working economically as well as legally.[105] In fact, by 1890, more than 40 percent of African Americans in North Carolina were tenant farmers, and they were paid less than their white counterparts.[106] The view of "mutuality" as a permanent arrangement was nearly fixed. Nine years later, when Booker T. Washington spoke in Atlanta, Jim Crow was becoming an established practice.

When Washington spoke in such an atmosphere, he had to weigh his words in a manner similar to that of black Republicans who had preceded him, but with the added realization that he was speaking to a regional, perhaps even a national, audience.[107] Washington chose a position like that of African Americans such as John Williamson mixed with the "mutual dependence" appeal of white Republicans later used by Henry W. Grady. Washington biographer Louis Harlan, like C. Vann Woodward before him, argues that with his call on whites to help African Americans for the sake of "mutual progress" and his "downgrading [of] civil and political rights in the black list of priorities," Booker T. Washington saw himself as a bridge between whites and African Americans in the midst of the downfall of African Americans as it took place throughout the South.[108]

The political writing of the 1870s in North Carolina supports their assessments. Rhetorically, Washington tried to join the moderate inheritors of the white Republicans who made vague appeals to "mutual dependence" and the African American Republicans who spoke with circumspection about "social equality." Given the strong similarities between political writings in the 1870s and the words of Grady and Washington, political debates seem to have filtered from statehouse to statehouse into the mix that made up the "New South" ideal. "Mutuality" did not begin with Grady—it was among the ideas that came in part from state capitals, if North Carolina is any indication. Part of what Washington did was take the residue of ideas that the less racist of southern whites presented on "mutual dependence" for mixed audiences, add it to the careful wording on "social equality" used by the most politically minded of southern African Americans for mixed audiences, and combine the two in a manner that would please whites without explicitly giving away African Americans' futures. In doing so, Washington was carrying on a legacy inherited as much from the contentious partisan battles of Reconstruction as from southern men of letters.[109] Unfortunately, by Washington's time, actions spoke louder than words. Whites associated "mutual dependence" not with the vague assurances of the white Republicans of the 1870s but with legalized segregation, and it was it too late to strike a compromise by remaining vague.

Notes

1. Paul M. Gaston, *The New South Creed: A Study in Southern Mythmaking* (New York: Alfred A. Knopf, 1970), 144, 37, 208.

2. Booker T. Washington, *Up from Slavery: An Autobiography* (Garden City, N.Y.: Doubleday, 1963), 160 (sentence quoted also found in Edward Ayers, *The Promise of the New South: Life after Reconstruction* [New York: Oxford University Press, 1993], 325); Gaston, *New South Creed*, 211; Louis R. Harlan, *Booker T. Washington: The Making of a Black Leader 1856-1901* (New York: Oxford University Press, 1972), 219.

3. Harlan, *Booker T. Washington*, 218-19. The term "mutuality" is used on 218. See also Joel Chandler Harris, ed., *Life of Henry W. Grady, Including His Writing and Speeches* (New York: Cassell, 1890), 303, quoted with commentary in Gaston, *New South Creed*, 207-8.

4. C. Vann Woodward, *Origins of the New South, 1877-1913* (Baton Rouge: Louisiana State University Press, 1951), 358; and Harlan, *Booker T. Washington*, 219, hint at this fact.

5. See Bertram Wyatt-Brown, "The Civil Rights Act of 1875," *Western Political Quarterly* 18 (December 1965): 765, on this social-legal distinction.

6. Harlan, *Booker T. Washington*, 218.

7. Ibid.; August Meier, *Negro Thought in America, 1880-1915: Racial Ideologies in the Age of Booker T. Washington* (Ann Arbor: University of Michigan Press, 1963), 101.

8. "Oration of Hon. Edward Cantwell, First January, 1875, to the Colored People of Wilmington," *Wilmington Weekly Post*, January 8, 1875.

9. Ibid. The phrase was published as a self-standing sentence in the speech.

10. See Ferald J. Bryan, *Henry Grady or Tom Watson? The Rhetorical Struggle for the New South, 1880–1890* (Macon, Ga.: Mercer University Press, 1994), vii, 9–10.

11. Gordon B. McKinney, *Southern Mountain Republicans 1865–1900: Politics and the Appalachian Community* (1978; Knoxville: University of Tennessee Press, 1998), 32; John Everett Huggins, "The Resurgence and Decline of the Republican Party in North Carolina, 1871–1876" (M.A. thesis, Wake Forest University, 1966), 62–63; Eric Foner, *Reconstruction: America's Unfinished Revolution 1863–1877* (New York: Harper and Row, 1988), 504; Marjorie H. Prim, "White Supremacy and the Jim Crow Laws in North Carolina" (M.A. thesis, Wake Forest University, 1966), 21–22.

12. Foner, *Reconstruction*, 367. Note 38 on page 367 cites the *Rutherford Star*, February 27, 1869, which Foner quotes. See also William Donaldson Cotton, "Appalachian North Carolina: A Political Study, 1860–1889" (Ph.D. diss., University of North Carolina at Chapel Hill, 1954), 273.

13. *The Legislative Manual and Political Register of the State of North Carolina, for the Year 1874* (Raleigh: Josiah Turner, Jr., State Printer and Binder, 1874), No. 19, Statistical Tables, 135 ("Seventh Congressional District") and 136 ("Eighth Congressional District"), strongly suggests overwhelmingly white voterships in the two districts. On the Conservative votership in mountain counties, see Cotton, "Appalachian North Carolina," 568–69 (Table 8, "Mountain Vote and Percentages"), 551–53; Thomas E. Jeffrey, "An Unclean Vessel: Thomas Lanier Clingman and the 'Railroad Ring,'" *North Carolina Historical Review* 74 (October 1997): 413, 413n49; and Thomas E. Jeffrey, *Thomas Lanier Clingman: Fire Eater from the Carolina Mountains* (Athens: University of Georgia Press, 1989), 204.

14. Kenneth Martis, *Historical Atlas of United States Congressional Districts 1789–1983* (New York: Free Press; London: Collier Macmillan 1982), 104, confirms Harper as a congressman for North Carolina's Seventh Congressional District in early 1872. *Index to the Congressional Globe for the Second Session Forty-Second Congress*, vol. 45 (Washington: Office of the Congressional Globe, 1872) (specifies the bill to which Harper is responding); *The Congressional Globe: Containing the Debates and Proceedings of the Second Session Forty-Second Congress; with an Appendix, Embracing the Laws Passed at that Session*, vol. 45, pt. 1 (Washington: Office of the Congressional Globe, 1872), 198 (records the introduction of Frye's bill); *Congressional Globe*, 42nd Cong., 2nd sess., vol. 45, pt. 4, 3073 (records Harper's asking to submit remarks to the *Globe*).

15. "Condition of the South. Speech of Hon. J.C. Harper, of North Carolina, In the House of Representatives, May 4, 1872, On the condition of the southern States," *Appendix to The Congressional Globe: Containing Speeches, Reports, and the Laws of the Second Session Forty Second Congress*, vol. 45, pt. 6 (Washington: Office of the Congressional Globe, 1872), 370.

16. Ibid.

17. Martis, *Historical Atlas*, 106, shows Robert Vance's service as following Harper's.

18. "Speech of Hon. Robert B. Vance, of North Carolina, in the House of Representatives, January 10, 1874," *North Carolina Citizen* (Asheville), January 22, 1874.

19. Ibid.

20. Ibid.

21. Ibid.

22. Ibid.

23. Brinsley Matthews [William S. Pearson], *Monon Ou or Well-Nigh Reconstructed. A Political Novel* (New York: E. J. Hale and Son, 1882), 56, 22; Karin L. Zipf, "'The WHITES shall rule the land or die': Gender, Race, and Class in North Carolina Reconstruction Politics," *Journal of Southern History* 65 (August 1999): 532. For a treatment on mountain Republicans and African Americans in states including North Carolina, see Gordon B. McKinney, "Southern Mountain Republicans and the Negro, 1865–1900," in *Appalachians and Race: The Mountain South from Slavery to Emancipation*, ed. John C. Inscoe (Lexington: University Press of Kentucky, 2001), 199–214.

24. See John Luther Bell Jr., "Constitutions and Politics: Constitutional Revision in the South Atlantic States, 1864–1902" (Ph.D. diss., University of North Carolina at Chapel Hill, 1969), 231–32; "Republican Meeting in McDowell," *Weekly Era*, March 21, 1872.

25. Tod R. Caldwell to George M. Arnold, January 30, 1872, in Tod R. Caldwell Papers, Perkins Library, Duke University, Durham, N.C.

26. Douglass C. Dailey, "The Elections of 1872 in North Carolina" (M.A. thesis, University of North Carolina at Chapel Hill, 1953), 40, identifies the *Weekly Era*'s Republican pedigree.

27. Tod R. Caldwell, "To the Colored People of North Carolina," January 19, 1872, in *Weekly Era*, January 25, 1872 (emphasis added).

28. "Legislature," *Hillsborough Recorder*, January 21, 1874.

29. Huggins, "Resurgence and Decline," 63–64; Otto H. Olsen, *Carpetbagger's Crusade: The Life of Albion Winegar Tourgee* (Baltimore: Johns Hopkins University Press, 1965), 192; *Journal of the House of Representatives of the General Assembly of the State of North Carolina, at its Session of 1873-74* (Raleigh: Josiah Turner, Jr., State Printer and Binder, 1874), 53, 65–66 (hereafter *House Journal 1873-74*); "Legislature," *Weekly Era*, November 27, 1873; *House Journal 1873-74*, 78; "Legislature," *Weekly Era*, December 4, 1873; *House Journal 1873-74*, 106–7; *Journal of the Senate of the General Assembly of the State of North Carolina, at its Session of 1873-74* (Raleigh: Stone and Uzzell, State Printers and Binders, 1873), 75–76, 183; "Legislative," *Weekly Era*, December 11, December 25, 1873; "Civil Rights," *Wilmington Journal*, December 5, December 26, 1873.

30. "Coming Home—The White Rads Dodging," *North Carolina Citizen*, January 29, 1874.

31. Ibid. Bowman's first name found in "Bowman, Jacob Weaver" card in "Legislators" card file, drawer A–C, Search Room stacks, North Carolina Division of Ar-

chives and History, Raleigh (hereafter Search Room stacks, NCDAH). Special thanks to Steven Massengill and Earl Ijames of the NCDAH for providing access to the archives' card file collection and other file information on state legislators. The files contain comprehensive information including full names, ethnicities, terms of service, and, in some cases, party affiliations of state legislators from the seventeenth century to the present. They also provide sources for all of the information they contain. Massengill and Ijames also pointed me to primary sources such as party tickets in newspapers.

32. "Remarks of Mr. S. Trivett," *Weekly Era*, January 29, 1874, February 5, 1874.

33. Allen W. Trelease, *White Terror: The Ku Klux Klan Conspiracy and Southern Reconstruction* (New York: Harper and Row, 1971), 385–87; Foner, *Reconstruction*, 454, 457.

34. "Remarks of Mr. S. Trivett," *Weekly Era*, January 29, 1874, February 5, 1874.

35. Ibid.

36. Ibid. (emphasis added).

37. Meier, *Negro Thought in America*, 117. Huggins, "Resurgence and Decline," 68, refers to the Republican position as a "counterattack."

38. See postscript under Caldwell, "To the Colored People of North Carolina," January 19, 1872, in *Weekly Era*, January 25, 1872. Some of the African American legislators sitting in the 1873–74 session are among the postscript's list of people who endorsed Caldwell's appeal during the 1871–72 session. Huggins, "Resurgence and Decline," 67, states that John Hyman later came out against the civil rights bill.

39. "Coming Home—The White Rads Dodging,"; "Remarks of John Williamson, Esq., The Able Colored Representative from Franklin, in the House, Jan. 19th on Resolution asking Congress not to pass a Civil Rights Bill," *Weekly Era*, January 29, 1874. The *Era* dates the remarks January 19, which was two days after the debate of the Houston resolution. Huggins, "Resurgence and Decline," 64, also puts the date as the 17th, and other primary sources tend to confirm Huggins.

40. "Remarks of John Williamson, Esq.".

41. *House Journal 1873–74*, 296; "Coming Home—The White Rads Dodging"; Huggins, "Resurgence and Decline," 64; John H. Haley, *Charles N. Hunter and Race Relations in North Carolina* (Chapel Hill: University of North Carolina Press, 1987), 32–33. A portion of this quote appears on page 32 of Haley's work. Huggins uses the entire quote.

42. "Coming Home—The White Rads Dodging"; "Legislative," *Weekly Era*, January 29, 1874. See also Huggins, "Resurgence and Decline," 64. The other Republican was Pasquotank County's F. M. Godfrey. Party affiliations during the time period could be fluid. The *Citizen* cites Bowman as the only Republican to vote against the substitute, as does the *Era*. However, the July 23, 1874, edition of the *Era*, discussing the vote on the Williamson substitute, states that "Mr. Godfrey was elected as a Republican, but the Democrats considered him with them."

43. *House Journal 1873–74*, 297; "Coming Home—The White Rads Dodging";

Haley, *Charles N. Hunter*, 32. Haley uses a version of this quote. Jones's first name verified in "Jones, Edmund III" card in "Legislators" card file, drawer Hon–Mac, Search Room stacks, NCDAH.

44. *House Journal 1873-74*, 299, has votes for Bowman, Blythe, Bryan, Dula, and Whisnant. Bryan's first name in "Bryan, Abraham C." card in "Legislators" card file, drawer A–C, Search Room stacks, NCDAH.

45. Bowe of Caswell is counted in this study as an African American, based on "The Colored Members of the Legislature," *Raleigh Daily Era*, December 4, 1872, reprinted in same, December 12, 1872. However, no other primary source used in this study lists him as an African American. See note 42 on Bowman and Godfrey. For votes on Williamson substitute, see *House Journal 1873-74*, 298. The Houston resolution with Jones's amendment seems not to have made it past the senate, although there is some uncertainty on the matter. The resolution does not appear in the published resolutions of the North Carolina legislature for the 1873-74 session. However, see John A. Hyman, "To the Editor of the Examiner," February 21, 1874, in *Weekly Era*, March 12, 1874; and "Civil Rights. Speech of Hon. A. S. Merrimon, of North Carolina, In the Senate of the United States, May 22, 1874," in *Congressional Record: Containing the Proceedings and Debates of the Forty-Third Congress, First Session*, vol. 2, pt. 6, appendix (Washington, D.C.: Government Printing Office, 1874), 318.

46. Ellison tried unsuccessfully to have the roll call on the resolution reconsidered, which may suggest that he supported the resolution only because he wanted to continue discussion of it. *House Journal 1873-74*, 299-300.

47. The fifteen Republicans, with their counties and percentage African American populations, are as follows (counties are in coastal plain unless marked otherwise): Foster (Caswell—piedmont) 59.0; Cobb (Edgecombe) 65.79; Corson (Beaufort) 35.60; Goodwyn (Halifax) 68.55; Gilbert, Gorman (Wake) 45.44; Gray (Dare) 13.57; Guyther (Washington) 42.62; Hampton (Polk—mountains) 22.64; B. Jones (Northampton) 57.70; Jordan (Montgomery—piedmont) 28.4; Lutterloh (Cumberland) 44.12; Miller (Bertie) 57.43; Scott (Jones) 53.10; Sneed (Granville) 53.78. The percentage of the state's population that was African American was 36.56. Information from "Population by Counties—1790-1870," in *Ninth Census, Volume I, The Statistics of the Population of the United States, Embracing the Tables of Race, Nationality, Sex, Selected Ages, and Occupations* (Washington, D.C.: Government Printing Office, 1872), 52-54 (table 2).

48. Huggins, "Resurgence and Decline," 64, suggests that the Williamson substitute itself was an attempt by Republicans to show in detail their position on the civil rights bill.

49. Ibid. See "North Carolina Republicans on the Civil Rights Bill," *Weekly Era*, July 2, 1874; and "Civil Rights in the North Carolina Legislature," *Weekly Era*, July 23, 1874, for analyses of the Williamson substitute similar to the one given in this study.

50. Hyman, "To the Editor of the Examiner."

51. "A Colored Republican," "To the Editor of the Era," n.d. (headline: "A Bombshell in the Radical Camp"), *Weekly Era*, January 22, 1874.

52. Hyman, "To the Editor of the Examiner."

53. McKinney, *Southern Mountain Republicans*, 49.

54. "Gen. R. B. Vance," *North Carolina Citizen*, May 7, 1874. The addition of the Eighth District in North Carolina is confirmed in Martis, *Historical Atlas*, 107.

55. "Civil Rights, Alias Necro [*sic*] Social Equality," *North Carolina Citizen*, June 4, 1874; Wyatt-Brown, "Civil Rights Act of 1875," 770.

56. Cotton, "Appalachian North Carolina," 281; "Vance and Pool Going West," *North Carolina Citizen*, July 16, 1874; "List of Appointments of Hon. R. B. Vance," *North Carolina Citizen*, July 16, 1874.

57. "Judge Merrimon's Speech on Civil Rights," *North Carolina Citizen*, June 25, 1874.

58. A. R. Newsome, editor, "The A. S. Merrimon Journal, 1853–54," *North Carolina Historical Review* 8 (July 1931): 300–301n1; Walter Clark, "Augustus Summerfield Merrimon" in *Biographical History of North Carolina: From Colonial Times to the Present*, ed. Samuel A. Ashe (Greensboro: Charles L. Van Noppen, 1917), 8:339.

59. *Congressional Record*, 43rd Cong., 1st sess., 1874, vol. 2, pt. 6, index, 238, shows the debate and vote for the legislation as being in *Congressional Record*, 43rd Cong., 1st sess., 1874, vol. 2, pt. 5, 4143–76. Pages 4164 and 4166 note the time of day of Merrimon's speech. The roll call for the bill is given on 4176.

60. "Civil Rights. Speech of Hon. A. S. Merrimon," 308, 313–15. Foner, *Reconstruction*, 529–30; and Rogers Smith, *Civic Ideals: Conflicting Visions of Citizenship in U.S. History* (New Haven: Yale University Press, 1997), 256–57, 328, provide information on the *Slaughterhouse Cases*. Wyatt-Brown, "Civil Rights Act of 1875," 764–65, gives a brief discussion of Merrimon's speech, and pages 765 and 767 provide additional information.

61. "Civil Rights. Speech of Hon. A. S. Merrimon," 315–18.

62. "Civil Rights, Alias Necro [*sic*] Social Equality."

63. Foner, *Reconstruction*, 534; "Mistakes its Position—The Pioneer and its Party—," *North Carolina Citizen*, July 23, 1874; "The Civil Rights Bill," *Asheville Weekly Pioneer*, May 30, 1874. See also Prim, "White Supremacy and the Jim Crow Laws," 18–19; and Huggins, "Resurgence and Decline," 63.

64. "The Civil Rights Bill," *Asheville Weekly Pioneer*, May 30, 1874 (notes the senate's passage of the bill); Cotton, "Appalachian North Carolina," 287–88.

65. "The Civil Rights Bill," *Asheville Weekly Pioneer*, June 6, 1874 (emphasis added). (Cotton, "Appalachian North Carolina," 288n41, cites this editorial.)

66. Cotton, "Appalachian North Carolina," 276.

67. Quoted in "Civil Rights Bill and Back Salary Grab Ignored," *Statesville American*, July 13, 1874.

68. "Democratic Tactics," *Wilmington Evening Post* (daily), May 16, 1874.

69. "Civil Rights," *Wilmington Evening Post*, June 10, 1874.

70. "Resolutions," *Wilmington Evening Post*, June 10, 1874 (emphasis added).

71. "8th Congressional District Official Vote," *Asheville Weekly Pioneer*, August 22, 1874; Cotton, "Appalachian North Carolina," 290. "The Southern Ballot-Box on Civil Rights," *Southern Watchman*, quoted in *North Carolina Citizen*, August 27, 1874. Huggins, "Resurgence and Decline," 71, reports that the one Republican victor was John Hyman. Martis, *Historical Atlas*, 106, 108, shows Robbins as the holder

of the Seventh District seat between 1873 and 1877. The boundaries of the Seventh District changed between the time that James Harper represented it and the time Robbins was elected. Page 257 shows that after 1872, the Eighth District, which was Robert Vance's district, was the westernmost district.

72. Wyatt-Brown, "Civil Rights Act of 1875," 771–72; Huggins, "Resurgence and Decline," 73.

73. Huggins, "Resurgence and Decline," 18; "Legislative Summary," *Weekly Era*, November 26, December 3, 1874.

74. *Journal of the House of Representatives of the General Assembly of the State of North Carolina, at its Session of 1875-'75* (Raleigh: Josiah Turner, Public Printer and Binder, 1875), 77–80; "Legislative Summary," *Weekly Era*, December 3, 1874. Mountain Republicans James Blythe and Eli Whisnant voted against the measure. John Garrison of Polk County also supported the measure. Some uncertainty exists about Garrison's party affiliation. He is listed as a Republican in all of the *Era*'s listings but as a Liberal Republican in the *Rutherford Star and West-Carolina Record*, August 29, 1874. Sadie Smathers Patton, *Sketches of Polk County History* (Hendersonville, N.C.: published by author, 1950), 109, lists him as a Democrat, but he probably was not. See R. A. Shotwell and Natt Atkinson, *Legislative Record, Giving the Acts Passed Session Ending March, 1877. Together With Sketches of the Lives and Public Acts of the Members of both Houses* (Raleigh: Edwards, Broughton and Co. 1877), 21.

75. *Journal of the Senate of the General Assembly of the State of North Carolina, at its Session of 1874-'75* (Raleigh: Josiah Turner, Public Printer and Binder, 1875), 98 (hereafter *Senate Journal 1874-75*); Foner, *Reconstruction*, 529.

76. *Senate Journal 1874-75*, 99.

77. Foner, *Reconstruction*, 529.

78. *Senate Journal 1874-75*, 100.

79. Huggins, "Resurgence and Decline," 75, states that the senate vote was a straight party vote, but it may not have been. Mountain senator Terrell W. Taylor, listed in the *Weekly Era* as a Republican, voted in favor of the resolution. The listed party affiliation of Taylor, however, is questionable. Reconstruction historian J. G. de Roulhac Hamilton did not count Taylor as a Republican in his own party analysis of another vote that took place that session. Taylor later served in the General Assembly as a Democrat, and other actions of Taylor's suggest Conservative leanings. See "Terrell Wilkie Taylor," in J. S. Tomlinson, *Tar Heel Sketch-Book. A Brief Biographical Sketch of the Life And Public Acts of the members of The General Assembly of North Carolina. Session of 1879* (Raleigh: Raleigh News Steam Book and Job Print, 1879), 48–49, copies in "Biographical Directory of North Carolina Legislators," folder TA-TE, file in Search Room stacks, NCDAH; Taylor's vote in *Senate Journal 1874-75*, 4–5; "Letter from Hon. T. W. Taylor, Relating to the Public Debt, &c.," *Western Expositor*, January 7, 1875; Taylor's first name and years of service in the state senate identified in "Taylor, Terrell Wilkie" card in "Legislators" file, drawer T-Z, Search Room stacks, NCDAH.

80. "Civil Rights Bill Passed the House," *North Carolina Citizen*, February 11, 1875.

81. "Messrs. Glenn, Foote and Dula," *North Carolina Citizen*, February 25, 1875; "The Legislature," *North Carolina Citizen*, February 18, 1875; Huggins, "Resurgence and Decline," 73–74.

82. Huggins, "Resurgence and Decline," 74. Several pieces in the *Weekly Era* (February 25, April 1, March 4, April 1, and March 11, 1875) confirm Foote's defection.

83. Huggins, "Resurgence and Decline," 74.

84. *Supplement to the Revised Statutes of the United States*, vol. 1, 2nd ed. (Washington, D.C.: Government Printing Office, 1891), chap. 114, 67–68, including margin note on page 68. Prim, "White Supremacy and the Jim Crow Laws," 18, gives a synopsis of the bill as it passed.

85. "A Colored Citizen," "To the Editor of the *Era*," March 2, 1875, in *Weekly Era*, March 11, 1875 (headline: "The Civil Rights Bill").

86. John M. Paschall, "To the Editor of the Era," March 6, 1875, in *Weekly Era*, March 18, 1875 (headline: "The Situation") (emphasis added). An earlier printing of the letter appears in *Era*, March 11, 1875.

87. Elizabeth Balanoff, "Negro Legislators in the North Carolina General Assembly, July, 1868–February, 1872," *North Carolina Historical Review* 49 (January 1972): 53; "A Colored Citizen," "To the Editor of the *Era*"; Paschall, "To the Editor of the Era."

88. Huggins, "Resurgence and Decline," 76; Frenise A. Logan, "Black and Republican: Vicissitudes of a Minority Twice Over in the North Carolina House of Representatives, 1876–1877," *North Carolina Historical Review* 61 (July 1984): 313–14.

89. Olsen, *Carpetbagger's Crusade*, 195; Huggins, "Resurgence and Decline," 77–78, 78n76, 80; untitled brief, *North Carolina Citizen*, October 14, 1875; William Durham Harris, "The Movement for Constitutional Change in North Carolina, 1868–1876" (M.A. thesis, University of North Carolina, 1932), 97; Bell, "Constitutions and Politics," 253.

90. Paul D. Escott, *Many Excellent People: Power and Privilege in North Carolina, 1850–1900* (Chapel Hill: University of North Carolina Press, 1985), 167; Huggins, "Resurgence and Decline," 81; Cotton, "Appalachian North Carolina," 295. Cotton quotes a primary source, but the citation is unclear. See 295n71.

91. Bell, "Constitutions and Politics," 259.

92. "Speech of John H. Smyth, of New Hanover, in the Constitutional Convention, on the Ordinance in Relation to the Separation of Races in the Public Schools—Delivered September 25th, 1875," *Wilmington Post*, October 8, 1875.

93. Ibid. Portions of the Smyth speech on the microfilm copy of the *Post* are difficult to read. For a compatible position given at the national level, see "Conditions of Affairs From a Colored Standpoint," *Wilmington Weekly Post*, December 25, 1874.

94. Huggins, "Resurgence and Decline," 82; Harris, "Movement for Constitutional Change," 51–52. Pages 51–52 include a quote attributed to the *Raleigh Sentinel*, July 26, 1875. See 52n30.

95. "The State Constitutional Convention," *North Carolina Citizen*, October 7, 1875, mentions that Barringer's speech was to be published.

96. Bell, "Constitutions and Politics," 254.

97. "Remarks of Gen R. Barringer, of Mecklenburg, on 'Separate Schools,' in the Convention, Sept. 27th, 1875," in *Weekly Era*, October 7, 1875.

98. Ibid.

99. Ibid.

100. *Journal of the Constitutional Convention of the State of North Carolina, Held in 1875* (Raleigh: Josiah Turner, State Printer and Binder, 1875), 135, gives the date and 138 the vote. Olsen, *Carpetbagger's Crusade*, 202–3, gives the vote count, along with a brief analysis of the vote.

101. Huggins, "Resurgence and Decline," 82, 83, 96–97; Harris "Movement for Constitutional Change," 97–99; Logan, "Black and Republican," 315; "Constitution of the State of North Carolina, as Amended by the Constitutional Convention of 1875," Article 9, Section 2, in *Laws and Resolutions of the State of North Carolina, Passed by the General Assembly at is Session 1876-'77, Begun and Held in the City of Raleigh, On Monday, the Nineteenth Day of November, A.D. 1876* (Raleigh: The News Publishing Company, State Printer and Binder), 30.

102. "Civil Rights. Speech of Hon. A. S. Merrimon," 315. The introduction to the abridged speech in "Judge Merrimon's Speech on Civil Rights," *North Carolina Citizen*, June 25, 1874, made a note of this prediction.

103. *Supplement to the Revised Statutes of the United States*, 1:67n1; Foner, *Reconstruction*, 587; Huggins, "Resurgence and Decline," 73.

104. "Grady's New South Speech," in Bryan, *Henry Grady or Tom Watson?*, 104 (appendix A: "Key Speeches of Henry Grady"). Bryan, on page 1, notes the financial destitution of the South at the end of Reconstruction.

105. Harlan, *Booker T. Washington*, 219–20, 223.

106. Frenise A. Logan, *The Negro in North Carolina 1876-1894* (Chapel Hill: University of North Carolina Press, 1964) 76–77.

107. Harlan, *Booker T. Washington*, 214–17.

108. Harlan "Booker T. Washington and the Politics of Accommodation," 3; Woodward, *Origins of the New South*, 357.

109. Ayers, *Promise of the New South*, 136–37.

STEVEN E. NASH

The Immortal Vance

*The Political Commemoration of
North Carolina's War Governor*

On June 22, 1916, an adoring crowd gazed in awe upon Zebulon Baird Vance's stout frame. Similar scenes had played out time and again in North Carolina when the "War Governor of the South" was on the stump. On this occasion, however, their "Zeb" was a bronze statue unveiled by the dead statesman's great-granddaughter, Dorothy Espey Pillow, who never knew the man whose likeness she uncovered in the nation's capitol building. Perhaps young Dorothy sat respectfully through the ceremony, or maybe she fidgeted a little, as William A. Hoke, formerly of the North Carolina Supreme Court, described Vance as "an illustrious citizen, distinguished for civic and military virtues—a great leader of his people in war and in peace, great in intellect, great in character and achievement, great in the breadth and quality of sympathy." While Hoke's tribute impressed Vance's "greatness" upon his audience, his characterization of the former legislator, congressman, soldier, governor, and senator repeated themes developed in white North Carolinians' memory since the end of the Civil War. Hoke concluded that Zeb's "hold upon the affections of the people of North Carolina endures and grows with the years."[1]

Judging by North Carolinians' reaction to the news of Vance's death on April 14, 1894, Hoke may well have been right. An outpouring of grief unlike that surrounding the passing of any other public figure swept the state. His body lay in repose in Raleigh for hours so people could pay their respects to the man who had spent roughly half of his sixty-four years in public service. Along the way to Asheville, where he would ultimately rest, people flooded the rail stations for a final moment with their idol. Three thousand mourners passed by the coffin in Durham "while 200 hands of the Durham Tobacco company's factory sang sacred songs in the negro dialect."[2] When the train stopped in Greensboro, "a steady stream of people poured through the car, taking a sorrowful glance at the features of the man whose name was a synonym for all that was great and good."

A "large party" from Winston included the Twenty-sixth North Carolina Infantry Regiment's band, whose members serenaded their former colonel with music suited to the occasion.[3]

Vance's funeral train arrived just as the sun rose over the mountains for his burial on April 18. Surviving members of the Rough and Ready Guards, Vance's Civil War company raised in Buncombe County, served as the honor guard over his body. Attendants carried the senator's remains to Asheville's First Presbyterian Church for another three hours of public viewing. After the final mourner passed, Vance's casket, flanked by Confederate veterans as well as state and national politicians, joined 110 carriages and 700 people in procession to Riverside Cemetery, where family and friends interred the body in his family's plot overlooking the French Broad River.[4]

With the so-called tribune of his people gone, North Carolinians were left to wrestle with his image and legacy. His memory, much like the man himself, remained closely associated with politics. Conservative white Democrats created a Civil War memory of white unity around the governor that ignored wartime divisions within North Carolina and fostered an illusion of unflagging popular devotion to the Confederacy. By portraying white North Carolinians as committed Confederate patriots, the Democratic Party, the defunct southern government's political heir, hoped to garner support for its vision of a "new" industrial South. In order to build such backing, Democrats had to craft a memory that neatly fit North Carolinians' political and emotional needs. Zeb Vance and his Democratic colleagues shared in the broader effort to celebrate the Confederate tradition, but in North Carolina, the Lost Cause was more about defending their state's war contribution than about their failed independence movement.[5] Even though Zeb's oft-contentious relationship with President Jefferson Davis led some to view him as an obstructionist, North Carolinians celebrated his "obstruction" as a "defense" of liberty. Their interpretation of Vance's record, born from the governor's deep inferiority complex during the war, rendered North Carolina the leading protector of states' rights in a region that allegedly seceded upon that doctrine.

While the construction and motivation behind such recollections are important, the use of these constructed memories is equally significant. References to the Civil War and Reconstruction were routinely used to overcome divisions, especially class differences, between white North Carolinians. The shared memory rooted in Vance's war record, which matured during the emotionally charged Reconstruction period, received confirmation amid another crisis roughly twenty years later as the Democrats hoped that Zeb Vance could unite whites in death as he did in 1876. Whereas an inferiority complex fueled Vance's and others' defense of their state in 1876, the issue in 1894 was more about the subordinate status of poorer whites in the Democrats' New South than about inferiority within the Confederacy. During the early 1890s, the war remained a potent rhetorical device, but it could create only a veneer of unity that papered over deep social divisions.[6]

One of the earliest cultivators of Civil War memory in North Carolina was Zeb himself, who passionately defended North Carolina's contributions to the southern quest for independence. Like many historians of his time and ours, Zeb thought seriously about the reasons for Confederate defeat and addressed the topic in numerous writings and addresses after the war. In a particularly caustic speech before the Southern Historical Society at West Sulphur Springs, West Virginia, in 1875, he voiced his opinion that "our civil administrators lost the cause of the South." Much as he had done during the war, North Carolina's war governor outwardly defended former Confederate president Jefferson Davis while simultaneously condemning his policies. Vance opined that "the causes of our ultimate failure" stemmed from the "neglect of those at home." One reason for this failure, Vance asserted, was the fact that the southern states seceded in response to "anticipated" outrages without tangible meaning to the people. If "a tenth of the outrages perpetrated since the war had been inflicted upon us, or even attempted, before a blow had been stricken," Zeb argued, "there would have been no flagging of popular enthusiasm, no desertion, no Appomattox, no military satrapies instead of States under the Constitution." Instead of such ideological nurturing, white southerners endured unfair conscription and tax policies that eroded their commitment to the Confederacy. The former governor felt that while northerners rallied around the banner of the Union, southerners clung primarily to the defense of slavery that could not "hold upon the popular heart." Perhaps shocking his audience, who were members of an organization founded by Virginians and devoted to Robert E. Lee, Vance lamented that "our people never recovered from the damper inflicted on their enthusiasm by the anomalous spectacle of beholding men hunted down and tied to make them fight for freedom and independence!"[7]

In his speech, the proud ex-governor established a dichotomy between the Confederacy and North Carolina that allowed him to honor the ideals embodied in the defunct southern nation by defending his state. While Zeb criticized Confederate national officials for failing to form a unifying ideology, he argued that North Carolina succeeded admirably. The former governor had a clear agenda, and it was no coincidence that he chose to give such a speech to a Virginia audience. During the war, Vance felt that Virginia newspapers regularly slighted North Carolinians' contributions to the war effort. Such critics often pointed to North Carolina's late secession, level of internal discord, and widespread desertion among its troops as signs of weakness in its commitment to the southern cause. Vance's response foreshadowed decades of historical scholarship in our time. Although "the great leaders of the war were furnished by other States," he argued that "in the number of soldiers furnished, in the discipline, courage, and loyalty, and difficult service of those soldiers, in amount of material and supplies contributed, in the good faith and moral support of her people at large, and in all the good qualities which mark self-sacrifice, patriotism, and devotion to duty, North Carolina is entitled to stand where her troops stood in battle, behind no State." Rather than continue to study the war through the eyes of great generals, Zeb advocated a social history of the conflict that accounted for the critical role the Confederate people played in the war's outcome. A shift away from the battlefield would acknowledge North Carolina's efforts to supply its people through state-sponsored blockade-running and various forms of aid to the soldiers' families.[8]

Similar Vance speeches rooted his image and the Confederacy's principles in a deeper context, justifying the South's secession as part of a democratic world history while ranking North Carolina's achievements above other southern states' accomplishments. The "Scattered Nation," delivered dozens of times across the nation, was, on one hand, a call for Americans to be both tolerant of Jews and appreciative of their achievements.[9] On the other hand, Zeb's assessment of ancient Jewish institutions and historic successes was another step in his defense of North Carolina. Vance established a parallel between white southerners, who had seceded from the Union in order to achieve a "purer" realization of the Founding Fathers' vision for their country, and the ancient Jewish kingdom. According to the former governor, the Jews' "model" democracy featured a broadly representative legislature and an organic legal code. He described their government as a confederation of tribes that "were to all extents and purposes independent States, joined together for common objects on the principle of federal republics, with a general government of delegated and limited powers," which many Confederates might have deemed an apt characterization of their own failed regime. If government form and philosophy were insufficient to create a shared past, he noted that both the Jews and Confederates also battled ruthless foes. The former Confederate governor criticized Christians' treatment of Jews much as he did the Yankee invaders' conduct toward the South. With praise that found expression in countless Confederate Veterans' camp meetings across the South, the old war governor lauded the Jews' "constancy, faithfulness and devotion to principle under the most trying circumstances to which the children of men were ever subjected."[10]

Zeb's reading of Jewish history also informed his belief that the Confederacy failed because its civil officials failed to hold the hearts of its people. From his description of the ancient Jewish regime, one can extrapolate Zeb's vision of an ideal democracy. He praised the Jews for their "protection of property, the enforcement of industry and upholding of the State" while instilling "the strongest impulse to personal freedom and national vigor." Ancient Jewish laws protected the rights of the people, much like the former governor's coterie believed he did in North Carolina during the Civil War. Unlike Confederate laws that hurt the lower classes the most, he praised the Jewish kingdom's laws, which he felt "secured the political equality of the people" and blocked the "appropriation of the whole territory of the State, by a rich and powerful landed oligarchy, with the consequent convulsing of the community from the deadly struggles between the patrician and the plebeian orders."[11] Taken to its logical conclusion, it seems again that Vance believed that if the Confederacy had been more careful in its dealings with its people, they might have succeeded in establishing a similarly pure democracy in the South.

Vance's construction of the past built toward a climax point when he called upon his audience "to judge the Jew as we judge other men — *by his merits.*" He decried the "abominable injustice of holding the *class* responsible for the sins of the *individual*," which he said Americans applied to no other group. Yet the old war governor never extended the same courtesy to African Americans, whom Zeb compared harshly to the Jews. He believed it ironic that in the United States, "where wars have been waged and constitutions violated for the benefit of the African negro, the descendants of barbarian tribes who for 4000 years have contributed nothing to, though in close contact with the civilization of mankind . . . and where laws and partisan courts alike have been used to force him into an equality with those whom he could not equal, we have seen Jews, educated and respectable men, descendants of those from whom we derive our civilization," discriminated against.[12] It was a familiar appeal for white unity. Although a different "race," Vance sought acceptance for Jews who shared similar values and beliefs with white southerners while excluding blacks.

Around the time Zeb may have been delivering his lecture for the first time, Reconstruction in North Carolina faced vociferous Democratic attacks. The "Scattered Nation" reflected Zeb's increasing anger with the Republican Party and its African American supporters. Convinced that the 1876 gubernatorial election represented a "do or die" political moment, the Democrats left little to chance. They recruited the popular Vance as their candidate in the hopes that the people would rally to their old governor. Their platform aimed to remove blacks from the body politic in a series of proposed state constitutional amendments, which, among other racially motivated changes, would topple the current system of elective county government and return control over local affairs to the Democratic-controlled state legislature. In response, Republicans stirred class tensions by claiming that such amendments sought to wrest power away from the people and restore a rigidly hierarchical social order. Democrats countered with frequent appeals to racial pride. The *Raleigh News* warned its white readers that "the negroes will vote in a solid mass against the constitutional amendments" and appealed to the whites' racial identity in order to drum up support for the Democrats' "wise and beneficent" proposals.[13]

The "Battle of Giants," as the election became known in North Carolina, revolved around three themes: race, class, and memory. Vance's opponent, Thomas Settle Jr., who played a leading role in the state's repudiation of secession, renunciation of slavery, and extension of equal civil rights to all citizens, was widely recognized as the state's most talented Republican. More immediately, Zeb's opponent goaded the former governor into a series of joint debates between July 25 and August 10. Zeb planned to solicit votes upon appeals to white racial identity and issues confronting the South at large, but Settle kept the focus closer to home. His decision to highlight state matters on the stump forced the former governor to confront his own past in a way that his public lectures had not. The resulting canvass featured bitter charges and countercharges. Democrats attacked the Republicans' corrupt Reconstruction administration, while the Republicans lashed out at the proposed state constitutional amendments that they believed would greatly restrict the power of poorer white and black North Carolinians.[14]

Before the state moved forward, the Republicans made sure that voters confronted its Confederate past. Democrats rallied around the former governor. Arguing that North Carolina adopted secession "with entire unanimity," Democrats defended Vance as doing his best "to redeem the pledges then made, and to preserve the plighted faith of his State." They offered "no apology . . . for his giving the cause of the south such an honest and zealous support that such Christian heroes as Robert E. Lee and Joseph E. Johnston felt, and expressed, admiration of his ability and patriotic course during those times of trial in the cabinet and in the field." His record, Zeb's supporters maintained, demonstrated a commitment to the supremacy of state laws, a fierce commitment to individual and property rights, and an overarching concern for his state's prosperity.[15] They reprinted various wartime papers to demonstrate that Zeb had worked tirelessly to uphold the rights and to provide for his people's well-being. They quoted from his November 17, 1862, message asking the legislature to block the exportation of items necessary for the state. Salt, leather, shoes, cloth, pork, flour, and various other goods were to be held within the state's borders unless expressly purchased for the aid of the southern armies. For the families of the state's "brave and self-denying soldiers," Vance advocated the creation within the interior of storehouses of foodstuffs needed to feed the home front.[16]

Democrats also praised the governor's efforts to uphold his constituents' rights, even if that meant conflict with his Confederate superiors. The author of the campaign broadside quoted approvingly from two letters from the governor to James A. Seddon, then the Confederate secretary of war, protesting impressments. In the first letter, Governor Vance characterized illegal seizures, principally by southern cavalry soldiers, as a sort of "plague" and held them accountable for the dissatisfaction among his people. A second missive renewed his complaints against the impressment officers. Vance told Seddon that the agents exercised too much power, often judging for themselves how much a farmer was able to give. Such irregular and unregulated seizures, Zeb wrote, produced considerable resentment among North Carolinians, and he asked the Richmond authorities for relief.[17] Within the context of the campaign, these letters conveyed the governor's displeasure with the policies of his Confederate superiors. Zeb's allies intended these letters to show the voters in 1876 that he always had their best interests in mind.

These carefully selected letters ignored the fact that more often than not, Zeb conformed to national demands at the expense of his state, which left his efforts to create a war memory that glorified his state and himself open to an onslaught of Republican derision. Playing upon the wounds left by the sharp divisions within the state during the war, Settle claimed that Vance sacrificed thousands of lives and tormented countless citizens to satisfy his thirst for power within the Confederate government. Settle depicted his opponent as determined to suppress all opposition to the Richmond government as the candidates toured the western and central counties, where dissent and Unionism thrived during the war.[18] He read excerpts from Vance's wartime correspondence calling for stronger laws and additional troops to deal with renegade conscripts and deserters. In particular, Settle also exploited a letter Vance wrote to Secretary of War Seddon advocating the creation of a military court to deal with deserters in late 1863. Since Vance's party condemned northern "abuses" and whipped up fear that occupation forces might return to aid in Settle's election, Vance must have resented the charge, couched as it was in his own words.[19]

Republicans also criticized a second major theme in the Democrats' celebration of the war governor, namely Zeb's alleged successes in alleviating material privation during the war. This particular element was equally important to the Republicans, who needed to convince poorer whites that Zeb and the Democrats were indifferent to their wartime struggles. Settle accused Vance of collecting three thousand dollars in gold after the war from Alexander Collie and Company, his London trading partner in his blockade-running scheme, while veterans and their families suffered unparalleled economic hardships. Reminding his listeners that Vance represented elite white North Carolinians, Settle claimed that Zeb had a vessel running back and forth to the Caribbean to provide himself and his family with such luxuries as sugar and coffee. The Republican sharpened his class rhetoric by constructing his own image of Vance. He told his audiences that while they fought for southern independence, their governor "sat in the shade in his easy chair, drank imported liquor, and enjoyed foreign luxuries with men exempted by the twenty Negro law while poor whites were hurried off to fight for the rich to enable them to keep their Negroes."[20]

Vance emerged victorious over Settle by a convincing fourteen thousand votes, seemingly indicating an equally important triumph of his version of the war over his opponent's interpretation. While white North Carolinians' dismissed Settle's version of the Civil War in favor of the more glorious narrative embodied by Vance, cracks lingered within the Democrats' newly cast order of party loyalty, racial solidarity, and industrial growth. Although the election results indicated strong support for Vance and the Democrats' constructed memory of the war among a majority of white voters, their version of the war was never quite so simplistic in whites' minds. Vance defeated Settle, but he garnered fewer votes than Democratic candidate Samuel Tilden polled in the presidential election later that year.[21] White farmers increasingly turned to organizations like the Farmers' Alliance and Industrial Union, which offered them hope within a cycle of debt wresting control of the land from them, while blacks remained politically active despite both discriminatory laws and increasingly virulent racism. The Republican Party, discredited but unbroken, refused to fade into oblivion, and divisions emerged inside the Democratic ranks as well. In 1884, younger, reform-minded members of the ruling party formed the Watauga Club to promote education and industrial development.[22]

The relatively complacent 1880s gave few indications of such festering divisions within the Democratic order. Little in Vance's image changed during the decade, partly due to his relocation to a larger political stage. In 1878, Governor Vance secured election to the United States Senate, a position he held until his death in 1894. During that time, the memory of the war advanced by Zeb and the Democratic Party remained unchallenged. Even as the senator moved away from the rhetorical devices he used so effectively against Settle and the Republicans, North Carolinians continued to praise Vance. In 1881, the state legislature carved out a new county from portions of Granville, Warren, and Franklin counties and named it "Vance." Predominantly African American in population and Republican in politics, Zeb's "black baby" stemmed from the Democrats' continuing efforts to both honor Vance and strengthen their party by gerrymandering the more densely black-populated areas into a new county to the advantage of white voters in the parent counties.[23] By and large, the 1880s seemed to be defined by a sense of contentment.

When a new political crisis shattered the comparative calm of the 1880s, the Democrats turned to Zebulon Vance to once again unite whites amid a divisive political maelstrom. During the war, his leadership kept North Carolinians fighting, albeit against the Yankees and each other. In 1876, Vance's war record helped the Democrats defeat the incumbent Republican Party and regain political control of the state. The threat to Democrats in the form of the Farmers' Alliance and the Populists gave new political immediacy to the commemoration of Vance. By the early 1890s, an agricultural depression, high railroad rates, deflation, and crippling debt made the state's farmers desperate for change, even if that meant abandoning the Democratic Party. Agriculturalists across the state joined the Farmers' Alliance and supported the subtreasury plan, which would allow farmers to store crops in subsidized warehouses to await the best market price. Vance presented the plan on the Senate floor out of respect for his white constituents but ultimately cast his lot with the elite conservatives opposed to the subtreasury. Some Alliance leaders condemned the senator's actions as a betrayal of his people and launched a campaign that succeeded in taking control of the state legislature in 1890. Despite bitter feelings and political squabbles, the new legislature reelected Vance. His popularity, however, had suffered a serious blow as it became clear that some farmers preferred economic reform to their aging Confederate hero. Two years later, in 1892, their frustration boiled over, and Alliancemen slowly began filling the ranks of North Carolina's own Populist People's Party.[24]

As if part of a Greek tragedy, Vance's death in early 1894 spared him from a possibly epic fall from grace. Even though Vance's popularity and party influence had been waning, Democrats felt his loss keenly in their dealings with the public. In times of crisis, whether during the war or Reconstruction, he had remained imminently popular despite deep class fissures. So it was only logical that the Democrats returned to Zeb Vance and the Civil War after his death to quell another class revolt. A correspondent for the *Daily Charlotte Observer* lamented their loss at a time "when we need him most." Divisions between Populists and conservatives made it "hard for them to distinguish between truth and policy; and even when we see the truth, policy is so astute in urging reasons why we should ignore it." Amid such confusion, he took heart from Zeb's example. "We remember what he always did," the newspaperman wrote, "how he never dallied with temptation, nor even glanced at the rewards held out by policy."[25]

Perhaps Zeb was the one politician capable of bridging the widening gap between the factions of his party, but when they desperately needed the man, the Democrats had to make do with his memory. A new wave of commemoration swept across the state in the wake of Senator Vance's death. Newspapers repeated and elaborated upon the image of the war governor put forth in 1876. Their eulogies exploited the perceived "Americanness" of their colleague's career in order to reconnect with dissatisfied farmers. A recurring theme in the short newspaper biographies published after the senator's death was Zeb's connection to the United States' revolutionary past. Not only were Vance's ancestors veterans of the American Revolution, thus binding Zeb to the country's founders, but it was also suggested that he shared a relative with former president Andrew Jackson. By connecting the state's leading Confederate to the nation's founding, eulogists sought a sense of continuity between the Confederate experience and American national history.[26] From this perspective, Vance's popularity stemmed from his deep American roots. His ancestors fought to create a people's republic, and he "shared blood" with the president most responsible for expanding democracy to the masses. Such a person could not help but be popular with the common people.

The Democrats' amplification of Zeb's "Americanness" sought to make political capital from the reunification spirit permeating national politics in the final decade of the nineteenth century. Commemorations after his death painted Vance as something of a man for all seasons. In the wake of the war and Reconstruction, he was the savior who led his people out of a corrupt Republican wilderness. Years later, Democrats revised Vance's image to fit the feeling of reunion sweeping the country. In quoting the *Baltimore Herald*, the *Daily Charlotte Observer* agreed that "as a soldier in the Southern army, as Governor of North Carolina, and as a member of the United States Senate, his bearing was always that of a true, typical and tried American."[27] Like George Washington and the other Founding Fathers, Vance sought to protect his people's natural rights. He fought centralization, first from Washington, D.C., and then from Richmond. Adding to this image were the connections sought between Zeb and more recent northern idols. Vance's admirers wrote of his similarities to George Washington but also compared him favorably with Daniel Webster and even Abraham Lincoln. Days after his death, the *Observer* said that in politics, Vance "represented [the people] and championed their cause" in politics like both Lincoln and the once-detested abolitionist Horace Greeley.[28] One man proposed that Vance and Horatio Seymour, the New York governor who also opposed the suspension of habeas corpus in his state, would "stand out as the two prominent figures of war days."[29]

Much like in the 1876 election, Civil War memory and Vance's image were used primarily to offset class divisions among whites. A key component of these newspaper celebrations after Vance's death was Zeb's portrayal as a stereotypical self-made American man who overcame humble beginnings to achieve greatness. Downplaying Vance's elite class status allowed his admirers to attribute his popularity with lower-class North Carolinians to his being one of them. Such an exaggerated version of Zeb's background sought to assuage the class divisions ripping the Democratic Party apart. Rather than continuing to celebrate Zeb as either governor or senator, the commemorations looked at the man himself in an effort to connect with poorer farmers. Although Vance's father had operated a prosperous drover stand and owned seventeen slaves at his economic peak, the newspapers focused on the adversity his family had faced after his father's untimely death.[30] This version of Vance's youth suggests that he struggled to gain more than a basic education. Kemp P. Battle wrote that young Zeb's early schooling consisted of little more than "Pike's arithmetic and Webster's spelling book." Reflecting a general bias in the state that equated "western" with uneducated, Battle neglected Vance's studies at an east Tennessee college and various mountain academies. His calculated oversight made Vance's alleged ascendance to first in his class at the University of North Carolina during his one year there in 1852 more a reflection of the man than of his class.[31] Newspapers consistently portrayed the former governor after the war as too honest to be wealthy, and they used his supposedly sterling character during Reconstruction and afterward as a political foil to allegedly rampant Republican corruption.[32]

Although death kept Vance from the campaign trail himself, newspapers tried to fill his shoes. Their eulogies served as a public campaign for unity based upon the past that revitalized the memories of Vance and the Civil War. The image that helped the Democrats overthrow Reconstruction gained renewed relevance as editors breathed new life into the traditional Vance image. They filled their papers with tributes concentrating on the most prominent elements of Vance's war record: civil liberties and supply. His perceived defense of civil liberties during a time of crisis raised North Carolina above the Confederacy, making it the pure realization of states' rights, retroactively placed at the war's heart by white southerners. The *Wilmington Morning Star* admired Vance's "nerve" in "maintaining State sovereignty against the assumed power of the Government at Richmond."[33] Democratic leader Samuel A'Court Ashe's *Raleigh News-Observer-Chronicle* noted that Vance executed the southern conscript laws "more promptly and satisfactorily than was done in any other State" and "in a constitutional way."[34] A Charlotte newspaper referred approvingly to the widely quoted biographical sketch by Battle, Zeb's friend and University of North Carolina president, which praised the governor for never allowing the military to subsume the civil authority. "It should be known," Battle wrote, "and remembered throughout the civilized world that all during the time when the Confederacy was vainly fighting for life, and when one-fourth of the State was overrun by contending armies, the great privilege of the writ of *habeas corpus* was never suspended." North Carolinians' good fortune was to have a "governor brave enough to enforce its mandates in the midst of conscript camps."[35]

Publication of the first full Vance biography in 1897 by his former subordinate officer and law partner, Clement A. Dowd, imbued the Vance legend with the force of history. In keeping with the broader goal of celebrating Zeb's life, this monograph carried clear civics lessons. Perhaps expressing the author's intentions, Dowd's publisher, the *Charlotte Observer*, praised the lessons conveyed in his *Life of Zebulon B. Vance* and recommended it as an apt gift for young North Carolinians.[36] Whatever values Dowd and his publisher hoped his volume would instill in its readers aside, his treatment of Vance during the Civil War followed his old partner's example by keeping civil liberties at the center of his war record. Still, Dowd and others grossly exaggerated the principles behind the governor's stand for individual rights as they continued to assert that Zeb entered office intent on preserving "personal liberty and property rights." This version of Vance made the governor more committed to freedom, and specifically white freedom, than even the Confederate government. Dowd portrayed Vance as a bulwark against the expansive Richmond government. Even divisive policies, such as conscription, failed to deter their Vance. In his contributions to Dowd's biography, Robert B. Vance wrote that his younger brother refused to compromise his people's rights in order to appease Confederate authorities, even though he knew that the draft policy was necessary to fulfill the southern republic's manpower needs. Robert believed that Zebulon upheld the power of the state whenever "the rights and liberties of any of its citizens were involved." Since state courts "were the highest and only constitutional tribunals for finally deciding such cases, Governor Vance was determined that their decision should be respected and obeyed."[37]

Vance's one-time junior law partner amplified his Civil War interpretation with a scathing condemnation of Reconstruction. Like most white Democrats, Dowd viewed Reconstruction and Republican-control of North Carolina at best as a crime or, more accurately, as an abomination. He resented congressional Reconstruction, which temporarily ripped political control from North Carolina's "better classes of citizens" and gave it to northern "adventurers," western deserters, eastern "Buffaloes," blacks, "a few respectable" native whites, and other "South haters." Drawing from Vance's acceptance speech in 1876, Dowd portrayed the Republican regime as corrupt and illegitimate because it drew strength from the enfranchisement of black men, "who had no right under the constitution and laws of the State or the United States to vote," while the best white men suffered disfranchisement. Dowd contrasted such denigration of civil rights sharply with Vance's war record. The war governor fought to uphold citizens' rights during the war, but the Republicans trampled upon those same rights after it. Habeas corpus again became a prescient political issue. Democrats championed Vance's warnings to Jefferson Davis not to violate the writ while condemning Republican William W. Holden for suspending it in 1870.[38] In the context of the time, Dowd's connection between Reconstruction and the war carried the threat of Republican rule forward to the present crisis. New horrors, his depiction of Vance made clear, awaited white North Carolinians if the Democrats again lost control.

While Dowd's book may have reached a wider audience, a more public declaration of esteem for Vance's memory took place in his native county of Buncombe. A few days before Christmas in 1897, a "large assembly" in Asheville gathered for a highly ritualized ceremony that featured local school children singing "America" and the entombing of several Confederate relics in the cornerstone of an obelisk monument being built in Zeb's honor. As the audience wiped the snow from their eyes, they lent their ears to Reverend Doctor R. R. Swope, the rector of All Souls Church in Biltmore, who offered a slightly different take on Zeb and civil liberties. More than any of the other major events praising Vance's memory, Swope's address in the former governor's native county showed how Zeb's war record could be spun from a negative obstruction to a positive defense of liberty. Neither a native North Carolinian nor an acquaintance of Vance's, Swope searched out details on his subject's life from his biographers.[39] Whether Swope had read *The Life of Zebulon B. Vance* prior to his speech or not, his contemplation of Vance's "greatness" differed from Dowd's interpretation. The clergyman believed that Zeb "resented all abuse of authority by the military powers" to the point of "being hostile to the Confederate cause." Here was Zeb Vance as an obstructionist, perhaps reflecting a competing image of the war governor from outside North Carolina. Still, Swope's oration twisted Zeb's resistance into the positive protection of liberty and slowly warmed his listeners. For southerners devoted to the cause of individual liberty, he argued, it was Vance's "proud distinction that in North Carolina, of all the states north or south, with possibly a single exception, the writ of *habeas corpus* was at no time suspended during the war." Despite leaving no lasting legislation bearing his name, Swope decreed, Vance provided the stability and continuity of policy that Americans truly wanted from their statesmen.[40]

This second wave of image-building after Vance's death also reassessed his blockade-running efforts, which constituted the second component of Vance's war record designed to foster white support. By nature, this second wave of memory-building was largely repetitive, since it grew out of previous speeches and political campaigns. Still, Vance's image drew continued strength from the Lost Cause belief that the Confederacy succumbed to Union armies blessed with overwhelming advantages in men and matériel. North Carolinians again claimed success where their national government had failed and specifically honored Vance's ingenuity in pursuing state-sponsored blockade-running. Newspaper eulogies again bolstered the image constructed after the war. In Wilmington, the center of the clandestine trade, they praised Vance for attending to "the welfare of our soldiers in the field who were clothed and otherwise provided for by the blockaders in the service of the State."[41] The *Raleigh News-Observer-Chronicle* concurred that Vance clothed North Carolina troops "better than was done by any other State."[42] Veterans in Fayetteville remembered gratefully "that it was through his foresight and watchful care that we were warmly clad and our wants supplied."[43]

Dowd's depiction of Vance's supply operation rendered the governor's attempts to furnish food and accoutrements for North Carolinians, at the front and at home, more symbolic. In his biography, the purchase of the blockade-runner *Advance* and the export of cotton to British markets made Vance a standard Lost Cause figure. State-sanctioned blockade-runners brought back "such articles as were most needed by the people of the State, such as cotton cards, spinning wheels and sewing and knitting needles, for the use of the good housewives in making clothes, and also with various kinds of machinery for the use of the cotton and wool mills in the State." According to Dowd, this risky trade "much enhanced the comforts of the soldiers and people."[44]

But unlike the 1876 campaign broadside defending Zeb's war record, Dowd kept the focus largely on the military. Citing a speech that Vance gave in Baltimore twenty years after the war's end, Dowd stated that North Carolina successfully imported an array of supplies through the *Advance* and other vessels. The former war governor gave vast estimates of the supplies he brought into North Carolina without the advantage of his wartime papers. Yet Dowd and others repeated as fact Vance's claims to have imported 60,000 pairs of hand cards, 10,000 grain scythes, 250,000 pairs of shoes, 50,000 blankets, enough cloth for 250,000 uniforms, 2,000 Enfield rifles with 100 rounds of ammunition, 100,000 pounds of bacon, and 500 sacks of coffee, among other items. The Lost Cause notion that the North simply overwhelmed the smaller armies of the South made Vance's, and later Dowd's, accounts of North Carolina's success appear greater in the context of Confederate failure. Dowd also added that the risky trade "much enhanced the comforts of the soldiers and people."[45] The characterization of North Carolina during the war distanced the Old North State from the Confederacy while simultaneously making it the ideal southern state. If only the Confederacy had been more like North Carolina, Judge Walter Clark opined, it might have garnered more supplies for its troops.[46]

But the situation in the 1890s was not the same as in 1876. By casting Vance as everyman, as a devout defender of white North Carolinians' rights, and as the provider for both soldiers and their families, Democrats appealed to white Populists through an imagined past in which racial harmony trumped class differences. Through Vance and Civil War memory, they hoped to establish continuity between the present Populist rift and the turmoil of the Civil War. Democrats held that North Carolinians stood behind the Confederacy through their beloved war governor, and they hoped that the memory of Vance could do what the man often had done in life: sustain political unity among white North Carolinians. Their depiction of Vance as a man of the people who overcame poverty to achieve greatness appealed directly to those likely to join the Alliance or Populists. Portraying Vance as a defender of civil liberties made the state's Democrats, through his example, appear sympathetic to poor farmers' anger over stock laws, trusts, and the perceived trampling upon their rights by wealthier citizens.[47] The Democrats' praise for Vance as a champion of people's rights sought to appease the Populists' concerns through appeals to the past rather than through an honest assessment of the present.

Although the Vance image's core appeal remained the same through the multiple stages of formation, the context around it had changed dramatically. During the contest with Settle, the image bound white Democrats to the former governor and reminded them what was at stake in the election. At the end of Reconstruction, appeals to the war carried an emotional weight that bound many whites together politically. Yet the cracks that existed in the Democrats' New South order never fully closed, leaving the restored hierarchical power structure vulnerable should the bonds uniting the Democrats splinter. This is precisely what happened in the 1890s. When the Populists split with the Democratic Party, they took with them their memory of the war and of Vance as well. Their commemoration of Vance after his death echoed the Democrats' own interpretation. A few weeks after his death, editorials in Populist and Alliance papers around the country lamented Zeb's passing. In Illinois, he was remembered as a "champion of the rights of the people." The editor of the Populists' state organ in Raleigh, the *Progressive Farmer*, gave Vance the most generous praise in asserting that "if the leaders of both old parties were half as good as Vance was, there never would have been a revolt." Walter Clark's piece on Vance, later included in Dowd's biography, went so far as to say the Confederacy might have succeeded if Davis had followed Zeb's example in North Carolina.[48] Populists remembered Vance in much the way that the Democrats did because they were once loyal members of the ruling party themselves. As such, they could join in the commemoration of the fallen governor without abandoning their current complaints against the Democrats. Unlike in 1876, the Civil War was no longer a deeply personal factor in the political life of most white North Carolinians, and the Populists privileged class interests over Vance and the Confederate past.

Such celebrations of his life, however, could not fully hide some Populists' lingering bitterness. One newspaper writer who harangued against

Vance in 1890 concluded cautiously four years later that Zeb had been an honest man with friends "among every class" and "admirers in all parties." As a man, he wrote, Vance was not perfect. Perhaps recalling the sense of betrayal he had felt after the senator rejected the subtreasury plan, the Populist editor noted that Vance, "like all men with convictions and ability . . . made enemies" and mistakes. But "when he raised his voice in the Senate chamber it was generally for the right," and "his votes were seldom, if ever, recorded in favor of a bad measure." Whatever his reservations, he opined that if more Democrats had followed Zeb's example, "our country would have escaped some of the horrors of plutocratic rule."[49]

White Democrats' failure to hold the Populists within their ranks produced their worst nightmare: a biracial political movement that united lower-class whites and blacks with the Republican Party. This political combination, often referred to as "fusion," defeated the Democrats in North Carolina for the first time since Reconstruction. Only a few months after Zeb's death, the Populist-Republican coalition won a majority in the General Assembly, seven of nine congressional seats, and control over the state supreme court and treasury. The Fusionist General Assembly chose Republican Jeter Pritchard as Vance's successor in the Senate in 1894 and sent Populist Marion Butler to join him two years later. Fusionists dismantled the Democrats' hierarchical power structure. New legislation made local officials subject to popular ballot rather than legislative appointment, and lawmakers revised election codes to allow blacks and Republicans to vote more freely.[50]

Frustrated in their efforts to lure the Populists back into the fold, Democrats took on harsher tactics, increasingly relegating Vance's memory to the backseat. Vance and the war remained popular distractions masking an intense and calculated racial campaign to stifle dissent. In Wilmington, a group of conservative whites orchestrated a political coup in which a white mob beat and cowed dozens of blacks over two days in November 1898. Led by former Confederate Alfred M. Waddell, the mob toppled the Republican city council, which included four African Americans, and replaced them with white Democrats. Far from an isolated incident, the Wilmington race riot was part of a larger campaign to reassert the political supremacy of the white aristocracy. A return to violent racial rhetoric smashed the biracial Populist alliance. Where race could not divide the Fusionists, the Democrats resorted to electoral fraud to achieve their counterrevolution in 1898. Once back in control of the legislature, they dismantled Fusion's reforms and moved to permanently disfranchise black and some lower-class white voters. Passage of a disfranchisement amendment slammed the door on political disagreement and secured a solidly Democratic North Carolina for 1900 and beyond.[51]

Democratic successes gave the final commemorative event held in Raleigh after the Populists' defeat the feeling of a victory celebration. Businesses, expecting festive crowds, advertised special sales to profit from the merriment while a statue of Vance was dedicated. On August 22, 1900, Zeb's friend and former secretary Richard H. Battle told his hot and tired listeners at the dedication that the energy and efficiency with which Zeb met the obstacles before him as governor pleased both his warmest supporters and some of his fiercest detractors. Once Vance "cast his lot with the South and pledged his faith to its cause," Battle declared, "that faith he thenceforth did 'bear of life and limb and terrene horror.'" While he acknowledged that Vance revered the Union, he reiterated that Zeb stood ready to "oppose the coercion of a seceded State, if any of them should exercise what he considered the revolutionary right of secession."[52] What separated Vance as the preeminent southern war governor was his defense of civil liberties. Battle remembered Vance being "as firm in preventing unlawful encroachments from the authorities in Richmond, or Confederate officers without authority, as he was to see that the laws of the State insuring justice between man and man were obeyed." Vance's former secretary believed that his boss's spirited defense of his people's rights should convince "any fair-minded man, however ardent a Confederate . . . that, through him and otherwise, this State was doing its full duty to the common cause."[53]

All in all, the cultivation of Vance's image as a Civil War hero had a mixed result in North Carolina. The Vance image worked within North Carolina to rehabilitate the state's checkered reputation within the Confederacy. Through the great "War Governor of the South," North Carolinians found a hero in the political sphere comparable to Robert E. Lee and Thomas "Stonewall" Jackson on the military side. In memory, their governor loomed larger than the defeated southern nation itself. For white North Carolinians, this was enough to convince them to reelect Zeb and rebuke the Republicans in 1876. But that image of racial unity never unified all whites politically. The Populists, like most whites, celebrated the Vance of legend, but that did not stop them from leaving the war governor's party in search of reform. Although the Vance image persisted, by 1900 Democrats could no longer depend upon Civil War memory exclusively to mobilize whites politically. Admirers continued to praise the war governor and the hardened foot soldiers of the Confederacy, but that imagined past could no longer be counted upon to provide political unity. His party was changing, and the Civil War and its governor became more window dressing upon a newly rigid racial order. Emotional racial rhetoric and the formal disfranchisement of black men and a number of poor whites clinched the conservative Democratic control that Vance and his colleagues desired after Reconstruction. Zeb remained useful, as later commemorations showed, but he no longer carried the immediate political force he once had.

Well after Richard Battle eulogized his old friend in 1900 and little Dorothy Pillow pulled the cover from her great-grandfather's statue in 1916, Zeb Vance was still seen as the ultimate guns and butter politician in North Carolina. Smaller commemorative activities took place across the state during the first half of the twentieth century. A church in Fletcher dedicated a tablet in honor of Vance's efforts to promote tolerance in the "Scattered Nation" speech in 1928. During World War II, preservationists took charge of Zeb's birthplace outside Asheville and his home in Statesville and turned them into museums dedicated to the war governor's life and career. North Carolina also paid respects to Zeb's wartime smuggling by naming the first "Liberty Ship" built in Wilmington after Vance. The legend created by the Democrats and Zeb continued to inform North Carolina history and politics long after his death. In the summer of 2005, the state unveiled the first of its new Civil War Trails markers at the state capital. North Carolina's first placard bore Vance's image. Although his record has been exaggerated and politicized in memory, Zeb remains the enigmatic public face of the Civil War in North Carolina.[54]

Notes

1. *Confederate Veteran* 24, no. 10 (October 1916): 442. Several newspapers and county meetings spoke of erecting a monument to Vance after his death. For examples, see *Raleigh News-Observer-Chronicle*, April 21, 1894, 2, and April 22, 1894, 2; and *Daily Charlotte Observer*, April 28, 1894, 2.

2. *Asheville Citizen*, April 18, 1894, 1.

3. *Greensboro Patriot*, April 18, 1894, 3.

4. *Asheville Citizen*, April 18, 1894, 1.

5. The Lost Cause possessed a variety of meanings, most of which centered upon the military aspects of the war. For instance, the standard Lost Cause position maintained that Confederate defeat was inevitable due to the Union's superiority in men and productive capacity. This interpretation upheld southerners' honor by praising their ability to fight bravely for so long against such long odds. In a broader sense, however, the Lost Cause was a worldview that connected the supposed racial and class stability of the Old South to the industrial New South. North Carolinians tempered their memory of wartime trials with triumph. With Zeb Vance at its center, the state's

Civil War memory was largely about overcoming the Old North State's critics and making it the archetypal Confederate state. On the Lost Cause and Civil War memory, see, for instance, David W. Blight, *Race and Reunion: The Civil War in American Memory* (Cambridge, Mass.: Belknap Press of Harvard University Press, 2001); Gaines Foster, *Ghosts of the Confederacy: Defeat, the Lost Cause, and the Emergence of the New South, 1865 to 1913* (New York: Oxford University Press, 1987); and Gary W. Gallagher and Alan T. Nolan, eds., *The Myth of the Lost Cause and Civil War History* (Bloomington: Indiana University Press, 2000).

6. Two excellent studies of Zebulon Vance have appeared in the past year. Gordon B. McKinney's *Zeb Vance: North Carolina's Civil War Governor and Gilded Age Political Leader* (Chapel Hill: University of North Carolina Press, 2004) is a definitive account of Vance's life, and Joe A. Mobley's *"War Governor of the South": North Carolina's Zeb Vance in the Confederacy* (Gainesville: University Press of Florida, 2005) identifies race and Confederate nationalism as the defining traits of his wartime administrations. Several solid studies of North Carolinians' memories of both Vance and the Civil War have also appeared in recent years. Of particular import are Gordon B. McKinney's "Zebulon Vance and His Reconstruction of the Civil War in North Carolina," *North Carolina Historical Review* 75, no. 1 (January 1998): 69–85, and Jeffrey J. Crow, "Thomas Settle, Jr., Reconstruction, and the Memory of the Civil War," *Journal of Southern History* 62, no. 4 (November 1996): 689–726. While these articles depict Zeb's role in reconstructing the cause for North Carolina's secession and war effort and summarize the opposition's competing narrative in the 1876 gubernatorial election, both stop in the 1870s. Vance remained a powerful political figure into the 1890s, when his memory underwent a second wave of construction. An examination of Zeb's place in memory as it evolved through the final decades of the nineteenth century reveals both North Carolina's deep insecurity about its place in the Confederate past as well as the limits of war memory in mobilizing the electorate. The changes wrought by New South industrialization seemingly weakened the power of the war and Vance to unify white North Carolinians.

7. "Address Delivered by Governor Z. B. Vance, of North Carolina, Before the Southern Historical Society, at White Sulphur Springs, West Virginia, August 18th, 1875," *Southern Historical Society Papers* 14 (January–December 1886): 516–17. Vance expressed similar opinions during the war as well. During his first inaugural address, he acknowledged public anger over conscription and promised to "protect the citizen in the enjoyment of his rights and liberties" against martial law. In 1864, the governor wrote Jefferson Davis complaining that the president had always been suspicious of North Carolina due to its late secession and that the Confederate conscription, impressments, and tax-in-kind policies had been unfairly enforced in his state. Still, Vance remained committed to the ideal of an independent Confederacy, which kept him and Davis in cooperation if not always on friendly terms. See Mobley, *"War Governor of the South,"* 34, 74–75, 118.

8. "Address . . . Before the Southern Historical Society," 509, 510–15, 517–18. The Conscription Act of 1862, which rendered all white men between the ages of eighteen and thirty-five eligible for the draft, was a particularly hard pill to swallow for the predominantly poorer white men subject to mandatory service because it granted an

exemption to one adult white male in every family owning twenty or more slaves. This last provision, derided as the "twenty-nigger rule," convinced many lower-class whites that the conflict was nothing more than a "rich man's war and a poor man's fight." Regardless of such problems, however, North Carolina sent more soldiers, roughly 125,000 including 21,348 conscripts, into Confederate military service than any of its sister states. See Paul D. Escott, *Many Excellent People: Power and Privilege in North Carolina, 1850–1900* (Chapel Hill: University of North Carolina Press, 1985), 35–39; and Richard Yates, *The Confederacy and Zeb Vance* (Tuscaloosa: Confederate Publishing Company, 1958), 34.

9. Clement Dowd, *Life of Zebulon B. Vance* (Charlotte: Observer Printing and Publishing House, 1897), 393. Dowd included the full text of the "Scattered Nation" in his biography. All citations to the speech are to that edition. It is unknown when or where Vance first delivered the "Scattered Nation," but Selig Adler estimated that Zeb wrote it sometime between 1868 and 1873. See Selig Adler, "Zebulon B. Vance and the 'Scattered Nation,'" *Journal of Southern History* 7, no. 3 (August 1941): 370.

10. Dowd, *Life of Zebulon B. Vance*, 377–85.

11. Ibid., 377–78. For example, see Vance's February 23, 1885, speech to the Association of Maryland Line in Baltimore entitled "Last Days of the War in North Carolina." In this speech, he roundly condemns William T. Sherman for his march through Georgia, South Carolina, and North Carolina. Of Sherman, Zeb said, "The manner in which this army treated the peaceful and defenseless inhabitants in the reach of its columns all civilization should complain." See Dowd, *Life of Zebulon B. Vance*, 467.

12. Ibid., 393 (emphasis in the original).

13. Escott, *Many Excellent People*, 166–67; Sandra Porter Babb, "The Battle of the Giants: The Gubernatorial Election of 1876 in North Carolina" (M.A. thesis, University of North Carolina at Chapel Hill, 1970), 25, 31–32, 40, 53–54, 61–62; *Raleigh News*, October 24, 1876, quoted in Babb, 61.

14. Babb, "Battle of the Giants," 38, 40; Crow, "Thomas Settle," 702.

15. "Gov. Vance's Record," *Raleigh Sentinel* print, 1876, North Carolina Collection, University of North Carolina, Chapel Hill (campaign broadside)

16. Ibid.

17. Ibid. The letters included in the campaign broadside can also be found in their entirety in Joe A. Mobley, ed., *The Papers of Zebulon Baird Vance*, vol. 2, *1863* (Raleigh: North Carolina Division of Archives and History, 1995), 344–45, 356.

18. Although most often discussed historically in relation to the western and central counties, all of North Carolina experienced internal rifts during the war. When Vance took the oath of office on September 8, 1862, much of the northeastern section of the state had already fallen to the Federals with little chance for the Confederates to recapture it. Meanwhile, a combination of conscription and the increasing trials of war convinced many North Carolinians to abandon the southern armies. Of the men North Carolina sent to the front, nearly 24,000 later deserted. Some of these rogue soldiers banded together in open defiance of the Confederate and state authorities. Deserter bands waged a guerrilla war in the mountain counties that aggravated that region's already divided allegiances. In the center of the state, a peace movement threatened

to undermine the war effort in Vance's backyard. For more on the internal divisions within North Carolina, see Richard Reid, "A Test Case of 'Crying Evil': Desertion among North Carolina Troops during the Civil War," *North Carolina Historical Review* 58, no. 3 (July 1981): 234–62; William T. Auman, "Neighbor against Neighbor: The Inner Civil War in the Central Counties of Confederate North Carolina," (Ph.D. diss., University of North Carolina, Chapel Hill, 1988); John C. Inscoe and Gordon B. McKinney, *The Heart of Confederate Appalachia: Western North Carolina in the Civil War* (Chapel Hill: University of North Carolina Press, 2000), esp. chaps. 4–6; Judkin Browning, "Removing the Mask of Nationality: Unionism, Racism, and Federal Military Occupation in North Carolina, 1862–1865," *Journal of Southern History* 71, no. 3 (August 2005): 589–620; and Barton Alan Myers, "Executing Daniel Bright: Power, Political Loyalty, and Guerrilla Violence in a North Carolina Community" (M.A. thesis, University of Georgia, 2005).

19. Babb, "The Battle of the Giants," 41. The governor's record against internal dissent is much more complex. In September 1862, he ordered the militia and two companies of North Carolina troops into the central counties known as the Quaker Belt to crack down on deserters. A few months later, Confederate regulars deployed against deserters. His Home Guard also garnered a reputation for brutality. On a number of occasions, they used force to extract information from women about their Unionist or deserter male relations. Whatever his objections to national policies, historian Joe A. Mobley concluded, Zeb usually conformed to national demands in the end. Therefore, it is far more accurate to view his actions through his commitment to the Confederacy than through some form of principled stand for states' rights. See Mobley, *"War Governor of the South,"* 43–48, 55–56, 163.

20. Babb, "The Battle of the Giants," 42–43. Like all Confederate states, North Carolina struggled to provide for its citizens at home and at the front. North Carolina established a number of state-owned granaries to increase its food supply under Zeb's direction, outlawed the distillation of grain into illicit spirits, and kept the Wilmington saltworks open to bolster the state's meager supply. The young governor captured lasting fame, however, for his approval of Brigadier General James G. Martin's suggestion that he purchase ships on the state's behalf to trade directly with British companies hungry for southern cotton. Under Governor Vance, North Carolina purchased a share in four blockade-runners—the *Advance*, the *Don*, the *Hansa*, and the *Annie*. Still, poor relief taxed county courts beyond their means, and the state legislature's allocation of funds fell far short of the people's needs. Yeomen women carried out "bread riots" in Salisbury and High Point and other protests elsewhere in the state. These demonstrators felt they were correcting a social wrong, and the majority of the public sided with the rioters. See Escott, *Many Excellent People*, 55–58, 66–67; Laura F. Edwards, *Scarlett Doesn't Live Here Anymore: Southern Women in the Civil War Era* (Urbana: University of Illinois Press, 2000), 93–94; and McKinney, *Zeb Vance*, 139.

21. Crow, "Thomas Settle," 724; McKinney, "Zebulon Vance and His Reconstruction," 77–80, 82–83; McKinney, *Zeb Vance*, 139; Glenn Tucker, *Zeb Vance: Champion of Personal Freedom* (Indianapolis: Bobbs-Merrill, 1966), chap. 15. Settle accused

Vance of running for office in 1862 as a peace candidate and then changing his position once in office. He also called the former governor to account for his vigorous enforcement of the Conscription Act, thereby provoking violence across the state. He also charged, and rightly so, that Zeb used his blockade-running enterprise not only to equip and feed the state but also to import goods for his family. Vance's defense stressed the themes that echoed through the later commemorations. Under Vance's administration, North Carolina allegedly provided more supplies to its troops and their families and more faithfully defended citizens' rights than any other southern state.

22. Escott, *Many Excellent People*, 171–72, 174, 179–87; James L. Hunt, "The Making of a Populist: Marion Butler, 1863–1895, Part I," *North Carolina Historical Review* 62, no. 1 (January 1985): 67.

23. Samuel Thomas Peace, *"Zeb's Black Baby": Vance County, North Carolina* (Durham: Seeman Printery, 1955), 10–14. Gubernatorial and presidential election results after Vance County's formation show a slow shift toward the Democrats in Granville, Warren, and Franklin counties. With the exception of Franklin, the Democrats never thoroughly dominated the other two counties until they barred black men from the polls in 1900. See R. D. W. Connor, ed., *A Manual of North Carolina Issued by the North Carolina Historical Commission for the Use of Members of the General Assembly Session 1913* (Raleigh: E. M. Uzzell and Co., State Printers, 1913), 987–92, 1003–6.

24. Alan B. Bromberg, "'The Worst Muddle Ever Seen in N.C. Politics': The Farmers' Alliance, the Subtreasury, and Zeb Vance," *North Carolina Historical Review* 56, no. 1 (January 1979): 20–21, 24–26, 31–35; Escott, *Many Excellent People*, 241–45, 247; Hunt, "The Making of a Populist, Part I," 68, 73, 75–77; James L. Hunt, "The Making of a Populist: Marion Butler, 1863–1895, Part II," *North Carolina Historical Review* 62, no. 2 (April 1985): 180–83, 188–89.

25. *Daily Charlotte Observer*, April 22, 1894, 4.

26. Ibid., April 16, 1894, 1. To make young Zebulon an even greater "southern" American, the sketch biography included an incident where a young Vance allegedly encountered John C. Calhoun. The prominent South Carolinian, supposedly struck by Vance's ability, encouraged the boy to work hard to develop those talents. In this telling of Vance's youth, it was Calhoun who convinced him to trade his mischievous ways for a path to greatness.

27. *Daily Charlotte Observer*, April 18, 1894, 2.

28. Ibid., April 16, 1894, 1.

29. Ibid., April 29, 1894, 6; *Raleigh News-Observer-Chronicle*, April 22, 1894, 2. Richard Battle opened his dedicatory address at the Raleigh ceremony by comparing Washington and Vance and by proudly asserting Zeb's claim to be honored alongside the father of our country.

30. David Vance's death left his wife with eight children and significant debt, but the Vance family was never in danger of starving or being homeless. His mother sold all but one of their slaves and moved the family to Asheville, where Zeb was able to continue his schooling despite assuming the duties of the male head of household. Re-

gardless, Vance's family was clearly a member of the upper echelon of western North Carolina society. His paternal grandfather served three terms in the state legislature, and his uncle was a United States congressman. See McKinney, *Zeb Vance*, 7–13.

31. *Asheville Citizen*, April 17, 1894, 2; *Fayetteville Observer*, April 19, 1894, 2; *Charlotte Democrat*, April 26, 1894, 2. Battle's account overstates Vance's performance at the University of North Carolina while simultaneously downplaying his early education. Vance never ranked first in his university class academically, although many of his classmates might have rated him first in wit and humor. In fact, Vance's class standing was never actually recorded, since he was a part-time student at Chapel Hill. Also, Battle's depiction of Vance as a sort of natural genius ignores the hard work Zeb did as a young man. While it is true that the family experienced hard times when his father died, Zeb had the benefit of a vast family library from which he voraciously studied the Bible, Shakespeare, and other popular works.

32. *Daily Charlotte Observer*, April 20, 1894, 2; *Fayetteville Observer*, April 19, 1894, 3; *Asheville Citizen*, April 16, 1894, 1.

33. *Wilmington Morning Star*, April 17, 1894, 2.

34. *Raleigh News-Observer-Chronicle*, April 17, 1894, 2.

35. *Charlotte Democrat*, April 26, 1894, 2. Battle's short biography was widely quoted and republished in the wake of Zeb's death. It was originally published, however, years before the senator's demise. See Kemp P. Battle, "Biographical Sketch of Senator Z. B. Vance," *University Magazine* 19 (n.s. 6), no. 7 (March 1887): 257–62.

36. *Charlotte Observer*, December 24, 1897, 3. When first approached by Robert B. Vance and his nephews about the project, Dowd declined. Their persistence, as well as their failure to contract a primary author, compelled Zeb's old colleague to accept, but only if men who knew the governor during periods of which he had no personal knowledge assisted him. The product comprises personal stories, second-hand accounts, and primary documents that demonstrate what Vance meant to North Carolinians. See Dowd, *Life of Zebulon B. Vance*, preface.

37. Dowd, *Life of Zebulon B. Vance*, 72.

38. Ibid., 142–45.

39. *Asheville Citizen*, December 22, 1897, 1, December 21, 1; *Daily Charlotte Observer*, December 23, 1897, 8; *Raleigh News and Observer*, December 23, 1897, 1; *Wilmington Morning Star*, December 23, 1897, 4; *Asheville Daily Gazette*, December 23, 1897, 5. Gordon McKinney identified Swope's sources as Senator Matt Ransom and Dr. Edward Warren. See McKinney, *Zeb Vance*, 407–8.

40. *Asheville Citizen*, December 22, 1897, 1–2, 4; *Asheville Daily Gazette*, December 23, 1897, 1, 5.

41. *Wilmington Morning Star*, April 17, 1894, 2.

42. *Raleigh News-Observer-Chronicle*, April 17, 1894, 2.

43. "A tribute of the Fayetteville Independent Light Infantry Company to the memory of Governor Zebulon B. Vance," in *The Papers of Zebulon Vance*, ed. Gordon B. McKinney and Richard M. McMurry (Frederick, Md.: University Publications of America, 1987, microfilm edition), reel 12; *Fayetteville Observer*, April 19, 1894, 3.

44. Dowd, *Life of Zebulon B. Vance*, 70–71. The *Advance*, also referred to as the *Ad-Vance*, may have taken its name from North Carolina's governor, although Zeb

himself said that was untrue. Vance's efforts to supply cotton cards for the women of his state to sew clothing were far less successful than Dowd claimed. Cotton and wool cards were scarce, and whatever surplus thread the state had went to make uniforms for the state's soldiers. See Mobley, "*War Governor of the South*," 131–33.

45. Dowd, *Life of Zebulon B. Vance*, 70–71; "Address . . . Before the Southern Historical Society," 507, 512–13; Tucker, *Zeb Vance*, 232; Mobley, "*War Governor of the South*," 145–46. It is unknown exactly how much Vance was able to sneak past the Federal blockaders because official records for the trade do not exist, but it seems others accepted his estimates as fact. In 1900, Richard Battle repeated Zeb's numbers but attributed them to the State Quartermaster's Department. Either Battle's true source was Vance, or the former governor had an impeccable memory for numbers. See *Raleigh News and Observer*, August 23, 1900, 2.

46. Walter Clark quoted in Dowd, *Life of Zebulon B. Vance*, 173.

47. Escott, *Many Excellent People*, 175–90.

48. *Progressive Farmer* (Raleigh), May 1, 1894, 2. Clark's obituary ran in the May 15, 1894, edition of the *Progressive Farmer*.

49. Ibid., April 17, 1894, 2.

50. Escott, *Many Excellent People*, 245–49, 251–53; James L. Hunt, "The Making of a Populist: Marion Butler, 1863–1895, Part III," *North Carolina Historical Review* 62, no. 3 (July 1985): 317–23, 335, 337–39. The emergence of the Populist Party in North Carolina happened gradually. In 1890, those in the Alliance secured a majority in the state legislature and unleashed a reform agenda unseen in North Carolina since Reconstruction. They chartered new banks, founded new schools (including institutions for blacks and women), and enacted a range of other legislation that rankled the old-line Democrats. When the old-line Democrats regained control and began dismantling these new policies in 1892, the agrarians' smoldering frustration exploded, and many found refuge in the People's Party. See Escott, *Many Excellent People*, 245; Hunt, "The Making of a Populist, Part II," 180–81, 187–89, 196–201.

51. Escott, *Many Excellent People*, 253–55, 258–61. Race was a major part of North Carolina's national restoration as well as an important motivation for Vance. During the war, he was part of a crackdown against black North Carolinians that followed Lincoln's emancipation edict. In 1863, the state legislature enabled the governor to call Courts of Oyer and Terminer to deal summarily with black lawbreakers. When asked to write his autobiography, which he started but never published, he stated bluntly that he converted to secession "not for the Confederate States [as] an object desirable in itself—but to avert the *consequences*—the abolition of Slavery." No matter "how much it was denied," he wrote as the fog of war dissipated, "and however much stress was laid upon the *Union*, and minor causes of irritation, the result has conclusively shown that the great desire of the North was to abolish Slavery and to humiliate the Slaveholders whom they had been taught to hate." See Mobley, "*War Governor of the South*," 79–85, 96–97; and Vance autobiography quoted in Joe A. Mobley, "Zebulon B. Vance: A Confederate Nationalist in the North Carolina Gubernatorial Election of 1864," *North Carolina Historical Review* 77, no. 4 (October 2004): 453–54.

52. *Raleigh News and Observer*, August 23, 1900, 1–2.

53. Ibid., 2.

54. McKinney, *Zeb Vance*, 409–12; Tucker, *Zeb Vance*, 513. The Civil War Trails marker is located across from the state capitol and addresses the final days of the war in North Carolina. Its text is largely an overview, but it addresses Vance's election in 1862 and briefly his role in negotiating the state's surrender.

Contributors

DAVID BROWN is lecturer in American studies at Manchester University in the United Kingdom. He has written about Hinton Rowan Helper in the *Journal of Southern History* and in his book, *Southern Outcast: Hinton Rowan Helper and the Impending Crisis of the South*, among other publications. Currently he is at work on a book-length study reinterpreting the "plain folk," the non-slaveholding whites of the antebellum South.

JUDKIN BROWNING, an assistant professor of history at Appalachian State University, has published in the *North Carolina Historical Review* and the *Journal of Southern History*. He is a 2003 winner of the Holmes Award for the best paper presented at an annual meeting of the Southern Historical Association. With Michael Thomas Smith, he edited *Letters from a North Carolina Unionist: John A. Hedrick to Benjamin S. Hedrick, 1862–1865*.

LAURA F. EDWARDS, professor of history at Duke University, is well known for her work on women, gender, and the law. She is the author of *Gendered Strife and Confusion: The Political Culture of Reconstruction* and *Scarlett Doesn't Live Here Anymore: Southern Women in the Civil War Era*.

PAUL D. ESCOTT is Reynolds Professor of History at Wake Forest University. He is the author of many articles and books, including *After Secession: Jefferson Davis and the Failure of Confederate Nationalism*; *Many Excellent People: Power and Privilege in North Carolina, 1850–1900*; and *Military Necessity: Civil-Military Relations in the Confederacy*.

JOHN C. INSCOE, a native of Morganton, North Carolina, is professor of history at the University of Georgia, where he is editing the *New Georgia Encyclopedia*. He is the author of many articles, edited works, and other works, including *Mountain Masters, Slavery, and the Sectional Crisis in Western North Carolina*. With Gordon McKinney, he co-authored *The Heart of Confederate Appalachia: Western North Carolina's Civil War*.

CHANDRA MANNING earned her Ph.D. at Harvard and teaches at Georgetown University. The 2003 winner of the C. Vann Woodward Award and the 2005 winner of the Holmes Award of the Southern Historical Association, she recently published *What This Cruel War Was Over*, on the views of Civil War soldiers about what caused the war and what it should have achieved.

BARTON A. MYERS is a doctoral candidate at the University of Georgia, where he is currently writing a dissertation that examines the intersection of hardcore Unionism, guerrilla violence, and military policy statewide in Civil War North Carolina. His first book, *Executing Daniel Bright: Military Incursion, Racial Conflict and Guerrilla Violence in a Coastal Carolina Community during the Civil War*, is forthcoming.

STEVEN E. NASH received his master's degree from Western Carolina University and is completing his Ph.D. dissertation at the University of Georgia. His article "Aiding the Southern Mountain Republicans: The Freedmen's Bureau in Buncombe County" appeared in 2006 in the *North Carolina Historical Review*.

PAUL YANDLE has taught history courses at West Virginia University, where he is completing his Ph.D. Yandle is the author of a two-part article, "Joseph Charles Price and His 'Peculiar Work,'" which appeared in the *North Carolina Historical Review*.

KARIN ZIPF received her Ph.D. from the University of Georgia before joining the Department of History at East Carolina University. She is the author of *Labor of Innocents: Forced Apprenticeship in North Carolina, 1715–1919*. She also has published articles in the *Journal of Southern History* and other scholarly journals.

Index

Dula, Thomas, 235
Dunkers, 10
Dunn, Jason S., 23–24
Duren, Charles, 87
Durham, N.C., 269
Durrill, Wayne K., 7

Edney, B. M., 16
Eleventh Pennsylvania Cavalry, 42
Elizabeth City, N.C., 39, 41, 42, 43, 44,
    47, 54, 55, 56
Elliott, John T., 44, 46, 52, 53
Ellis, John W., 14, 21
Ellison, Stewart, 232, 235
Emancipation, 3, 4, 118, 222; by U.S.
    Army, 44, 51, 71
Emancipation Proclamation, 38, 69, 71,
    78, 110
Emanuel, James E., 207
Enforcement Act of 1870, 232
Escott, Paul D., 7, 12, 28
Evans, Augusta, 132

Families: and political decisions, 16,
    26–27; suffering of, 25–26, 275–76;
    and support of deserters, 21
Farmers, tenant, 10
Farmers' Alliance and Industrial
    Union, 276, 277, 284
Faust, Drew Gilpin, 27
Fayetteville, N.C., 26, 130, 135, 144,
    147, 282
Fayetteville Observer, 111, 135
Ferguson, Garland, 118
Ferrill, John L., 202
Fifteenth Amendment, 177
Fifth Pennsylvania Cavalry, 42
Fifth U.S. Colored Troops, 42, 44
Fifty-fifth Massachusetts, 42
First North Carolina Colored Volun-
    teers, 42
First U.S. Colored Troops, 42
Fletcher, N.C., 287
Foote, James H., 252

Ford, Lacy, 30
Fort Macon, 82
Fort Sumter, 8, 13
Forty-eighth North Carolina, 108
Forty-ninth North Carolina, 117
Foster, John G., 85
Fourteenth Amendment, 177
Foust, J. H., 20, 24
Fowle, William B., Jr., 69
Franklin County, N.C., 234, 277
Franklinville, N.C., 20
Free blacks. See African Americans
Freedmen's Bureau, 90, 208
Freehling, William W., 11
Frye, William, 227
"Fusion," 285

Gahagan, George W., 195
Gales, Joseph, 158
Gallagher, Gary W., 7
Galloway, Abraham, 84, 208
Gardner, Sarah E., 132, 148
Garner, Eliza, 82
Gaston, Paul, 221
Gaston, William, 158
Gates County, N.C., 39
Gender roles, 2, 4, 80, 81, 194, 214; and
    legal system, 163, 166, 167, 174, 214;
    and marriage, 200, 202–4, 211–12;
    and peace of community, 174; and
    privy examination, 211, 214; and
    women writers, 132–33, 147, 148
General Assembly, 195, 196, 211, 214
Gibbs, Hilliard, 91
Gibson, Private James William, 15,
    16, 19
Gilliam, Jordan, 163
Gilmer, John, 14
Glenn, William B., 252
Godfrey, F. M., 235
Goldsboro, N.C., 112, 130, 139, 144, 147
Grady, Henry, 221, 222, 259, 260
Graham, William A., 139, 140, 141, 142
Grandy, John J., 56

Granville County, N.C., 13, 277
Greeley, Horace, 279
Green, G. N., 88
Greensboro, N.C., 10, 139, 140, 141, 143, 207, 269
Gregory, Major D., 48
Griffin, Joel R., 45
Grimes, Jacob, 81
Gross, Ariela, 162
Guerrilla forces (Confederate), 37–58 passim; characteristics of, 52–53; described by General Wild, 52; execute black soldier, 57
Guilford County, N.C., 10, 14, 22, 23
Guirkin, R. R., 50

Habeas corpus: suspension of, 107, 279, 280, 281
Hahn, Stephen, 30
Hale, Edward J., 135
Hall, Thomas, 91–92
Hancock, Winfield, 102
Hanes, Jacob, 109
Harlan, Louis, 259
Harper, James C., 227, 228, 230, 231, 232, 233
Harris, George W., 76
Harris, James Henry, 207, 208, 209
Hart, Robert D., 193
Hathaway, W. W., 206
Haywood, John, 158, 169
Hedrick, Benjamin S., 10
Hedrick, John, 85
Hefner, Marcus, 108
Helper, Hinton Rowan, 10
Henderson County, N.C., 16, 232
Heroes of America, 18, 22, 115
Hertford, N.C., 44, 47
High Point, N.C., 17, 28
Hill, Edward H., 246
Hill, Robert, 108
Hinton, James W., 44, 45, 52
Hinton's Crossroads (Hintonsville), N.C., 47, 64 (n. 41)

Hoke, Robert, 116
Hoke, William A., 269
Holden, William W., 4, 111, 113, 114, 118, 139, 281; as candidate for governor in 1864, 101, 102, 109, 110, 114–16; leads peace movement, 106–8; responds to Vance's speeches, 115; suppression of votes for, 102; suspends publication, 115; threatened by Virginia troops, 109
Home Guard, 20, 21, 23, 24, 25
Hood, James Walker, 207, 208, 211
Hopkins, Martha A., 193, 195, 196, 207
Hopkins, William T., 193
Hostages, 44, 57
Houston, R. B. B., 231, 244
Houston resolution, 234–40, 241
Howard, Oliver O., 90
Howe, Julia Ward, 210
Howes, John, 163
Huggins, Alex, 77
Hughes, Edward, 79
Hyde County, N.C., 90, 91
Hyman, John A., 240, 241

Impressments, 2, 29, 104, 275
Indiantown, N.C., 38, 48
Industrial development, 276, 277
Inflation, 27, 105
Inner civil war, 19–23, 30, 56
Iredell, James, Sr., 158
Iredell County, N.C., 15, 21
Irregular troops. *See* Guerrilla forces

Jackson, Andrew, 278
Jackson, Thomas "Stonewall," 286
Jacobs, Harriet, 73
James, Horace, 74, 80, 82, 90
Jim Crow, 178, 221, 222, 224, 225, 256, 259
Johnson, Andrew, 90, 138
Johnson, Reese, 201
Johnson, Samuel, 116

supported by Republicans in 1870s, 225, 232, 233, 242, 244, 252

Segregation, 221, 222, 223, 224, 225, 233–41, 257–58, 260; and Constitutional Convention of 1875, 256, 257, 258; and stance of political parties, 225, 227, 229, 234–40, 242–46, 256

Settle, Thomas, Jr., 274, 275–76

Seymour, Horatio, 279

Shannonhouse, James, 56

Sherman, William T., 129, 130, 139, 140, 141, 142, 145, 147

Shoe, Edmund, 15, 16

Shroyer, Edward, 199–200, 205

Shroyer, Mary, 199–200

Simmons, Edmond, 50

Sinclair, James, 14–15

Singleton, William Henry, 72–73, 74, 83

Sixty-eighth North Carolina State Troops, 52, 57

Sixty-second Georgia Cavalry/Partisan Rangers, 45, 46

Sixty-sixth North Carolina State Troops, 52

Skinner, William S., 193

Slaughterhouse Cases, 242, 246, 251

Slaveholders: attacks on blacks, 69, 79; attempts to keep blacks in slavery, 69; and secession, 12, 17; view slaves as content, 71–72

Slaveholding, 9

Slavery, 2, 9, 10–11, 30; defended by Vance, 110–14

Slaves: and legal system, 166–67, 170

Smyrna, N.C., 76

Smyth, John H., 256, 258

Social equality, 221, 224, 229, 234, 241, 243, 244, 256, 260

Soldiers (Confederate): concerns for families, 103, 105; dissatisfaction with Confederate government, 103–5; lack of shoes, 105; motives to fight, 102; sentiment for Holden, 101, 108, 109

Southern Claims Commission, 17, 22, 23, 78

Southern Historical Society, 271

South Mills, N.C., 39, 42, 50

Spencer, Cornelia Phillips, 4; background of, 133–34; begins writing articles, 134; defends Swain, 143–47; defends Vance, 137–43, 148; emphasizes northern atrocities, 137; friendship with Swain and Vance, 132, 134, 137; pioneers in defending North Carolina and its men, 129, 132, 148–9; reacts to Nichols' book, 135–36; and reputation of North Carolina, 130–31, 136

Spencer, James Munroe, 133

Spencer, Julia, 133

Stanley, Edward, 77, 78, 87

Stanton, Edwin M., 57, 75

Stanton, Elizabeth Cady, 210

Statesville, N.C., 287

State v. A. B. Rhodes, 206

Stephens, Alexander, 132

Storey, Margaret M., 21, 79

Sumner, Charles, 225, 228, 231, 241, 242, 243

Susan Cooke v. Henry L. Cooke, 206

Sutton v. Askew, 212, 213

Swain, David L., 132, 137, 139, 140, 149, 158; career of, 134; concern for reputation, 131; and son-in-law, 143–47; urges Spencer to write history, 131

Swain, Eleanor, 143

Swope, R. R., 282

Taxation, 29; ad valorem, 12

Tax-in-kind, 104, 108

Teachers, 86–89

"Tewksbury," 42, 43, 44, 47, 53

Third Battalion, North Carolina State Troops, 105

Thomas, Eliza A., 26

Thompson, David, 114

Tilden, Samuel, 276